CREATING A HEALTHIER WORLD, ONE PERSON AT A TIME

CREATING A HEALTHIER WORLD, ONE PERSON AT A TIME

JEFFREY L. RODENGEN

Edited by John Fakler, Christian Ramirez, Joseph Demma, and Heather Lewin
Design and Layout by Elijah Meyer

Write Stuff Enterprises, LLC
1001 South Andrews Avenue
Fort Lauderdale, FL 33316
1-800-900-Book (1-800-900-2665)
(954) 462-6657
www.writestuffbooks.com

The publisher has made every effort to identify and locate the source of the photographs included in this edition of *Creating a Healthier World, One Person at a Time*. Grateful acknowledgment is made to those who have kindly granted permission for the use of their materials in this edition. If there are instances where proper credit was not given, the publisher will gladly make any necessary corrections in subsequent printings.

Publisher's Cataloging in Publication

(Prepared by The Donohue Group, Inc.)

Rodengen, Jeffrey L.
    Creating a healthier world, one person at a time / Jeffrey L. Rodengen ; edited by John Fakler … [et al.] ; design and layout by Elijah Meyer ; [foreword by Roy Spence].

    p. ; cm.

    Includes index.
    ISBN: 978-1-932022-49-0

    1. Healthways (Firm)—History. 2. Disease management—United States. 3. Health services administration—United States.
4. Employee health promotion—United States. I. Fakler, John.
II. Meyer, Elijah. III. Spence, Roy. IV. Title.

RA399.5 .R63 2012
362.1/0973
2011932562

Among Jeffrey L. Rodengen's Current Titles:

The Legend of Chris-Craft

The Legend of Dr Pepper/Seven-Up

*The Legend of Stanley:
150 Years of The Stanley Works*

*The Legend of Goodyear:
The First 100 Years*

The Legend of Cessna

The Legend of Mercury Marine

The Legend of Pfizer

*Office Depot:
Taking Care of Business—
The First 20 Years*

*A Passion for Service:
The Story of ARAMARK*

The Legend of Brink's

Completely produced in the United States of America

10 9 8 7 6 5 4 3 2 1

Table of Contents

Preface

By Henry Herr, Tom Cigarran, and Bob Stone

Healthways' purpose has always been predicated on the principle of doing the right thing for the individuals, customers, and communities we serve, and for the colleagues of the company who make what we do possible. Our conviction was, and is, if we consistently adhered to that principle, the business would take care of itself.

The manifestation of this principle is that, for Healthways, improving the health and well-being of individuals is our business, our only business. We don't sell supplies, devices, pharmaceuticals, or any of the other items that individuals might need in their pursuit of better health. Our services are not a loss leader for some other more profitable product. Our mission and our focus are clear and perfectly aligned with those of our customers. At the end of the day, we are about proving, repeatedly, that "Healthier People Cost Less and Perform Better" by providing the solutions that make that happen.

Health care in America is driven by supply-side economics because we have a system that is focused on treating people *after* they get sick. But people are getting sick at a greater rate and to a greater degree than ever before, and treating them after they get sick is expensive and likely to become even more so.

While there are many contributing factors to the rising cost of health care in America, it is this increasing demand that is principally responsible. Healthways' objective is to improve the health and well-being of individuals, organizations, communities, and countries, thereby increasing the vitality of each. We pursue that purpose through the development and delivery of comprehensive solutions that keep healthy people healthy, reduce or eliminate lifestyle risk, and assure optimized care for those with chronic disease or persistent conditions.

Healthways' history has been characterized principally by a constant and consistent expansion of the population to which we have delivered such solutions: the acutely ill; those suffering from addictive diseases; people with diabetes, arthritis, or cardiac disease; individuals with lung conditions; the persistently ill; and now, the healthy and the at-risk as well.

Similarly, one can view our expanding and evolving service distribution channels as recognition of additional ways to reach an even broader segment of the population through varied markets which include hospitals we owned, hospitals with which we contract, physicians, health plans, self-funded, employers, government entities, and pharmacy benefit management (PBM) clients. About five years ago, we added international customers as well, and it would not be a stretch to imagine that within the not-too-distant future, our services will be available in the retail channel.

Obviously, the more people we serve, the greater impact we can have. But, unlike nearly everyone else in the health care market, we don't get paid based on the volume of people we serve. We get paid based on the number of people whose health we improve and the savings and performance that improvement generates as compared to what would otherwise be spent or lost. Improved health always comes first— the value we create is a by-product of our success in that effort.

Today, our effort makes a significant contribution to the health and well-being of individuals throughout the world. But our job is not done. And so, we are driven, every day, to pursue our goal: *to be universally acclaimed for creating a healthier world, one person at a time.*

Foreword

By Roy Spence

WHAT IS PURPOSE? SIMPLY, IT'S A DEFINITIVE STATEMENT ABOUT THE DIFFERENCE YOU ARE trying to make in the world. If you have a purpose and can articulate it with clarity and passion, everything makes sense, everything flows. You feel good about what you're doing and clear about how to get there. When you unleash the power of purpose, it creates a sea change in the category in which one competes. Organizations, leaders, and brands with a real and genuine purpose are primed to deliver success not only in the marketplace, but where it really counts—in the lives of others.

Over the course of my career, I've had the privilege of working with a few companies and individuals who understood the power of purpose. Healthways is such a company, its CEO, Ben Leedle, and its two active founders, Tom Cigarran and Bob Stone, are such individuals. None of the other companies with which I've worked have had a purpose statement so literally focused on improving people's lives as Healthways' *Creating a Healthier World, One Person at a Time*. What greater goal could any of us have than to be part of that journey?

From its roots as a hospital ownership company 30 years ago, Healthways' course to its current status as the recognized global leader in improving well-being for

individuals, companies, communities, and governments is a lesson in staying true to one's purpose. Like most companies, it's enjoyed good times—when adhering to purpose is easy—and tough times—when purpose provides the North Star by which an organization's true course is maintained. That is the only sure way to know you will reach the destination you have set for yourself; a destination so important to every person on Earth that noted author of the best-selling *Good to Great* and respected business researcher Jim Collins charged you with "an obligation to succeed."

From its very first day, Healthways has pursued Frost's "path less traveled" and followed Emerson's injunction to "go … where there is no path, and leave a trail." In doing so, this extraordinary company created new markets and solutions for addressing the critical challenges facing health and health care, both domestically and overseas. It created value for customers by providing solutions that have made millions of individuals healthier, repeatedly proving that healthier people cost less … and perform better. It has risen to Shaw's challenge to "dream of things that never were, and ask 'why not?'" then created those things and brought them forth in waves of innovation possibly unequalled by a non-tech, non-product organization.

While having a purpose is critical, it must be supported by a culture that enables every employee to work "on purpose," and tolerates nothing less. Defining such a culture is relatively easy. Nurturing and maintaining it is not. But Healthways leaders walk the talk, assuring all colleagues the same support for their well-being as it provides to the nearly 40 million individuals it serves every day. As a result, its nearly 3,000 colleagues are quick to note that Healthways is a different kind of place to work: a special place, a place where they can do their best to help other people be their best.

Clearly, Shaw was right in his observation: "Give a man health and a course to steer, and he'll never stop to trouble about whether he's happy or not."

It has been my privilege to know the leaders and colleagues of Healthways and to have the opportunity to play a part in pursuit of their purpose. I am proud to be an unabashed fan of what the company stands for. Its colleagues are purpose-inspired, passionate about what they do, and anchored in a culture and a set of values whose sole objective is to enable them to do their best work.

My final words on the occasion of Healthways' 30th anniversary are reserved for the people who make Healthways the extraordinary company I know it to be. You have accomplished much in the past three decades and have reason to be proud. But you stand on the verge of something even greater; by your efforts, you can change the world. Keep on. Keep going. Never waiver. Never doubt. Never give in or give up. The world needs you to be steadfast to your purpose. Healthways is a company that does the right thing and does it right. If I didn't work for my own company, I would be honored to work for yours.

Be well, my friends.

Roy Spence

Ride at Dawn

Best-selling author Roy Spence is cofounder and chairman of GSD&M Idea City, a leading marketing, communications, and advertising company. His agency has developed brand awareness for corporate clients including Walmart, DreamWorks, and the PGA Tour. A national brand expert with a special passion for entrepreneurship, he has been named Ad Man of the Year and Idea Man of the Century.

Acknowledgments

HEALTHWAYS

MANY DEDICATED PEOPLE ASSISTED IN THE RESEARCH, PREPARATION, AND PUBLICATION OF *Creating a Healthier World, One Person at a Time.* Research Assistant Sandy Smith conducted the majority of the archival research, while senior editors John Fakler, Christian Ramirez, Joseph Demma, and Heather Lewin managed the editorial content. Graphic Designer Elijah Meyer brought the story to life.

The insights of Healthways' management team were of paramount importance to the project. No one was more integral to the publication of the book than Healthways cofounder Bob Stone, who shared so much of his time and intimate knowledge about the origins and evolution of the company. His project direction, research, and editorial assistance proved invaluable in developing this corporate history of one of the world's most unique health care organizations.

Several key individuals associated with Healthways and its previous corporate entity, American Healthcorp, assisted in the development of the book from its outline to finished product. Gratitude is extended to those serving on the book review committee: Ben R. Leedle, Jr., Healthways president and CEO; Thomas Cigarran, Chairman Emeritus and cofounder; and Henry D. Herr, cofounder.

All of the people interviewed—Healthways employees, retirees, and friends—were generous with their time and insights. Those who shared their memories and thoughts include: Rick Bailey, Stefen Brueckner, Janet Calhoun, Mary Chaput, Chris Cigarran,

Emily Cook, Ryan Daniels, Jim Deal, Bill Evans, Robyn Fulwider, Dave Godwin, Shiela Hayes, Mary Hunter, Stan Kantanie, Matthew E. Kelliher, Kathy Kirk, Michael Klein, Martin "Mike" Koldyke, Steve Lindstrom, Alfred Lumsdaine, Patricia Lynch, Carol Murdock, James E. Pope, Steve Samples, Sue Schmidt, Regina Seider, Justin Smith, Gerrye Stegall, Glen Stettin, Paul Wallace, Charles Wilhelm, and Dana Williams. Special gratitude is owed to branding expert and company friend Roy Spence, who contributed the book's foreword.

Additional thanks is extended to Kaz Smith, Amy Wickes, and Ashley B. King for coordinating the massive amounts of data in storage and making it readily available; Kim Eden, for coordinating photos from Healthways International; Nancy Mangold, for identifying photos from the 1980s; Carolyn Peacher, for photographing many company events over the past few years and making her vast collection available; Laura Perkins, for access to historical HR records; and Catherine Lane, Chris Mason, and Bryan McClarey, for photo assistance. Gratitude is also extended to the following care enhancement center contacts for assistance in photos from their sites: Kim Matthews (Pittsburgh); Michael Vasper and Cory Canyete (Hawaii); Amy Strom and Courtney Shirley (Raleigh); Joe Wachtler (Minnesota); Bonnie Jones and Malinda Lowney (Phoenix); Holly Barbour and Rebecca Detig (Baltimore); Aaron Mickelson (Seattle); Tamara Porterfield (St. Louis); Stephen Watkins (Des Moines); and Cash Bradley (San Antonio).

Lastly, special thanks are extended to the staff of Write Stuff Enterprises, LLC: Elizabeth Fernandez, executive editor; Sandy Cruz, senior vice president/creative design; Danielle Taylor, graphic designer; Lynn C. Jones and Abigail Hollister, proofreaders; Mary Aaron, Barbara Martin, and Patti Dolbow, transcriptionists; Donna M. Drialo, indexer; Amy Major, executive assistant to Jeffrey L. Rodengen; Marianne Roberts, president, publisher, and chief financial officer; and Stanislava Alexandrova, marketing manager.

Healthways Care Enhancement Centers are an integral part of Healthway's disease management services. Pictured above are (top row, left to right) Pittsburgh, Hawaii, Raleigh, Minnesota, Phoenix, (bottom row) Baltimore, Seattle, St. Louis, Des Moines, and San Antonio.

Above: The acquisition of Hospital Affiliates International by Hospital Corporation of America dominated the local news on April 20, 1981. It would be the singular event that would launch the establishment of American Healthcorp, a new health care company created and driven by former Affiliates executives. *(Image courtesy of the Nashville Public Library, Special Collections Division.)*

Opposite: On August 25, 1981, Henry Herr's daily to-do list was filled with HAI activities and the note "Leave for Chicago," where he and other American Healthcorp founders would pursue investors.

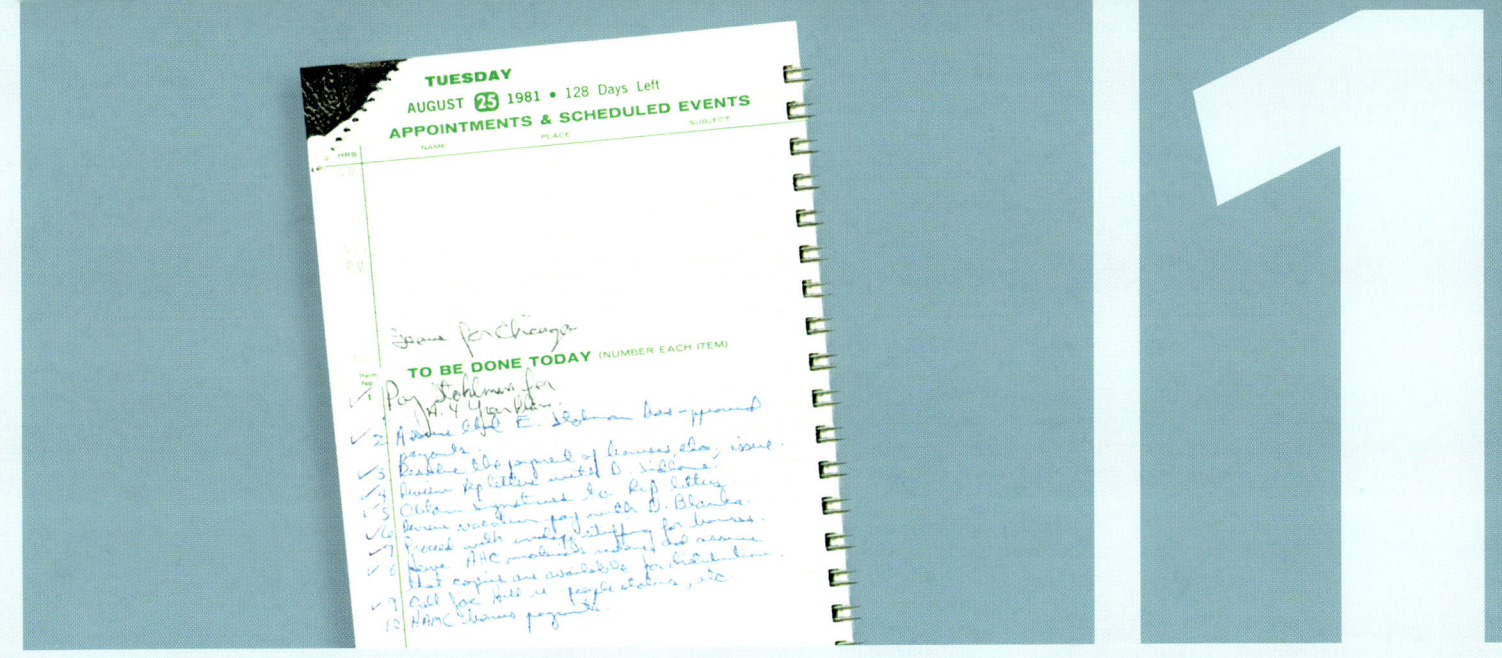

We weren't interested in [job] security. We were interested in doing something that would be ours. And I say "we" because anyone who says he or she is responsible for a company is crazy. It doesn't work that way.[1]

—Tom Cigarran, 1989

"THE PURPOSE OF A BUSINESS … TO HAVE A PURPOSE, TO DO SOMETHING that matters."[2] Thirty years ago, Healthways was established to do just that: to make a difference in the lives of people. The past three decades chronicle its journey from a new company with six employees and no business to the worldwide leader in health and well-being improvement, serving nearly 40 million people domestically and abroad. It is a track record of sustained and meaningful progress toward its purpose: *to be universally acclaimed for creating a healthier world, one person at a time.*

Providing solutions for improving people's health and well-being, and thereby reducing health care cost and improving personal and organizational performance, has been the hallmark of Healthways since day one, September 2, 1981. Through the design, development, and implementation of solutions to keep healthy people healthy, reduce or eliminate lifestyle risks, and ensure optimized care for those with a chronic disease or condition, Healthways has set the standard for health promotion, prevention, acute

care, and chronic care management, both in the United States and internationally. As a result of its steadfast adherence to its purpose and a business model based on "doing the right thing," today, Healthways is recognized as the world's leading well-being improvement company. But, as with every successful company, this took strong leadership, innovative ideas, focus, and hard work.

The Beginning

The seeds for the company that would become Healthways were sown in an April 1981 phone call to Tom Cigarran, then senior vice president of development at Hospital Affiliates International (HAI), based in Nashville, Tennessee. Cigarran was at a dinner party with friends when he took the call that would change his life and the lives of millions of people in the United States and around the world. The caller was his boss, Jim Buncher, HAI's president and CEO. Buncher told him that their company had just been sold to crosstown rival Hospital Corporation of America (HCA), a company that HAI had

competed against "hammer and tongs" for more than a decade.[3]

Cigarran went numb.

"I literally had to sit down after the phone call," Cigarran said. "We had this company that was really going to go someplace, and, all of a sudden, it's being sold. It was totally unexpected."[4]

It wasn't just Cigarran who was caught off guard by the announced $650 million sale. In a letter to HAI personnel, Buncher wrote: "I must admit that I, along with you, was not prepared for the events of the past week. Therefore, I have no canned message or preplanned thoughts to share with you."[5]

An Entrepreneurial Spirit

Once the shock wore off, Cigarran moved into action. The first order of business was to try and secure jobs at HCA for any of his staff who wanted to remain. Once staff needs had been met, he could then turn his attention to his own career. Although he had a job offer in California, he wanted to continue to raise his family in Nashville, where he'd moved four years earlier.

Cigarran thought he might open his own business and, on a whim, took a piece of paper and made a list of the names of those whom he would want to work with to launch a new venture. It became his "dream team:" Henry Herr, HAI's vice president and controller; Stan Kantanie, who had been a hospital administrator, regional director, and group vice president–operations at Hospital Affiliates; and Bob Stone, HAI's assistant vice president–development. He envisioned these three men filling key roles. "I've always believed that you had to do something. You couldn't just sit. So I made this chart, and I had these people identified," Cigarran said.

Enter Bob Hilton, Hospital Affiliates' chief financial officer. "He came in one day," Cigarran recalled, "and said, 'I've thought about starting a company.' I laughed." Cigarran showed him his list and Hilton told him, "I think I can raise the money."[6]

That fateful conversation and piece of paper were the cornerstones in the foundation of American Healthcorp. The team Cigarran hoped to assemble had experience and knowledge gleaned from the "hard-charging, entrepreneurial" environment of HAI. The "dream team" was about to become a reality.

Defining the Vision

The team was made up of Cigarran, Hilton, Kantanie, Stone, and Herr—five strong leaders, all of whom had worked together at HAI. Their backgrounds were varied, and each excelled in specific areas. Hilton, the former chief financial officer at Affiliates, had worked for more than two decades in the financial arena. Prior to that, he had been with Genesco, a Nashville-based specialty retailer and wholesaler of branded footwear. Slated to be American Healthcorp's chairman and CEO, he would line up the needed funds for basic operations and hospital acquisitions.

Cigarran would be the president and chief operating officer. Prior to joining Affiliates, he had run a division of Dun & Bradstreet in the occupational medicine field. At HAI, he had been tasked with buying and building new hospitals, strategic planning, and development of new lines of business.

Herr was appointed American Healthcorp's senior vice president of finance, using skills developed as an auditor

Bob Stone (left), and Dana Williams both had hospital management experience in their early careers. Stone was responsible for business development, regulatory affairs, and marketing at American Healthcorp. Williams' first position with the company was as administrator of the Russell County Medical Center in Virginia.

at Arthur Young and Company and in various financial positions with American Medicorp. He had joined HAI in 1978 as a division controller and had advanced at the time of the sale to the position of vice president and controller.[7]

"To this day, anybody who has ever worked with Henry, not just inside [our company] but throughout the industry, has said that there's no chief financial officer anywhere as good as [he is]," Cigarran later said.

Kantanie would serve as senior vice president of operations. "He could operate anything—a motel, for example—and produce quality," Cigarran said. "People loved working with him. He had a strange sort of old-world style to him."[8]

Stone, whose career included experience in public, private, and academic health care facilities and as director of the Certificate of Need (CON) program for Massachusetts, would support Cigarran in business development and be responsible for regulatory affairs and marketing. Together, the pair had a long track record of success at HAI in purchasing and winning government approval for new hospitals, and their skills would soon lead to similar success for American Healthcorp.

But titles and job descriptions were for the convenience of those outside of the office. Because the company was just starting out, the founders would pitch in and do whatever task was necessary. Shiela Hayes, hired as a junior accountant in 1982 after working at HCA, realized that each founder had a role to play, and it was not always reflected in their titles.

"Bob Hilton was easygoing, quiet, and focused," Hayes said. "He was a motivator. Tom was the guy who took all the chances. He was the one with all the ideas who went out to find new things. He was the adventurer. Stan was the anchor. Bob [Stone] would develop the plans to do everything that Tom came up with. Henry handled the finances. He was very serious but a kindhearted, caring person."

It was a strong management team. But what was the new company's business going to be? Hospital Affiliates had been in the business of owning and managing hospitals, and that seemed to be the best way for American Healthcorp to gain a foothold in the industry. Clearly, the first requirement was to develop both a financial plan and a business strategy.

Cigarran explained:

We had to raise money. We had to have a business plan. We had to prove that whatever business we were going into, we knew how to do it, and we had a successful track record in every slot, every job. There was only one business we could do that in … the hospital business. We did not want to be in the hospital business long-term, but to get a company built, we had to do that.[9]

Securing Investors

The HCA–HAI merger was announced in late April 1981. That summer, with the knowledge and approval of both HAI and HCA management, the Healthcorp team made a trip to Chicago in August to meet with two venture capital firms. Both agreed to lead the venture capital financing, and by September, the team had secured $6.5 million in investments from a number of firms, including Continental Illinois Venture Capital, First Chicago Venture Capital, Frontenac Company, William Blair & Company, Smith Barney, Bessemer Securities, Foster Management Ltd., and Citicorp Venture Capital.[10] The response was encouraging.

"We didn't have any hospitals [by September 2, 1981, our first day of business], but we'd managed to raise $6.5 million in the past 30 days, and we were ready to start negotiating in the Southeast, where we intended to concentrate our efforts," said Hilton.[11]

The company acquired a $27 million line of credit so that funds were available when an appropriate hospital had been identified.[12] Although it had millions in the bank, its first offices—at 3814 Cleghorn Avenue, Nashville—were hardly lavish. According to Hayes, the company had about 2,400 square feet of office space. Cigarran recalled that the offices were so small that one had to stand in the doorway to speak with the person inside.[13]

"[We had] horrendous multicolored shag carpets—the unbelievable shocks I'd get in the wintertime," Herr recalled. "I'd crawl over the top of my desk to get in and out because it was so small."[14]

"Bob Stone and I bought used office furniture, and Tom Cigarran came in on the weekend and wallpapered the boardroom himself. It was grass cloth," said Annetta Burgess, the administrative

When meeting with potential investors, each of the five founders offered a brief summary of his work experience and his role in the new company. Henry Herr's notes were handwritten on blue-lined paper and included a reminder to thank Stan Kantanie, who preceded him.

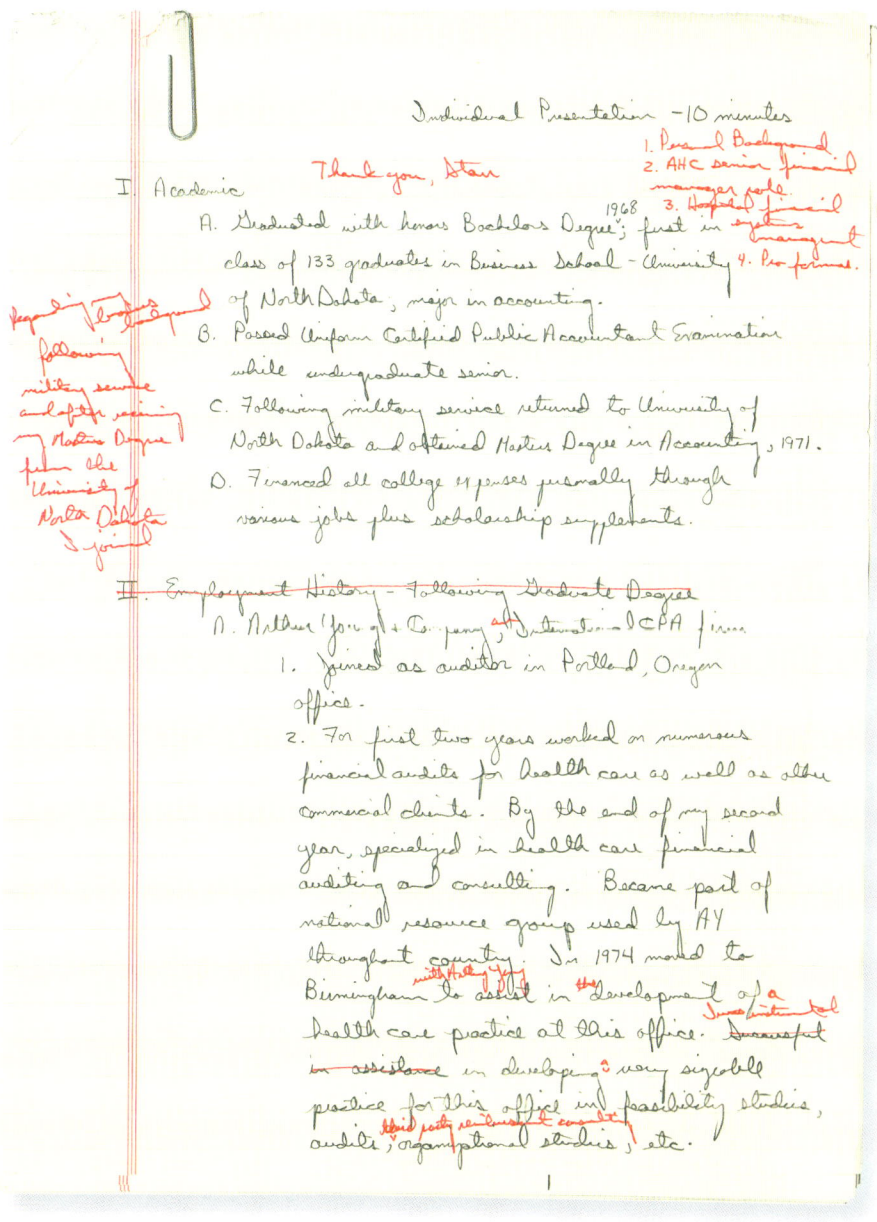

Expanding the

Hospital Corporation of America (HCA) and Hospital Affiliates International (HAI) were both founded in 1968 with physicians in central roles. Although the two firms had similar business models, the comparisons ran much deeper as the businesses grew.

Up until the mid-1960s, most hospitals were charitable institutions that also served as default social services agencies. Medicare, which was signed into law in 1965, changed that. Suddenly, virtually every American over the age of 65 had some form of insurance, provided they received Social Security. Prior to Medicare, seniors were the most likely demographic to be living in poverty, and only half had some form of health insurance.[1]

The time was right for investor-owned hospitals to compete with the charitable institutions that had provided most of the health care coverage in the decades prior. Not only did these investor-owned hospitals now have a tremendous market—millions of Americans could now afford medical care thanks to Medicare—they also benefited from economies of scale in purchasing supplies and equipment.

Government spending became an increasingly large portion of a hospital's budget, accounting for 55 to 60 percent of a hospital's revenues by the early 1980s.[2] As a result, financial predictability increased tremendously. "Medicare paid hospitals on a cost basis, which gave some level of security to those patients with Medicare, and provided a certain known amount of reimbursement and manageable cash flow [to the providing facilities]," said Henry Herr, co-founder and longtime chief financial officer.[3]

Creating the Industry

At the time of the HCA–HAI merger in 1981, HCA owned 137 hospitals and managed 63 others, and HAI owned 54 hospitals and managed another 100. The merger would give HCA 49,943 beds under its umbrella, which was 20 percent of all privately owned hospital beds in the United States.

Along with General Care Corporation, which HCA purchased a year before it bought HAI, these companies helped create the vibrant hospital management industry that would rival music publishing and recording as the signature industry in Nashville. Today, a "family tree" produced by the Nashville Health Care Council, an arm of the city's chamber of commerce, traces nearly 650 health care company offspring to HCA or HAI.[4]

Health Care Field

The council also identified three other industry segments that were "created or fostered by Nashville-based companies: … freestanding outpatient surgery centers, physician practice management groups, and disease management."[5] In 2008, Nashville-based health care companies generated $50 billion in revenue and supported 310,000 jobs worldwide.[6]

HCA and HAI also have ties to the politics of health care. Former Tennessee Governor Phil Bredesen is an HAI alumnus.[7] After leaving Hospital Affiliates, Bredesen founded HealthAmerica, a health maintenance organization that eventually had 6,000 employees and was publicly traded.[8] HCA was founded by the family of former Senate Majority Leader Bill Frist, a respected transplant surgeon before he turned to politics. After leaving the Senate, Frist founded Hope Through Healing Hands, an international nonprofit that uses "health as a currency for peace."[9]

The strength of the Nashville health care industry is a potent pull. By 2010, nearly 56 health care companies were headquartered in the area.[10] Nearly 30 years after the merger of HCA and HAI—and more than 40 years after each company began—the industry continues to shape the economic future of Nashville.

"As you look at the next 25 years in the United States, health care is going to be a growing and dominant part of that economy," Jack Bovender, former chairman and CEO of HCA, told *HealthLeaders* magazine in a special Nashville-centric supplement.

CEO Jim Buncher explained the merger with HCA and what he expected from HAI employees during the transition.

AMERICAN HEALTHCORP

assistant and first employee of the new company. "The boardroom was so small that when they sat down on a chair, it would bang up against the wall. I'd never worked for a company that was a startup before. I loved every minute of it."

Burgess also had new technology to learn—a Xerox 850 single-line typing system, a forerunner to the computer with a separate keyboard, printer, and monitor. "I'd never sat down to one before," she said. "Bob Stone would stand behind me with the user's manual and literally show me how to use the machine."[15]

American Healthcorp also invested in human capital, tapping a number of former HAI personnel to join the company. In addition to Hayes and Burgess, David Sidlowe joined as controller and Jim Deal as vice president of operations. Dana Williams and Mary Hunter, who had worked at HAI-owned hospitals, were chosen as administrators for the first hospitals American Healthcorp acquired.

A Crowded Field

Things proceeded smoothly in the company's first few months as the team pursued a number of potential hospital acquisitions. But the hospital management field was crowded. HCA, already the largest investor-owned hospital chain in the country, continued to extend its lead. Similarly, Humana, American Medical International, and National Medical Enterprises—the industry's No. 2, 3, and 4 firms—were enjoying robust growth and were all reporting revenues of more than $600 million.[16]

While it was a boom time for the hospital management industry, uncertainty ruled the day nationally and politically as the country tried to come to grips with the hangover of inflation, high interest rates, and government spending that had soared during the final years of the Carter administration.[17] Presidential candidate Ronald Reagan ran on a campaign of balancing the federal budget while instituting massive tax cuts and increasing defense spending. Reagan would propose cutting programs as well, with expectations in the 4 to 5 percent range, according to a report by Montgomery Securities published in *Surgical Business* in April 1981. Given that health care costs had been rising 12 percent annually, the report predicted that any cuts would be substantial:

We believe the next four years will be challenging for the health care industry. The Reagan administration will be tough, and economic pressures will force a number of changes, e.g., hospital consolidation. However, we also believe that progressive hospital leadership will view this as an era ripe with opportunities in delivery systems, operational techniques, organizational structure, and community and governmental relations. Health care leaders in the first half of the 1980s may focus their creative energies on areas such as unique corporate structures, multihospital involvement, satellite clinics, and freestanding ancillary services.

Investor-owned management companies should prosper in a restrictive spending environment in which emphasis will be on management efficiency and strategic planning.[18]

The report lined up perfectly with the American Healthcorp business plan, and the team believed it could turn potential negatives into assets, reassuring prospective investors that its small size would make it more flexible in competing against the industry giants.

"We were going to focus on [the market of] medium-sized suburban or rural hospitals, and we were going to run them with a very focused effort, get a lot of

community involvement in the success of our institution, build loyalty around that hospital, and be known as the place to get your health care," said Williams. "The challenge was, of course, that we had to run lean and mean."[19]

Despite the "lean and mean" goals, American Healthcorp would still invest significant resources to upgrade and modernize the facilities it was purchasing to "protect and improve their market positions and long-term value."[20]

Reaching the First Goal

American Healthcorp's initial business plan aimed to have five hospitals with 420 beds under management within its first year of operation, and the company moved quickly to fulfill that pledge. By the end of 1981, according to Herr, most of the company's efforts were spent negotiating purchase agreements. There were a number of candidates still on the short list as well as some other facilities American Healthcorp knew were for sale.

"Most of these, particularly hospitals that were in the range of 75 to 100 beds, usually didn't have sophisticated financial or clinical management systems," said Herr. "However, these hospitals many times were

UNIVERSITY MEDICAL CENTER HOSPITAL

the sole hospital in the community and were positioned to benefit significantly from targeted physician recruitment, the addition of needed medical services, and professional management."

Herr elaborated:

The value that we could bring to potential acquisitions was more than just financial. We brought new and needed medical services to the smaller market communities that they had not had prior to our arrival.[21]

The first agreement, to purchase University Medical Center (UMC) in Lebanon, Tennessee, was announced in late 1981, a mere three months after

funding had been secured.[22] The acquisition would take nearly six months to complete, and in the interim, two other hospitals were acquired.

Tepper Hospital, a 64-bed pediatric hospital in Chattanooga, Tennessee, was the first acquisition actually completed and became the company's first operating facility in January 1982. Founded by Dr. Jack Tepper in 1954 as a clinic, the 35-bed hospital was added in 1969 and a $1.5 million annex in 1974.[23] Its physician base was limited to pediatricians affiliated with Tepper's practice. On the day of the purchase, the hospital only had six patients.[24]

American Healthcorp purchased Tepper for $3.9 million and immediately changed the name to Metropolitan Hospital. Renovations increased the number of private rooms. Metropolitan Hospital would become the site of the pilot for the company's hospital-based Diabetes Centers of Excellence business, which would go on to create a new market offering that would achieve national recognition as Diabetes Treatment Centers of America.[25]

Above: Founders Tom Cigarran (left) and Bob Stone oversee a proposal to purchase another hospital. As American Healthcorp purchased new hospital facilities, it devoted significant resources to modernize them.

Right: American Healthcorp's purchase of University Medical Center in Lebanon, Tennessee, was the company's first hospital acquisition and took nearly six months to complete.

Just six weeks later, American Healthcorp acquired the Russell County Medical Center in Lebanon, Virginia, a 78-bed general hospital that was in Chapter 11 bankruptcy.[26] The $8 million purchase included a medical office building and a Certificate of Need for a skilled nursing facility.[27] It was a rural area, but the population of the community had grown 17 percent during the previous decade.[28] Hospital Affiliates alum Dana Williams, then 26, was the appointed administrator.[29]

"All I had was energy, some experience, and a willingness to provide sweat equity, but I believed in these guys, and I think they believed in me," Williams said. "They took the greatest gamble they could take—to have a venture capital–backed company with the debt and the growth expectations they had and hand a big part of it over to a 26-year-old and say: 'Make it work.'"[30]

By May 1982, the $14.6 million acquisition of UMC in Lebanon was completed, and American Healthcorp added a 125-bed acute care hospital, 14 licensed nursing home beds, and a medical office building to its growing list of properties.

According to Gordon Bone, administrator of UMC prior to American Healthcorp's purchase, the sale would allow the facility to continue to uphold a condition of its charter—to support Cumberland College with profits generated from the sale of the hospital.

Unlike its two previous purchases, UMC was not as financially troubled as

RUSSELL COUNTY
VIRGINIA

a county with room to grow.

From the beautiful valleys with green pastures, to cool fishing streams and small lakes, to the scenic mountain peaks, Russell County has bountiful treasures that play an important part in human joy and well being. But aside from the sensual pleasures of beauty that Russell County has to offer, it is a fresh start, where one can be a part of planning an exciting future.

With the booming technology of the coal industry, combined with farming, retail, industry and commerce, Russell County has grown in great strides, not only in population, but financially as well. There is still plenty of "elbow room" to grow with four hundred eighty-three square miles located in the center of Southwest Virginia that is only an hour's drive from Tennessee, Kentucky, West Virginia and North Carolina.

Look us over and discover a fresh new dimension for yourself and your business.

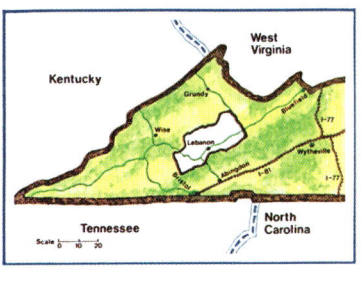

above top: Russell County's existing courthouse located in downtown Lebanon, Virginia
above bottom: Russell County's second courthouse used from 1799 to 1918. Restored in 1979

the bankrupt Russell County or the nearly vacant Tepper. As with its other properties, the company made quick improvements at UMC, expanding the intensive care unit and adding two operating rooms, obstetrics, and a same-day surgery program. Mary Hunter, who also had worked at Hospital Affiliates, was named administrator.

American Healthcorp's fourth hospital purchase—Harton Memorial Hospital in Tullahoma, Tennessee—epitomized the competitive and complex nature of hospital acquisitions. Those who followed the sale saw its price increase with each passing headline: "Two Firms Offer Over $10 Million for Hospital," the *Tullahoma News* reported

In the early 1980s, Russell County, Virginia, billed itself as "a county with room to grow." But when Dana Williams went there to revive a bankrupt hospital, one of his first tasks was rebuilding the medical staff. *(Photo courtesy of The Industrial Development Authority of Russell County, VA. russellcountyida @bvunet.net)*

on March 10, 1982. A week later, a headline read: "3 Firms Now Vying for Hospital." By the next week, it was: "Fourth Firm's Offer Is $11.5 Million."

American Healthcorp was the third company to enter the competition. HCA and Methodist Healthcare Systems (Memphis) had already submitted initial bids. And Humana would follow with a fourth offer.[31] "It was just like being back at Affiliates, duking it out with HCA," Stone said.

"The investor-owned hospital industry was really taking off," Herr said. "There were a lot of targets that were bigger, and therefore, we didn't see much in the way of competition for the first couple of

hospitals. It was in our backyard, and we decided that we wanted to make a real good run at that hospital. As a result, we found ourselves in competition with three other big players in the industry."

Although American Healthcorp's offer was ultimately selected, selling the hospital was a contentious issue in an area where the next closest hospital was 12 miles away. Public hearings drew hundreds of locals, and the Tullahoma Board of Aldermen even debated allowing a public referendum on the issue.

The mayor promised to cut property taxes by 40 percent if the sale went through.[32] For its part, American Healthcorp pledged to continue a

$7 million hospital expansion project that would add an operating room, emergency department, and pharmacy and expand physical therapy, radiology, and laboratory services.

"We won that competition with the bigger chains because we convinced the city fathers that as a smaller, Tennessee-based company, we could give the community and the hospital the attention from the senior managers that they probably wouldn't be able to get from a larger company," Herr said.

"There's no question in my mind that we were successful in Tullahoma because we approached it differently than the bigger firms, who treated it as pretty much just another acquisition," Cigarran added. "Bob Stone practically lived in Tullahoma for six months. We became part of that community and engaged civic groups, political leaders, financial institutions, hospital employees, and the citizens at large in our vision for what the hospital could become. At the end of the day, the town trusted us more than they did the other guys."

It was a hard-fought battle in Tullahoma but one that allowed American Healthcorp to get within reach of its goal. Although it did not have the five hospitals targeted in its initial plan, it did attain its targeted number of owned beds. By the end of its first year in business, American Healthcorp was in the black, posting $2,000 in monthly net income on $2 million in revenues.[33]

Obstacles to Acquisitions

Despite American Healthcorp's success in acquiring four hospitals in its first year, there were no new hospitals added to its portfolio in the subsequent two years. While its primary focus was on restructuring and growing the four hospitals it owned, it continued to look at additional hospital acquisition opportunities. In fact, management reported on a dozen potential hospital acquisitions in various stages of discussion at the September 1983 board of directors meeting.

Giles County Hospital, a 95-bed facility in Pulaski, Tennessee, was among them. Giles County had been managed by Hospital Affiliates and, later, HCA. The Giles County Commission explored selling the facility outright and sought bids. National Medical Enterprises (NME), a California-based hospital management company, offered $3 million more than American Healthcorp, HCA, and Republic. The county opted to negotiate exclusively with NME.[34] Soaring prices were slowing the growth of American Healthcorp's hospital business. Although American Healthcorp was by then a $75 million company, it elected not to get caught up in a bidding war. "We just were not prepared to pay more than we thought these facilities were worth," Cigarran noted. "We were active, but prices were unrealistically high during this period of feverish acquisition."

"I think the acquisition prices for hospitals right now are much, much too high," Hilton told the *Tennessean* newspaper. "I think that the prices will come down, and it may very well end up being a buyer's market someday rather than a seller's market."[35]

Before that could happen, though, the government—typically one of any hospital's largest sources of business— announced sweeping changes to the Medicare and Medicaid payment system. The new Prospective Payment System (PPS) called for predetermined payments regardless of the actual cost of treatment. Patients were grouped into categories called Diagnosis-Related Groups (DRGs), based on their reason for hospitalization and certain geographic, demographic, and medical factors. Hospitals were then paid a set fee to treat all patients who fell into this grouping, regardless of how long they stayed in the hospital or what additional care might be required.

Previously, Medicare had reimbursed the hospital for the costs incurred in treating each individual patient. The company felt that, over the course of a year, its government payments would average the same amount, but there would be initial delays as the new system was created as well as continuing uncertainties over payments.[36] This was of great concern, since as much as 50 percent of revenues at the four American Healthcorp-owned hospitals were from Medicare.[37]

"It could have created difficulties in planning and in growing the business," Stone said.[38]

Cigarran added:

Whenever the government switches from one system to another, there is a big delay in payment, and we didn't have the cash to withstand that. You had a chance to work on being more efficient and more effective and actually making more money, but we couldn't deal with the cash flow issue. We couldn't deal with the government holding our payments for six months. It could put us under.[39]

"I think the changes will, perhaps later rather than sooner, force hospitals to find particular niches and become very good and recognized in those niches," Hilton said. "Right now, everybody tries to be everything to everyone."[40]

Hospital Division Sold

Although American Healthcorp hospitals were doing very well under the existing reimbursement environment, the impending Medicare changes and the high prices for potential hospital acquisitions led the company to determine it could not compete effectively with the larger players in the industry. Because of the high prices, however, the company could maximize the value it had created under its ownership. As a result of those two factors, by September 1984—the end of its third year of business—American Healthcorp was in discussions to sell all four of its hospitals to NME, which had entered the Tennessee market through its successful $14.2 million acquisition of the Giles County Hospital the previous year. The discussions concluded with American Healthcorp receiving $52.3 million for the hospitals.[41]

"With only four hospitals, we could not effectively put together the kinds of services—such as ambulatory surgical care, home health care, and preferred provider arrangements—that could be provided for hospitals which are part of a system like HCA, Humana, or NME," Herr said.[42]

This sale was primarily about strategic positioning and marked American Healthcorp's ability to understand where the industry was heading: to sell its noncompetitive or regulatory-threatened businesses at the right time, and to launch new ones just ahead of emerging trends. The hospital

acquisition market was about to decline. But that no longer mattered to American Healthcorp; it had sold its hospitals at the very top of the market.

"We recognized that efficiency and specialization would prove to be keys to our future success," Stone said. "Hospital administrators rapidly learned that the only way you maintained your margin, or any margin, under the new payment system was to shrink length of stay, increase standardization, and find new services that could help them grow census. And administrators did shrink length of stay. As a result, overall average hospital census in the country dropped dramatically, creating significant unused capacity. Understanding what is happening in the health care market and addressing those issues with appropriate solutions not only helps patients, but it is also a solid business [model]."

Two such solutions that the company had been incubating for about a year would usher in the next chapter of American Healthcorp's success.

American Healthcorp's board of directors in the mid-1980s, left to right: John L. Hines; Wilbur H. Gantz; Martin J. Koldyke; Robert C. Hilton; John E. Sloan Jr.; John C. Brothers, MD; Thomas G. Cigarran.

Making a New Market

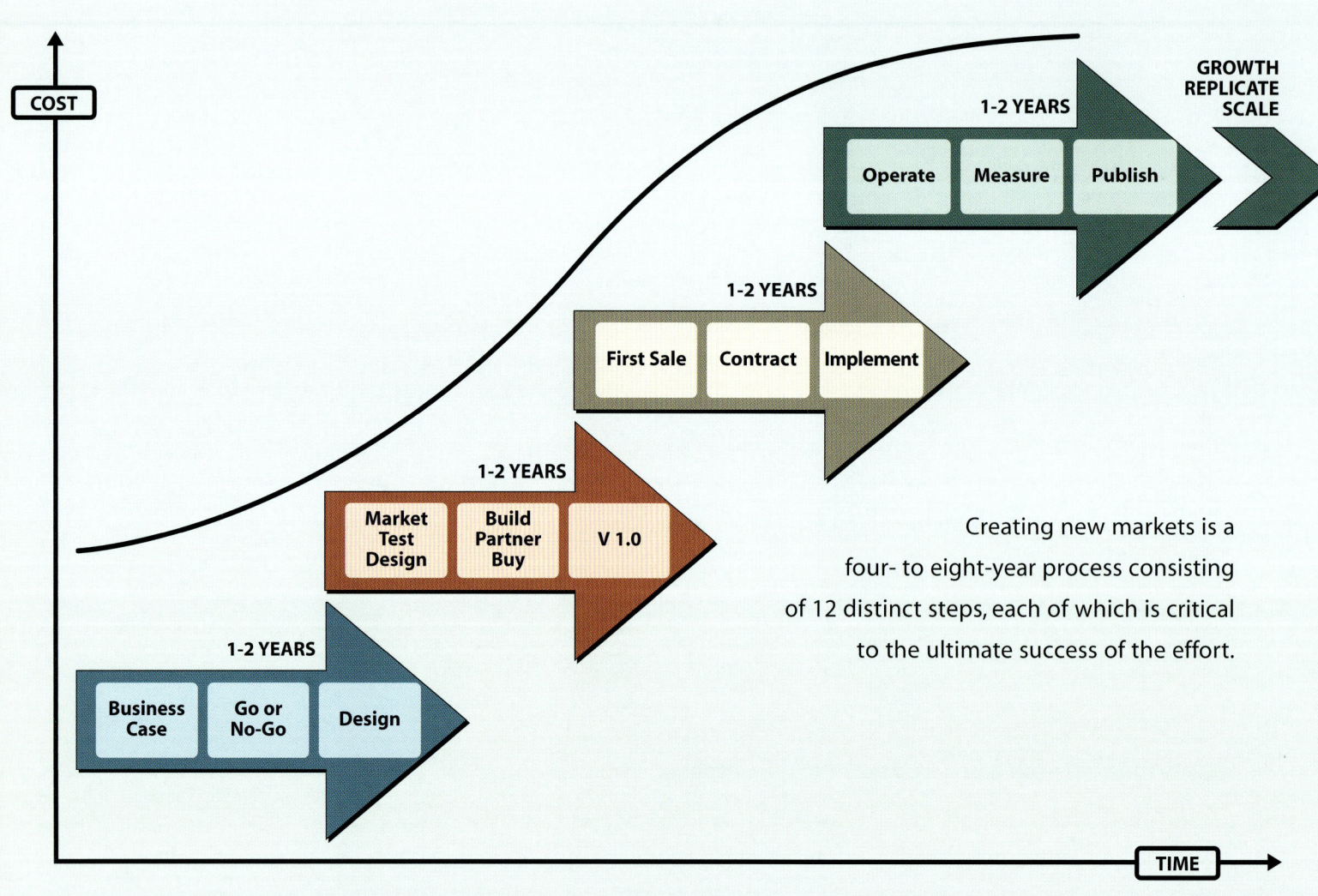

COST

1-2 YEARS
Operate	Measure	Publish

GROWTH REPLICATE SCALE

1-2 YEARS
First Sale	Contract	Implement

1-2 YEARS
Market Test Design	Build Partner Buy	V 1.0

Creating new markets is a
four- to eight-year process consisting
of 12 distinct steps, each of which is critical
to the ultimate success of the effort.

1-2 YEARS
Business Case	Go or No-Go	Design

TIME

SINCE ITS INCEPTION IN 1981, Healthways has pursued its purpose by creating solutions that respond to current and anticipated market needs. This market-driven approach has required the company to continuously innovate to expand the depth and breadth of its solutions. As a result, the number of people around the world who benefit from the company's efforts has grown from a few thousand in 1981 to nearly 40 million today. Making a new market requires a disciplined process that cannot be rushed. There are 12 distinct steps to the process, which, on average, requires four to eight years of investment before broad adoption by the market occurs.

Each of the four major processes in making a new market—reflected by the arrows shown in the graph (opposite page)—contain three key steps that must be decided on, created, tested, and/or applied. Provided the results are favorable throughout each phase, the level advances to the next process of work and decision-making.

Over its first three decades, Healthways' growth from a startup hospital company to its current position as the industry leader in well-being improvement can be seen (as reflected on the following two pages) in three significant and successful new market

development efforts. The first was the creation of solutions for facilities the company didn't own and included offerings in diabetes, arthritis, and physician practice-based single specialty surgery centers. Leveraging the success of the diabetes solution, the second new market effort was focused on payers, including health plans, employers, and governments. This market, while originally limited to domestic customers, was subsequently extended internationally. The third, and current, new market process not only adds communities and individuals to the list of actual and potential clients but, in the aftermath of health care reform, returns the company to its roots with new solutions for hospital and physician organizations.

Like all good stories, the 30-year evolution of Healthways from hospital company to diabetes company to disease management company to well-being improvement company has been characterized by successes, challenges, and moments of high drama. Its successful adaptation to the ever-changing landscape of the highly complex health care industry is testament to its unswerving commitment to its purpose: *To Create a Healthier World, One Person at a Time.*

Market-Driven Solutions

Diabetes care, disease management, and developing solutions to improve well-being are the "three great stages" of Healthways' market evolution. The three stages provide a natural growth strategy, moving from excelling at improving the lives of those with one disorder to benefiting everyone, regardless of their current health level.

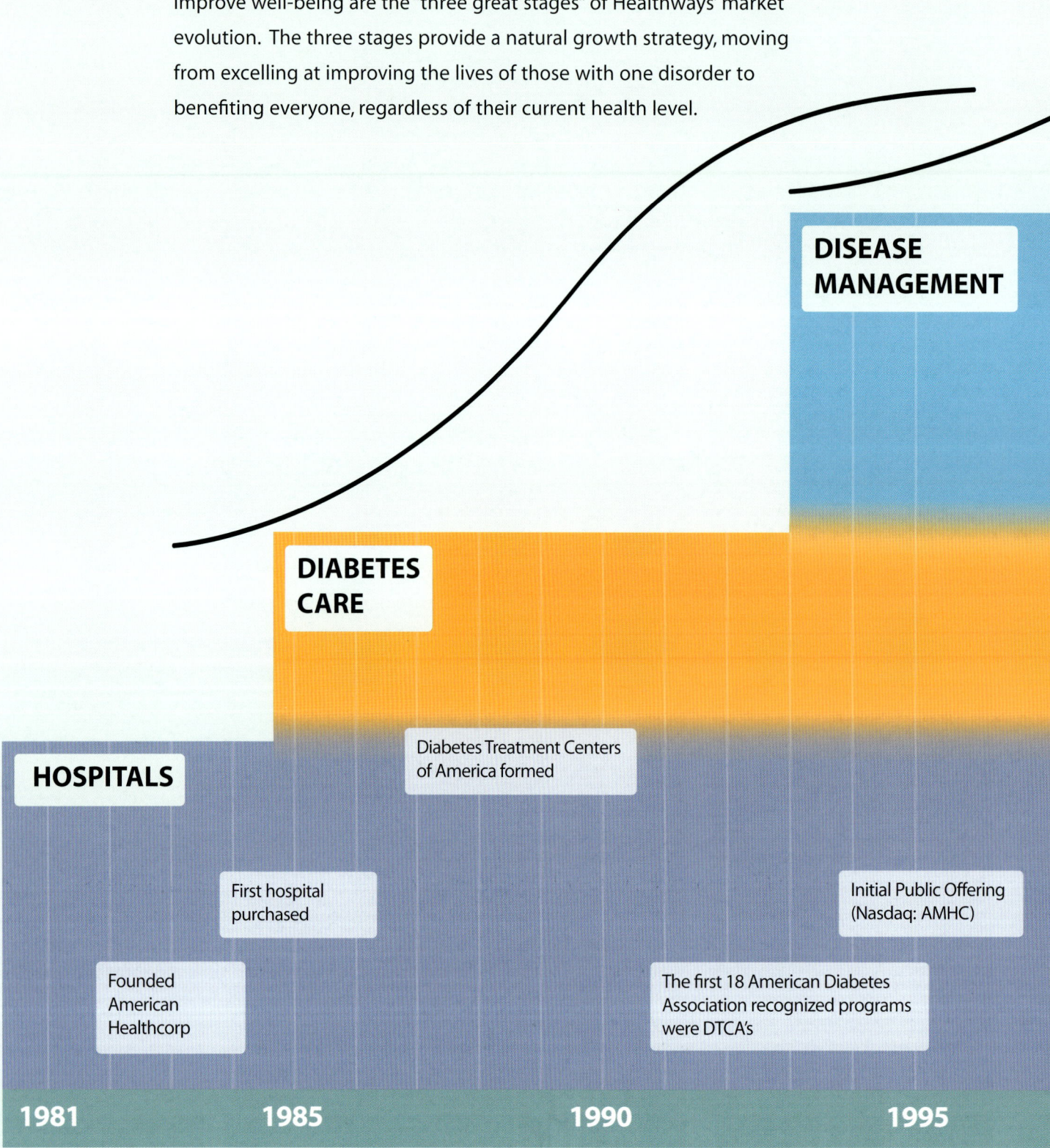

DISEASE MANAGEMENT

DIABETES CARE

HOSPITALS

Diabetes Treatment Centers of America formed

First hospital purchased

Initial Public Offering (Nasdaq: AMHC)

Founded American Healthcorp

The first 18 American Diabetes Association recognized programs were DTCA's

1981   1985   1990   1995

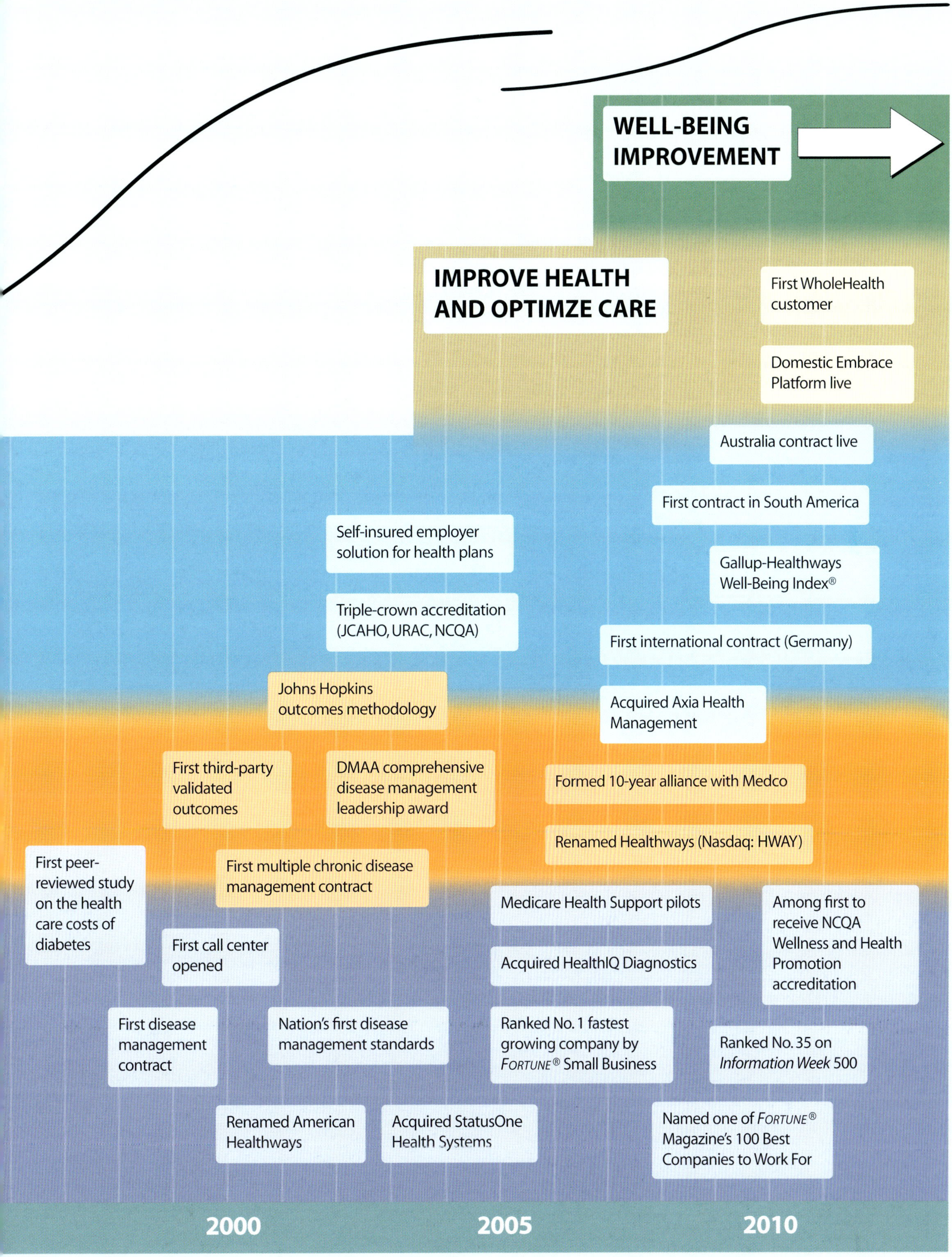

WELL-BEING IMPROVEMENT →

IMPROVE HEALTH AND OPTIMZE CARE

First WholeHealth customer

Domestic Embrace Platform live

Australia contract live

First contract in South America

Gallup-Healthways Well-Being Index®

Self-insured employer solution for health plans

Triple-crown accreditation (JCAHO, URAC, NCQA)

First international contract (Germany)

Johns Hopkins outcomes methodology

Acquired Axia Health Management

First third-party validated outcomes

DMAA comprehensive disease management leadership award

Formed 10-year alliance with Medco

Renamed Healthways (Nasdaq: HWAY)

First peer-reviewed study on the health care costs of diabetes

First multiple chronic disease management contract

Medicare Health Support pilots

Among first to receive NCQA Wellness and Health Promotion accreditation

First call center opened

Acquired HealthIQ Diagnostics

First disease management contract

Nation's first disease management standards

Ranked No. 1 fastest growing company by *FORTUNE*® Small Business

Ranked No. 35 on *Information Week* 500

Renamed American Healthways

Acquired StatusOne Health Systems

Named one of *FORTUNE*® Magazine's 100 Best Companies to Work For

2000   **2005**   **2010**

Above: Koala's broad range of services and focus on excellence helped make it one of the leading substance abuse treatment programs in the country.

Opposite: Koala Centers' mission statement—*to help people achieve and maintain recovery physically, emotionally, and spiritually, one day at a time*—recognized that sobriety was a journey, not a destination.

[Koala] was very successful for us. We had developed Koala into one of the leading alcohol and substance abuse treatment providers in the country. One of the things we saw beginning ... we saw cracks in insurers who were beginning to say, "We're not going to cover this as we have in the past."[1]

—Henry Herr, founder,
former executive vice president
and chief financial officer

A S THE REVENUES AND PROFITS FROM ITS FOUR HOSPITALS BEGAN TO FLOW, American Healthcorp began the process of diversifying its lines of business. "Our goal was to find segments in health care in which we could be a market leader," Tom Cigarran said. "We knew from the beginning that our hospital business was only a means to that end."

In its 1981 business plan, American Healthcorp indicated that ownership and management of psychiatric hospitals, including drug and alcohol programs, would "receive significant management attention."[2] By 1983, the company had the resources to act.

Unfortunately, the psychiatric hospital market was heavily dominated by the big four hospital companies. Unwilling to engage in another round of highly competitive acquisitions, the company chose to focus on the less-penetrated market opportunity of alcohol and substance abuse treatment.

An Area of Great Need

While alcoholism and drug abuse were not new health care issues, by the early 1980s, much had changed with respect to the understanding of the diseases and their treatment. Nevertheless, the impact of substance abuse on families, businesses, and society in general was significant. Alcohol was a factor in six out of every 10 automobile crashes, and in this era of designer drugs that could be made at home, access no longer required a clandestine visit to a dealer.

The American Medical Association had declared alcoholism a "disease" in the mid-1950s. By the early 1980s, though, that theory was still debated and hardly a majority viewpoint. The TV program *Nova* reported in early 1984 on groundbreaking research that alcoholics were often genetically predisposed to alcoholism.[3]

The country was in the midst of its "Just Say No" phase as well. First Lady Nancy Reagan hosted an international conference on drug abuse at the United Nations.[4] Substance abuse was estimated to cost $180 billion per year in health care, lost productivity, and the like.[5]

By 1988, an estimated 16 to 24 million Americans were abusing alcohol and drugs. Of those, about 10 million needed treatment, and 1.5 million were ready to enter a treatment program.[6]

The Koala Centers, including this one in Lebanon, Indiana, were based on an inpatient strategy, with those seeking help staying a month or more.

Recognizing the need, the opportunity it presented, and the market's compatibility with the company's vision, American Healthcorp entered the space with the purchase of Koala Centers, an investment that would provide significant financial strength for the company in the years following the sale of its hospitals.

Acquisition and Opportunity

The privately held Koala Centers operated two facilities in Indiana. Named after the Australian marsupial that doesn't drink, deriving most of its fluids from chewing on eucalyptus leaves, Koala was founded in 1976. Its first center, an adult treatment facility in Lebanon, Indiana, was opened a year later. A 60-bed adult center in Columbus, Indiana, was opened in 1982.

By the time American Healthcorp purchased Koala in 1983 for $8.6 million, the six-year-old Lebanon facility was operating in excess of 80 percent occupancy, and patient stays averaged slightly more than three weeks.[7] Two more facilities were scheduled to be built in Indiana—one in Plymouth, and one in Indianapolis. When construction of the two new facilities was complete, 265 beds had been added to American Healthcorp's management.[8]

Operations at the Koala Centers were more standardized than the operations at general hospitals, where patient stays varied depending on illness and health conditions. At Koala Centers, the typical patient stayed three to five days for detoxification, then another 21 to 25 days for rehabilitation. During the final week, the patient's family stayed onsite and participated in rehabilitation. A one-year outpatient program was recommended.[9]

"Everything about it was first-rate, including the reputation, the people, the facilities, and the way it was run," Cigarran said. "People were proud to be associated with it."[10]

Within a year, the company had four Koala Centers in operation and added three others by purchasing Professional Care Services, Inc., (ProCare) for $13 million in April 1984. ProCare, which operated 264 substance abuse beds in Florida, Pennsylvania, and Missouri under the White Deer name, was an attractive acquisition.[11]

"There is a growing need for these services," Cigarran said at the time. "There is an increased awareness of the benefits to society of effectively treating alcoholism early, before additional medical complications arise."[12] The acquisition also added relationships with outpatient treatment providers for United Auto Workers union members.

Koala Centers and White Deer merged into a new subsidiary, American Treatment Centers, but continued to operate under the Koala Center name. By early 1984, the subsidiary had seven

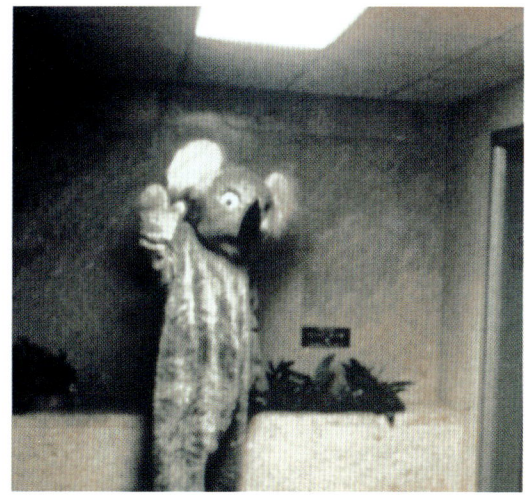

Koala Centers featured a marsupial mascot who occasionally made appearances at events.

freestanding centers, two under construction, and three operating in hospitals. Within a year, three more Koala centers were under construction. In 1985, the division provided $16.5 million in revenues to the company.[13]

A Major Contribution

Koala was a strong business line for American Healthcorp throughout the 1980s. After the sale of the hospital division, it was Koala that kept the company strong. Koala was also emblematic of the company's philosophy when entering a new market: "We have no interest in entering a market where we cannot be the dominant or one of the dominant players," Cigarran told the *Wall Street Journal.*[14]

By the late 1980s, Koala was one of the largest providers of substance abuse services in the country. American Healthcorp had nine freestanding and six in-hospital facilities with another 25 outreach offices.[15]

Koala had inpatient alcohol programs aimed at women, adolescents, and older adults, and was also addressing the top drug crisis of the time with a cocaine treatment program. Inpatient services were supplemented with outpatient treatment and aftercare programs, providing a variety of access points for patients and ensuring the continuity of intervention recognized as being critical for effective treatment. All had one thing in common: results. Participants in Koala's various programs had impressive long-term sobriety rates.

Koala also showcased the company's understanding that health issues had widespread impact. American Healthcorp listed the program's benefits beyond those that affected the patient specifically: reduced employer costs in areas such as health insurance, absenteeism, and hiring and training costs and reduced associated societal costs resulting in unemployment, crime, and accidents.

Sensing the Future

By all accounts, Koala was an unqualified success—for the patients who chose to enter treatment at the centers as well as American Healthcorp. During the first five months of fiscal year 1988, Koala accounted for more than 61 percent of American Healthcorp's revenues.[16]

But the industry was about to change. Driving the changes were rising health care costs, which were increasing at 15 percent per year. Employee health plans had been a large customer of substance abuse centers, but to offset the rising costs, strict limits were placed on substance abuse treatment. "They couldn't do anything about someone who had an appendectomy or if they broke their leg," Cigarran said. "But an employee who couldn't stop drinking, they thought, 'We can change the way we pay for their care.'"[17] Inpatient treatment options were tightened, if not eliminated,

Business Awards

1987 Advantage Business Awards
Company of the Year: Koala Centers

"... Koala's expansion can also be attributed to its operators' constant efforts to find the best ways to treat addiction. Recognizing that all addicts are not alike, Koala has innovatively designed separate treatment programs for men, women, adolescents, older adults, relapsed addicts and cocaine addicts. Recently, the company began a program for a newly recognized illness called co-dependency ..."

Annually in its August issue, *Advantage* asks its readers to nominate "the company that has excelled over the past year beyond others in its field. The company will have displayed measurable success in meeting the demands of its industry, while also helping to set a standard for corporate responsibility."

Koala Centers Can Help

Koala is constantly finding new ways to help troubled people with different needs achieve the same goal — recovery from substance abuse.

Koala Adolescent Center - Nashville

Koala Center of Tennessee Christian Medical Center

More than 40 Koala treatment programs are dedicated to treating the growing disease of addiction in Indiana, Michigan, Missouri, Pennsylvania, Florida, North Carolina, Louisiana, Arkansas, Kentucky, Tennessee and surrounding areas.

In 1987, Koala Centers is proud to have received this honor from *Advantage*, and national recognition from *Forbes*, which cited Koala as one of the country's 12 best providers of alcohol and drug treatment.

For more information on specific substance abuse treatment programs call **1-800-433-3009**. Or see your local telephone directory for the Koala Center nearest you.

KOALA CENTERS

and strict limits to how often an employee could use outpatient options seemed imminent.

American Healthcorp became concerned about the long-term prospects for its substance abuse business. That unease led to the $62 million sale of Koala Centers in 1989.[18] Its predictions of future changes "gave us a reputation of having advanced knowledge of what was happening in the market," said Henry Herr, chief financial officer at the time. "It isn't here yet, but we don't want to take the chance. And we were right. Within about a year or a year and a half … insurers started to cut back on coverage for alcohol and substance abuse. So it became a much more difficult market out there. It didn't disappear, but the financials became much more problematic. It would have been much more difficult for us."[19]

While others may have questioned how American Healthcorp was able to read the market so clearly yet again, it was an instance in which the company's small size was a help.

Herr believed:

We were close to our customers. We were close to the people who were paying the bills. Because we weren't this gigantic company … we heard things a little bit earlier, and we felt things a little bit earlier than a lot of the bigger companies that were out there, and we were able to react accordingly at that time.[20]

In the company's history, its ownership of Koala Centers was brief. But it showcased several elements that would become deeply ingrained in the company's culture: anticipating health care needs before they were widely understood, perceiving the ripple impact of disease on employers and society, and knowing when—and being willing—to change.

Bill of Rights for Persons with Diabetes

Preamble

We, the Medical Directors of Diabetes Treatment Centers of America, believe that persons with diabetes have fundamental rights that derive from their complex health care needs. We believe that many people with diabetes are being denied these rights. And, we believe that all physicians have an obligation to act as patient advocates in the dissemination of and pursuit of these rights on behalf of the person with diabetes.

Rights

1. All persons with diabetes have the right to enjoy an active and fulfilling life.

2. All persons with diabetes have the right not to suffer job discrimination on the basis of their disease.

3. All persons with diabetes have the right to have access to state-of-the-art diabetes care including comprehensive educations.

4. All persons with diabetes have the right to have affordable healthcare insurance which will provide payment for treatment, education and supplies.

5. All persons with diabetes have the right to be informed about the implications of diabetes control and its effect on their ultimate health and well-being.

6. All persons with diabetes have the right to have access to an endocrinologist or other qualified diabetes specialist.

7. All persons with diabetes have the right to have access to other forms of specialty care, such as eye, foot and kidney care.

8. All persons with diabetes during pregnancy have the right to be treated by an endocrinologist or other qualified diabetes specialist.

9. All persons with Type 1 diabetes during pregnancy have the right to receive care by a high-risk pregnancy team, including an endocrinologist or other qualified diabetes specialist.

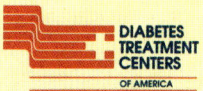

DIABETES TREATMENT CENTERS OF AMERICA

Above: Physicians affiliated with Diabetes Treatment Centers of America (DTCA) created a Bill of Rights for Persons with Diabetes stating that people with diabetes "have fundamental rights that derive from their complex health care needs." The bill detailed nine specific rights, including access to specialists and specialty care, and the right to enjoy an "active and fulfilling life."

Opposite: Tepper Hospital, a former children's hospital in Chattanooga, Tennessee, was the birthplace of the DTCA program.

If you are open, if you are flexible, if you have the right outlook toward what is going on, you can function and thrive no matter which direction the company is moving.[1]

—Steve Samples, senior vice president–finance

AMERICAN HEALTHCORP'S MARKET INSIGHTS WERE TO PAY OFF AGAIN WITH ITS ENTRY into the business of contracting with hospitals to provide inpatient centers of excellence for people with diabetes. As an outgrowth of its experience with a pilot program developed at the company's Metropolitan Hospital in Chattanooga, Tennessee, Diabetes Treatment Centers of America (DTCA) would become the nation's leading provider of services for people with diabetes and a key player in translating rapidly emerging new treatment science from academia to the patient care setting.

In the early 1980s, the most effective way to treat diabetes was a matter of significant professional debate. While many physician specialists believed that maintaining blood glucose levels as close to normal as possible was key to enabling patients to live longer and more normal lives and to reduce the incidence and/or severity of diabetes' well-known complications, there was no scientific evidence to support that contention. At the same time, new technologies such as self-directed blood glucose monitors and insulin pumps were being introduced, offering real options for more effective patient self-management of the disease.

"As is often the case with great business decisions, the timing was perfect for our entry into diabetes care," Tom Cigarran noted. "We had a clinically successful and financially viable model in Chattanooga. Hospital census was declining nationally as the result of Diagnostic Related Groups, hospital administrators wanted to fill those beds, and physicians and patients wanted new and more comprehensive services."[2]

Current Healthways president and CEO Ben Leedle recently reminisced:

Looking back, the development of DTCA was the company's first experience in making and then leading a new health care market. While the dynamics of that market have changed significantly over the past 27 years, the need for effective services for people with diabetes has not; in fact, it's grown. This increase has occurred—despite all the advances in treatment, monitoring, and self-management that have been introduced over that time—principally as a result of a rapidly increasing incidence of the disease resulting at least in part from personal dietary choices and sedentary lifestyles. While the financial growth of DTCA was slower than we experienced with Koala, the need to provide services aimed at improving the lives of people with diabetes has proved to be long-lived. Our original centers of excellence model is still being provided to some 50 hospitals today, but more importantly, our experience in diabetes through the 1980s and into the early 1990s provided the experiential foundation for the company's next market-making effort—our move into chronic disease management.[3]

It All Began with a Figure Skater

When American Healthcorp had purchased its four hospitals, all were struggling to fill empty hospital beds. The Tepper Hospital in Chattanooga, Tennessee, was particularly challenging. It had begun as a children's hospital and faced stiff competition from a new 100-bed children's hospital at the nearby Erlanger Medical Center.[4]

Under state law at the time, children's hospitals could treat adults as long as the adult census was less than 50 percent of licensed bed capacity. In 1982, the company began to aggressively recruit physicians for Tepper, which by then had been renamed Metropolitan Hospital, adding an obstetrician/gynecologist; an ear, nose, and throat specialist; and a family practitioner. Seizing on the momentum to expand, American Healthcorp inadvertently found an opportunity that would eventually become the mainstay of its business.[5]

Dr. Robert Creech was a physician at the Diabetes Hospital at the University of Alabama–Birmingham and had built a successful regional practice. An ardent proponent of what was known as "tight control," Creech, a diabetes patient himself, taught his patients how to monitor themselves and more effectively manage their blood sugars to keep the levels as close to normal as possible.

But getting him to relocate his successful practice from a diabetes specialty facility that was part of a university teaching hospital to the company's little-known—and arguably less-prestigious—facility, resulted from a family, rather than a clinical, desire. Creech's daughter was a budding figure skater, and his wife drove her to skating lessons in Chattanooga twice a week—a 300-mile round-trip. While Metropolitan offered Creech the opportunity to direct his own program, eliminating that twice-weekly trip made the decision to relocate much easier to reach. Following a regimen developed at the Joslin Diabetes Center in Boston, Massachusetts—where he did his fellowship—Creech and Metropolitan Hospital began to offer diabetes patients a program for lifetime control of their diabetes. This included an inpatient admission during which the patients worked with a dietitian, a nurse educator, an exercise specialist, and a counselor to learn what caused their blood sugars to rise and fall and how to make the dietary, exercise, and behavioral choices that would help keep them under control.[6]

Within weeks of his arrival in Chattanooga, participation in the diabetes program had increased the hospital's average daily census significantly. "Due to complications and related disorders, people with diabetes are hospitalized a lot more than the average individual without diabetes," said Henry Herr. The number and severity of these associated outcomes are directly related to how successful the patient is in controlling blood sugar levels. "There was a big consumer demand. There were a

New career/practice growth opportunities for the physician with a special interest in the patient with diabetes.

The Regional Diabetes Treatment Center

A quality care program

DIABETES TREATMENT CENTERS OF AMERICA

The Diabetes Treatment Centers of American (DTCA) model began with identifying an appropriate location, then reaching out to physicians who could champion the effort.

lot of people … with diabetes, and our general knowledge as we learned what was going on in the diabetes marketplace was that most of them—and their physicians—were dissatisfied with the care that they were receiving," Herr recalled.[7]

"Bob [Creech] helped us develop what essentially became the prototype program that Diabetes Treatment Centers of America then provided under contract to other hospitals around the nation," explained Bob Stone. "He said, 'I need a nurse educator. I need a dietitian. I need an exercise specialist and a counselor.' Patients came in who, other than their diabetes, were essentially healthy. Dr. Creech recognized that these patients needed to know how to take care of themselves since about 99 percent of their lives occur outside of the doctor's office."[8]

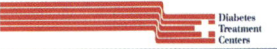

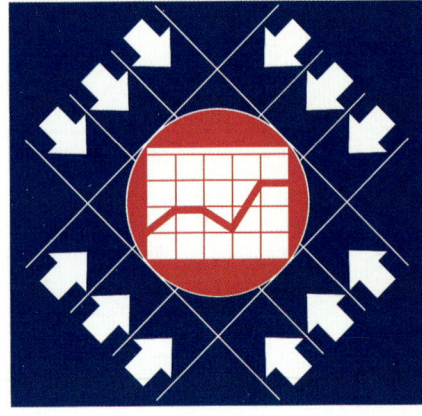

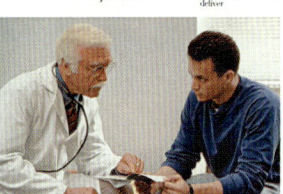

Practice Transcript.

Outcomes Reporting
For Diabetes Populations

Helping Physicians Provide Proof Of Value

Purchasers of health care services are demanding evidence that proves they are receiving real value–better outcomes at lower costs–from health care providers

The Opportunity.

Physicians who can successfully document outcomes for their patient populations with diabetes can:
• Demonstrate the clinical effectiveness of their patient care services
• Continuously improve the quality of care they deliver
• Enhance their credibility
• Improve the likelihood of and facilitate achieving ADA Provider Recognition
• Create and maintain a competitive advantage in their marketplace
• Increase their market share

Until now, the resources, systems and processes necessary to capture the data required to document outcomes for populations with diabetes were beyond the horizon of most physician practices. Now Practice Transcript provides a solution.

Practice Transcript Outcomes Reporting System.

Practice Transcript is the first outcomes reporting system for populations with diabetes developed by the physicians who treat those populations. Over 40 physicians, including members of DTCA's prestigious Medical Director and Scientific Advisory Councils, participated in the creation of the data collection tools, the outcomes standards, and the report formats for Practice Transcript. Through seven months of refinement and testing, they helped create a fully functional process to enable physicians to document the care they provide to their patients with diabetes.

Specifically, Practice Transcript is designed to:
• Facilitate the recording of critical diabetes patient data
• Provide data entry into the DTCA Practice Transcript database
• Provide data segmentation and analysis
• Generate reports that validate treatment protocols, lead to improved treatment methods, and document clinical outcomes

Practice Transcript requires a minimal investment of physician time as compared to the significant benefits it offers. Quarterly reports provide each participating physician with detailed information about their practice and benchmark comparisons to other DTCA physicians as well as practices external to the DTCA network.

Practice Transcript Provides The Proof That Payors Demand.

You know you are a good doctor. Unfortunately, your knowing it is no longer good enough. You have to be able to prove it –continuously–to payors and, increasingly, to patients. By taking the lead with Practice Transcript, you will be uniquely positioned in your community to document the clinical outcomes you are achieving. While other physicians can only assert their value, you will be able to document yours. That is competitive advantage in an environment where "seats at the table" are becoming increasingly difficult to secure and maintain.

Moreover, Practice Transcript measures what should be measured. The data collected is specific to the outcomes that are meaningful for a population with diabetes. They are not the general population standards so often used by payors to evaluate physicians. And by using Practice Transcript you are helping to assure that its diabetes-specific standards will be the only standards by which your work with patients with diabetes is judged.

Sign Up Today and Prove Your Worth.

Enclosed you will find samples of a Physician Header form, data collection forms, Practice Transcript reports, and chart stickers that form the basic tools of the system.

If you want to realize the benefits of Practice Transcript to improve your competitive advantage and market position please completely fill out the Physician Header form to enroll in the program.

Your DTCA program manager will answer any questions you may have about the Practice Transcript process and benefits.

The Practice Transcript™ Outcomes Reporting System helped doctors demonstrate the effectiveness of their patient care.

Physician referrals to, and patient demand for, the new program were so great that Creech was soon working 16-hour days, six days a week, according to Stone. By September 1982, Chattanooga's Metropolitan Hospital had a daily average of 27.7 patients, which was significantly higher than the six patients it had when American Healthcorp purchased the facility.[9]

Because the practice in Chattanooga filled very quickly, American Healthcorp began talking to other endocrinologists about relocating to Chattanooga and helping Creech deal with the increasing demand. While the response was overwhelmingly positive to the idea that tight control of blood sugar levels was the right approach to maintaining the health of those with diabetes, no one was willing to move to Chattanooga.[10]

"The doctors we spoke with said, 'I'd really like you to come and convince the administrator of my hospital that this makes business sense. In fact, if you can't convince the administrator of my hospital, but you can convince the administrator of the other hospital in town, I'll move my practice over there,'" said Stone. "We didn't have to hear that too many times before we realized we had a valuable offering that was both scalable and marketable."[11]

When American Healthcorp realized the widespread need for the program and the level of physician support it garnered, the company began offering its innovative treatment concept to other hospitals, not just the ones it owned. Lakewood Hospital in Long Beach, California, and Shallowford Community Hospital, near Atlanta, were the first two to sign on.[12] As hospitals began to feel the census impact of DRG reimbursement, the floodgates opened, and the company added 18 additional contracts in 1985.

With each new program, the company hired a team of doctors, a diabetes nurse educator, a dietitian, an exercise specialist, and a counselor, along with a dedicated, onsite program manager. In Wichita, Kansas, the exercise specialist was Leedle, who joined the company in 1985 during the rapid growth of DTCA. A graduate of Emporia State University in Emporia, Kansas, with a master's degree in exercise physiology, he had originally planned to teach physical education and coach sports following graduation.[13]

"It's easy to look back 25 years and see just how lucky I was to have fallen into the opportunity to be in this company," said Leedle, who would be named president and chief operating officer in 2001 and CEO in 2003. "What would have happened if I had taken a different job or done something different? The company gives people chances—regardless of their formal preparation in life—to learn the business and share in it, and if they're passionate about it, to contribute in very different roles over time."[14]

For physicians and other health care professionals, it meant a chance to be on the cutting edge of health care and to shape the models of delivery to improve patient care at all levels.

"We were creating curricula and materials and programs and training for the nurses as well as the patients," said Pat

Lynch, who joined DTCA in Atlanta as a dietitian in 1984. "It was very new, and there was a lot that we could do on our own to create things that would be helpful to the company."[15]

DTCA was also expanding its reputation within the health care industry. In 1987, the Diabetes Treatment Center at Georgetown Hospital was the nation's first hospital awarded recognition by the American Diabetes Association (ADA) for program excellence.[16] Of the additional 20 programs the ADA would recognize that year, the next 17 were all affiliated with DTCA. Ultimately, all of the company's diabetes treatment centers became ADA Recognized.

Expanding DTCA

By 1990, Diabetes Treatment Centers of America and American Healthcorp were essentially synonymous. Following the sale of Koala in 1989, DTCA was the only business line the company had in the market. The company was dedicated to helping patients with diabetes learn how to best manage their

Above: Diabetes Treatment Centers of America (DTCA) provided valuable assistance to its patients, even as the company widened its scope, supported by clinicians and staff strongly tied to the communities in which they served. DTCA centers even sent out holiday cards.

Left: Tom Cigarran, left; Phil Stuart, center; and Kathy Kirk, right; celebrate new contracts for DTCA centers.

DTCA Foundation

S TAYING ON TOP OF THE LATEST RESEARCH WAS VITAL TO THE DIABETES TREATMENT Centers of America (DTCA). In 1985, American Healthcorp created the DTCA Foundation, a nonprofit organization, to fund clinical research that could lead to new treatments to improve the lives of those with the disease.

The DTCA Foundation provided grants to young researchers, with applications vetted by leading diabetes physicians and researchers who served on the foundation's scientific advisory board. Those members, along with the directors of the DTCA facilities around the country, held semiannual meetings.

"It provided an opportunity for the academics and the clinicians to get together on a regular basis and talk about what was going on in their relative spheres," said American Healthcorp cofounder Bob

Stone. "They were working to try and deal more effectively with people with diabetes."[1]

After a few years, the foundation concluded that the research funded by the grants was not creating the kinds of outcomes it had hoped to see for the patients served through DTCA.

In 1989, the DTCA Foundation was closed. However, the physician meetings provided such a valuable opportunity for leading researchers to come together to share information, to hear about the latest

disease and enjoy the best possible state of health. The resources provided by the sale of its substance abuse division allowed the company to focus all of its efforts on strengthening the DTCA model. By 1991, there were 57 centers in operation, and the company had identified 300 additional potential sites, with 35 in active discussion.[17]

By this time, both the sales and operational models were streamlined and effective. The company would identify a potential market location, approach endocrinologists and diabetologists in that

area, discuss the need for resources, and demonstrate how DTCA could deliver those resources for the physicians and their patients.

"We'd get [the physicians] all excited about the possibility of having those resources and have them take us to the hospital administrator," said Kathy Kirk, who joined DTCA in sales in 1986. "The good news was that the administrator knew there was physician support. The bad news was that the administrator could feel coerced by the physicians."[18]

research, and to spark ideas for new treatments that the meetings continued as the Annual Physicians Meeting.[2]

The legacy of the DTCA Foundation, and its testament to the company's recognition that the fundamental interaction in health care is between patient and physician, was a continuing commitment to provide physicians with the opportunity to provide input into both the company's programs and critical issues in health care. The focus of these annual meeetings would continue to change to reflect emerging trends in the delivery of health care services. The first such

evolution was to an Annual Outcomes Summit in conjunction with the company's relationship with Johns Hopkins. Today, the purpose of these annual meetings continues through the Healthways Well-Being Summit.

The Diabetes Treatment Centers of America Foundation provided grants for diabetes research.

Despite the proven success of the model, it was not always an easy sell.

"There were hospitals that didn't have an appreciation of the needs of patients with diabetes. We would hear things like, 'We don't admit people for diabetes, because they didn't know that 20 percent of the people in their beds had diabetes, which aggravated whatever other health issues they had," Kirk said. "We used to call diabetes the 'Rodney Dangerfield of diseases,' in a hospital administrator's mind. It wasn't high-tech like cardiac. And

sometimes the hospitals that did understand wanted to treat it themselves."[19]

But as the DTCA model grew, American Healthcorp provided the statistics to demonstrate the program's success. The company offered two versions of the program. In the first, American Healthcorp hired the professional staff and paid the medical director and marketing expenses. In the second, only the center manager was hired by the company. Both arrangements also carried incentives.

"It seemed doable," said Emily Cook, who joined DTCA in 1989 as a center program manager. "[We wanted] to have an excellent program with good service that would attract more and more patients to that hospital. It helped people, [and] it was abundantly clear that it was up to me to hit the targets, to lead a team of people to hit the targets, and there were suggestions and tools about how to get there. But I knew where the accountability was, and that was with me. I liked that."[20]

Focusing on diabetes helped the company as well. In 1992, the company had revenues of $30.1 million and earnings of $1.39 million.[21]

In addition to 300 larger prospective markets—those with populations of 250,000 or more—management also had identified some 1,200 smaller markets for potential expansion in which the need for diabetes services was significant. The need for services that DTCA had identified nearly a decade earlier had not decreased; if anything, it was growing. The challenge for the company was in identifying and recruiting the highly qualified colleagues it would need to serve that growing need. In typical Healthways fashion, the company

decided that the best way to find new talent to manage its growing diabetes business was to grow its own.[22]

The Healthways Director-in-Development Program consisted of a one-year curriculum designed to give high-performing managers across the business the tools they needed to take on greater responsibility as the company grew. The first class comprised eight corporate and DTCA colleagues, including Leedle, who at the time was the DTCA program manager in Charleston, South Carolina.

"It was a hell of a commitment," Leedle remembered. "You and your family moved to Nashville without knowing where your next job would be. The company spent a full year exposing you to all elements of the business, and at the end of that year, you had to agree, in advance, to go wherever the company needed you to go."[23]

About nine months into that year, Leedle was tapped to move into business development. His initial response was a rather direct "I don't think so. I'm not a salesperson—I'm on the operating side. I understand how to make these things work."[24]

Convinced to give sales a try, Leedle ended up having the time of his life. "The way I thought about it was that there were communities in this country that didn't have the advantage of having a center of excellence," Leedle recalled. "I was able to find those places and meet new people who cared about doing better for people with diabetes and who wanted to lead from a medical

Registered nurses have always played a critical role in patient care, and working with American Healthcorp has given many RNs an opportunity to move into senior executive roles. JoAnne Westerfield (center) and Patty Orr (right), standing beside CEO Tom Cigarran, both became vice presidents at the company.

standpoint as a physician or as hospital administrator. [They wanted to] create a center of excellence in their community. I've had lots of fun in the company, but I can't remember having more fun than doing that."

Leedle sold contracts for five new centers in his first 18 months in the position.

"I had a really deep belief that what I was involved with, through this company, was one of the most important things going on in the world," Leedle said. "You could really make a great difference for people in their communities. How could they not have this program?"[25]

Federal Study Supports DTCA Model

In 1993, DTCA received another boost from a landmark, nine-year government study. The Diabetes Control and Complications Trial (DCCT) provided strong evidence that the very glucose control methods Diabetes Treatment Centers of America had taught for nearly a decade produced significant reductions in complications for those with diabetes.

Specifically, the DCCT findings showed that strictly controlling blood glucose levels reduced the risk of eye disease 76 percent, the risk of kidney disease 50 percent, and the risk of nerve disease 60 percent.[26]

American Healthcorp continued expanding its treatment of diabetes patients, with 67 diabetes treatment centers in 29 states by 1993. That year, American Healthcorp brought in $44 million in revenue with $5.5 million in profits. The company's small sales team helped identify new areas where DTCA could best expand its services to support the existing medical community.

"I don't think it was anything magical," said Leedle, describing why he considered the sales team so successful. "I think it had to do with a really deep belief that what we were doing—what the company was doing—was really important and making a difference."[27]

A Challenging Year

Despite the promising success of 1993, the next year proved exceedingly challenging. The entire health care industry faced a period of difficult transitions.

"Everyone in health care—physicians, hospitals, managed care executives, and insurers—is on a journey to a new delivery

Left: As DTCA's concept proved increasingly successful, the company shared statistics indicating dramatic cost savings. Cofounder Bob Stone is shown here at a press conference at the National Press Club in Washington, DC, reporting on the company's clinical and financial outcomes.

Below: Patty Schultz, DTCA executive and senior vice president of the ADA, often represented the company at key industry functions, including the International Diabetes Foundation meeting in 1991. She appeared with national spokesman and comedian Tom Parks, a diabetic and founder of the Comedy Crusade Against Diabetes.

Diabetes Increasing

DIABETES CONTINUED ITS ONSLAUGHT ON THE AMERICAN POPULATION IN THE 1990s, a decade marked by a rapid increase in the number of people being diagnosed with the disease.

By the end of the decade, this trend showed no signs of slowing, and its impact affected all demographic and age groups. The one commonality throughout the population was Americans' burgeoning waistlines, according to a report by the Centers for Disease Control and Prevention (CDC).[1]

The report showed a 33 percent increase in the overall prevalence of diabetes, with increases occurring in all ages, ethnic groups, educational levels, and in almost all states. The dramatic growth in the number of cases came after a relatively calm 15 years (1975–1990) that showed no increase in the percentage of Americans with the disease.[2]

There was a glimmer of good news in the report, though. "The recent increases in the public's awareness of diabetes might explain some of the increased prevalence we found," the authors wrote.[3] A previous study, conducted from 1976 to 1980, showed that about half of the total diabetes population was undiagnosed, a figure that had dropped to 44 percent in the 1990–1998 study.

The Diabetes Treatment Centers of America (DTCA) model had grown along system, whether they want to go or not," stated an editorial in *Hospitals & Health Networks*. "They know that they should be going somewhere; they just don't know how to get there. In fact, figuring out how to get to the new system is one of the toughest problems facing health care executives today."

The editorial went on to raise several questions:

For example, can you really look at yourself in the mirror in the morning and say, "The hospital is a cost center?" Of course, you can't. It's not a cost center. In fact, it's generating the revenue to support development of the new emerging organization. It will be one day, but what do you do in the meantime?[28]

The fear and uncertainty in the industry made it exceedingly difficult for American Healthcorp to successfully promote DTCA's proven "center" concept. For the first time in a decade, the number of diabetes centers did not

with the prevalence of diabetes. In 1990, the year that the American Diabetes Association noticed an upswing in diagnoses, 47 DTCA facilities were in operation.[4] By 1998, the same period that the CDC reported the increase in diabetes diagnoses, the DTCA had 72 hospital-based centers and contracts with health plans that covered 92,000 people with diabetes.[5]

Patients who were receiving aggressive treatments like those offered by the DTCA were benefiting, but the CDC anticipated diabetes trends were going to get worse. "When an increase of 33 percent in diabetes in just eight years is considered with the disturbing reality that the effects of the obesity epidemic have not fully unfolded, an alarming scenario [can be predicted]," the CDC report stated.[6]

The American Diabetes Association noticed an uptick in the obesity rates in 1986, four years before the increase in diabetes rates began, giving some time for obese patients to get weight under control before diabetes set in.[7]

A study earlier in the decade, commissioned by American Healthcorp and conducted by Lewin-VHI, Inc., had shown just how many more health care dollars diabetes patients consumed than those without the disease.

The CDC report, which estimated the cost of health care was $98 billion for diabetes patients in 1997, underscored the scope of the problem. With its new population-based disease management program in place, American Healthcorp was positioned to be a major part of the solution.

increase, dropping instead to 63 by the end of 1994.[29] The losses were due to the ending of existing relationships with hospitals as well as a reduction in the launch of new centers, down to eight compared with 10 the previous year. In 1994, American Healthcorp shut down nearly a dozen centers, three times the number the company had closed in 1993.[30] The 1994 Annual Report described it as "one of the most difficult years in our company's history."[31]

Expanding Diabetes Care

DTCA's strong relationships with physicians and hospital customers helped the company persevere during the uncertain period of system transition. In 1994, 63 percent of all diabetes patient costs were related to inpatient hospital stays, but few of those stays were necessitated by the need for treatment of the patient's diabetes. The company subsequently restructured its DTCA program, adding individual and

DTCA Purpose Statement

IN 1990, THE COMPANY RELEASED ITS FIRST PURPOSE STATEMENT, WHICH would go on to influence the company's continued purpose throughout ·the coming decades:

To create value for physicians and hospitals
by helping them improve the lives of individuals with diabetes.

The statement was carefully worded to ensure that every colleague understood the company's bedrock belief that the fundamental interaction in health care is the one between patient and physician and that our role was to help make that interaction both more effective and more efficient. Simply put: doctors treated, and the company supported the doctor's plan of care, both in the hospital and out.

group outpatient programs for continuing education and support and focusing the center staff on providing optimum care for every diabetes patient in the hospital— wherever they were housed and whatever their admitting diagnosis was.[32]

The company also used its experience in owning and managing hospitals, and the knowledge it had gained in nearly 10 years of providing diabetes services, to develop programs designed to help physicians and hospital staffs improve their care delivery systems and practices. The goal, simply, was to help them reduce the total cost of providing inpatient care. As part of these programs, the company compiled data from its hospital customers, creating databases and developing new benchmarking systems organized by Diagnostic Related Groups (DRGs). The company then offered its clients a customized DRG-specific improvement plan, helping hospitals reduce their costs while improving care.[33]

During this period, American Healthcorp also took its first steps toward outcomes-based diabetes population management while helping hospitals make the transition to performance-based managed care. The company helped hospitals acquire contracts with self-insured employers in their service area in an effort to help them better manage the direct and indirect costs of their employees with diabetes. An important contributor to the success of this effort was DTCA's development of new analytical systems and models that enabled it to identify people with diabetes and then design personalized plans—including intensive education, monitoring, and ongoing support that would enable those individuals to more effectively manage their disease.[34]

A New Business Model

The DTCA model had taken off and matured, and by 1994, it had peaked. Though contracts would remain in place for many years to come, the hospital-based model was clearly not the future. Revenues exceeded $41 million in 1994 before dropping 11 percent to $36 million in 1995.[35]

"We were doing everything we could to jump-start DTCA: applying different economic models, trying to do cardiac or senior care or other things to wrap around the program and get hospitals' attention," said Kirk, a sales vice president at the time. "We knew we were in a very mature, declining business, and we knew we needed something else."[36]

What that "something else" would be was anybody's guess at the time, but the results of the Diabetes Control and

Complications Trial (DCCT) suggested that the real value in improving the care of the nation's growing number of people with diabetes lay in improving their health and thereby reducing the cost of their care. The natural beneficiaries of such an approach would be the insurance companies and employers who paid for that care. Developing and proving the model that could do that outside of the hospital setting would take three years and ultimately provide American Healthcorp with its next opportunity to make a new market.

"I think our leadership has been particularly good at recognizing market trends and deciding what to do about those,"[37] said Emily Cook. Regina Seider, director of sales analytics, added, "Nobody reads the market perfectly, but I think we react accordingly and are proactive in trying to find new things and look at things differently. I think we keep an entrepreneurial spirit here. Part of our agility is that it doesn't matter what your job title is. You'll pull in who you need and people are willing to do the work to get it done."[38]

"It would have been easy for people to be concerned about the future of the company from '94 to '96," Stone noted. "The bloom was off the DTCA rose, and nobody was quite sure what would come next. But those are not the kind of colleagues we have at this company. They hung in there, they persevered, and they were confident that we would find a new way to meet the needs of people with diabetes."

Colleagues who had worked for DTCA for five years received gold service pins. The embedded stone shown here symbolized passion and vitality, characteristics that were critical elements for success in DTCA's work with physicians and patients.

Above: American Healthcorp published its first Annual Report in 1991. It featured testimonials from both physicians and patients.

Opposite: As American Healthcorp evolved, it remained dedicated to helping people stay as healthy as possible for as long as possible by providing evidence-based interventions that would help them avoid or delay the next episode of illness.

make one person healthier
and you create a better life

make a thousand people healthier
and you create immeasurable value

I see us as a significantly larger company involved in three or four different areas of health care, all of which take advantage of our multilocation management abilities, which we think are substantial, our strong financial position, strong balance sheet, and what we've learned … in terms of relationships with physicians and hospitals. We understand those relationships very well and know how to successfully work with them. We see ourselves as a larger company with as many as three or four different specialty areas.[1]

—Tom Cigarran, American Healthcorp
chairman, president, and CEO, 1992

AMERICAN HEALTHCORP'S SUCCESS WITH KOALA AND DIABETES TREATMENT CENTERS of America did not diminish its efforts to find other specialty lines of business in which it could deliver critically needed services to improve the health and reduce the cost of care for those in need. As a result, the company made three significant investments in other specialty service lines between 1988 and 1992. Results were mixed.

"Trends in health care delivery systems will be such that a specialist in an area or a function will be more effective than a generalist," former CEO Bob Hilton wrote in a proposal to the board of directors in 1984. "While I will never underemphasize the role of the medical doctor in the delivery of health care, I feel that more and more of the decisions concerning health care will be patient-made and that the forms of delivery of health care will be patient-decided."[2]

But Hilton was equally concerned that American Healthcorp could be pigeonholed as a "substance abuse and diabetes company" rather than the specialty health care company it had always intended to be.[3] As early as 1984, Hilton was outlining criteria for a new investment that might well have served as a road map for any future American Healthcorp acquisition:

1. Room for growth;
2. Potential for value-added services;
3. Opportunity to achieve leadership among competitors;
4. Existing, sufficient, and realistic resources available;
5. Potential for an attractive return within a reasonable time frame.[4]

While the company looked for that opportunity, it was clear that it would look much more like the diabetes model than hospital ownership, "more of a business through contract than through owning real estate,"[5] Hilton wrote.

Arthritis Treatment Centers

Though American Healthcorp had sizeable resources to invest, finding a new line of business would not be easy. The board discussed and decided against markets such as nursing homes, extended-hour doctors' offices, surgical centers, and home health care.[6] Cancer care was given strong consideration, due to both the scope of the disease—which had more than 100 recognized forms—and service delivery methods, including diagnosis, treatment, and psychological assistance to patient and family.

The company eventually decided on arthritis. The scope of the problem was

Hoping to replicate the success of the diabetes centers, the company founded ArthritisCare Centers of America to help patients learn how to better manage their disease.

significant: More than 36 million Americans suffered from the disease. And, as was the case with diabetes, most of those who had arthritis were often unsatisfied with their current course of treatment, usually in pain, and aggressively pursuing treatment.[7] Hoping to follow a model similar to diabetes, ArthritisCare Centers of America was launched. Rheumatologists were brought in as experts. But the diabetes model

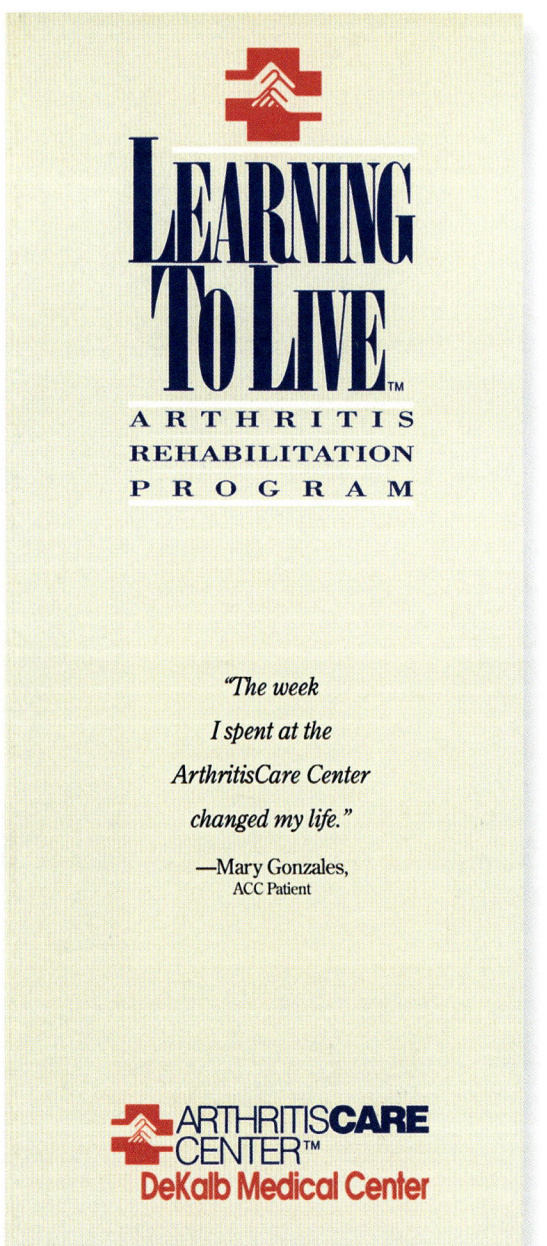

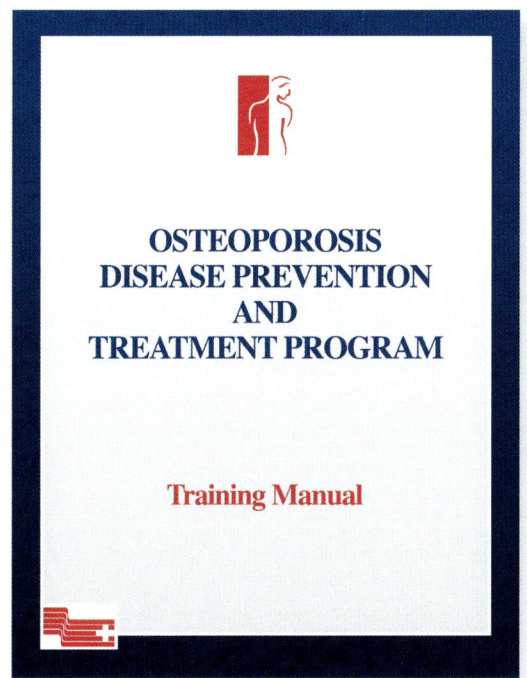

**OSTEOPOROSIS
DISEASE PREVENTION
AND
TREATMENT PROGRAM**

Training Manual

could not be fully replicated because arthritis lacked one single, scientifically proven treatment approach that would relieve symptoms and/or complications.[8]

"There was a lot that we could do clinically for these people, but we couldn't develop a business model to make it work financially," said former chief financial officer Henry Herr.

In 1988, there was just one ArthritisCare Center, with two more planned. While that number grew to 11, initial hospital agreements were not renewed after the initial term. By 1992, the company only had two centers in operation, and plans for further expansion were on hold. The diabetes model that had previously proven successful in improving the health of so many individuals had not proved as effective in treating arthritis.[9]

The arthritis division never prospered, but it was not for lack of effort. "Arthritis

is a huge problem, and we have an aging population," Cigarran told the *Wall Street Journal*. "But it's primarily an outpatient business. So the present reimbursement system doesn't provide enough incentive for physicians or hospitals to provide needed services in the face of shortages of people in the rehabilitation area and other conditions of the system today."

Medical Weight Loss Treatment

In 1989, American Healthcorp purchased Medical Weight Management (MWM) and the Houston Center for Health Promotion, for $2.5 million.[10] On paper, it should have been an ideal match for the DTCA concept, as many patients with diabetes are also overweight or obese. Finding a medical weight-loss solution would mean an expansion of the services for those with diabetes as well as others with significant weight challenges.

Internal data supplied by MWM showed that 65 percent of patients using MWM and the Houston Center for Health Promotion lost weight in their program, which began with a 16-week period during which time patients were limited to a high-protein liquid diet along with extensive nutrition education and counseling.[11]

Medical weight loss programs had also caught the public's attention in late 1988 after Oprah Winfrey showed off her blue-jean clad, size-10 figure on her TV

The training manual for the company's ArthritisCare program was expanded to include osteoporosis care and prevention in 1996. The program was closely modeled on the diabetes care program, with a physical therapist providing therapy and a dietitian offering counseling on the importance of vitamin D and calcium in managing the disease.

Changes at the Top

BY 1988—THE TIME AMERICAN HEALTHCORP HIT THE SEVEN-YEAR MARK—THE venture capitalists that had provided the critical startup funds for the company wanted to cash out.[1] That meant American Healthcorp had to be sold or taken public. But the climate for a public offering was not good as a result of the October 19, 1987, stock market crash that put an end to a five-year run of successful IPOs.

"Now more than ever, being a private company is in vogue," the *Nashville Banner* reported. "I don't really see the advantages [of public ownership]," Bob Hilton told the newspaper. "We have no need for capital, and in fact, even as a privately held company, we are more conservatively capitalized than many public companies that have raised equity."[2]

Despite Hilton's statement, there was pressure from investors to do something to raise enough capital to buy them out. The pressure revealed a difference in

philosophy between Hilton and Cigarran, who had been surprised when his previous employer, Hospital Affiliates, Inc., had been sold. "I thought of Healthcorp as our company," Cigarran said. "We had these investors. We had to respect them and give them a return, but it wasn't their company. It was our company. Bob [Hilton] believed that we were the servants of the investors."[3]

While the two executives discussed their differing philosophies, it was the board that had the ultimate say, and the board was heavily populated by venture capitalists. Investment bank Lazard Ltd. was contracted to represent the board in a sale of the company.

During a board meeting in Jacksonville, Florida, Martin "Mike" Koldyke asked Cigarran privately if he supported the sale.[4] Cigarran said, "No." Koldyke, who had founded The Frontenac Company in 1971[5] and was one of the original venture capitalists in American Healthcorp, told

Mike Koldyke (center), played a key role in American Healthcorp's leveraged buyout. Shown here with Tom Cigarran (left) and Ben Leedle (right), Koldyke remained on the American Healthcorp board for more than two decades.

Cigarran, "This is the best management team I've seen," and offered to line up financing for a leveraged buyout.[6]

Cigarran relayed the conversation to the three other founders: Stan Kantanie, executive vice president of operations; Henry Herr, executive vice president of finance and administration; and Bob Stone, then senior vice president of DTCA, and they agreed to move forward without Bob Hilton.

As a result of Koldyke's belief in the company and the management team, the four, along with Jim Deal, president of the DTCA, purchased American Healthcorp for $65 million in 1988 with Frontenac's backing.[7]

"There's no change in the way the company operates," Cigarran said at the time. "It's just a change in the way we are financed."[8] There were also slight changes in titles. Cigarran became CEO and chairman of the board while retaining the president's title. Kantanie was named chief operating officer.

The economy brightened, and after resisting a push to go public in 1988, when the original venture capital firms wanted to harvest their investments, American Healthcorp began an aggressive

"road show," presenting itself to investors in 1991. The first stop was Minneapolis, on July 23, 1991. The last stop, a month later, was on Wall Street. American Healthcorp had become a publicly traded company on August 1, 1991, with shares traded on the NASDAQ under the symbol AMHC.[9]

On the first day of trading, shares opened at $10, on par with what the company expected.[10] The stock closed at $10.75 that first day on 115,000 shares traded. The company sold 1.3 million shares of stock in the offering, raising approximately $12 million that was used to pay off a significant amount of debt.[11] Frontenac, which had been a critical player in 1988 during American Healthcorp's leveraged buyout, was able to cash out much of its investment in the company, reducing its ownership to 25 percent.[12] Koldyke remained on the board of directors.[13]

The changes during the company's first decade had been dizzying. In just 10 short years, American Healthcorp had transformed itself from a company that owned hospitals and was largely owned by several Chicago venture capital firms to one that was primarily a diabetes treatment company and now publicly traded.

DTCA President Jim Deal joined Tom Cigarran, Stan Kantanie, Henry Herr, and Bob Stone in the 1988 leveraged buyout of the company.

show. She had lost 67 pounds in four months on OPTIFAST®, a medically supervised, stringent, clinic-based diet program limiting intake to 400 calories per day.[12] Winfrey's TV show, in which she famously pulled a wagon laden with 67 pounds of fat, triggered a broad but short-lived wave of interest in medical weight loss.

Cigarran was not totally convinced this was the right venture for American Healthcorp, but swayed by the low cost of entry into the field and the excitement of his team, he approved the purchase. Within a month, he was enthusiastic enough to mention it at a company meeting to which American Healthcorp had brought its scientific advisers and physicians.

During dinner, Cigarran mentioned the 65 percent weight-loss success rate to Dr. Rena Wing, a professor at the University of Pittsburgh and a member of the DTCA scientific advisory council. Dr. Wing, an internationally renowned expert on weight loss and diabetes, replied that 10 percent was the standard long-term success rate for anyone, regardless of the program's approach.

Cigarran remembers her words clearly. "Tom, I have spent the last 15 years of my life researching all of these weight-loss programs, and the answer is always 10 percent," Cigarran recalled Wing saying. "I got back to the office from this meeting, and I called the management team together, and I said, 'OK, I want some really smart people who understand

epidemiology to look at the results and tell me the truth,'"[13] Cigarran added.

While the epidemiological research was being done, Los Angeles Dodgers manager Tommy Lasorda, challenged to lose 30 pounds by two of his players, Kirk Gibson and Orel Hershiser, in a spring training bet, vowed to drop the weight by the summer's All-Star break. Win or lose, the wager would benefit the Sisters of Mercy, a Nashville convent whose building had been condemned.[14] Lasorda soon had an endorsement deal with Slim•Fast®, and by the time the research was completed, Lasorda was appearing in print and TV advertisements promoting the "two shakes a day and a sensible meal" plan. He had single-handedly saved the convent, helped fund a $2 million facility, and reinvigorated the weight-loss industry.

However, medical weight loss proved exceedingly costly. American Healthcorp's program averaged $1,900, and most patients needed health insurance to cover the cost. Slim•Fast® powders, in comparison, cost less than $20 a month.

The answer to Cigarran's question about weight loss success was, as Wing said, 10 percent. Yo-yo weight loss, in which a patient's weight fluctuates, would not help those with diabetes manage their disease; in fact, it could potentially cause greater harm. In what Stone points to as one of the best management decisions in the company's history, Cigarran set a deadline of 60 days to sell or close the weight-loss business.

"We did all the rigorous stuff," Cigarran said. "But we missed something, and we didn't find out about it until way down the road. When we finally figured it out, we just cut our losses and moved on."[15]

The weight-loss venture had failed due to key fundamentals in American Healthcorp's business model. The company could not enter the market and dominate by offering programs backed with science. "We weren't going to be able to do it. No one else would be able to do it," said Herr. "One of the good things that happened, we got into it, but we got out of it in a hurry without suffering any kind of major disaster. That was a hard business, an up-and-down business, a yo-yo business with our customers. It was just not a business that could provide real value to providers and patients."[16]

The AmSurg Investment

Despite the setbacks in arthritis and weight management, American Healthcorp continued to look for ways to diversify, especially in areas of health care that offered the solid value proposition of better care and lower costs. In 1992, the company found such an opportunity and acquired a majority share in AmSurg, investing $5 million in the company for 58 percent ownership.

AmSurg was a privately owned Nashville company that operated physician practice–based surgery centers.

AmSurg, which operated independently of American Healthcorp, worked with physician practices to create single-speciality, outpatient surgery centers physically located in conjunction with the doctors' offices. Each AmSurg center typically dedicated itself to one specialty. Armed with a new business model and resources from Healthcorp's investment, AmSurg completed deals for three new centers in the ensuing year.

"Nobody's doing what AmSurg is doing," Cigarran said at the time. "This is what the health care system is looking for—lower cost, higher quality, and greater patient satisfaction."

In just a few short years, AmSurg had become an industry leader in physician practice–based surgery centers, an emerging segment of the health care industry. By 1995, AmSurg had a total of 25 centers in operation or under construction, up from 16 the previous year,[17] and was contributing about one-third of American Healthcorp's revenues.[18]

Standing on Its Own

AmSurg had met the exact criteria to which American Healthcorp held itself: better outcomes for patients at lower costs. But within five years, it had grown so large so quickly that it needed to stand on its

CTREATMENT
Coordination

ROUTCOME
Reporting

SPATIENT
Support

IDATA
Integration

ESELF-CARE
Education

SPROVIDER
NETWORK
Support

DIABETES
TREATMENT
CENTERS
OF AMERICA

AMERICAN HEALTHCORP ANNUAL REPORT 1997

By 1997, American Healthcorp had put the pieces in place to transform itself into a disease management company. It had been a long haul, but as a 1997 letter from Tom Cigarran to stockholders attested, there was "tangible and mounting evidence" that the company was progressing.

own. As a separate company, AmSurg could acquire the capital that it needed to fund its continued growth.[19] It would also have the ability to become publicly traded.

The move was clearly well timed. By the end of 1997, the year in which the spin-off occurred, AmSurg increased from 24 centers to 39, increasing revenues from $34 million in 1996 to $57 million.[20] It was a popular company on Wall Street as well, where UBS Global Research put a "buy" recommendation on it the day after the company was spun off. "We project a 35 percent EPS [earnings per share] growth over the next five years through a

combination of new center development, acquisitions, and same-center growth," UBS advised investors.[21] The report also labeled AmSurg the "clear leader in physician practice–based surgery."[22]

Spinning the company off gave American Healthcorp investors a boost as well. The company distributed all of its shares of AmSurg stock to its shareholders, minus the $17 million it had invested in AmSurg throughout the years. Wise planning allowed the company to receive IRS approval for its plans, meaning the spin-off occurred virtually tax-free.

The spin-off also included a bit of restructuring for AmSurg. Tom Cigarran had been chairman and CEO at AmSurg since Healthways' initial investment. Following the spin-off, Cigarran retained the chairman position, and Ken McDonald, who had been AmSurg's chief operating officer since 1994, became CEO. Herr had also done double duty, serving on the AmSurg board, and for a while, filling the position of its chief financial officer.[23]

AmSurg, the first company to be spun off from American Healthcorp, continued its rapid growth, closing 2010 with a majority interest in more than 200 surgical facilities and $700 million in revenue.[24]

Rethinking the Future

There were clear successes—and one outright failure—as American Healthcorp attempted to expand its services. But the company held tightly to its vision of improved health care at lower costs. As it had done with hospital management and substance abuse, it proved it knew when to hold on to struggling ventures and when to let go.

But by 1994, the writing was on the wall. The future for AmSurg was as a separate company. ArthritisCare Centers of America was not going to be the next DTCA, and the decade-long growth of the DTCA model was beginning to fade. The world of health care was changing, and the company would need a new model to bring value-creating services to the health care marketplace and the people who depended on it.

Standards
For
Disease
Management
Programs

Above: American Healthways helped to define the entire disease management industry, and used its leadership and experience to develop guidelines, convening a panel of primary care and specialty physicians to create an initial draft of industry standards. "The value of disease management to people with chronic diseases, their physicians, and society as a whole cannot be sacrificed to the immaturity of the industry," the guidelines asserted.

Opposite: Janet Calhoun began her American Healthcorp career as a diabetes educator at the Diabetes Treatment Center in Portland, Oregon. She was one of a handful of people charged with ensuring that the early diabetes disease management contracts were successful.

We never referred to individuals as diabetic. We regarded them as people who happened to have a chronic disease. In our program design and in our interactions with the people we serve, we've always looked at the whole person and what that individual needs to live a healthy, productive life.[1]

—Janet Calhoun, senior vice president–product development

A S THE DEMAND FOR NEW HOSPITAL-BASED DIABETES CENTERS OF EXCELLENCE CONTINUED to decline, American Healthcorp, for the second time in its 12-year history, found itself faced with the challenge of creating a new market for its proven capability to improve health and reduce cost. In identifying the customer for that new market, management asked the critical question: "Who benefits?" While it was clear that patients with diabetes were the ultimate beneficiaries of the company's programs, it was immediately obvious that the real financial winners were those responsible for paying the bills for health care services, namely health insurers and their employer customers. But, in the absence of scientifically proven standards of care for the treatment of diabetes, insurers were not yet convinced that there was a real value proposition associated with more intensive treatment and support. And, even if there had been, they were also not convinced that the value could be achieved within the three-and-a-half years that the average individual was a member of their plan.

"We knew that there were significant benefits we could bring to individuals with diabetes," said Ben Leedle, Healthways CEO. "We also knew that selling our services to insurance

Dr. Richard Corlin, former Speaker of the American Medical Association's House of Delegates, vouched for the Diabetes Treatment Centers of America model at a 1996 press conference. "Getting people with diabetes involved in programs like those provided by DTCA and their affiliated physicians will improve their health status, reduce both short- and long-term complications, keep them out of the hospital and the emergency room, and save a great deal of money," he said.

companies would enable us to reach much larger percentages of the population much more quickly, but the theoretical value proposition lacked two critical factors: a solid scientific basis and a real-world demonstration showing that the health and cost improvements could be achieved."[2]

The solution to the first of these challenges came in June 1993, with the release of the findings of the Diabetes Control and Complications Trial (DCCT). The DCCT was a 10-year, prospective randomized control trial funded by the National Institutes of Health and conducted at 29 academic medical centers. It ended a year early because of the profound nature of the results. The DCCT validated the benefits of "tight control" of blood sugars in avoiding, delaying, and/or diminishing the severity of diabetes' most common costly complications: kidney disease, leading to dialysis and transplant; retinopathy, leading to blindness; and neuropathy, leading to lower limb

amputation. Based on the DCCT findings, the entire diabetes community came together to rapidly develop new standards of care for the treatment of people with type 1 (insulin-dependent) diabetes.

The findings of the DCCT for type 1 patients were subsequently confirmed for people with type 2 (insulin-resistant) diabetes by the United Kingdom Prospective Diabetes Study. According to Oxford University, which conducted the study and published the results:

The UK Prospective Diabetes Study (UKPDS) was a landmark randomised, multicentre trial of glycaemic therapies in 5,102 patients with newly diagnosed type 2 diabetes. It ran for 20 years (1977 to 1997) in 23 UK clinical sites and showed conclusively that the complications of type 2 diabetes, previously often regarded as inevitable, could be reduced by improving blood glucose and/or blood pressure control.[3]

These findings further solidified the scientific basis for the standards of care for all people with diabetes.

The results of the DCCT galvanized American Healthcorp's management team. "We knew that health insurers would have to begin covering DCCT-like services for people with diabetes,"[4] remembered Steve Samples, then DTCA's chief financial officer and current Healthways senior vice president of finance. But the DCCT also introduced a whole new issue that insurers and physicians would have to face.

"Participants in the DCCT were followed for nine years," Calhoun noted. "It was a longitudinal intervention, as opposed to the more typical acute medical intervention with which the entire health care system was familiar. Moreover, the primary method of delivering the intervention to the study participants was through the use of multidisciplinary teams of health care professionals, under the direction of a physician, but not by the physician directly."[5]

The similarity to the program model being used in the DTCA centers was unmistakable, but a significant challenge had to be overcome. Both the DCCT and the DTCA models were facility-based; how could those services be mass customized and delivered in a manner that maintained the DCCT's effectiveness at a cost point that would create a meaningful value proposition for the entities that were paying the bill?

Interestingly—although the financial question was not part of the DCCT evaluation—the DCCT Research Group subsequently concluded that it would cost about another $3,200 (in 1993 dollars) annually to provide DCCT-like services to an individual with diabetes, a cost that they felt was worthwhile given the significant future costs associated with complications that could be avoided. "We thought those numbers were wrong then," Samples said. "Looking back, it would appear we were right."[6]

Coming to the conclusion that they couldn't answer the question of how much money could be saved by treating people with diabetes in accordance with the new standards of care without having a good understanding of how much people with diabetes actually cost, American Healthcorp commissioned Lewin-VHI, a nationally respected health care research firm, to find out.

The landmark Diabetes Control and Complications Trial provided strong evidence confirming the benefits of many of the methods employed by DTCA for nearly a decade, providing critical data that helped American Healthcorp make the shift to disease management. Published in the *New England Journal of Medicine*, the study proved that strictly controlling glucose levels leads to dramatic improvements for patients while lowering the risk of complications. *(Reprinted with permission, from the NEW ENGLAND JOURNAL OF MEDICINE. [ISSN 0028-4793] Vol. 329:977-986 [September 1993]. Copyright © 1993 Massachusetts Medical Society. All rights reserved.)*

Vol. 329 No. 14   INTENSIVE DIABETES TREATMENT AND COMPLICATIONS IN IDDM — NATHAN ET AL.   977

THE EFFECT OF INTENSIVE TREATMENT OF DIABETES ON THE DEVELOPMENT AND PROGRESSION OF LONG-TERM COMPLICATIONS IN INSULIN-DEPENDENT DIABETES MELLITUS

THE DIABETES CONTROL AND COMPLICATIONS TRIAL RESEARCH GROUP*

Abstract *Background.* Long-term microvascular and neurologic complications cause major morbidity and mortality in patients with insulin-dependent diabetes mellitus (IDDM). We examined whether intensive treatment with the goal of maintaining blood glucose concentrations close to the normal range could decrease the frequency and severity of these complications.

Methods. A total of 1441 patients with IDDM — 726 with no retinopathy at base line (the primary-prevention cohort) and 715 with mild retinopathy (the secondary-intervention cohort) were randomly assigned to intensive therapy administered either with an external insulin pump or by three or more daily insulin injections and guided by frequent blood glucose monitoring or to conventional therapy with one or two daily insulin injections. The patients were followed for a mean of 6.5 years, and the appearance and progression of retinopathy and other complications were assessed regularly.

Results. In the primary-prevention cohort, intensive therapy reduced the adjusted mean risk for the development of retinopathy by 76 percent (95 percent confidence interval, 62 to 85 percent), as compared with conventional therapy. In the secondary-intervention cohort, intensive therapy slowed the progression of retinopathy by 54 percent (95 percent confidence interval, 39 to 66 percent) and reduced the development of proliferative or severe nonproliferative retinopathy by 47 percent (95 percent confidence interval, 14 to 67 percent). In the two cohorts combined, intensive therapy reduced the occurrence of microalbuminuria (urinary albumin excretion of ≥40 mg per 24 hours) by 39 percent (95 percent confidence interval, 21 to 52 percent), that of albuminuria (urinary albumin excretion of ≥300 mg per 24 hours) by 54 percent (95 percent confidence interval, 19 to 74 percent), and that of clinical neuropathy by 60 percent (95 percent confidence interval, 38 to 74 percent). The chief adverse event associated with intensive therapy was a two-to-threefold increase in severe hypoglycemia.

Conclusions. Intensive therapy effectively delays the onset and slows the progression of diabetic retinopathy, nephropathy, and neuropathy in patients with IDDM. (N Engl J Med 1993;329:977-86.)

"Interestingly, no one had ever asked that question before," said Bob Stone. "The American Diabetes Association produced annual reports on the health care cost of diabetes, but no one ever looked at the cost questions from the perspective of the whole individual."[7]

Stone recalled:

Lewin's findings, published in the Journal of Clinical Endocrinology and Metabolism *were astounding. On average, the health care cost for people with diabetes was 3.6 times greater than for those who did not have the disease. For certain subsets of the population, such as those covered by Medicare and Medicaid, the multiple was as high as 13 times greater. Overall, the Lewin report found that America's 11 million people with diabetes cost $119 billion, accounting for 14.7 percent of the nation's total health care costs. American Healthcorp's 1993 Annual Report put it this*

way: "Stated differently, 4.5 percent of the population accounted for nearly 15 percent of the total direct US health care expenditures."

Building a Solution

Armed with the scientific findings from the DCCT and the cost findings from the Lewin study, a small team of executives tasked with reinvigorating American Healthcorp began meeting in Stone's basement. From those meetings emerged a confirmation of the company's firm desire to expand its core focus. According to Tom Cigarran, "The original vision was that, someday, we would be more than a hospital company. Our experience with DTCA provided a path for us to begin to realize that goal. But health plans didn't know us. They were a new market with a different set of dynamics that we had

0021-972X/98/$03.00/0
Journal of Clinical Endocrinology and Metabolism
Copyright © 1998 by The Endocrine Society

Vol. 83, No. 8
Printed in U.S.A.

Clinical and Economic Impact of Implementing a Comprehensive Diabetes Management Program in Managed Care*

ROBERT J. RUBIN, KIMBERLY A. DIETRICH, AND ANNE D. HAWK

The Lewin Group, Fairfax, Virginia 22031

ABSTRACT
Diabetes mellitus places a significant burden on the U.S. health-care system. Because of the potential to reduce diabetic complications and costs through intensive management, diabetes has become a primary target for disease management programs. We performed a retrospective analysis of short-term baseline and follow-up clinical, economic, and member and provider satisfaction data from approximately 7,000 people with diabetes being treated through seven managed care plans using Diabetes Treatment Centers of America's Diabetes NetCare^{SM}, (Nashville, TN), a comprehensive diabetes management program. Our analysis indicates that Diabetes Net-Care^{SM} achieved gross economic adjusted savings of $50 per diabetic

member per month (12.3%), with gross unadjusted savings of $44 (10.9%) per diabetic member per month. Hospital admissions per 1,000 diabetic member years decreased by 18%, and bed days fell by 21%. Patients with diabetes were more likely to get HbA1c tests, foot exams, eye exams, and cholesterol screenings while enrolled in the program. These data suggest that implementation of a comprehensive healthcare management program for people with diabetes can lead to substantial improvements in costs and clinical outcomes in the short-term. It is expected that improvements will increase over time, with continuing improvements in health status and a reduction in the number of future diabetic complications. (*J Clin Endocrinol Metab* **83**: 2635–2642, 1998)

ONE of every seven dollars spent on health care in the United States is spent on behalf of a person with diabetes (1). According to data from the most recent National

period, which averaged 7 years, there was a 50–75% reduction in risk between the intensive treatment group and the standard treatment group in the development of long-term

to learn and understand before we could even begin to suggest that our diabetes expertise could deliver a meaningful value proposition."[8]

The team focused on ways to reinvent the American Healthcorp model to position its diabetes program for payers—employers, government entities, and ultimately, health plans—rather than a hospital customer.

Calhoun explained:

Those discussions were hugely energizing because what we knew was that we could help. From our hospital-based diabetes business we knew that what we were really good at was helping people make sustainable, life-changing behavioral changes. We knew that we could help physicians and their patients become a stronger team by us coaching them, if you will. … We knew in our hearts that the expertise and the skills we had as a company to work with people to help them take better care of themselves could be taken out of the hospital into a non-acute setting—that when people were healthier, they cost less, and there had to be somebody out there who would be willing to pay for that. We took this concept first to a large employer and then to a state Medicaid program. While they were intrigued, they were not willing to be pioneers. As a result, we extended our reach to health plans because we were convinced we could help them provide a better service to the members, and that service would save them money. What's not to love about that business model?[9]

The conversations in Stone's basement rapidly made it clear that providing services for thousands, even tens of thousands, of health plan members would require a new approach. "Our DTCA model, and even the DCCT model, was to deliver services mostly to small groups on a face-to-face basis," Leedle recalled. "That was not a scalable approach. Our solution was to build a model that relied on interacting with health plan members by phone and mail (whichever they preferred). We felt that if we hired the right clinicians and supported them with state-of-the art patient management software and infrastructure, whatever we gave up in the intimacy of face-to-face contact, we would more than gain back through frequency and continuity."[10]

Charged with the responsibility to design, develop, and sell services to health plans, the company engaged product design consultants from Electronic Data Systems (EDS) to support Leedle in his leadership of a team of roughly 20 colleagues in designing, building, and—ultimately—selling a new model for the delivery of services. Over the course of 16 weeks, this team conceptualized, defined, and fleshed out the requirements and interdependencies of every aspect of the new solution.

While Leedle went on to lead the team to construct the guts of the new solution, Calhoun and Stone hit the road, ultimately calling on nearly 100 health plan medical directors and executives. "These 'sales' calls were very informative," Calhoun recalled.

New Jersey BMS Employees:

Your diabetes doctor has a whole new staff

Introducing "Beating Diabetes"—confidential, convenient, customized free support services specially designed for people with diabetes.

Call 1 800 2 ENROLL to join the Beating Diabetes program from **Diabetes Treatment Centers of America**

Bristol-Myers Squibb Company

DIABETES TREATMENT CENTERS OF AMERICA

American Healthcorp partnered wih Bristol-Myers Squibb in a $1 million pilot program that chose 113 of the pharmaceutical giant's employees in the New Jersey area.

"Each call provided us with new insights into how health plans thought and worked, what their solution requirements would be, how quickly we would have to demonstrate the effectiveness of our solution, what the financial and risk parameters of a contract were likely to be, and what concerns and objections we were going to have to overcome in order to secure a relationship."[11]

Even in the early stages of development, well before the first contract was signed, the company forecast its potential for success with its new disease management model. The company's 1995 Annual Report stated prophetically, "We anticipate that … the market for diabetes disease management will offer American Healthcorp a growth [opportunity] unlike any in its history."[12]

The focus on creating a new market and solution presented some challenges internally at American Healthcorp. Hospital teams knew the future was in disease management. But in the interim, they had to keep hospital business strong to fund development of the new plan. "At times, we felt that the train was leaving the station without us,"[13] said Kathy Kirk, then DTCA's senior vice president of sales. But change had to happen as DTCA business continued to shrink. In 1994, hospital-based revenues peaked at $41 million, before dropping 11 percent in 1995.

A Living Laboratory

"Disease Management" was a concept first introduced by the Boston Consulting Group in 1993 and originally designed as a value-added service that pharmaceutical companies would supply to health plans in exchange for preferred positions on the plan's drug formulary. While that model proved to be unattractive to health plans, many leading pharmaceutical companies spent significant energy during the period from 1993 to 1996 either building a disease management solution for diseases that their drugs treated or seeking to partner with a disease management company to provide those services for them.

Nevertheless, management was somewhat surprised when they were approached by executives from pharmaceutical giant Bristol-Myers Squibb, a leading supplier of drugs for blood glucose management in type 2 patients. Concerned that they didn't have the time to develop their own diabetes disease management program and stay competitive, Bristol-Myers Squibb proposed a joint development pilot and sales effort while they decided whether or not they needed to be in the disease management business at all. "They offered us $1 million for a two-year agreement," Stone recalled, "and another million if we would agree for that two-year period not to sell the company to another entity while they decided what their ultimate strategy would be. Given the amount of money we were spending building the new solution, it was an easy decision for us to reach."

Operationalizing the pilot was a bit more difficult, Leedle recalled. "All we had at the time were notebooks. We had design upon design upon design, but we didn't have the capital as a business to just go out and build it because you had to have a population to work with. We had to find a willing partner for our proof-of-concept pilot. Bristol-Myers Squibb was made to order for us."[14]

Bristol-Myers Squibb made a perfect partner, as it already had a firm understanding of diabetes and its complications, having previously released several medications designed to treat the disease and manage its symptoms. For the pilot program, 113 employees in the New Jersey area were chosen, all with a less than 30 percent compliance rate for 12 widely established diabetes care guidelines. The low compliance rate surprised Leedle. He explained:

We thought, "How could this be?" It was dismal. Everything was under 30 percent. These were proven, empirically validated, National Institutes of Health guidelines that should have been followed by all people with diabetes regardless of their circumstances, but the US health care system was only getting it right one out of every three times.[15]

As a result of the interventions provided to the Bristol-Myers Squibb employees during the pilot, standard of care compliance improved during the first year to an astounding near-100 percent, which in turn led to a dramatic reduction in diabetes complications and costs for participants. These improvements also led to a significant number of the pilot participants ceasing to require medication to effectively manage their blood sugars.

The early success of the pilot program provided American Healthcorp with the final piece it needed to sell its diabetes disease management program to health plans more effectively. "We had the science on improving health for people with diabetes from the DCCT, we had a financial model that we knew provided us lots of opportunity to reduce cost, and as a result of the Bristol-Myers Squibb pilot, we had proof that we could do both. Now, all we had to do was go out and sell it," Leedle said.[16]

While the Bristol-Myers Squibb pilot produced the results American Healthcorp needed to take its new disease management

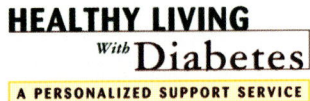

Introducing

HEALTHY LIVING
with Diabetes
A PERSONALIZED SUPPORT SERVICE

It's like having a diabetes counselor in the family

✦ Bristol-Myers Squibb Company

Bristol-Myers Squibb made an ideal partner for American Healthcorp as it already had a firm understanding of diabetes and its complications.

program to market aggressively, it also brought important refinements to the original program design. "Participants in the Bristol-Myers Squibb pilot had to self-identify," Calhoun recalled, "[and] 113 did, but I'm convinced to this day that there were many more who didn't."

Based on the evidence from the pilot, American Healthcorp abandoned the "opt-in" model and adopted an "opt-out" methodology that rapidly became the industry standard for all disease management programs. "People don't voluntarily say, 'I have diabetes. Put me in the program,' " said Dana Williams, a veteran of the company who had remained in the hospital-based program while the insurer-based plan was being developed. "To make an impact on the population, you really need to design a program that they did not have to 'opt in' to. In order to find out who had diabetes, we would analyze claims data to identify eligible participants and then proactively contact them about the program. Unless they 'opted out' by telling us not to contact them anymore, they were participants and we were responsible for their results. The idea that 'You're in unless you choose not to be' doesn't seem so significant today, but at the time it was a game-changer for the whole industry. By the time other disease management companies figured out what we were doing, we had literally hundreds of thousands of individuals participating in our programs."[17]

From Pilot to Implementation

Healthways' first disease management business model was a "carve-out" design, which they tested in a large endocrinology practice in Florida. Under this model, the company would create its own small physician and hospital networks and have those physicians provide all medical services to health plan members with diabetes. Despite management's conviction that this model would provide the best value proposition for payers, the health plans the company approached balked. Their two most valuable assets were their membership base and their provider networks, and they were not about to give up control of either. As a result, American Healthcorp had to retool its approach based on a "carve-in" model in which services would be provided to members irrespective of which doctors were treating them.

The timing for American Healthcorp's entry into the field of disease management was clearly promising, as managed care organizations focused on reducing costs and increasing efficiency.[18] In spite of management's excitement with the opportunity and the results of the pilot, creating the new market for its diabetes disease management program ultimately cost more than $9 million.[19] Despite the significant start-up costs, company executives and board members remained firmly determined to create an entirely new health care delivery system. According to Stone, "One of the most significant events in that time period was the commitment of the board, including the outside members, to commit the resources of the organization so we could build this new model."

Samples recalled the transition:

You just had to get comfortable with change because, particularly once we started defining our version of disease management in the early 1990s, we didn't know a lot. So we had to keep changing and modifying as we marched along. You just became comfortable with the idea of saying, "OK, that didn't work. Now let's go try this," in terms of addressing some of the challenges we ran into.[20]

During the transition, American Healthcorp employees remained enthusiastic about the prospect of finding new ways to have a positive impact on the lives of patients. "What you have to do is have tremendous confidence in your product," Cigarran said. That enthusiasm helped propel the sales team to successfully pitch their new vision for managed care to the nation's major self-insured companies.

As Leedle recalled:

They thought we were a little bit crazy. The good thing about people when they're excited about something, even when it's hard to understand, is that attention gets paid. Even today, when we leave a prospect or a client, they're probably thinking, "You know, those guys are awfully excited about something. I'm not quite sure what it is, but we probably ought to meet with them again to keep trying to find out. They're either the happiest people in the world, or they really are on to something we don't understand."[21]

As Cigarran had suggested, the framework for the sale of the new disease management program was the company's credibility in diabetes through the DTCA approach, and its track record of providing hospitals with cost-saving opportunities while ensuring that both patients and providers remained satisfied by improving the quality of care. In order to reinforce that link, the company decided to continue to use the DTCA brand to market the new program. "That credibility was important," Stone remembered, "but it only got us in the door and got us a chance to tell our story. We had to make some pretty big promises in our early sales proposals in order to get health plan chief financial officers to sign off on what they saw as an essentially untested, unproven, innovation. That reality is what led us to guaranteeing that the first-year financial results would be break-even or better. We took the risk out of the deal for our first customers."

American Healthcorp projected that it could save small managed care organizations with 100,000 enrollees at least $29 million per year in health care costs related to the 4.5 percent of members, on average, with diabetes.[22] That translated into a savings of 40 percent for diabetes patients and an overall savings for the entire health plan of 3 to 4 percent.[23]

American Healthcorp also pledged to underwrite the cost of the program in return for a portion of the savings generated. It was a risky strategy, but one that the company often employed as it sought to expand its disease management footprint. "We told them we were going to succeed," said Rick Bailey, senior vice president of finance at the time. "That's something that had been brought from the hospital business. 'Expect to be paying us incentives because we will succeed, and that is our mind-set, and we will not let ourselves fail.'"[24]

First Customers

After nearly three years of designing, testing, and introducing its disease management services to the health plan market, the company received its first two contracts virtually at the same time. Principal Health Care in Rockville, Maryland, agreed to a five-year shared savings contract that grew to include seven markets and an estimated 11,000 people with diabetes.[25] Just seven days later, Blue Cross Blue Shield of Florida's subsidiary Health Options, based in the Orlando area, added another 65,000 members, including an estimated 1,800 to 2,000 with diabetes.[26]

While it may have seemed as if the company's new program was an overnight success, these contracts were the result of years of hard work, predicated on the company's vision to improve health and cut costs. Bill Evans, director of managed care sales at the time, had spent the previous two years in Florida, flying in every Monday morning for a week's worth of sales calls, working his way through a chamber of commerce report that listed the largest employers and insurance companies.

Sales call teams included financial professionals and clinicians with a book of educational materials that had proven successful with patients in the hospital-based diabetes program.

The Principal Health Care and Health Options contracts were a gamble for the company. "We used to get kidded [by American Healthcorp finance personnel], 'Please don't do another deal real soon because we're taking on more risk here,'" Evans said. "It was a joke that every time we did a deal in those early days, our stock went down. They knew … we were sticking our necks out."[27]

It was a risky time, to be sure. But the attitude internally among those responsible for worrying about such things was that the stakes were more secure than they appeared. The company so firmly believed in its program that what looked like a gamble to an outsider was in reality an opportunity for American Healthcorp to deliver on the promise that healthier people cost less. But the reality was that failure was not an option. "The company was not that big at the time," said Bailey. "While we still had a strong balance sheet, and the capabilities to underwrite this risk, it wasn't going to go unnoticed if we didn't succeed."[28]

The new business model was problematic for some Wall Street analysts. The company had gone public based on the rather predictable revenues from its DTCA business. The uncertainty of a shared savings plan—in which American Healthcorp would not be able to project earnings for contracts until the first operational year was up and the data had been received and analyzed—created unpredictable earnings. "There was a lot of flexibility back then," Bailey said. "A lot of that has become more black and white, whereas back then it was gray, because we were a new player and it was a new industry. People didn't know it. Accountants didn't know it. The auditors didn't know it. Even

DTCA focused on hiring skilled workers essential to managing its expected growth. American Healthcorp signed nine DTCA hospital contracts for fiscal 1998, up 50 percent from fiscal 1997.

we, back then, took a relatively conservative view of it, not being able to forecast because we hadn't done it before."[29]

Early Success Breeds More Success

Just as the pilot program with Bristol-Myers Squibb had given the company a boost to reach its first insurers, the early managed care contracts provided another push. The company had intended to implement the contracts—six sites for Principal Health Care and one for Health Options—by March 1997. But the rollout proceeded more smoothly and at a lower cost than anticipated, allowing American Healthcorp to implement all seven sites by October 1, 1996—five months earlier than projected.[30] The early accomplishments in implementing the contracts provided further support for the efforts of the sales team.

"It was easier to walk in there—with a lot more confidence—knowing you had seven health plans that had started this program with you," Evans said. "You still had people who didn't think it was going to work, but you were confident that they were going to listen to you and take you seriously."[31]

Principal and Health Options soon had more than sales presentations to rely on. Seeing the early results was enough to convince Principal to add a seventh market—and another 35,000 covered lives—by December 1996. The success with Health Options brought another Florida Blue Cross Blue Shield company on board in early 1997,

adding 95,000 more enrollees. Just as the company had believed all along, delivering the results of improved health and lower cost would lead to continued success.

Improving Health, Saving Money

Early success in the disease management business had a positive impact on DTCA's hospital-based business as well. Taking a different approach from Principal and Health Options, US Healthcare chose DTCA to provide outpatient diabetes education services to its members with diabetes. The model was different, and so was the payment mechanism. While DTCA was charging fees on a per-member/per-month basis for its disease management programs, the US Healthcare contract was a fee-for-service agreement, since US Healthcare did not believe that diabetes education and support needed to be provided longitudinally. The US Healthcare agreement was essentially the outpatient model for the company's hospital customers, delivered to a health plan population. The services included patient assessment and short-term educational, behavioral, and motivational support, as well as outcomes tracking and reporting.

A similar contract was entered into by United Healthcare of Georgia, resulting in access to a specially designed outpatient program for all of its Atlanta-area enrollees (240,000 people). Both of these contracts were profitable in that they used resources from existing DTCA hospital-based programs, which lowered start-up costs and helped fuel revenue at a time when the disease management contracts were not yet fully paying off. At the end of the day, however, the company's concerns about "opt-in" models and the scalability of face-to-face interactions proved correct, and both programs ended at the conclusion of their first contract term.

However, at the time, these new contracts added a boost to hospitals desiring a DTCA facility as well. By 1996, hospital-based DTCA centers were growing again, expanding to 70 facilities in 1996. The company had 26 contract renewals, relocations, and new contract signings in 1997, up from 20 the previous year. The rate of contract terminations had dramatically improved as well, with only one in 1997, compared to 11 in 1996.[32]

Despite the brief respite in the hospital business, and although DTCA hospital programs exist to this day, the opportunity for American Healthcorp was clearly in health plans. In 1997, the hospital division provided 91 percent of the company's revenues, but in 1998, this proportion had dropped to 60 percent.[33]

CIGNA Contract Requires More Innovation

Building on the key lessons from its early programs, American Healthcorp was able to continuously refine its diabetes disease management program using what

the company described as an "all-win" approach—diabetes patients received improved health care, insurers saw costs fall, and American Healthcorp earned a healthy reward. But even those refinements weren't sufficient for the company's next client. At the end of 1997, after almost a year of negotiation, the company was chosen by CIGNA HealthCare to provide services to, initially, 87,000 members with diabetes in six of the insurer's 29 markets. CIGNA had powerful reasons for choosing American Healthcorp—its members with diabetes accounted for 3 percent of its membership, yet represented 17.5 percent of the

American Healthcorp announced in a 1997 press release that it had inked a deal with CIGNA HealthCare to provide services to 87,000 members with diabetes in six of the insurer's 29 markets.

AMERICAN HEALTHCORP

NEWS RELEASE

One Burton Hills Boulevard / Nashville, Tennessee 37215
FAX 615/665-7697   PHONE 615/665-1122

FOR IMMEDIATE RELEASE

Contact: Howard S. Drescher   Henry D. Herr
            CIGNA Healthcare   Executive Vice President and
            860-726-3578   Chief Financial Officer
                                        American Healthcorp, Inc.
                                        (615) 665-1133

**CIGNA HEALTHCARE AND AMERICAN HEALTHCORP, INC.
SIGN AGREEMENT FOR DIABETES MANAGEMENT SERVICES**

Bloomfield, Conn. and Nashville, Tenn.(October 6, 1997) — CIGNA HealthCare (NYSE:CI) and American Healthcorp, Inc. (Nasdaq/NM:AMHC) announced today that CIGNA will contract with Diabetes Treatment Centers of America (DTCA) to provide diabetes disease management services for members of CIGNA HealthCare managed care programs.

Under the three-year agreement, the services of DTCA, a wholly-owned subsidiary of American Healthcorp, will be a key component in CIGNA HealthCare's comprehensive approach to helping members and their physicians improve the quality of diabetes care.   DTCA will provide, through a fee-based arrangement, a tailored version of its NetLink™ teleservices-based diabetes management program.

"We are very pleased to be working with DTCA and using their innovative methods to improve the care of our members with diabetes," said Victor Villagra, M.D., Vice President Care Management, CIGNA HealthCare. "DTCA's long involvement in the intensive management of diabetes, along with its innovative products and national presence, are the foundation for this agreement. We see this as a model program for diabetes care management."

"This contract is a first of its kind for DTCA," said Tom Cigarran, Chairman and Chief Executive Officer, American Healthcorp. "In addition to strengthening our position in the national health care marketplace, the contract provides further evidence of the reputation and substantial potential of DTCA's comprehensive diabetes management programs."

CIGNA HealthCare and DTCA plan to implement the contract beginning in March, 1998, and be in operation in six markets by the end of the year.

-MORE-

The relationship between CIGNA and American Healthcorp was so complex that the company provided a supplement to *Healthcare Business* magazine (shown above left) detailing how the two had teamed up to create a winning strategy. "There were a number of companies out there, but none had the pedigree or national scope of American Healthcorp," Victor Villagra (below right), CIGNA's vice president of quality and strategic medical affairs, told the magazine.

company's total medical costs.[34] The specialized services CIGNA had offered to its diabetes members had failed to achieve the desired result, even though they were standardized across all CIGNA markets. "We knew that we did not have all the core competencies to arrange for the provision of intense diabetic care to patients, or to assist them in self-management," Victor Villagra, CIGNA's vice president of quality and strategic medical affairs, said at the time.[35]

"Victor was very up-front with us," Leedle remembered. "He told us that he loved what we were doing and how we had built the program. He wanted to buy it, but he only had so much to spend. If we could deliver the program for that amount, the contract was ours. The opportunity was too large for us to decline the challenge, so we went back to the drawing board to figure out how to make our delivery model even more efficient."

It was a significant challenge. CIGNA required a rapid deployment in multiple locations, and the typical model wouldn't work. "In Central Florida, we had an executive director who ran the business for us, and then we had nurses who were in the market, and they were making local telephone calls to members who had diabetes," Bill Evans said. "CIGNA said, 'We have people in Butte, Montana; we have people all over the country. You cannot afford to [use] in-market nurses. You need a different solution.' "[36]

"To meet CIGNA's expectations, we had to rethink the distributed model, which in turn helped us to see the light about the efficiencies we could achieve by providing calls from a centralized location, using automated telephone technology and a comprehensive, centralized patient record," said Steve Samples. "As we looked at the total price tag and the price points, it was just inescapable that the only way you could get there was to have [one] very efficient operation, not these little ones

that were scattered all around the country."[37] The resulting development of the company's first Care Enhancement Center (CEC) in Nashville enabled American Healthcorp to meet CIGNA's cost requirements.

Dr. Villagra was so convinced of the clinical and financial benefits of the diabetes disease management program that he also got CIGNA management to agree that he could offer it free, for one year, to CIGNA's self-insured employer customers. If, at the end of the year, those employers wanted to keep the program, they would have to begin to pay for it. That decision led to a rapid increase in program participants beyond CIGNA's 87,000 fully insured members, and proved to be the genesis of significant growth for American Healthcorp's new business as the company took the idea to other health plan customers.

There were other significant differences between the CIGNA contract and the earlier ones American Healthcorp had entered into, reflecting both the maturing of the disease management market and CIGNA's confidence in the company's ability to deliver the promised results. CIGNA was less interested in a shared-risk model, so the financial structure included a one-time implementation fee, plus a fixed fee for monthly services based on the number of members covered (a fee structure that came to be known as PDMPM—per diabetes member per month). While American Healthcorp gave away performance upside

using this approach, revenues became much more predictable, and the promised reward for good performance in the first six markets was expansion of the program to CIGNA's other 23 plans. The CIGNA program also adopted the recommended "opt-out" member engagement approach as the best way to ensure maximum member participation. The predictability of revenues and earnings helped lessen Wall Street's concerns as both the company and analysts were able to forecast company performance with much greater precision.

The company built its second CEC in Pittsburgh to serve the members of

THIRD QUARTER REPORT TO STOCKHOLDERS

Fellow Stockholder:

We are greatly pleased to report significant progress at DTCA with the signing of three new multi-year contracts with major managed care organizations. Two of these contracts, with Principal Health Care and Health Options, Inc., an HMO subsidiary of Blue Cross and Blue Shield of Florida, relate to DTCA's new comprehensive healthcare management services and are the first in the country to provide HMOs with these services for their enrollees with diabetes. The other contract, with U.S. Healthcare, involves providing outpatient diabetes management services to its enrollees through existing DTCA hospital centers. Combined with the Bristol-Myers Squibb contract signed in the second quarter, these contracts demonstrate DTCA's continuing leadership in the diabetes management services industry. They are also tangible examples of the exciting opportunity DTCA has to provide higher quality of care at lower cost for people with diabetes through the comprehensive management of their healthcare.

Although DTCA's prospects have improved significantly through the signing of these contracts, its third quarter financial results reflected both the continued turmoil in the healthcare market and the expenses associated with DTCA's diabetes disease management efforts. Total American Healthcorp revenues for the quarter, which ended May 31, 1996, were $16.0 million compared with $14.4 million for the third quarter of fiscal 1995. Net income for the latest quarter was $653,000, or $0.08 per share, compared with $875,000, or $0.11 per share, for the same prior-year period.

The Principal Health Care and Health Options contracts are five-year "shared savings" contracts covering seven markets and approximately 435,000 covered lives. We estimate that there are currently approximately 13,000 enrollees with diabetes in this population. These HMOs will continue to be at risk for 100% of their members healthcare costs under these contracts, and DTCA will be at-risk for the costs of operating its comprehensive healthcare management system. Cost savings produced by the system will be shared according to ratios set forth in the contracts.

We anticipate that revenues from the Principal Health Care and the Health Options contracts will be more heavily weighted toward the later years of their terms and that during the first year of operation at each of the seven market sites initially involved in these contracts, revenues will be slightly less than operating costs. Implementation at two of these sites has already been initiated and will continue on a staggered basis through March 1997. As a result, DTCA's profitability will

DIABETES TREATMENT CENTERS OF AMERICA

A wholly-owned subsidiary, DTCA is the leading provider of specialized, comprehensive diabetes treatment services designed to improve the quality and lower the cost of care for individuals with diabetes. DTCA created the business of hospital based diabetes treatment centers and has also created a comprehensive diabetes disease management program which it markets to managed care organizations, large employers and other at-risk healthcare organizations.

ASC AMSURG CORP

A majority owned subsidiary, AmSurg develops, acquires and manages single specialty physician practice-based ambulatory surgery centers. AmSurg provides high quality outpatient surgical care in the lowest-cost settings for people undergoing frequently needed low-risk surgical procedures. It is also entering the field of specialty care networks.

Three new multiyear contracts for DTCA with Principal Health Care, Health Options, Inc., and US Healthcare were announced in a 1996 letter from Tom Cigarran to American Healthcorp stockholders.

Registered nurses like Karen Holland, comprehensive care manager, were a critical element in the success of the Care Enhancement Centers. The centers, in turn, were critical for rapid growth once American Healthcorp began reaching health plans, allowing for faster and more cost-efficient implementation.

Highmark Blue Cross Blue Shield, its next large health plan contract. As the CIGNA relationship continued to expand, a third call center was built in Phoenix to serve its central and western state members. Both CECs were staffed with nurses who would reach out to the insurance plan's members around the country via telephone and mail, delivering compassionate care, encouragement, and education aimed at engaging members to manage their disease more effectively. It marked yet another transition for American Healthcorp's corporate colleagues as they came to realize the company had more employees in Pittsburgh than it did in Nashville. But Healthcorp was a company that thrived on change, particularly the change that came with creating and leading a new industry.

As Samples recalled:

We started off thinking of the be-all and end-all approach, which was having very small units of these [clinicians] literally sitting in the health plans' back door. We had to adapt and change our delivery and management models because the people who were running these very small units of maybe five, six, seven people also had a lot of direct customer impact, as well as the [responsibility for] management of these nurses, generally. In the care enhancement model, we really separated those duties. So we had people who were operations people running a center of 100 or 150 nurses that might have little if any direct customer interaction. And then you had the account management side, which had all the direct customer relationship, but didn't control those centers. So we wired ourselves to make certain that what we were telling the customers was what these people over here were actually delivering, and vice versa.[38]

Clinicians were there to provide not only information, but also inspiration. "There were always two goals—the [health plan members'] goals and the nursing goals," said Deb Hagemann, a clinician at the time. "Diabetes patients may have their own personal goal to, say, 'go on a vacation in the next six months,' but right now they aren't feeling well enough. The nursing goal would be to support the member's goals, and the way we did that was to encourage them to get them to adhere better to the standards of care and get their hemoglobin tested regularly, monitor their blood sugar, eat right, exercise, and follow the recommended diet and their physician's plan of care."[39]

Landing CIGNA was just the beginning of the hard work. To launch the CIGNA HealthCare Well Aware Program for Diabetes in Houston, American Healthcorp spent three months working with CIGNA's provider network to inform them about the new program. The company also installed the first version of PopulationWorks, a $20 million software program and platform that would allow the two firms to exchange data, ensuring that those in the CECs had access to a member's clinical history along with claims, administrative, and utilization data, all of which were used to stratify each individual's severity and risk and to help guide the clinician through an appropriate intervention plan.

As the number of contracts increased, CECs were opened in other cities. Today, the company has 13—four of which are located overseas to support programs in France, Brazil, and Australia. "There are cultural sensitivities that have to be understood and respected," Calhoun noted. "It would be hard, for example, for a clinician in Pittsburgh or Nashville or Austin to interact effectively with a patient in Hawaii."

The CIGNA agreement, which still represents the largest disease management relationship in the industry's history, was made possible because Healthcorp management listened to what the customer wanted and then found a way to deliver. It was an important lesson that still resonates with Healthways colleagues today. "Listening to the customers not only leads to significant improvements in how we do what we do, it

helps us help them design their strategies and meet their objectives. It's a core competency at Healthways and has been critical to our ongoing success,"[40] noted Robyn Fulwider, senior vice president–Nashville Business Unit, who added:

My entire tenure at Healthways has really been based on a philosophy of developing deep and intimate and strategic relationships with the customers. It is what is key to our success—the customer-facing, the customer service, delivering on our promises to our customers, being strategic with them, building opportunities together, and looking for opportunities for efficiency, and at what we can standardize. But at the same time, there's a focus on what we need to customize to be very specific to the needs of those customers. I think that's been key to our success, and sometimes our challenge is to be able to do that and do it in an efficient manner.[41]

The CIGNA relationship was foundational to future development of new disease programs, new delivery models, and a focus on efficiency, as well as effectiveness. It is a powerful alliance, and one that continued to shape the care that CIGNA's members receive and the plans that American Healthcorp created for years to come.

Turning Potential into Reality

After millions of dollars, and years in development, American Healthcorp's outreach to insurers was finally starting to show more than just promise. CEO Tom Cigarran was justifiably proud in telling stockholders: "Fiscal 1998 was a year in which American Healthcorp turned potential into reality. In addition to maintaining an unchallenged leadership position in its hospital diabetes treatment center business, DTCA conclusively demonstrated that it was living up to the bold slogan for its managed care business, 'Helping Fulfill the Promise of Managed Care.' Helping … as in present tense; that is, now."[42]

Cigarran had every right to be optimistic about the managed care line. The company had ended 1997 with 11,304 diabetes patients under management, a figure that increased fivefold to 57,000 lives under management by the end of 1998, with another 35,000 in backlog.[43] The additional participants came via seven new contracts signed with managed care organizations, including Highmark Blue Cross Blue Shield of Western Pennsylvania and John Deere Health Services.[44]

Blue Cross Blue Shield of Florida added a third market to its lineup that year—a powerful testament to how it viewed the savings it was realizing from the program. The company's success with the Health Options program in Central Florida was directly responsible for its expansion into the Miami and Tampa regions.[45]

The company also experienced its first contract loss when Coventry Health Care acquired Principal. Coventry wanted to pursue a different strategy and settled the early termination of the agreement for $3.6 million.[46] "With Principal, we started out with a great buy-in because the chief medical officer very much wanted it and helped us sell it within the company," Evans said. "Then they were purchased by Coventry, whose business model was designed to push financial risk downstream to the delivery system. In that model, there was no value proposition for them to continue as a customer."[47]

Putting Outcomes on the Board

American Healthcorp's early successes with its disease management programs were the result of excellent design, flawless implementation, and consistent execution. "We always intended to differentiate ourselves from our competitors by our results," Leedle said. "We made sure that we had the tools, the solutions, and the people to be confident that we could do that."

By 1998, results started to roll out. One company study showed that those using DTCA services had a hospitalization rate 67 percent below the national average for people with diabetes and 82 percent fewer emergency room admissions. "It is significant to note that these utilization rates were not the result of reducing care to this population," Stone told reporters. "In fact, in nearly every category of clinical outcome analyzed, including blood sugar control, complication rates, and adherence

Diabetes Treatment Centers of America Operations

LOCATIONS IN OPERATION UNDER DEVELOPMENT

- ● Hospital Sites
- ▲ Diabetes NetCare℠/Diabetes NetLink℠ sites
- ☐ Arthritis and Osteoporosis Care Centers

DTCA had centers in 72 hospitals in operation or under development on August 31, 1998. Locations included hospital sites, diabetes care sites, and arthritis and osteoporosis care centers. American Healthways advertised in The Endocrine Society reprint of the report by The Lewin Group, appealing to health plans to implement cost-saving disease management solutions.

to treatment plans, the results were better than national averages. If the country's entire diabetes population had similar utilization patterns, up to $49 billion in annual savings could be realized."[48]

Another company study showed a 26 percent—or $141 per member per month—reduction in direct health care costs within six months of a health insurance plan's implementation of the company's diabetes disease management program.[49] "It

is well understood that focusing the right resources in the right way can improve clinical outcomes and reduce costs for persons with diabetes," Stone said at the time. "In short, improving the health of this population reduces the cost of their health care. Until now, however, there has been no real-world evidence of the magnitude or timing of these savings and improvements."[50]

A third company study showed that the number of diabetes patients receiving a retinal eye exam—a critical factor in preventing blindness—increased from 28 to 80 percent, far above the national average of 37 percent. Those receiving an annual foot exam increased from 2 to 25 percent. Most important, though, was the measurement of hemoglobin A1C, the most accurate predictor of complications for diabetes patients. The company's data showed this critical measure was improved by 9 percent for type 2 patients and by 11 percent for type 1 patients.[51]

The capstone to these outcome studies was an independent analysis of the company's results, both individually and in the aggregate, for the six Principal health plans. Published in the *Journal of Clinical Endocrinology and Metabolism*, this Lewin analysis found that over the course of the first program year, the program generated, on average, a $50 reduction in direct health care costs per diabetes member per month. For a typical health plan, this meant that the new diabetes model offered an annual

savings of $600,000 for every 1,000 members with diabetes.[52] Perhaps equally as important, the Lewin analysis verified that these savings were not the result of reducing care, and that the results were replicable across multiple plans in different geographic areas.

American Healthcorp had a goal of 10 percent savings in the program's first year.[53] The Lewin-VHI study proved it was exceeding this goal (averaging 12.3 percent).[54] American Healthcorp's internal data showed that figure reached 17.3 percent after 18 months of participation in the program, and the company continued to push to achieve a 30 percent reduction over time.[55] The philosophy remained simple: prevent the 80 percent of diabetes patients who were relatively healthy from joining the sickest 20 percent of the population by aggressive intervention in the early stages of the disease.[56]

Every new piece of data made the diabetes disease management program an easier sell—or at least opened new doors. "It became an easier conversation," said Rick Bailey. "It doesn't stop your customers, though, from constantly changing the risk/gain relationship—[i.e., saying] 'we want you to take risk on this' and then, as they see that you hit [that goal], start morphing it into something different, always trying to get it a little bit [beyond] what they expect the performance to be—so the risk never completely goes away."[57]

American Healthcorp's board of directors in the mid-1980s: front, left to right: Thomas G. Cigarran, Henry D. Herr; standing, left to right: Martin J. Koldyke, Frank A. Ehmann, William C. O'Neil Jr., C. Warren Neel, PhD.

That risk became more manageable as the company shifted to a fixed payment schedule and thus assumed less of the financial liability of some of the early contracts. The new payment approach also allowed the company to forecast its earnings more accurately. As the company repeatedly demonstrated success, customers and prospects became less interested in the risk/reward contract model. As a result, by the end of 1998, even the early contracts had been converted to a fixed-fee schedule.[58]

American Healthways advertised in a journal of The Endrocine Society, appealing to health plans to find economical solutions to disease management care. The August 1998 issue reprinted the landmark Lewin Group report.

Converting existing clients to fixed-fees was not as difficult as it may sound. "As we began to demonstrate outcomes that were repeatable and reliable, the health plans were writing us bigger and bigger checks. Clients [began] saying, 'I know you can do this. I don't want to give you the gain share anymore,'" said Calhoun. "We said, 'All right, we won't take gain share, but you no longer get 100 percent fee risk, and we want longer term.'"

No longer were stock prices dropping every time a contract was signed. Buoyed by the various reports, CEO Cigarran held a conference call with stock analysts showcasing results from the earliest contracts. Within two weeks, the company's stock price was up 34 percent.[59] "The people who have been buying stock in the last 10 days are bullish on the fact that this is going to work," Cigarran told the Bloomberg Forum. "And when it does, it'll be huge."[60]

CIGNA's Disability Solutions for Chronic Conditions

your
COPD
workbook
chronic obstructive pulmonary disease

make a *personal* commitment to your health

596137 07/05

Above: The company's growing relationship with CIGNA underscored its move into disease management. The brochure *Your COPD Workbook* explored facts, guidelines, and solutions to assist patients in managing chronic obstructive pulmonary disease.

Opposite: Of the five men who founded American Healthcorp in 1981, only Tom Cigarran (left) and Bob Stone (right) remained active in the company's daily activities by the time both addressed the company during its 20th anniversary celebration.

*There were serious questions in the investment community about whether there were idiots
managing the company and if anybody here knew how to manage anything. Then what we
were doing started to work and work well. All of a sudden, we became geniuses. The truth was
we'd been pretty smart all along. Not as smart as they think we are now but never as dumb as
they thought we were during the years we were investing.*[1]

—Tom Cigarran, cofounder, chairman, and CEO, American Healthcorp

JUST TWO YEARS AFTER LANDING ITS FIRST DISEASE MANAGEMENT CUSTOMERS, AMERICAN
Healthcorp was the acknowledged leader in diabetes disease management. The
company's programs led to increased savings for its health plan customers,
repeatedly delivering on its promise that "Healthier People Cost Less." Revenues
were reaching record levels, while the number of lives under management
achieved new milestones with each passing year.

By 1998, however, health plans—the principal purchasers of disease
management services—were about to fundamentally change the way they bought
those services. For the previous five years, health plans had focused on a "best-in-class"
strategy, selecting their disease management services from organizations that provided
evidence of success in one specific disease. As a result, it was not uncommon for a plan
to have multiple relationships for management of each disease. The chronic diseases
included diabetes; cardiac disease, including coronary artery disease (CAD) and
congestive heart failure (CHF); and respiratory disease, including asthma and chronic

The end of the century brought a new name for the company— "American Healthways" —and later, a new look. The new image for the company was largely driven by its move away from hospitals and into disease management.

obstructive pulmonary disease (COPD). What the best-in-class purchasing strategy failed to take into account, however, was that as many as a third of all health plan members with chronic disease had more than one. In those instances, the member was receiving services from more than one supplier, each of which was claiming credit for the member's overall health improvement and lower cost. As a result, plans began to seek a single solution for all members that had one or more of what came to be known as "the core chronic diseases."

American Healthcorp was particularly advantaged as a result of this change in the purchasing behavior of

health plans because of the way its diabetes program had been designed. "Because of our [extensive] experience in working with people with diabetes, we understood that diabetes affects all other health conditions and vice versa," said Janet Calhoun. "As a result of that understanding, our diabetes program was never limited to just treating the member's diabetes but was designed instead to accommodate and support all of the member's health challenges. A diagnosis of diabetes was merely the requirement to participate. Once a member was in our program, we managed their diabetes and all of their complications and comorbidities."[2]

As then-executive vice president Ben Leedle stated:

It was a race, and the first to the overlap [of multiple chronic conditions] was going to emerge as the dominant firm in the disease management industry. Since we already had the protocols and systems in place to manage cardiac and respiratory disease for people who also happened to have diabetes, separating those elements into standalone programs was not a major conceptual or development challenge.[3]

What's in a Name?

The change in health plans' disease management purchasing strategy also provided the opportunity for the company to address a subtle but nonetheless significant concern among the management team: the company's name.

American Healthcorp's name was suitable when the company was founded as a hospital management firm in 1981. It had even been appropriate as the company diversified into drug and alcohol treatment, surgery centers, and hospital-based diabetes treatment centers. But by the mid-1990s, American Healthcorp was essentially a diabetes treatment company, and its subsidiary name, "Diabetes Treatment Centers of America" was used to market services to hospitals and health plans. In management's opinion, the company's transition from owning facilities to providing services for individuals had rendered the name "Healthcorp" less suitable.

"We felt 'corp' was fine when we were a corporation that owned facilities," Healthways executive vice president Bob Stone recalled. "Now we were in the business of delivering services to people, and we wanted a name that reflected that and that was less suggestive of an institutional base. 'Healthways' reflected the sense of what we were doing— providing individuals with chronic disease ways to improve their health."[4]

Eventually, the name "Diabetes Treatment Centers of America" posed challenges as well. "We were out marketing [diverse disease management services] to the payers as 'Diabetes Treatment Centers of America.' That didn't make any sense," Leedle said. "Our brand just had so much equity in the area of diabetes that it actually made it very difficult to get out from underneath the diabetes-only umbrella and to cascade [our service offerings] across more conditions. So it was time to change our name."[5]

As a result—except for the ongoing hospital-based diabetes programs—the DTCA name was phased out and the rest of the company's offerings carried the new American Healthways name. "It didn't take us long to convince ourselves that

The company headquarters in Nashville's Green Hills area received a facelift when the new logo took its place at the front of the building. The "Embrace" logo replaced the long-held medical cross logo, marking a step into a more collaborative approach to a patient's health care.

The Company

THE DAWN OF THE NEW MILLENNIUM BROUGHT SIGNIFICANT CHANGES TO American Healthcorp, which first shed its corporate-sounding name in favor of "American Healthways" in 1999. By 2001, the company would make another major change.

The familiar red stripes emblazoned with a medical cross and blue lettering would be replaced by a new logo that better symbolized the company's purpose. The well-known red and blue would remain, but the medical look would give way to a more personal one.

The new logo was called "Embrace." The design was an abstract depiction of an embrace between two people as seen from above, symbolizing partners reaching for a common goal, with a shared mind to achieve it.

"The 'Embrace' stands for the link we all share in achieving positive health outcomes," the company explained. "It is this personal relationship, this one-on-one embrace, that fosters healthy behavior. Put simply, success requires a human connection."[1]

'American Healthways' really was a better banner for the company to fly under than 'Healthcorp'; you could fit a lot underneath [it]," Leedle said.[6]

"It was the right name for the time," then-CEO Tom Cigarran noted. "The common use of 'Healthways' in our new corporate name, and across all product lines, told both our current and potential customers, 'There are ways to improve the health of people with chronic diseases,'

which is exactly what our programs and services are designed to do."[7]

As Cigarran anticipated, the new name offered brand flexibility. The company's diabetes program became "Diabetes Healthways," cardiac programs were branded "Cardiac Healthways," and respiratory programs became "Respiratory Healthways." These product names were used not only for marketing the programs to customers but also to

"Through our care enhancement services, we can add significant value to every health care interaction. Physicians and other providers are empowered to provide better care in an environment that restores and supports the primacy of the physician-patient relationship, while patients are helped to be healthier than they otherwise would have been, and health plans achieve lower cost and more satisfied customers."[2]

The "Embrace" also reflected the company's goal of closing the gaps in care that "routinely result in poorer patient outcomes than could be achieved if evidence-based standards of care were followed. These less favorable clinical outcomes yield higher-than-necessary costs and contribute to the current and projected double-digit increases in the nation's health care expenditures."[3]

Along with the Embrace, the company introduced a new tagline—*improved health is the outcome*—to better reflect its overall purpose. The introduction of the Embrace was the first logo change since American Healthways' founding and came as the company celebrated its 20th anniversary.

In 2006, American Healthways changed its name to "Healthways" in an effort to better reflect its function as a global well-being company.

brand program materials for participating health plan members.

But neither the name change nor the relative ease of modifying existing systems and protocols proved to be a magic wand in providing the company immediate entry into the management of other diseases. In 1998, the first year it was offered to the market, Cardiac Healthways was purchased by only one customer, adding about 2,500 lives to

the company's total number of individuals being served.[8]

As Leedle noted: "You end up marketing, believing that you're building a plan in one area, and the market digests it as, 'Boy, if you really want to get diabetes right, you ought to see these guys.' How hard was it to expand our brand to represent multiple chronic diseases? Harder than we thought. In a sense, we were rebuilding the market. We needed that first

customer to give us a shot, and we needed to deliver the outcomes."[9]

Technology Critical to Growth

Above: Colleagues like Lou Cabacungan at the Hawaii Care Enhancement Center helped drive the success with the Hawaii Medical Service Association, which was one of the company's largest accounts.

Right: The Hawaii CEC marks Christmas with green and red floral leis. Though key elements of the company culture are maintained at each site, the company also embraces the unique local and regional flair at each location.

The rapid expansion of diseases for which services were being provided, and the number of people to whom American Healthways was providing those services, created an increasing need for revision of the company's PopWorks platform and infrastructure. The software and hardware had not changed significantly since version 2.0 had been introduced in 1998 to support the change from the distributed delivery model to the centralized CEC model. "While the new disease management programs were being delivered on the PopWorks platform, each disease state was essentially a standalone component. Just as our customers wanted an integrated solution from us, providing that solution required the development of an integrated platform

if we were going to be able to continue to be the most efficient provider of services, not just the most effective," Calhoun remembered. "There was also an increasing customer demand for more sophisticated and timely reporting."[10]

With two new CECs in Phoenix, Arizona, and Kapolei, Hawaii, joining the company, it was essential to upgrade the proprietary technology system to fully integrate care processes for participants with more than one disease or condition, and to handle the increasing volume. The revised program, known as PopWorks 3.0, integrated all of American Healthways' computer technology programs and facilitated information exchange between the company's care coordinators, health plans, and physicians. It also housed patient and care data and monitored program activities.[11]

By 2000, American Healthways' clients were located throughout the United States, and centralized program delivery through the CECs had become even more important to the company's success. It now had more than 250 nurses working in the centers, which were staffed six days a week, 12 to 18 hours a day. Nurses were available to receive calls

from participants during evenings, nights, and weekends.[12] The company also received 150 to 175 inbound calls per day, with people reaching out to their assigned nurses to ask questions.[13] The bulk of CEC activity was directed at making outbound calls, welcoming new people into the program, setting goals, providing guidance and support for improved health behaviors, and monitoring progress once goals had been set.

Operationally, each program participant was stratified into one of four levels based on the risk of health compromise. The healthiest were termed Stratification (Strat) 1, whereas the riskiest were deemed "Strat 4." Stratification levels changed dynamically as each participant's condition changed. PopWorks 3.0 suggested the initial stratification level, but each nurse could override that recommendation based on his/her own judgment and assessment of each individual's circumstances.

Nurses hired to work at the CECs were screened for empathy based on an assessment tool developed by American Healthways in conjunction with the University of Tennessee. "We needed the nurses to be able to interact in a manner that engendered immediate trust with each participant," Calhoun noted. Newly hired nurses also attended a six-week training program before going "live" on the phones and were monitored by supervisors through the first several weeks of their tenure.

Working in a care enhancement center required a "totally different mindset,"

explained Gerrye Stegall, who joined the company in 2001 to help further develop Cardiac Healthways and train the nurses who would be interacting with participants with cardiac disease. "Hospital systems are very established. They've got all their processes and rules in place. When I came here, there weren't a lot of processes or rules."[14]

Stegall added:

It was really, OK, what are you going to talk to the person about first? What's going to make the most difference the fastest? What are you going to work on for the longer term? How are you going to help them understand how to take care of symptoms or problems that they might have along the way? So if an individual has a new chest pain, what do they do about that? Do they have an action plan? Do they know who to call? Do they dial 911? Do they know how to take their nitroglycerin?

Early treatment after the onset of symptoms is very important, so that's another process in the education of people with cardiac disease, particularly. We had to change the teaching strategy to make people more effective at self-managing their disease. "Here is a problem. You try to figure it out, and we'll give you the resources to help you do that and make sure you've got it right."[15]

In addition to the release of PopWorks 3.0, American Healthways made investments to ensure that its telephone systems were designed to enable the CEC nurses to be even more

In 2000, the company's structural changes showed the importance of both the hospital-based business and health plans as Mary Hunter, senior vice president and chief operating officer–hospital group; and Ben Leedle, executive vice president and chief operating officer–health plan group; joined Bob Stone (left) and Tom Cigarran (right) at the executive level. Both Hunter and Leedle had longevity with the company and had begun their careers in the field. Hunter began hers as administrator of the company's Lebanon, Tennessee, hospital, while Leedle's first job was as an exercise physiologist at the Diabetes Treatment Center in Wichita, Kansas.

.

effective and efficient. The company installed a $7-million state-of-the-art dialing system with call routing and information access technologies at each of the CEC centers.[16] "The goal was to always be able to reinvent because things aren't static, and that's why the technology has to keep moving," Stegall said. "You can't rest on your laurels."

The company also teamed up with a number of different technology partners to develop voice and data networking, databases, and at-home support for cardiac disease management program participants, which in turn allowed for integrated pulse, weight, and blood pressure monitoring. Information was transmitted over a secure phone line to PopWorks, which would compare the data to treatment targets and clinician expectations. Anomalies were flagged by

the care manager, who would then contact the patient. The system was also programmed to alert clinicians to check on patients whose data was not transmitted in a timely manner.[17]

"These companies recognize the important role their technologies play in developing solutions that improve the effectiveness and efficiency of health care delivery while addressing the need to reduce costs," said Stone. "Their participation will help ensure the availability of hardware, software, communications, and network solutions for even more effective and efficient delivery of large-scale care management programs like the ones we offer. We are pleased to initiate this effort, which we believe will ultimately raise the technology bar for the industry and allow American Healthways to continue to shape the health care environment in the future."[18]

Health Plans Become the Dominant Business Line

By early 2000, with the addition of respiratory disease programs the previous year, the company was providing management for the three most common and costly chronic disease groups—

diabetes; cardiovascular disease, including CAD and CHF; and respiratory disease, including asthma and COPD.[19] Once again, the company's timing was perfectly in tune with the market, as was made clear in that year's Annual Report, which proclaimed, "Fiscal 2000: The Disease Management Log Jam Breaks."[20]

The company was expanding contracts and adding new ones as quickly as it could. In 2000, the number of lives under management increased from 132,000 to 212,000. Within the first month of 2001, another 100,000 were added.[21] The six-year-long effort to become a sole-source chronic disease management company was proving successful. Disease management surpassed the hospital business by 1999, the same year the company's operating revenues topped $50 million for the first time.[22] Disease management revenues represented 61 percent of the company's total in 2000.[23]

This growth demonstrated that American Healthways was continuing to listen and learn from its customers. "The experience that drove it to deal with more of these diseases than just diabetes had revealed that we, the payers, needed programs that addressed all the comorbidities, not just the single disease," said Dr. Charles Wilhelm, who, as chief medical officer with Principal Health Care, had been one of the company's first diabetes disease management clients. "You have to look at the whole patient."[24]

More and more health plans were beginning to do just that. Vytra Health Plans of Melville, New York, contracted for diabetes, cardiac disease, and respiratory disease services—marking the company's first multiple disease contract. In doing so, Vytra was also the company's first client for Respiratory Healthways, a program designed for members with COPD and asthma.[25]

"At one point, I can remember our strategy being based on our conviction that the company that's able to do diabetes, cardiovascular, and respiratory conditions on a common platform, with an integrated database and a service model that can be counted on to deliver results, is going to really get a big wind in its sail," Leedle said. "So, along the way, there were steps where you could just see how the market was going to move, and that if you could do 'XYZ,' you were going to push yourself far out into the front. We were fortunate. We got there first, and we delivered on outcomes early … [and those factors] carried us through the first seven or eight years of this decade."[26]

Success Breeds Success

The company's historic success with its diabetes program proved to be a powerful lever in the sale of additional programs to existing customers. Health plans looking for a credible, sole-source supplier as they disengaged from the best-in-class model would often look to the supplier of the most successful program as their first choice to provide programs for the core chronic diseases. More often than not, American Healthways, having proven the effectiveness of its diabetes solution, was that first choice.

In 2000, CIGNA, which already offered diabetes programs to 60,000 members in 17 markets, added another nine markets, comprising 35,000 additional lives.[27] The new agreement expanded American Healthways' relationship with CIGNA to 20 states and the District of Columbia. As further evidence of their satisfaction with the success of the existing relationship, CIGNA also expanded the term of the contract through 2004.

CIGNA increased its American Healthways offerings again in mid-2000, adding Cardiac Healthways to its services. The plan, which would be phased in throughout 2001, covered 50,000 cardiac patients and made the company the largest provider of cardiac disease management services in the industry.[28]

In May 2000, the company signed a five-year contract with the Hawaii Medical Service Association (HMSA) to serve approximately 20,000 members with diabetes.[29] The HMSA contract also covered Medicare clients, a population that was showing dramatic improvements through the use of Diabetes Healthways' services. A company analysis showed a 17.1-percent drop in total health care costs for Medicare beneficiaries through its programs, accounting for $1.36 million in savings for every 1,000 Medicare members with diabetes.[30]

"Studies have shown the impact comprehensive diabetes disease management programs can have on members of commercial HMOs," Stone wrote. "This is the first large-scale analysis, however, to confirm that this approach also works for the Medicare population, who by virtue of their age and health status typically need more health care services and are at higher risk for chronic conditions. This analysis validates our belief that healthier people cost less."[31]

While the growth in the number of agreements for individual and combined chronic disease management services was energizing both the organization and Wall Street, American Healthways was not content. "Our chronic disease programs were only reaching 8 to 10 percent of our customers' total population," Leedle recalled. "While we were making a significant contribution in terms of improving health and bending the cost curve, it wasn't enough to overcome the significant upward pressure on health care costs and increasing prevalence of disease."[32] The company responded with a new offering for 12 "impact conditions"—high-cost disease states with prolonged duration for which there were evidence-based standards of care. Based on those criteria, the company was convinced that they could be managed just like the core chronic diseases, leading to both clinical improvement and cost savings.

Once again, the timing was right, and in 2001, Blue Cross Blue Shield (BCBS) of Minnesota stepped to the plate by executing a 10-year agreement with the company to provide both core chronic and impact condition services to all of its health plan members. Both the scope and the duration of the agreement were industry firsts.

The momentum increased a few months later when the company signed a similar agreement with HealthSpring, a plan that served Middle Tennessee Medicare members.[33] Because of their age, Medicare members often have more health issues than members of a commercial health insurance plan. American Healthways' services would affect the 50 percent of HealthSpring's members that accounted for 75 percent of the plan's total medical costs.[34]

At the end of the first year of using American Healthways services, both BCBS Minnesota and HealthSpring saw impressive results. HealthSpring's members had reduced hospital admissions and emergency room visits, which lowered the company's expenditures by about 3 to 4 percent of its total costs.[35]

In Minnesota, American Healthways' BluePrint for Health® program again demonstrated the company's ability to deliver on all aspects of its value proposition: improved health, cost savings, and member satisfaction. The program's intense focus on the 14 percent of the population that represented 45 percent of the plan's medical costs saved more than $41 per American Healthways program participant per month.[36] Those savings were paired with improved health outcomes and reduced utilization among participating

You Are Here.

BluePrint for Health® care support

Right where you are standing, Blue Cross and Blue Shield of Minnesota is changing the way health care is delivered. You will see dedication and innovation. You will see how our BluePrint for Health® Care Support Program uses the miracle of 21st-century technology to deliver clinical excellence to hundreds of thousands of people without losing the human touch.

Watch the future of health care take shape. Right here. Right now.

Welcome to the Care Enhancement Center.

BlueCross BlueShield
BluePlus
of Minnesota
Independent Licensees of the Blue Cross and Blue Shield Association

members, including a 14-percent decrease in hospital admissions and an 11-percent decrease in emergency room visits. In all, BCBS Minnesota estimated it would save $36 million to $45 million in its first year of the program.[37]

These cost savings also flowed to the health plan's employer clients, as they noted indirect savings due to a reduction in days missed from work or school for their employees and dependents.[38]

A company survey revealed that health plan members were satisfied with the program, as reflected in the fact that

Blue Cross Blue Shield of Minnesota signed a contract with American Healthways to service all of its health plan members—an industry first. This move was based on the premise that "healthier people cost less."

95 percent of eligible members participated. In addition, about 84 percent of members with chronic disease and 64 percent of those with impact conditions reported they had more control of their health as a result of their participation in the American Healthways programs.[39]

"We believed in American Healthways and in our mutual vision of what was possible if we could broaden our reach beyond just one or two chronic diseases, and the results have exceeded our expectations," said Dr. Bill Gold, chief medical officer for BCBS Minnesota. "I believe the implications for the future of health care to be nothing short of profound."[40]

The millions saved by health plans were impressive: $850 million between 1996 and 2003. But American Healthways management and colleagues, harking back to the company's original guiding principle— "if we do the right thing, the business will take care of itself"—were more passionate about the lives that were improved as a result. Fewer hospital stays and emergency room visits, for instance, represented lives uninterrupted, not just lower costs. In an address to investors, Cigarran opined:

We would make a lot more money if we were in the cosmetics business. Of course, it would say on our tombstones that we invented the best lipstick color of 1995. That's not a very satisfying epitaph. Colleagues [from our company] sleep well at night because they know that, every day, they make a meaningful difference in people's lives.[41]

Calhoun expressed it this way:

Regardless of what business we've been in, there's an underlying theme—helping [people] live healthier lives. Even when we were the Diabetes Treatment Centers of America, our goal was to help people with diabetes live the most productive, active lives that they could, [even though] they had a chronic disease. So when you have an organization of people whose passion and mission is to get up and think about how to do that better, faster, cheaper, and easier, it's easy to be entrepreneurial because the mission is just so wonderful.[42]

Staying Ahead of the Curve

American Healthways' seemingly uncanny ability to sense market changes and react in a timely manner is the result of management's refusal to ever conclude that what the company offers and how those services are delivered is as good as it can ever be. "If there's one question that's on a leader's mind, it's, 'What's next?'" Leedle noted. "A contract service business model requires constant innovation. Customers are always evaluating the cost of buying services versus the cost of providing those services themselves. If we're not constantly doing it better and less expensively—if we're not always a step ahead in terms of what the market's next requirements are going to be—we'll see customers come to the 'wrong' answer on the 'make or buy' question."[43]

Improved health was the goal, and evidence of success was critical both for making sales presentations and for proving that the methods worked. A key component of the sales process was intense data analysis that led to a keen understanding of each prospect's opportunity. The results of this analysis were compiled in a comprehensive "Milestone Report" that showed [the customer] examples of what we thought we could achieve specifically for them. "We told them, 'If you do this, you'll save X amount of dollars over the next five years,' and 'These are the clinical savings we guarantee,'" said Regina Seider, director of sales analytics. The data was also used to promote potential savings from a specific product addition for existing clients. "The information is invaluable to the client, who is often unable to get their own technology department to parse its records to provide it."[44]

To stay as far advanced on the innovation curve as possible, the company created a technology advisory council to develop the next generation of integrated care management tools. This group brought together both American Healthways' current partners and outside industry experts for collaborative brainstorming.

Acquiring Capabilities

In 2001, American Healthways acquired Empower Health, a Connecticut-based compiler of market research data, and CareSteps, a predictive modeling firm that initially had been a member of American Healthways' technology council.

The acquisitions, which were completed almost simultaneously, came during what the *Nashville Business Journal* called a "money-draining infrastructure buildup."[45] Stock analysts reacted favorably, however. "It makes quite a bit of sense. Obviously it's a dilutive transaction, at least for this year, because Empower Health doesn't have any revenue, but there are a lot of long-term benefits to this," Arthur Henderson, senior equity research assistant with Jefferies & Co., told the newspaper. "They put up a lot of money [that] was never capitalized into their IT system. … Everything is in place and ready to go."[46]

The pairing of American Healthways and Empower Health made so much sense, in fact, that Empower had attempted it first. "Empower Health was interested in acquiring both CareSteps and American Healthways," said Mary Chaput, who retired as Healthways' chief financial officer in 2010. "They couldn't get the money together to do it. So American Healthways turned around and bought Empower Health for $20 million."[47]

Chaput also came on board during the acquisition, replacing Henry Herr, who had been chief financial officer and one of the company's founders. Herr had anticipated the purchase attempt by Empower and had made plans to retire.

"After more than two decades with the company, it was time to turn the finances over to someone else. The Empower Health deal would bring in some new people for

As the company grew, so did its leadership team. Mary Chaput became executive vice president and chief financial officer when American Healthways acquired Empower Health.

W HEN AMERICAN HEALTHCORP LAUNCHED ITS DIABETES TREATMENT CENTERS OF America Foundation (DTCA), the intent had been twofold: fund research by qualified young scientists and build relationships with some of the top diabetes researchers in the country, who would then assess the research proposals.

Though the DTCA Foundation was relatively short-lived in terms of the company's history, it led to the company's ongoing pursuit of scientifically verifiable data, which was then shared with top physicians throughout the country.

One significant outcome of the DTCA Foundation was the company's annual Physicians Summit, where leading health care professionals gathered to listen and present the latest research in the field.

When American Healthways partnered with Johns Hopkins University in 2001, the Physicians Summit was transformed into the annual Outcomes Summit, which brought together researchers and other experts to explore topical issues related to health care and develop consensus on ways to improve it.

"At the end of the day, the fundamental interaction in health care is between the patient and the physician," said Bob Stone. "The rest of the system exists or ought to exist solely for the purpose of making that interaction more efficient or more effective or preferably both. We recognize the role that physicians play—have to play, should

play—and make them part of the solution. It has been a part of our DNA, and I would tell you it's part of our success."

The Outcomes Summits also produced important and valuable consensus papers on some of the key issues facing health care. Each year, more than 200 practicing physicians, physician executives, thought leaders, and subject matter experts gathered to tackle these issues. A steering committee met regularly prior to the summit to create a draft document, which was then debated and changed during the summit. The entire group participated in writing the final consensus report.

For practicing physicians, the summits provided an opportunity to hear the latest research while academicians received valuable insight into what was occurring in doctors' offices.

Through the years, the summits produced work that included:

- *Specialty Referral Guidelines for Cardiovascular Evaluation and Management*, which offered primary care physicians a set of clinical thresholds that indicated when patients needed referral to a specialist;

- *Standard Outcome Metrics and Evaluation Methodology for Disease Management Programs*, which measured disease management programs that were implemented under real-world conditions rather than in a controlled experiment, providing ways to measure outcomes and calculate returns on investment;

- *Defining the Patient-Physician Relationship for the 21ˢᵗ Century*, which identified the ideal patient-physician relationship to improve the quality of care;

- *Outcomes-Based Compensation*, which explored physician incentives in support of quality improvement; and

- *Improving Care through Physician-Disease Management Collaboration*, which explored ways in which the health care system could better integrate care.

The 2006 Outcomes Summit focused on health care organizations and wellness—ways in which the health care community could become more involved in disease prevention rather than focusing solely on treatment. It also marked the evolution of the annual gathering itself,

which, three years later, would shift its focus—and change its name—to better reflect the purpose of American Healthways: well-being improvement.

Today, the company's annual Well-Being Summit brings together key leaders to discuss ways to improve overall well-being.

The Well-Being Summit also provides a forum for those interested in transforming the health of a specific population—including employers, community leaders, and health care professionals.

The 2011 summit featured some of the world's best-known well-being professionals, ranging from Dr. Deepak Chopra to Dan Buettner, author of *The Blue Zones*, to Daniel Pink, author of several books on finding satisfaction in the workplace.

Each session of the summit also included a review of company case studies on the implementation of well-being programs and their impact on the workforce's productivity.

On the surface, the Well-Being Summit looked a lot different than the early DTCA Foundation meetings. However, there is a consistent thread that connects these annual forums: a desire to bring together thought leaders to share information and hone improvements in health care and well-being for their constituents.

Notable well-being professionals Deepak Chopra (top), Dan Buettner (center), and Daniel Pink (bottom) were featured speakers at the company's 2011 Well-Being Summit.

the next step as far as the company was concerned. We had a very good candidate who had great experience and had done a great job with it in line to take my role," Herr said. "I saw other people in the organization who had joined at various times develop into great managers and come out very well in terms of where they wanted to be. I guess you feel like you don't have a whole lot of things you need to

make up for or additional things you have to do. You're able to leave and say you have no regrets."[48] Herr remained a member of the board of directors until 2009.

Although American Healthways ended up as the purchaser, Herr continued with his retirement plans, and Chaput was hired as chief financial officer.

"None of it had happened yet when I was first contacted," Chaput said. "So it was like, 'I'm not sure who is going to be the boss,' but by the time of my interviews, American Healthways had prevailed, and I knew I would be working for Tom Cigarran."[49]

At the same time, the purchase of CareSteps and its sophisticated neural network predictive modeling technology allowed American Healthways to identify health plan members who were at risk and to predict who, without intervention, were most likely to incur significant health compromises, utilization, and costs within the next 12 months. The accuracy of the CareSteps predictive models was unmatched in the industry. American Healthways clinicians used the models, in addition to data from PopWorks and their own input after each patient encounter, to ensure that program participants were highly stratified irrespective of their current health status. As a result, the company could mitigate costs significantly by intervening earlier than might otherwise have been the case.

Recognizing the potential value of the information and expertise it had garnered over the years, the company launched the

A VISIT TO OUR SITE *could help you avoid* A VISIT TO THIS ONE.

EMERGENCY

careSTEPS
PERSONAL HEALTH ADVISOR

Healthways purchased CareSteps, a company that appraised individuals' health risks based on a personal inventory and then provided them with a customized wellness plan.

American Healthways Center for Health Research, whose role included analyzing company data to better understand the drivers of health outcomes, ensuring that the company's knowledge base was reflected in the development of solutions and enhancements and providing scientific analysis necessary to continuously support the company's results.

In 2001, the company also formed an alliance with Johns Hopkins University that would independently certify the clinical integrity of its programs and verify its program results. Originally funded as a $1.4 million, five-year project, the alliance continues to this day.

"We think it's a company with a good idea, and we liked the role we could play," said Steve Libowitz, then a senior director at Hopkins Health, the division that would help coordinate work by Johns Hopkins researchers involved in the project.[50]

Together, American Healthways and Johns Hopkins launched the Outcomes Summit, which brings academics and practicing physicians together to discuss—and ultimately create solutions for—critical issues in the health care system.

The relationship with Johns Hopkins also led to the creation of the Outcomes Evaluation Program, in which Johns Hopkins faculty and clinicians provided independent analysis of the effectiveness of American Healthways programs and their clinical and financial results.

The company also initiated a collaboration with both the Massachusetts

Institute of Technology (MIT) AgeLab, which designed strategies for the elderly and their caregivers, and, later, Pro-Change Behavior Systems Inc., which had 30 years of experience with evidence-based science research.

MIT and Pro-Change would form the backbone of American Healthways' strategic partnerships. Later partners would include the Center for Health Transformation, a collaboration of public and private leaders attempting to create a health care system that lowered costs while improving care; Medco Health Solutions, a pharmacy benefits manager with which American Healthways worked to create integrated health programs; and

Healthways partners with a number of health care providers, including Pro-Change Behavior Systems and the MIT AgeLab, to help improve the lives of seniors. Here AgeLab founder Joseph Coughlin, PhD, demonstrates a simulator that tests the affects of aging on driving skills. *(Image ©Jason Grow/ All Rights Reserved).*

the Partnership to Fight Chronic Disease, a national and state-based coalition aimed at raising awareness of death, disability, and rising health care costs related to chronic diseases.

Raising the Bar on Quality and Results

Though disease management was still a relatively new industry, American Healthways had become the acknowledged industry leader with a compound annual growth rate (CAGR) of more than 40 percent. "Our growth was predicated on our always having something new for the market and our unfailing ability to deliver on our outcomes promise," Steve Samples said. "In addition, we always tried to set the performance bar for the entire industry, doing what was 'right' even if it wasn't necessary at the time. We were committed to being the best, bar none."[51]

Apparently, the industry agreed that American Healthways was moving in the right direction. The company was the first to receive the "triple crown" of accreditation, with certification from the National Committee for Quality Assurance (NCQA), the American Accreditation Healthcare Commission (URAC), and the Joint Commission on Accreditation of Healthcare Organizations (JCAHO). It also won the Disease Management Association of America (DMAA) Leadership Award three times— the only company in the industry to ever

do so—including two years running, in 2002 and 2003.

Following its receipt of the Leadership Award, American Healthways' relationship with the DMAA was further expanded when Stone was elected president of the association in 2003.[52]

At the time of his appointment, Stone said:

DMAA has already made significant strides in gaining a broad understanding of what disease management is and in promoting the quality of disease management services through pursuit of external accreditation and certification. Now we must move on to demonstrate unequivocally that disease management can and does deliver on its basic value proposition of improving health, improving patient and physician satisfaction with the health care experience, and, as a result, reducing the overall costs of care. I look forward to having the opportunity to help shape the programs and initiatives that will lead to that goal.[53]

The recognitions and accreditations were extremely important market differentiators for American Healthways as the industry grew. "The minute people saw where this thing was going, 200 companies came out of the woodwork—big companies—well-established, brand-name, FORTUNE® 50 and FORTUNE® 100 companies," said Leedle. "Health plans themselves and a million 'out-of-the-garage' folks with any kind of [venture capital] funding could stick their tent out there underneath this broad thing called disease management. That was a time in which we were the only public company doing this for a long time, and the market received us well."[54]

The stamp of approval that came from the three accreditations, the DMAA awards, and 20 years of experience, helped American Healthways stand out from those who were new to the field. But the principal driver of American Healthways' growth through the first few years of the new century was the success it was documenting on behalf of its customers.

Wall Street Responds

From its inception, American Healthways had been determined to be the leader in whichever field of health care it entered. Now, it was making good on that commitment, and investors were taking notice. Both the company and the industry were growing at an accelerated rate. The *Wall Street Journal* forecasted a $20 billion industry in just a few years. After seven years of single-digit growth, the company's stock price increased 800 percent from January 2000 to July 2001. "For much of our first decade, Wall Street wasn't quite

sure how to value us and was skittish about the unpredictability of our revenues and earnings," Cigarran said. "As the industry matured, and our financial results stabilized, they came around."

In 2003, American Healthways earned the No. 1 spot on *Fortune*® magazine's list of the 100 Fastest Growing Small Businesses and was No. 5 on its list of 100 Fastest Growing Companies in America. The company was also included in *BusinessWeek's* 100 Hot Growth Companies list and in Standard and Poor's Small Cap 600 Index. In response to this growth, as well as investor demand, the company gave its shareholders a two-for-one stock split.

Though most business analysts focused on improvements to a health plan's bottom line, American Healthways kept its eye on improved health for the individual, believing that success in that effort was a required precursor of sustained savings. "We have never wavered from our understanding that all the elements of our value proposition are connected by the word 'and,'" Leedle said. "It's easy to reduce cost or improve health; it's not quite as simple to do both. Our success results from figuring out how to do just that."

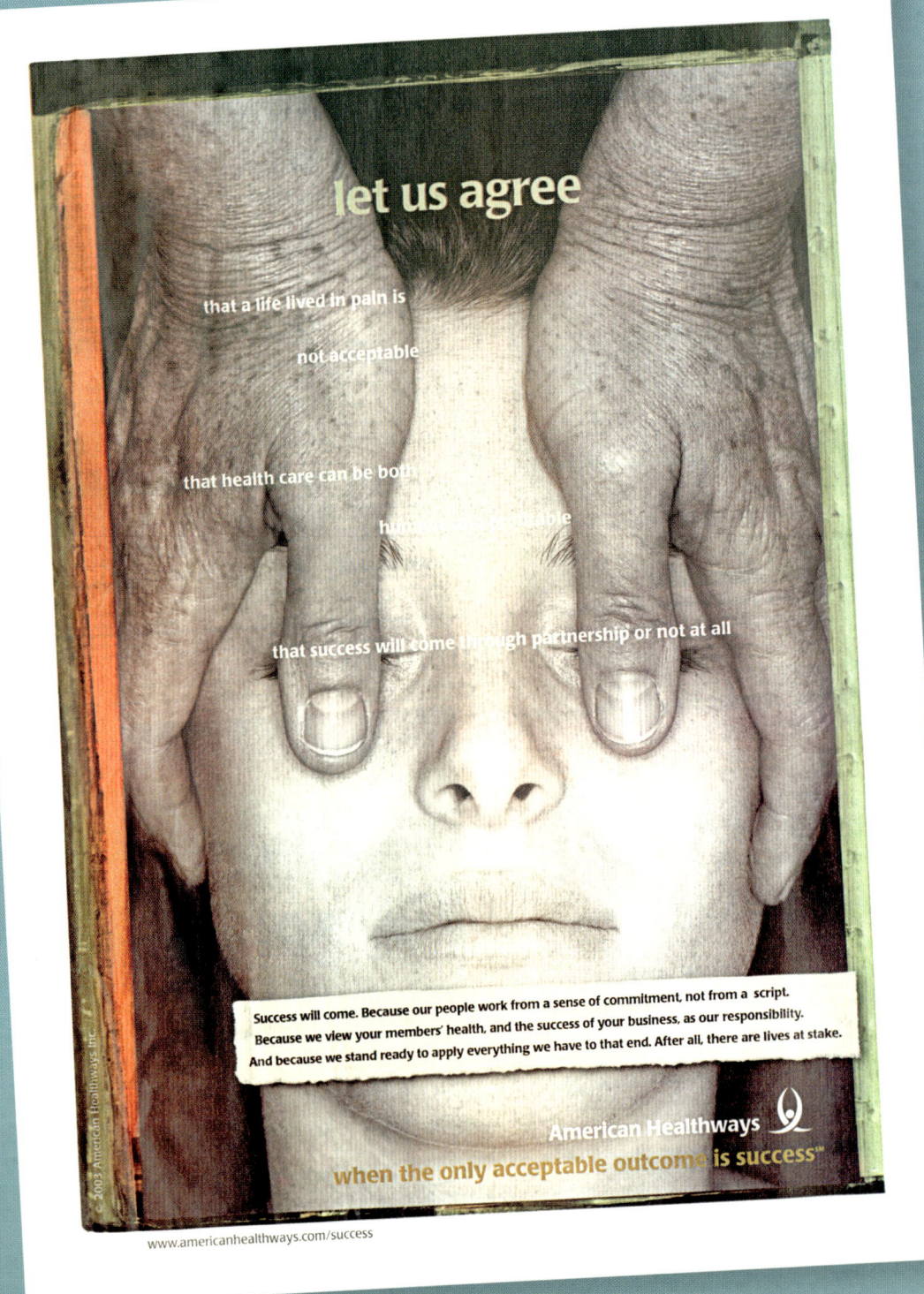

Above: This advertisement appeared in an American Healthways–sponsored supplement in the *New York Times*, which explained disease management to the National Managed Health Care Congress in 2003.

Opposite: The relationship between patients and physicians has always been considered a major ingredient in developing and maintaining the health and well-being of those in American Healthways' disease management programs.

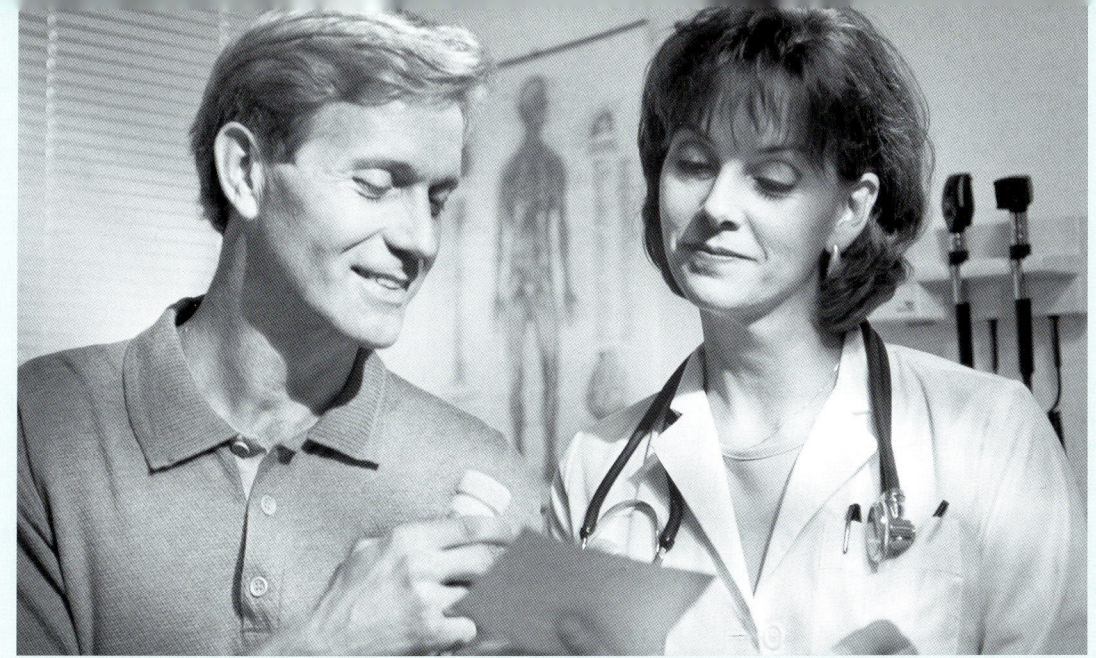

Getting the patient to be involved in anything that has to do with modifying their behavior to improve their health is not the easiest thing in the world, but overall, once the patients understood what the program was all about, the patient buy-in was very good. … Get enough patients to buy into the program, and you get the outcome that you're looking for.[1]

—Dr. Charles Wilhelm, former chief medical officer, Principal Health Care

AMERICAN HEALTHWAYS WAS POISED AT THE TOP OF ITS INDUSTRY. BUOYED BY THE results achieved at Blue Cross Blue Shield of Minnesota, Hawaii Medical Service Association (HMSA), and HealthSpring, demand for the company's programs continued to grow. To service the new business, the company had to grow, too, but that growth needed to be managed in a way that didn't jeopardize American Healthways' hard-earned reputation for excellence in design, implementation, execution— and most importantly—outcomes.

StatusOne was a company that had carved out a niche in the case management business, providing intensive one-on-one interventions to the highest-risk health plan members. Its patient services were much more focused than those offered by American Healthways, they were at the greatest risk for incurring significant medical costs over the coming year, proving to have a major impact on health plan costs.

Above: Matt Kelliher joined the company when American Healthways acquired StatusOne, which he founded.

Right: StatusOne filled in significant gaps, targeting its services to high-risk populations.

Below: HealthSpring patients who participated in Healthways' programs received information and a handy checklist to take to their next physicians appointment.

Proving just how small the world of financial investors is within the realm of health care, in 2002 StatusOne was working on capital-raising strategies with an investment bank that had close contacts with American Healthways.[2] "There was lots of interest in our company because we were actually an Internet [application service provider] as well as a service organization," explained Matt Kelliher, founder of StatusOne. "[But] we were not looking for a strategic investor."[3]

The investment bank had different ideas and asked StatusOne to consider meeting with American Healthways. "For the first round, we didn't [engage with Healthways]. We weren't at all clear that

Innovations Forum
Del Mar, CA - 2003

Healing Words
A Deeper Dialogue in Care Management

L'Auberge Del Mar Resort and Spa
Wednesday, May 28 – Friday, May 30, 2003

there would be a good mix of cultures,"[4] Kelliher said. "After the first round, our investment bankers sort of begged us to at least let them participate. So in deference to our investment bankers, with whom we had a good relationship, we let American Healthways have a copy of our [business] book. Then we wound up letting them in, and American Healthways, to be honest, convinced us that the culture wasn't that different and that there was a lot of benefit to having the two organizations together."[5]

American Healthways later purchased StatusOne for $65 million,[6] and although Kelliher had intended to leave one year after the merger, he eventually decided to stay on to solicit and operate new contracts for the company's new high-risk case management solution.[7] Within a few months of the acquisition, American Healthways sold its first contract for its expanded complement

LIPID PROFILE
A lipid profile is a lab test that measures the amount of certain fats and cholesterol in your blood. High lipid levels can lead to a heart attack or cause your heart disease to worsen. You should have a lipid profile at least once a year. The "bad" cholesterol (LDL) should be less than 100mg/dl, and triglycerides (also bad) should be less than 150 mg/dl. The "good" cholesterol (HDL) should be greater than 40 mg/dl. Talk to your doctor about helping you meet these goals.

BLOOD PRESSURE
High blood pressure (hypertension) can lead to a heart attack, heart failure or kidney failure. Blood pressure lowering medications can help, but your dosage may need to be adjusted and lifestyle changes made to achieve the best results. The American Heart Association recommends blood pressures of less than 130/85 for people who have heart disease and less than 130/80 for people with diabetes. Check your blood pressure regularly and talk to your doctor about how to reach your blood pressure goals.

SMOKING CESSATION
If you smoke, QUIT. Cigarette smoking is a strong risk factor for heart disease. As soon as you quit, your blood vessels begin to return to normal. Talk to your doctor about ways to help you QUIT.

DIABETES SCREENING
Have your blood sugar checked at least once a year. Early detection and treatment of high blood sugars will help prevent complications associated with diabetes.

MEDICATIONS
Several medications can help treat and prevent progression of heart disease in many people, especially those who have already had a heart attack or heart failure. Talk to your doctor about aspirin, beta blockers, ACE inhibitors and statins.

HealthSpring
Cares

of services. The customer, Regence Group, provided health plans to 3 million participants in Washington, Oregon, Idaho, and Utah, and eventually purchased comprehensive care enhancement (disease and impact condition management) and high-risk management services as well.[8]

A Close Call

Expansion, either internally or through acquisitions, continued to be a major thrust of the company as a way to enable it to provide its services to more people. The company would identify a gap it needed to fill, and then identify the optimum target. Most of the time—but not always—the merger or acquisition was a success.

In mid-2005, the company purchased Health

IQ Diagnostics for $3 million.[9] It was later transformed into the proprietary model known as MyHealthIQ℠, which assigned health scores to individual members, using lab results in lieu of self-reported information to help members understand their health risks and motivate them to take action to maintain optimum health.

The company then looked to expand its disease management footprint and began to study as many as 10 potential acquisitions to determine a good fit. It eventually decided upon a $307-million purchase of South San Francisco–based LifeMasters, which had a significant book of business in providing services to both Medicare and Medicaid populations.

However, by October 2006, the deal, which had been agreed to by both parties, came apart when American

Inset: Despite all the hard work, some members of the 2002 executive team found time for a little fun, with Mary Hunter (left), Don Taylor (standing, left), Tom Cigarran, Bob Stone, and Mary Chaput donning disguises.

Left: The more formal photo of the 2002 executive team was in the company's Annual Report and included Ben Leedle (standing, center).

The leading worksite wellness program from Healthways

Healthways purchased Health IQ Diagnostics, which would later become MyHealthIQ℠. The $3 million acquisition added a vital assessment tool as Healthways moved into wellness. The web-based program used lab results and scientific evidence to assess a person's health risks.

Healthways discovered a major error related to LifeMasters' financial projections.[10]

Bruce Crosby, who worked in business development at the time recalled:

We had actually executed the documents and were ready to wire the funds when a material adverse change occurred—a MAC, as it's known in the M&A business. LifeMasters was participating in the [Medicare Health Support] pilots with the government. There were these performance reports … in the government project that came on a quarterly basis, and based on your performance, as determined in these quarterly reports, you were able to recognize revenue or not because your revenue was based on performance. LifeMasters had reported that they were

performing and therefore had recognized the revenue. We believed what they were reporting and had given them credit for the revenue. Then, literally the week before funding the acquisition, the report came in, and they were not performing. It could have been just devastating to the organization had we not caught the error.

New Channel, New Alliance

Notwithstanding the LifeMasters setback, American Healthways continued to lead the market in capturing new customers. In April 2006, the company began offering a complement of services to the 750,000 members of the [Blue Cross Blue Shield] CareFirst health plan, which served Maryland; Virginia; Washington, DC; and Delaware.[11] In addition to disease management services, American Healthways would provide health promotion services to all CareFirst members, using outcome-driven methods.[12] First, members would be evaluated using the MyHealthIQ℠ health risk assessment tool. Those whose scores indicated a high risk would receive Healthways' lifestyle coaching. Members with a lower risk would receive electronic communications through a partnership between Healthways and Pro-Change Behavior Systems.

American Healthways opened a new channel to bring its programs to even more people a few weeks later, signing a 10-year alliance with Medco Health Solutions, the country's largest pharmacy benefit manager (PBM). Through the Optimal Health program, the 55 million individuals who received their prescription medications through Medco would now also have access to American Healthways' services. Equally as important, since members' pharmacy data was available on a near real-time basis, and as much as 6 to 8 weeks before claims data would become available, American Healthways' clinicians could interact with program participants much sooner than usual and at a time when the individual was already thinking about his or her health.

The alliance allowed Medco to sell American Healthways services and offer competitive pricing and value-added benefits to the pharmacy benefit manager's existing clients. Some at American

Healthways were reluctant to go down this road. "We had to convince [some of our stakeholders] that another distribution channel—through a partner other than a health plan—would be beneficial," said Bob Stone. "It was a game-changing deal."[13]

"One of the reasons we did the deal with Medco is that there was very little overlap in our client base," said Janet Calhoun. "So a lot of the clients were new to American Healthways—we didn't have [them] anywhere else in our health plan or employer business."[14] The Medco relationship proved to be successful almost immediately, with American Healthways adding 30 new customers within the first full year following the agreement.

The Medco agreement also reflected American Healthways' growing belief that it could not completely fulfill its purpose by itself. "In today's complex health care world, the key to excellence and continued growth is collaboration," Ben Leedle said at the time. "No single company can have all of the core competencies necessary to make the meaningful changes in our health care system that will further enhance health care delivery and reduce the cost of care."[15]

By 2008, the alliance with Medco was so successful that the two companies built a joint facility—the Medco Center for Health Action—in San Antonio, Texas. The ability for clinicians from both companies to work literally side by side further enhanced the comprehensive support that could be delivered to patients.

THE COMPANY ENTERED FAMILIAR TERRITORY IN 2005 WHEN IT BEGAN A three-year pilot program offering diabetes and cardiac disease management services to Medicare patients. The company would offer its services to the oldest and sickest Medicare beneficiaries, proving that its methods could save the federal government money.

The government's Medicare Health Support (MHS) program launched the pilots to test disease management programs that had proven successful in the commercial market to see if the same benefits could be derived for Medicare beneficiaries, and the government, in its role as payer. American Healthways was tapped to provide services to 20,000 patients in Maryland and the Washington, DC, metropolitan area. Its longtime partner Cigna landed another 20,000 enrollees in Georgia and hired American Healthways as the subcontractor.[1]

"It's a big deal for our company, it's a big deal for the industry, and it's a big deal for the future of health care," CEO Ben Leedle said at the time.

The potential was even greater, as diabetes and heart failure affected 14 million Medicare patients. Leedle added, "Even if we got 10 percent of those 14 million, that would be 1.4 million lives. Trust me, it's a big opportunity."[2]

However, this potential was fraught with challenges. The patients in the pilot represented the most acute end of the health spectrum, not the broader population with which the company usually engaged. On average, they were 78 years old, treated by 8 to 10 different doctors who generally had no interaction with each other, and taking 12 different prescription medications each day. They also tended to have multiple health challenges. The company would need to save 5 percent (a criterion that was later changed to "break even") or return fees on a prorated basis.[3]

The Maryland pilot began August 1, 2005. Early results were promising, but, as the pilot drew to a close in August 2008, the results were unclear. Eight months earlier, in January 2008, the Centers for Medicare and Medicaid Services (CMS) had announced that none of the eight pilots was meeting Phase 1 requirements, including savings goals, and therefore the program would end at the conclusion of the three-year pilot term. American Healthways publicly asserted that CMS' announcement was "premature" and that there was a real possibility that the program would achieve all of the pilot objectives, including those for cost savings. Nevertheless, the impact on the company's reputation and market value was immediate, resulting in the loss of nearly $500 million in market capitalization in a matter of days.

Because of documented issues with the conduct of the pilot, American Healthways, Cigna, and the other program sponsors entered into negotiations with CMS—and, ultimately, the US departments of Health and Human Services and Justice—to negotiate a financial settlement with respect to the fees that had to be repaid to the government.

"The negotiations were about the money," Leedle noted, "and we were delighted that they were satisfactorily concluded. At the end of the day, however, we were much more interested in finding out whether or not the program worked for the Medicare beneficiaries who participated in the pilot. So we began a two-year process with leading scientists from Harvard and Emory to answer that question for us."

When the scientists reported back, their answer was an overwhelming "yes." The program had achieved the pilot objectives,

both clinical and financial, achieving an extremely high participation rate and even higher levels of satisfaction among participants and their physicians. Ultimately, CMS, in final reports prepared by the agency's third-party evaluators, concluded the same thing. Based on the findings of the CMS contractor, American Healthways had achieved improvements in the key clinical metrics and had saved more than it had charged, thereby exceeding the break-even target.

Because of the economic issues associated with health care for seniors, the company published peer-reviewed findings on all of its solutions for that age group, including the results of the Medicare Health Support pilot, in a special supplement to *Population Health Management*, the official peer-reviewed journal of the population health management industry.

"American Healthways participated in the MHS program to demonstrate the effectiveness of our solutions, to gain insight on how to make those solutions even more effective and efficient, and to further establish our unique capability to deliver solutions that improve the health, and reduce the costs, of the nation's rapidly growing, high-cost Medicare population," Leedle said in a company statement. "We accomplished all of those goals."

A vision for the future.
Making disease management
work for you.

significant increase in participant engagement and adherence.

Expanding the Company's Reach

Initially, American Healthways had grown its business by providing a hospital-based program to help people with diabetes better manage their disease. Later, it provided remotely delivered program support to help people with any number of chronic diseases achieve the same end. Throughout this transformation process, the company's customers had changed from hospitals to health plans and employers, and the number of individuals who could be served grew exponentially.

But despite the magnitude of the outcomes achieved for customers of the company's disease management programs, "We weren't making a big enough difference," Leedle recalls. "Saving 3 percent of a health plan's costs was huge on its face but wasn't enough to overcome the overall increases in the cost of care. We needed to bring something more to the market."

In typical fashion, American Healthways' management team initiated what would become the third and perhaps most challenging market creation effort in the company's history. At the strategic level, the objectives were clear: Help more people improve their health, and, in doing so, reduce health care costs to a degree that

American Healthways expanded its business from a hospital-based disease management program for people with diabetes to remotely delivering support to people with a number of chronic diseases, including cardiac and respiratory conditions.

The alliance has continued to be a strong one in terms of additional customer relationships for Healthways and contributing to the success of those who use the combined services of the two companies. In 2011, American Healthways and Medco were finalists for the URAC Awards for Best Practices in Health Care Consumer Empowerment and Protection. The companies submitted results of their integrated solution showing a

mattered to those who paid the bills—health plans, employers, government entities, and individuals.

Recognizing that incremental improvements in the company's existing programs would not be sufficient to overcome the apparently inexorable annual increase in health care costs, the obvious question became, "What would?" The answer, elegant in its simplicity, was to create a solution that would help people from becoming chronically ill in the first place. After all, if, as the company had maintained for years, healthier people cost less, then helping everyone in its customers' populations stay as healthy as possible for as long as possible had to be the right recipe.

The idea wasn't totally new to the American Healthways management team—previous exploration of the concept had led to the acquisitions of CareSteps and MyHealthIQ℠. But the rapid growth and expansion of the company's disease management business and the lack of market readiness at the time had precluded successful adoption of the company's previous programs. Based on its experience in developing the diabetes treatment centers and disease management markets, the company knew that, on average, developing creative solutions for new markets took four to eight years, and significant growth of those markets would follow two to four years later. As Leedle recalled, "It was clear to me that it was time, perhaps past

time, to make the investments necessary to design, develop, test, and implement this new market offering."

Up to this point in American Healthways' history, its growth—from facility ownership to facility-based diabetes programs, to remotely based diabetes programs, to programs for a wide variety of chronic diseases—could be considered evolutionary. Like the rest of the health care industry, the company had grown by focusing on and promoting healthier behavior for people who were already sick and helping their physicians find ways to improve their patients' health and avoid or minimize the impact of complications, co-morbidities, and disease progression. While the new vision would incorporate all that had come before—"We weren't going to throw the baby out with the bathwater," Steve Samples recalled—it was quite literally revolutionary. "Fully 80 percent of the population has either limited or no interaction with the health care delivery system," Samples added. "By definition, our population health management offering had to include services for them as well."

As the management team began the process of determining what it would take to turn the new vision into a viable market offering, three things became clear immediately. "We had no services for people who weren't sick," Calhoun recalled. "We had no way of finding them in traditional health plan claims or administrative data. Our existing data platform and infrastructure, PopWorks 4.0,

Strike Up the Band

AMERICAN HEALTHWAYS COLLEAGUES HAVE TO BE CAREFUL WHEN DISCUSSING HOPES AND dreams in the office hallway. When music lovers were discussing a desire to form a company band, Ben Leedle overheard and signed them up for their first gig—the company's annual meeting, which was to be held in less than a month.

At the time, the band had no name and hadn't even scheduled its first rehearsal, but it was the precursor of the American Healthways group that now performs at company functions such as annual meetings and family days.

"Being in a rock-and-roll band has been a lifelong dream for many of us," said vocalist and cofounding member Robin Davis, director of knowledge management and proposals. "And like a lot of other people here in Nashville with careers outside of the music industry, we're [still] musicians at heart."[1]

The band, first formed in 2005, quickly named itself "Strat 5," a riff on the company's stratification system that classified the health status of its member clients in one of four levels, with "Strat 4" comprising those most in need of intervention. "We thought if Strat 4 is severe, Strat 5 must be extreme," Davis said.[2]

The band, whose other cofounding members include Nadine Conley, Jeff Elkins, and Marty Leinwand, is often tapped to perform at company events. But its music has made it outside of American Healthways' halls as well. It was one of 18 groups that participated in *FORTUNE®* magazine's annual Battle of the Corporate Bands in 2007 and was a contender again in 2009, when it won the 9th annual battle. It also performed prior to the keynote address at the 2008 World Health Care Congress

wasn't designed to address the needs of either a healthy or at-risk-but-not-sick population, and we had no way of assessing their initial health status or of measuring their status and our performance over time."

While there were any number of ways for the company to address these identified gaps—in services, in the data platform and infrastructure, in assessment, and in measurement—Leedle made it clear to his leadership team that any solution had to adhere to the fundamental business concepts that had guided the company from day one. Solutions would have to 1) be science-based and consistent with a value-creation,

and on the floor of its convention hall.

The group has included as many as 15 band members at a time playing every type of guitar plus drums, keyboards, harmonica, mandolin, horns, and banjo. Leedle occasionally sits in on cowbell.

For those who were passionate about both their jobs and their music, the gigs provided an opportunity to live like musicians, traveling as a group, promoting both American Healthways and the music.

"American Healthways has always been passionate about instilling a culture that inspires our colleagues to do their best work," explained Chris Cigarran,

Healthways' band, Strat 5, performs at company and industry events. It had as many as 15 members at one time, including (standing from left to right) Mark Paul, Marty Leinwand, James Davis, Victor Mattingly and (seated) Nadine Conley, Emy Stewart, and David Lakey.

then American Healthways' senior vice president–human resources. "One of the ways we do that is by supporting each other's goals and interests. Supporting Strat 5 also provides the company with its own house band, which brings both rock-and-roll and blues performances to and further invigorates even the liveliest of events."[3]

value-share business model; 2) produce superior outcomes across all dimensions of the value proposition; and 3) position the company to continue its leadership position as the market matured. As long as those criteria were met, everything was on the table.

"As is often the case when starting to design something new, there was a huge

temptation to build it all ourselves," Mary Chaput remembers. "We had done pretty well with that model for a long time, but as our business became more complex, we grew much more intelligent about making the 'make or buy' decision. While we would always own the elements of any solution that constituted the 'secret sauce,' we were no strangers to buying or partnering for capabilities that we didn't have. Given the scope of this effort, that turned out to be a good thing."

Of all the identified gaps, the services area offered the greatest potential for a financially beneficial solution in the short term. For almost two years, Leedle had been meeting regularly with Ben Lytle, chairman of Axia, one of the nation's largest and fastest growing companies in the areas of health promotion, prevention, and wellness. A purchase of Axia by American Healthways would go a long way to addressing the company's need for services for both healthy and at-risk populations while at the same time providing significant new revenues and margins.

American Healthways had tried to acquire Axia previously (when Leedle and Lytle first met) but was politely rebuffed. Leedle recalled the meeting:

Ben [Lytle] and I met for dinner here in Nashville, and at one point I said to him, "Ben, you should be a part of American Healthways. Let us buy out your [venture capitalists]. Even though you haven't done anything yet, you come on board at American Healthways. Build out this thing on behalf of American Healthways, and then we'll have some big upside in it for you."

I actually put a term sheet on the table for Ben to look at, and he politely declined, which was a wonderful move for him since, at that time, I thought we could buy the company for about $100 million."

Best in Class

American Healthways kept a watchful eye on Lytle's company and watched it absorb five major health and wellness companies over a period of 18 months. The first was a merger with HealthCare Dimensions (HCD), a company founded by Mary Swanson in 1992. Swanson was inspired to found the company as a result of her father's heart attack at age 51 and his commitment to maintaining a healthy lifestyle through physical activity. HCD founded the popular SilverSneakers® program, which offered a comprehensive fitness program specifically designed for seniors.[16]

Just as American Healthways had done throughout its history, Axia continued to expand into new product lines, increasing the population to whom it could deliver solutions. It acquired American WholeHealth Networks in mid-2005, which added complementary and alternative medicine (CAM) to Axia's lineup.[17] QuitNet, an Internet-based smoking cessation program, joined the list of acquisitions in late 2005.[18] Harris Health Trends, which offered personalized coaching for lifestyle behavioral changes, was acquired in early 2006.[19] The acquisition of My ePHIT, an online prevention and wellness community, rounded out the buying spree a couple of months later.[20]

Axia had grown quickly, amassing 500 employees and more than $150 million in revenues in less than two years.[21] But "they weren't pulled together," Lytle said of his acquisitions. "[The subsequent acquisition by American Healthways] was an opportunity to aggregate the best in class among these people and to build a much larger platform that could deliver integrated service nationally or even internationally."[22]

Not only were the Axia companies not pulled together, but overall growth had been so rapid that many of the company's operations were not yet merged into one headquarters. Yet Axia's appeal as the base for the complementary services required for American Healthways population health management offering was too much to resist: 3,000 certified health improvement instructors, 10,000 fitness centers, 30,000 health and alternative care providers, and a suite of popular web applications.[23] The SilverSneakers® program alone was being delivered to more than 3 million Medicare members in 42 states, and QuitNet, the nation's most successful smoking cessation program, had more than 300,000 users.[24] Further, there was essentially no overlap between American Healthways and Axia's customer base, providing real cross-selling opportunities for a combined entity. All in all, an American Healthways–Axia merger would cover 120 unique health plan customers serving 165 million members.[25]

The empathetic, sustained personal connection that applies science and experience to improve lives.

HEALTHWAYS SIGNS DEFINITIVE AGREEMENT TO ACQUIRE AXIA HEALTH MANAGEMENT

Combination to Offer Industry's Broadest Spectrum of Coordinated WholeHealth Solutions

NASHVILLE, Tenn. and TEMPE, Ariz. – October 11, 2006 – Ben Leedle, president and CEO of Healthways, Inc. (NASDAQ: HWAY), the nation's leading provider of Health and Care Support[SM] services, and Ben Lytle, CEO of Axia Health Management, LLC (Axia), the leading national provider of preventive health and wellness programs, today jointly announced they have signed a definitive agreement whereby Healthways will purchase Axia. The $450 million acquisition, which is anticipated to be accretive to Healthways' financial results for fiscal 2007, is expected to close before the end of the calendar year, subject to the satisfaction of customary closing conditions, including obtaining Hart-Scott-Rodino (HSR) clearance. The transaction will be financed through a combination of cash on hand and committed bank debt.

Strategic Fit
"Our agreement to purchase Axia represents a major step forward in our continuing strategy to provide, or enable our customers to provide, WholeHealth solutions, a full spectrum of integrated, personalized, proven and evidence-based interventions to maintain or improve health and productivity," Leedle said. "Axia's programs, when combined with our current set of Health and Care Support[SM] services, will transform the market and clearly position us as the industry leader and partner of choice for commercial and Medicare Advantage health plans, employers and government. Further, the addition of Axia's unique national network will enable consumers to obtain everything from in-person health coaching, fitness center access and online communities of interest, to telephonic lifestyle management, condition and disease management, high-risk care management and end-of-life support in the manner that best suits their needs and lifestyles."

Axia President Hugh Lytle said, "Axia brings best-in-class interventions in physical activity, nutrition and weight management, smoking cessation, stress relief and early detection and screening. Axia also brings new, high-touch delivery platforms for those interventions through its network of 10,000 fitness centers, 3,000 Axia-certified health improvement instructors, 30,000 health and alternative care providers and robust web applications. Through this unique nationwide network, Axia creates select venues and providers that are specific to the consumer's needs and motivation for better health.

- MORE -

In December 2006, American Healthways acquired Axia for $467 million, and Lytle joined American Healthways' board. Despite the short-term challenges of purchasing what were virtually five separate companies all at once, American Healthways focused on the long-term benefits. Owning Axia not only gave American Healthways an entry into wellness and prevention but also allowed it to become the leader in that market overnight.

After numerous attempts, American Healthways ultimately acquired Axia in 2006 for $467 million, which opened the door for American Healthways to become the leader in the wellness and prevention market overnight.

W HEN AMERICAN HEALTHWAYS OUTGREW ITS GREEN HILLS OFFICES, IT UNDERTOOK a massive expansion, building a new facility in nearby Franklin, Tennessee. This was not just a building project, however. The design incorporated lush green space, an open architecture plan, and special features that encourage American Healthways employees to get moving and improve their health.

"Ben [Leedle] was very passionate about his vision for this project," said Sue Schmidt, director of facilities, who joined the company mid-expansion in 2006. "It was very important to him that we create an environment that fostered collaboration and communication, created a sense of family, and ensured that each colleague would be comfortable in the environment. [He] just wanted people to be able to do their best work, to be inspired by the space that was around them—to feel the energy."[1]

Designing the corporate headquarters to reflect the company's philosophy

Healthways' corporate headquarters in Franklin, Tennessee, boasts an innovative and efficient design.

required a new way of thinking and drew acclaim throughout the process.

"This building is different in so many ways, particularly with respect to the use of natural light," Schmidt said. "Everybody gets a window seat. The Green Hills office was very traditional 'corporate America' with all of the private offices lining the windows. So for anybody that was in a workstation in an interior space, it was very dark and dreary. In the new building, things are very bright, with natural light."[2]

The new building is filled with nontraditional features, including numerous small meeting rooms. The layout of the workstations is what Schmidt termed "deliberately random." "The desire there was to create 'accidental collaboration,' so to speak. There is no one way through an area."[3]

Private offices were omitted from the design. Even top executives sit in a "bull-pen"–style area with walls no higher than 51 inches. "The only thing that makes the executive floor here different than any other floor is that the executives are on it," Schmidt said.[4]

Matches the Purpose

A centralized "copy hub," in keeping with the company's "move to health" concept, is designed to help colleagues adopt health-promoting, risk-reducing behaviors. "You don't need to be sitting at your workstation all day long. Get up, get the blood flowing, get some oxygen, get the cobwebs out. I personally have found I'm not printing nearly as much as I was [prior to the new building] because I really don't need to. The other thing that we implemented with the copy hub was a technology that allows for secure printing—certainly because of the personal health information that we have, but also [due to the] demonstrated cost savings from the perspective of paper usage. [With the new system] you [send] something to print, and it's held at the central printer/copier area until you go to pick it up and scan your security card. The other thing that's great about [the new system] is that you can send your print job to any machine enabled with the technology and get your document. So if you're on the fifth floor, running to a meeting on the second floor, you can send something to print and breeze by the nearest machine and get your document."[5]

The unique nature of the building has not only worked well for American Healthways but has also garnered attention from outside the company. There are frequent requests for tours from organizations building new facilities and groups such as the International Facilities Managers Association, which conducted a group visit to view the new design. The new building design has proven so successful that many of the same elements were instituted when the Chandler, Arizona, offices moved to a new facility.

"We didn't set out to build a building so that we could win awards or garner attention," Schmidt said. "We built a building that was very personal to American Healthways. It was very important that we get it right and that it be right for what we do—that it speaks to our culture, that it supports our culture."[6]

The new building's interior was designed to include numerous open meeting rooms and access to natural light.

"To those who didn't have a clear idea of where Ben [Leedle] was leading American Healthways, it probably seemed like an odd acquisition. Clearly we were buying a new set of capabilities, but to what end? Looking at the deal from the outside in, it would be hard to understand how those capabilities fit operationally into American Healthways' existing business," said Justin Smith, who joined the company's corporate development team just prior to the acquisition. "I was comfortable with the acquisition, largely because we didn't make the mistake of counting on the benefits of [the merger]. We just basically modeled [both companies'] base business as it was."[26]

A Learning Experience

Acquiring a company as large and diversified as Axia provided American Healthways with a number of new learning opportunities, beginning with the financing of the deal.

Alfred Lumsdaine, American Healthways' chief financial officer, recalled the process:

Our previous acquisitions had been paid for in cash or through the use of our revolving credit line. For the Axia deal, we secured a $600 million credit facility, which required our debt to be rated for the first time. Even the reporting was very unique because of the way the Axia companies had been brought together. The SEC rules [were] less than clear in defining

exactly what statements we had to provide in terms of the predecessor companies, and we sort of had to work with our auditors to infer what we were even required to file.[27]

American Healthways initially intended to leave Axia operations intact, but "that engendered some market confusion. The company began to detect some early but real market interest in an integrated solution. Confusion on one hand and interest on the other made letting Axia operate as an independent entity untenable, so we changed plans," Emily Cook said.[28]

Rick Bailey, American Healthways' senior vice president–finance, recalled:

We changed our minds about how we [were going to bring] them in at least three times— what we were going to do with them, what we were not going to do with them, and what we were really going to do with them. For a while, we also had the challenge of how to integrate the Axia companies with each other, in addition to trying to figure out how to best integrate Axia into American Healthways. So, sometimes, even our colleagues were confused. But the vision became clearer as we better understood what we got with the acquisition, and we now have a lot of clarity around where we want to take it— and lots of excitement.[29]

Axia paid off almost immediately, adding revenues and earnings in addition to a significant expansion of the population to whom American Healthways could deliver services. But American Healthways' management would long remember the challenge of integration. "American Healthways is a learning organization in that people don't forget pain," Cook said. "Now, when we get into circumstances that look similar, people immediately identify the situation with the Axia acquisition: 'This looks familiar to me. We're not going to do that again. We're going to do it differently this time.'"[30]

Despite the challenges of integrating and aligning six organizations around one culture, one business model, and one purpose, "Axia was a great acquisition," said Mary Hunter, then executive vice president. "It provided new services and capabilities—things we didn't have but

were going to need to have if we were truly going to provide a solution for every member of our customers' populations. While we were figuring out what 'version one' of our population health management offering would be, Axia provided us with services that the market wanted in its own right. Other, more forward-looking customers were also beginning to sense the value of integration—[having] one supplier for all their population health management needs—and rapidly recognizing that American Healthways was uniquely capable of helping them move in that direction. The Axia acquisition made the company an exciting place to be. It was a great acquisition—a great match."[31]

Together, we can change
the future of healthcare.

HEALTHWAYS

Above: The company's decision to take its services global was reflected in its international sales brochure from 2006. That same year, the company changed its name to Healthways to give it wider brand appeal.

Opposite: (seated left to right) Mary Chaput, Kathy Kirk, Carol Murdock, and Emily Cook gather at the company's 2006 Spring Town Hall meeting.

I don't think there's a person who works in our company who doesn't desire to bring the magic of what we do to more and more people across the globe. We are interacting with and influencing so few people when you compare it with how much opportunity there is. … One of the most gratifying things about working with Healthways is that—either by intellect or by chance or by the grace of divine intervention—we have, at the right time, determined when we need to reinvent ourselves both to satisfy new market demands and to create new markets. We are a market-driven company, always ready to redirect our energy and capability in directions that align with our purpose.[1]

—Emily Cook, vice president, American Healthways

AMERICAN HEALTHWAYS ENTERED 2007 UNIQUELY POSITIONED TO PROVIDE SERVICES across the spectrum of a population's needs. The Axia acquisition had combined the industry leaders in health and care support, enabling customers and prospects to access all those services from the only entity in the industry capable of supplying and integrating both.

The company had also broadened its customer base from health plans, which had accounted for virtually all of the revenue in 2002,[2] to include employer contracts, which in 2007 contributed about a third of the company's revenue.[3] In 2007, the company would serve 100 domestic and international health plans and 800 major employer customers,[4] generating $615 million in revenues, a nearly 50 percent increase over the previous year's $412 million.[5]

The market for the company's services had expanded dramatically as well. In 1984, the year the company began, the industry for health support services was about $150 million.

It had grown to $1.5 billion by 1996 and to $20 billion by 2005.[6] An illustration in the company's Annual Report for 2007—an image of the Earth—hinted at what was to come.

Going Global

In adopting its Purpose Statement, American Healthways clearly contemplated providing services outside the United States. By the end of 2006, fueled by its understanding that all developed nations share the problem of aging populations with escalating health care costs and knowledge that potential competitors were becoming more active internationally, management and the board concluded that the time was right to pursue opportunities overseas. The first step, however, was the second name change in the company's history, in this case simply dropping "American."

"Changing our name to Healthways removed the domestic-only brand implication and eliminated any potential negative overseas reaction to engaging with an American company," Matt Kelliher recalled.

Expanding internationally took a significant research effort and outlay of capital. "Making the decision to offer our services overseas required significant patience on Healthways' part," said Kelliher, who had been tapped to be president of Healthways International. "International wasn't something you flick a switch on, and all of a sudden you've got successful operations all over the world. It just isn't that simple."[7]

"There were many cultural hurdles to overcome. A lot of American companies think that they're going to get a quick return going into international [markets] much like they do when expanding in the US and that they'll be able to support the same kind of margins," Kelliher said. "So a lot of them will go into a market, find out that's not possible, and pull out, and that's created credibility problems for American companies around the world."

The other critical mistake US companies often make, Kelliher said, is treating the overseas branch like a field office of the American company. "Those who've been successful have actually viewed it differently. In principle, they're visualizing the process as starting companies in new countries, in new markets, where the objective is to transfer intellectual property, technology, and the capital to start a new company, led by and run by people in the markets as opposed to a field office or franchise of a US-based company," Kelliher said. "We learned both from those who did it wrong and those who did it right and came to the conclusions about what seemed to make sense and what didn't make sense and then how we would apply those findings to Healthways."[8]

Healthways International was ultimately created as a wholly owned subsidiary, with each country essentially functioning as an autonomous enterprise with a general manager overseeing both business development and operations.

The company worked with consultants to identify which countries would be the best fit for its services. After assessing 28 developed nations, "we rated them and scored them and classified them into essentially two different markets," Kelliher said. "One was primary markets. These were markets where, given the level of interest and awareness of our products and services, we would expect to be able to see a contract within two years. Based on that assessment, we could focus on them and make investments."

Kelliher's time estimate was accurate. After two years of development activity and $10 million of investment, some of which was for an international-friendly version of the company's software platform, Healthways signed its first international agreement with one of Germany's largest health plans, Deutsche Angestellten-Krankenkasse (DAK). Healthways would provide service in two regions, Bavaria and Baden-Württemberg,[9] and work with about 50,000 health plan members with heart disease and respiratory conditions.[10]

"The new market is the rest of the world," Kelliher said. "Interestingly enough, if you listen to Wall Street and the investors around the world, there is and has been a lot of interest in international [markets]. They view that, of course, as probably one of Healthways' biggest strategic opportunities."

The agreement in Germany benefited from the groundwork that the company had accomplished before the signing of the contract. DAK had 6.2 million members, making it the country's second-largest "sick fund," as health insurance is called there.[11] The Healthways contract was implemented on time and was profitable by the end of the first year.[12]

"It was a big breakthrough," Kelliher said. "We were going to be operating in a foreign country, with a lot of visibility in Europe and a lot of interest from people on the sidelines to see how well it went. We had a great management team. Germany was a very ripe market for us."[13]

Off the Tracks

Healthways had exploded from a small, Tennessee-based, four-facility, 418-bed hospital management firm to an international population health

Employees Sabine Glatz (left) and Martina Hager (right) prove that the Healthways culture, which includes bell ringing to celebrate success, translates to the office in Germany.

management company with 27.4 million lives in its care.[14] By the end of 2007, about one out of every 11 Americans was using, or eligible for, some form of Healthways' services. The growth opportunity seemed unlimited and that fact was reflected in the company's $68 stock price at the end of the first week of 2008.

At the end of January 2008, the Centers for Medicare and Medicaid Services (CMS) would announce that all of the Medicare Health Support pilots were failing to achieve the targeted outcomes, and were unlikely to do so in the future. In February, long-term customer Blue Cross Blue Shield of Minnesota advised the company it would be terminating its agreement at the end of the calendar year.

The effect of this one-two punch shocked the industry as well as Wall Street. Shares of Healthways stock tumbled to $34 in the first week of March and would ultimately reach a low of $6 by Thanksgiving. Potential customers were no longer sure that Healthways represented a "sure thing," and even existing customers began to actively evaluate whether or not they would be better off with another supplier or providing disease management services in-house. At the end of the year, the company would respond to the actual and projected revenue decline with its first-ever layoffs.

The uncertainty about Healthways' future was to be further compounded at the end of 2008 by the general collapse of the country's economy, the election of a new president, and the commitment of the new administration to a fundamental reform of the nation's entire health care system.

Bob Stone recalled:

It was a grim time. A few of us—those who had been around in 1993 and lived through the transition from the diabetes hospital center business to disease management—had seen it before and were confident that over time, the company would right itself. But a significant number of colleagues began to doubt that Healthways had the magic touch, and doubt can be insidious.

The challenges facing health care systems, both domestically and internationally, hadn't changed; they had just become larger and more acute. Our management team knew we had the "right" answer and that the company was on the right path to bring that answer to the market. Our real challenge was to simultaneously keep the core business as solid as possible while accelerating the development, testing, and deployment of the new market solution. Put another way, we had to keep everyone on "purpose."

Purpose-driven focus on execution, outcomes, and innovation was the hallmark of Healthways' repeated market successes. At the beginning of 2009, the management team was convinced that that formula would prove successful again. "It's all about commitment to purpose and belief in the model," Ben Leedle said to colleagues at the time. "If you don't believe that we are headed in the right direction and aren't 'all-in' in making sure that we both deliver on our promises to our existing customers and advance along that path toward creating our new well-being improvement solution, this is going to be a very uncomfortable place for you to work."

Shoring up Healthways revenues and earnings would be hindered for the next two years by a confluence of factors over which the company had little or no control. The global recession had hit with full force resulting in massive increases in unemployment. That, in turn, meant a significant reduction in the number of people receiving health insurance—and thus access to Healthways programs—through their employers. Health plan decisions about new initiatives were significantly slowed, compounding the effect of unemployment, as plan leaders waited to see how health care reform would ultimately pan out.

As it turned out, a significant contribution to company operations would come from two sources: rapid growth in its health and wellness programs—particularly SilverSneakers®—and new contracts overseas.

Saving Grace

The growth in SilverSneakers®, the company's award-winning fitness program

for seniors, resulted from three identifiable factors: proven outcomes, participant satisfaction, and expanded access. The SilverSneakers® program, which blends activity, lifestyle, and social considerations into a fitness program for older adults, showed nearly immediate and dramatic changes in patients with diabetes. According to a study published in *Diabetes Care*, the official journal of the American Diabetes Association, participants saw a $1,633 reduction in health care costs in their first year of participation in the program. For those who attended a SilverSneakers® program at least twice a week, the reduction was more than $1,200 for the second year of participation.[15]

A second study showed that those who participated in SilverSneakers® at least twice a week for a year saw a reduction in risk of depression, an issue that affects between 5 and 10 percent of all seniors.[16]

"These studies are proof, once again, of the dramatic positive impact physical activity and disease prevention can have on the economic burden that chronic conditions place on older adults, on the health care system, and on our society," Leedle said in announcing these results.

The SilverSneakers® fitness program, which encourages older adults to exercise, was named Best All-Around Fitness Initiative in 2006 at the Consumer Directed Health Care and National Health, Wellness, and Prevention Awards.

"You have the obvious cost savings, which are outlined in these two important reports, but SilverSneakers® also enables older Americans to get more out of life, to interact socially, and to reclaim an element of freedom that may have been fading for them."[17]

The two studies combined to show what Healthways had asserted for years: better lives and lower costs create a win for all. Not long after the studies were released, SilverSneakers® partnered with Curves International, the world's largest fitness club franchiser. The move tripled the number of health clubs that offered the program to nearly 10,000.[18] In late 2010, the Snap Fitness franchise joined SilverSneakers®,

bringing the total number of participating health clubs available to more than 11,000.

Continental Shift

The nearly two-year dry spell following Healthways' first international contract with German sick fund DAK in 2007 ended in late 2008 with the announcement of a new agreement with Fleury, Brazil's premier medicine and health company. Because the agreement would go operational late in the year, the full financial benefit would not begin to be realized until the second half of 2009.

The agreement with Fleury was followed in December 2008 by an

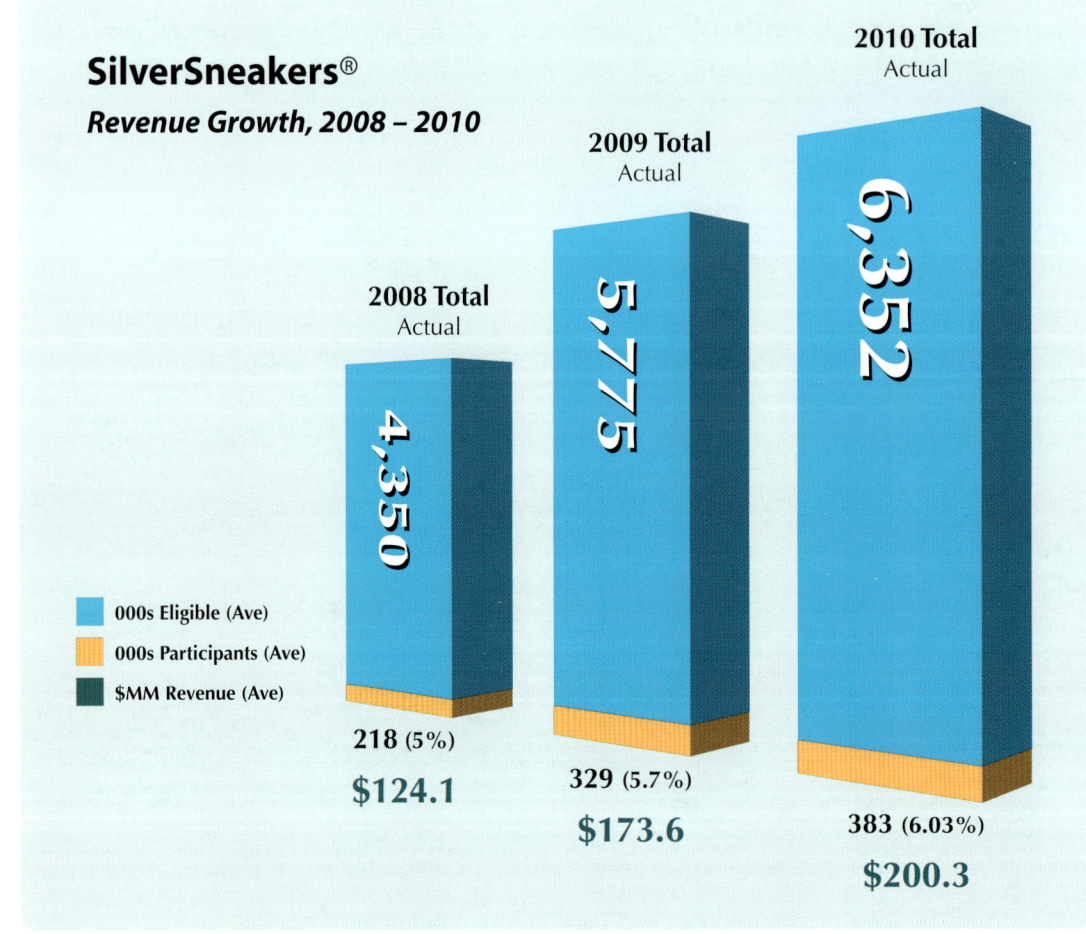

SilverSneakers®
Revenue Growth, 2008 – 2010

Revenue from the company's SilverSneakers® program grew from $124 million in 2008 to more than $200 million in 2010.

2008 Total Actual
4,350
■ 000s Eligible (Ave)
■ 000s Participants (Ave)
■ $MM Revenue (Ave)
218 (5%)
$124.1

2009 Total Actual
5,775
329 (5.7%)
$173.6

2010 Total Actual
6,352
383 (6.03%)
$200.3

When Healthways partnered with Fleury S.A. in Brazil it moved into Latin America with a mixture of local employees and Healthways veterans, a key element of the company's strategy for international success.

agreement with the Hospital Contribution Fund of Australia (HCF), one of the largest health insurers on the continent with over 1 million members. As was the case with Fleury, the late signing meant that the full financial benefit of the agreement would not be realized until late in 2009, and the full value of both agreements would not be felt until 2010.

International growth continued into 2010, despite the expiration of the DAK contract, with an expansion of the HCF agreement and a new agreement with Teachers Health Fund, Australia's seventh-largest health insurer.

Broadening its reach across the globe was part of fulfilling the company's strategy to institute a presence overseas and "to expand its footprint on each continent, because once you have operations, you

have easier scalability, and you have the ability to have market awareness," Kelliher said. "So now we're in Europe, Latin America, and Australia."[19]

Experiencing a surge in morbidity rates, countries throughout the world were struggling against a growing epidemic, with the World Health Organization attributing 35 million deaths worldwide to chronic diseases and predicting a 17 percent increase by 2018.[20]

"Without a doubt, the main interest in the international arena, including international/multinational corporations, is still for disease management solutions," Kelliher said. "Most of these developed countries have the same problems we have in the [United States]: an aging population, an explosion in chronic disease, and a health care system that's not responding to the challenge very well. So, there's a niche

Setback Leads to New Strategy

HEALTHWAYS DID NOT TAKE THE BLUE CROSS BLUE SHIELD (BCBS) OF Minnesota termination lying down. In 2008, the insurer opted to bring the services that Healthways had provided in-house.

A significant portion of the population BCBS served in Minnesota were employees of large Administrative Services Only (ASO) employers serviced by the plan. ASO customers are self-insured companies whose health insurance provides only enrollment, network administration, claims processing, and payment.

Based on the success that Healthways' programs had achieved for these companies as evidenced by improved health and reduced health care costs, Healthways approached the companies directly. They were reminded who provided the services to the employees, and the results that had been achieved on their behalf.

In the end, five of the six largest employers purchased Healthways services directly when the company's contract with BCBS ended.

there that people are looking to us to be able to fill, and one in which we've demonstrated that we can scale up and be effective–that's key."[21]

New Science Emerges

While there were elements of behavior change in Healthways' clinical models for both its diabetes treatment centers and disease management programs, both models were developed primarily based on the results of rigorous medical research, the best medical science, and evidence-based standards of care. To ensure that those models were consistent with the science, Johns Hopkins verified and validated that nothing had been lost in the translation of science to practice. "We had that process down cold," noted Dr. James Pope, vice president and chief science officer of Healthways.

As the design work on the company's population health management solution progressed, it became clear that traditional medical research was not going to provide the scientific basis for new models, particularly for those who were healthy or at risk. Helping people who were healthy stay healthy and helping people who were at risk reduce or eliminate that risk required a deep understanding of human behavior, and proven techniques to help people change poor behaviors to good ones.

As Leedle explained:

If changing people's habits were as simple as providing them with the right information, doctors all over the country would be as busy writing prescriptions for periodicals as they are for pills. But research—and the alarming rates of obesity and chronic disease worldwide— prove that it takes more than just information to motivate people to take better care of themselves. We have 2,000 nurses on the front lines of our daily work here at Healthways who are specially trained to recognize a person's readiness to change and then provide them with the right tools at the right time and in the right way to get results. We have driven extremely good outcomes based on our current model, but we can do better by combining our practical experience and our "living laboratory" with cutting-edge science and content in the field of behavior change.

In the field of behavior change science, no one was more renowned than Drs. Jim and Janice Prochaska at the University of Rhode Island. Creators of the Transtheoretical Model of Behavior Change, the Prochaskas had authored more than 250 papers on behavior change for health promotion and disease prevention. Programs developed by Pro-Change drew on more than 25 years of effort, millions in funded grants, and information generated by 120,000 research participants. Dr. James Prochaska's research had been instrumental in changing how health professionals understood and implemented programs to modify high-risk behaviors.

Back in 2005, American Healthways signed an agreement that would provide it with access to Pro-Change's lifestyle management programs, which address topics such as smoking cessation, weight management, and medication adherence, while integrating those programs with the company's own MyHealthIQ℠.

The relationship with Pro-Change provided American Healthways with access to the leading research on behavior change in entire populations. It also provided the company with access

Above left: As Healthways moved into Brazil, some of its key staff became world travelers, such as Deb Hagemann, senior director of international clinical solutions.

Above right: Hagemann took time out from setting up the Australia office to view local wildlife attractions such as the koalas and kangaroos.

Left: In the ongoing effort to keep its beneficiaries fit, the company entered into an agreement with Pro-Change to gain access to its lifestyle management programs.

BRINGING LARGE NUMBERS OF NEW EMPLOYEES INTO AN ORGANIZATION, WHETHER through acquisitions or through organic growth to meet increased service demands can create significant stress for both new and existing employees, and perhaps more importantly for the fundamental culture of the organization. As a purpose-driven and culture-anchored company, Healthways makes every effort to keep every colleague aligned with the culture and the underlying values it has adopted.

"We're very protective of the culture," said Healthways' former chief financial officer Mary Chaput. "It's the glue that holds us all together despite the fact that we have colleagues scattered across the globe. One example is the annual all-colleague winter holiday shopping event. Every company facility around the world shuts down for part of a day so the colleagues can shop for at-risk children. Each location identifies a local charity or two focused on the needs of these kids and each colleague is given $150 to spend, with half dedicated to clothing and half to toys. We also do some shopping at a facility level for their moms."[1]

"You see the best of people and it's a wonderful community-building thing that we do," said Chris Cigarran, senior vice president–human resources. "There have been wonderful stories of nurses getting back to their desks in the call center after doing this the first time and picking up the phone and calling their friends, saying, 'You're not going to believe what this crazy company that I

to two prestigious researchers. Dr. James Prochaska joined the company's Strategic Advisory Board and Dr. Janice Prochaska joined the company's Scientific Advisory Committee.

Just as the acquisition of Axia helped to close the services gap that management had identified as a critical element of the population health management solution, the relationship with the Prochaskas and Pro-Change assured the company and its

customers that the service delivery model was based on years of research and validation by the leading scientific minds in the field.

The company's relationship with MIT AgeLab also brought significant credibility and resources. Joseph F. Coughlin, PhD, AgeLab's founder and director, is a worldwide leader in aging and technology. He published significant research in aging, business, and policy

work for now just paid me to do. I just got paid to shop for needy kids.' It's things like that that make this place special."[2]

The holiday shopping tradition began when a group of administrative assistants who had traditionally picked company holiday gifts for all colleagues and organized the company's holiday lunch asked Tom (Cigarran) if the company would be willing to take the same amount of money and spend it on something for a local charity instead. "I loved the idea," Cigarran recalled, "so much, in fact, I told them we'd spend twice as much on shopping as we did on the party." Today, that thoughtful gesture has spread throughout the company. "It's part of the lure of the organization. [Giving back] is an important part of who we are."

To make the holidays special for at-risk kids, Healthways employees take part in a yearly shopping tradition that began when a group of administrative assistants grew tired of the usual turkey and ham holiday function.

journals and consulted with organizations as diverse as the American Association of Retired Persons (AARP), the American Business Collaboration for Quality Dependent Care, Johnson & Johnson, and the White House Office of Science and Technology Policy.

The MIT AgeLab is a partnership between the Massachusetts Institute of Technology, industry, and the aging communities to improve quality of life for older adults and their caregivers, focusing on housing, transportation, health, communications, leisure, and workplace issues.

The pairing of Healthways and AgeLab came at a time when the population of those over 60 was predicted to quadruple to 2 billion by 2050, causing a significant burden on the health care system. In the US, at least 80 percent of seniors had at least one chronic condition and half had two.[22] Chronic conditions accounted for about 75 percent of health care costs.

Since the partnership began, AgeLab and Healthways collaborated on a number of joint research projects, intending to improve the overall well-being of a significant—and often health-challenged—segment of the population.

Relationships with some of the country's leading researchers into health issues provided Healthways with valuable insight and credibility as it created ground-breaking solutions in all areas of well-being.

A Partnered Solution

Unbeknownst to the company, a solution for closing the critical gaps related to identification, assessment, and evaluation for its new market solution would shortly present itself. For some time, Healthways had been a member of the Center for Health Transformation, an organization founded by former House Speaker Newt Gingrich and dedicated to improving the delivery of health care services and reducing the cost of care. After gaining a better understanding of what Healthways did and what its purpose was, Gingrich told Leedle, "You need to get together with Jim Clifton," CEO of the Gallup Organization, which was also a Center member.[23]

"Newt told me that he had told Jim the same thing," Leedle recalled. "Our first meeting was in Washington and during that meeting Jim showed me the Gallup World Poll and introduced me to the

Newt Gingrich, former Speaker of the US House of Representatives, founder of the Center for Health Transformation, and speaker at Healthways' 2008 kickoff.

science of behavioral economics on which the analyses of poll results were based. While not exactly what we were looking for, there was enough there to get me thinking about how the two organizations could come together, create something truly unique, and meet our needs for a scientifically valid instrument that would enable us to find, assess, and measure progress against some uniform scale for every person in a customer's population, irrespective of their health status."

Apparently Clifton was intrigued, but wanted to make sure that he had a committed partner in Healthways before he undertook to commit Gallup to the formidable task of completing 1,000 surveys every day for the next five years. At the next meeting, held at Gallup University in Omaha, "Clifton tested our commitment," Stone remembered, "telling us that our share of the cost for the project would be $5 million a year for five years. Without batting an eye, Ben said, 'Done. But we want a 25-year term for the agreement. We'll figure out the financing arrangements for years 6 to 25 later.'"

Surveying for the Gallup-Healthways Well-Being Index® began in January 2008

and the two organizations shared the results from the first 100,000 surveys of the new Gallup-Healthways Well-Being Index® in April of that year.

The partnership between Healthways and Gallup in the creation of the Well-Being Index® (WBI) was a natural alliance, designed to explore the correlation between where people work and live and how those factors influence their health and well-being. While the index offered a monthly report of the nation's well-being, its results could also be tailored to assess the health and well-being of individuals. That information could then be used to design individual well-being plans and improvement plans as well as to identify community and work site issues that needed to be addressed to meet the broad needs of that specific population.[24]

Gallup-Healthways Well-Being Index® respondents are asked questions about their current and future life perspective, physical health, healthy behaviors, emotional health, access to health care and health-related goods and services, and work environment. All have proven to relate to overall costs of health care. Ongoing research showed that those who are considered to be thriving (based on their life evaluation score) have health care costs 20 percent lower than average, while those who are struggling have costs that are 50 percent higher.[25]

"Nobel Prize winner Joseph Stiglitz said, 'If you don't measure the right thing, you don't do the right thing,'" said Leedle.

"Gallup and Healthways created [the WBI] because we both care deeply about the health and well-being of this country, and without this knowledge we don't know where to go first and communities don't know where to look first to make real, sustainable changes and improve life for their constituents. Now each community, big or small, can take notice of what's driving the well-being of people in their area and respond thoughtfully to those needs."[26]

Together, Gallup and Healthways use the Well-Being Index® responses to determine the overall well-being index score and the scores for each of the six subdomains that are evaluated.

"The power of the approach used in the Gallup-Healthways Well-Being Index® is in its size and scope," said Dr. Julie Gerberding, then director of the Centers for Disease Control and Prevention (CDC). "Surveys and studies that get information from large numbers of people have the potential to provide a lot of information that can be used to shape and deliver programs that improve health. Having a daily snapshot of how Americans view their own health and well-being can also provide insights that can help guide public health

The Gallup-Healthways Well-Being Index® was billed as the "Dow Jones of Health."

A joint Gallup - Healthways press release announced the deal with Wellmark Blue Cross and Blue Shield, making it the first Healthways customer in the nation to measure the well-being of its health plan members and employees.

policies."[27] To stay abreast of daily polls, Healthways' headquarters is one of seven locations in the world to house a Gallup World Poll monitor.[28]

Wellmark Blue Cross and Blue Shield in Iowa and South Dakota was the first Healthways customer to sign on for the WBI, commissioning surveys for both its members and its employees.[29]

"Wellmark took an important first step in conducting this survey to set internal benchmarks for its members and its employees. It has seen the value of adding the new data provided by the WBI to create a full picture of the needs of its customers and employees," Leedle said at the time. "The ongoing evaluative nature of the WBI will provide continuing insights and data to health plans, governments, communities, and employers to continuously measure the effects of their efforts to improve the health and well-being of their populations."[30]

Prior to the creation of the Gallup-Healthways Well-Being Index® and the collection of what is already the world's largest empirical behavioral economics database, how well-being was intertwined with daily life was unknown. "We didn't know the impact that elements such as happiness, anger, stress, health status, employment status, and neighborhood safety had on the whole," said Nikki Duggan, a Healthways' WBI analyst. "Through these million people sharing their lives, we have uncovered incredibly valuable insight for our country and its people. We have heard both concern and hope over the past three years of our surveying."[31]

New Platform and Infrastructure

The remaining originally identified gap that had to be closed related to technology platform and infrastructure. Healthways was already seeing the strain imposed on PopWorks associated with the increased population it was serving as a result of the Axia acquisition. Unlike the solutions that had been identified for closing the other gaps, however, the company was unwilling to outsource the development of the new platform. "The science, logic, and intervention algorithms built into our platform and the platform's integration into the Care Enhancement Center (CEC) systems, the web, and social media, are key contributors to our success," noted then-Chief Information Officer Scott Blanchette.

Fortunately, the design of the new platform did not have to start from scratch. Because of the unique nature of the company's international contracts, the international division had been given the license to develop a platform that would address the program designs those contracts reflected. Closer in concept to the company's envisioned population management solution, the international platform would provide a valuable starting point for the designers and engineers who would be responsible for creating an even more robust and fully integrated platform known as Embrace.

In the first year of operating Embrace, however, it became clear that the complexity of both operating and building out functionality to realize the full vision of a next generation, fully integrated platform was beyond the internal capacities of the Healthways team and its existing contract-for-hire technology partners.

After an exhaustive search process for external partners, Healthways concluded that Hewlett-Packard, with its deep health care expertise, offered the best capability to enhance an already powerful platform with greater scalability and sustainable, timely innovation at a lower cost.

At the same time, the company also realized that Embrace's first version web portal, while clinically sound, did not deliver on the full engagement promise required for a prescriptive behavior-change application. Recognizing that the web portal needed to be more than what could be found in traditional static medical information websites, the company engaged Roundarch, a leader in digital technologies, to develop its next generation online and mobile offerings, wellbeingGo™ and Well-Being Connect™.

With over half a billion dollars invested in integrated platforms, applications, and capabilities, these new partnerships relieved the company of its historical need to be an expert in emerging technology and positioned it for singular focus on the design, implementation, scalability, and delivery of its proactive Well-Being Improvement Solution.

HEALTHWAYS
The Health/Care Trust Channel

for health plans

Above: As Healthways has expanded its services, it has continued to be a vital component in reducing health plans' costs while increasing the services offered to its customers.

Opposite: A commitment to training, both initial and ongoing, is a regular part of Healthways' care enhancement centers.

Every time it seemed like people were able to get a sense of where growth might be, we innovated and took another step. Analysts love to take great joy in identifying where the edge of your growth is; we take great satisfaction in being able to extend that limit every time they think they've found it.[1]

—Ben Leedle, president and CEO, Healthways

H EALTHWAYS LEADERSHIP WAS MORE CONVINCED THAN EVER THAT THE ultimate solution to the challenges facing health care systems around the globe could only be met with an increased focus on the entire population: the healthy, the at-risk, and those already chronically ill. "Our historic solutions have been effective in bending the health care cost trend for our employer and health plan customers," the company told shareholders. "However, annual inflation of those medical costs at a rate that is two or three times greater than general inflation led us to conclude that our historic solutions, while critical, were simply not enough. We recognized that an effective solution had to not only address the needs of the sick but also be effective in helping people avoid becoming sick in the first place."[2]

An approach that helped people avoid becoming sick had the potential to bring improved health and well-being to all, offering a measurable impact on individuals, their families, employers, communities, and nations. It was a tall order, but as it had done many times in the

POTENTIAL MEDICARE SAVINGS THROUGH PREVENTION & HEALTH RISK REDUCTION

A Report from The Center for Health Research
July 2009

past, Healthways looked to the future. "The market is nearing an inflection point. The demand for WholeHealth [the first name for the company's total population management approach] will, over the next few years, surpass demand for less comprehensive solutions that address only components of the value proposition,"[3] according to the 2008 Annual Report.

In 2009, Healthways began to coalesce these concepts around the principles of well-being. Relying on the definition of health adopted by the World Health Organization (WHO) in its 1946 charter— *Health is a state of complete physical, mental, and social well-being and not merely the*

absence of disease or infirmity[4]—the company began the process of communicating its broader value proposition, including for the first time, the value of improved individual and organizational performance to customers, employers, and governments.

The logic behind the slogan "Healthier People Cost Less" was inescapable; once again, however, Healthways faced the challenge of quantifying a value proposition that had never been delivered, let alone proven. "We knew that we had to move the discussion from the theoretical to at least the plausible," Bob Stone noted. "We had to answer the question 'what's possible?' and we didn't have the all-encompassing science of a multiyear research trial to point to as we did 15 years ago with the DCCT."

Returning to the strategy that had proven successful in the transition from the DTCA to disease management business, the company engaged Ingenix, a highly regarded health actuarial firm, to quantify the savings that would be realized for each percent reduction in risk for the Medicare population. The answer, based on a relatively modest reduction in risk, approached $700 billion over a 10-year period. Equally as important, the

potential for another $700 million in savings over a 10-year period. "Taken together, these two studies enabled us to state the case for a comprehensive, integrated, total-population Well-Being Improvement Solution in a way it had never been able to be made before," Stone said, "and stakeholders began to listen."

Armed with an actuarial model of potential savings, the company nevertheless wanted a way to make valid estimates as to what would happen if its existing programs were applied to a general population. Turning to the internal predictive modeling experts at the Center for Health Research, with assistance from the Boston Consulting Group, a new, proprietary simulation model was developed that used both traditional claims and administrative data along with data from the Gallup-Healthways Well-Being Index® to make forward projections based on proven levels of health improvement and savings from Healthways' existing and planned suite of programs. The validated simulation model also enabled the company to show each customer and prospect what costs would look like for their populations without intervention and how those costs,

model demonstrated that a similar risk reduction in the 55 to 64 (pre-Medicare) population would push the cost savings to more than $1.4 trillion.

"The congressional debate on health care reform actually helped us in our initial efforts to change the conversation from 'sick care' to 'health and well-being,'" recalled Vicki Shepard, director of government relations. "The publication of the Healthways/Ingenix white paper gave us a strong argument to use on the Hill for expanding the health, wellness, and prevention services provisions of the bill." Healthways and Ingenix subsequently produced a similar study and white paper showing the effect of risk reduction in the population aged 18 to 64, which indicated

Left: WholeHealth was the first name for the company's total population approach.

Below: Vicki Shepard, Healthways' director of government relations extolled the virtues of the Healthways/Ingenix white paper as an argument for expanding service provisions during the congressional debate on health care reform.

both direct and indirect, would change as a result of the Healthways solution.

Healthways took other steps in 2009 to support its emerging new market well-being improvement strategy. "We've always played a long game," Ben Leedle said. "While we obviously keep an eye on how Wall Street evaluates us, our objectives are not governed by quarterly earnings reports. Ultimately, it is more important for us to do the things that expand our ability to effectively pursue our purpose, even if some of those things take years to put in place."

Again taking a chapter from its historical playbook, Healthways committed resources to pursue the kind of third-party validation activities that effectively raised the performance bar for the entire industry. As a result, the company was one of the first to receive accreditation from the National Committee for Quality Assurance (NCQA)

Healthways was one of the first companies to receive accreditation from the NCQA for its wellness and health promotion programs.

for its wellness and health promotion programs. The company's performance reporting was also designated as "Accredited," a level beyond standard accreditation, for submitting a specific number of results for NCQA's Wellness and Health Promotion Performance Measures. In addition, Healthways was among the first organizations to receive accreditation from the Utilization Review Accreditation Commission (URAC) for its comprehensive wellness plans, which included both program evaluation and performance measurements.[5]

The Official Statistic

Throughout 2009 and 2010, Healthways and Gallup continued the daily polling of 1,000 Americans and monthly reporting on overall changes in the Gallup-Healthways Well-Being Index® and its six major domains. As the size of the database grew, the joint effort enabled the release of increasingly discrete findings. The first annual assessment of well-being by state and congressional districts was published in 2009. The first report on the well-being of the nation's 188 largest Metropolitan Statistical Areas (MSAs) accompanied the second state and congressional district report published in early 2010. Later that year, the Gallup-Healthways Well-Being Index® would record its 1 millionth survey.

"Originally designed to provide actionable information for the large percentage of the population that does not actively use the health care system, the Gallup-Healthways Well-Being Index® has proven to be an effective and comprehensive resource for determining a population's baseline well-being, identifying specific opportunities for improvement at both the individual and population levels, and measuring progress over time," Leedle said. "As such, it provides clear insights for government, related agencies, and business leaders charged with shaping the policy responses necessary to improve health, increase individual and organizational performance, lower health care costs, and achieve sustained economic growth. The WBI is rapidly becoming the 'official statistic' of well-being in the [United States], and we anticipate it achieving similar status in the UK and in other nations around the world."[6]

As the longitudinal view of well-being began to develop, it became increasingly clear that annual variation was real. Even in the depths of the continuing US recession, some states got better while others got worse. Perhaps more significantly, change also occurred closer to home at both the congressional district and MSA level. The finding that well-being was clearly not static also provided important support to the company's conviction that carefully designed interventions could change it for the better. Most importantly, the rapidly increasing database allowed Healthways researchers to undertake a variety of studies that repeatedly demonstrated that well-being scores were highly correlated

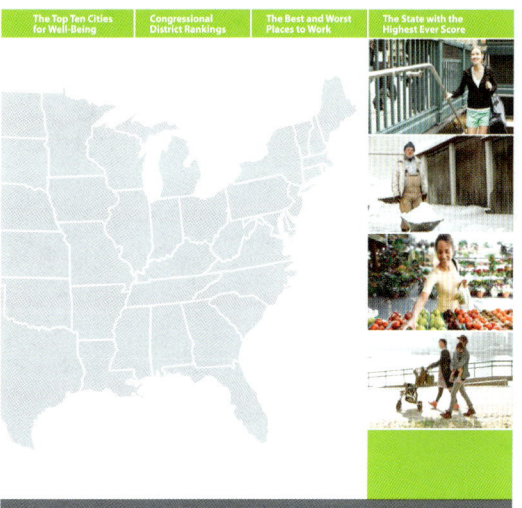

The *State of Well-Being 2010* report was based on data collected from the Gallup-Healthways Well-Being Index® (WBI). Later that year, the WBI would record its 1 millionth survey.

with more traditional measures of health care utilization, quality, and cost.

While the results from the daily surveys created an ever-clearer picture of well-being in America and the impact of the six domains that yielded the overall score, Healthways understood that the scores were generated by random survey. The data was extraordinarily important as a guide to the development of the company's Well-Being Improvement Solution, but the company needed a method for measuring individual well-being that was less costly, more scalable, and more personalized to convince individuals with poor survey scores to adopt healthier behaviors and its customers to accept changes in their population's well-being score as proof of program effectiveness.

As a result, Healthways used the insights from the Well-Being Index® to create the Well-Being Assessment (WBA), a web-based questionnaire that combined elements of the daily survey with high-value questions from traditional health risk assessments (HRAs). As most employers were already conducting HRAs for their employees, the company felt that the additional value of collecting both HRA and Well-Being Index® data with one instrument would appeal to employers who might prove reluctant to add another questionnaire to their annual workload and budget. The WBA met that need, often at a cost lower than employers were paying for the HRA alone. By the end of 2010, several organizations representing a total of 4 million individuals had signed up to use the WBA.

"The database compiled by the Gallup-Healthways Well-Being Index® is a researcher's dream," said Carter Coberley, director of Healthways' Center for Health Research. "Our biggest challenge is to make sure that we are using it to answer the most important questions first!"

Advancing the Well-Being Improvement Solution

Carter Coberley, PhD, director of Healthways' Center for Health Research.

While the company made meaningful strides in changing the conversation from "health care" to "health" to "well-being," and in continuing to produce world-class-level research about the outcomes of its various programs, management knew that it didn't have unlimited time before the market would want to see the solution. Accordingly, significant investments continued to be made, particularly around the Embrace platform and infrastructure.

"We had to have a functional model, at least a version 1.0, before we could start to pilot the solution," Leedle said. "Embrace was the critical element of that model because that's where all the elements— data, identification algorithms, intervention protocols, communications, and reporting—come together."

But Embrace was much more than a software program designed to house and use data. It promised a customized view for individuals, customers, health professionals, and Healthways colleagues. Using real-time information, it could prompt action by a Healthways team member or generate a personalized message to an individual (e.g., if an insurance claim or contact indicated a change in the individual's health status). It also allowed for interactions using the modalities the participant favored most, including chat, text, phone, e-mail, or interactive voice response.

Embrace was also designed to serve as a clearinghouse for all of the employer's health plans and health-related data, including data drawn from the Healthways Well-Being Assessment, which would provide a baseline for each individual's well-being, generate individualized health improvement plans, and measure progress in improving well-being over time.[7]

The software also supported Healthways' traditional disease management, wellness, and prevention programs, since it was unlikely, at least in the near term, that every customer would step up and buy the Well-Being

Improvement Solution right out of the box.

In late 2008, Healthways secured a relationship with a *FORTUNE*® 50 company that would enable the company to test an early version of the new platform, specifically its ability to collect and integrate data from multiple sources. After working through the kinds of issues that emerge with new, complex applications, Embrace performed well. Encouraged by this preliminary result, the company continued to release various components of the platform throughout 2009. Later that year, it was also decided that implementation for all new customers would be done on the Embrace platform. Existing customers would be migrated to Embrace from the legacy PopWorks system according to a mutually agreed upon schedule.

Healthways also took advantage of its strong cash flow and the lowered market expectations with respect to financial performance to add to its capabilities and effect positive behavior change in the populations it was, and anticipated, serving.

In late 2009, Healthways purchased HealthHonors, a company created by two Harvard-trained physicists that specialized in behavior change through the use of incentives. HealthHonors' scientifically

Contact:
Mary Chaput
Chief Financial Officer
(615) 614-4486
mary.chaput@healthways.com

HEALTHWAYS ACQUIRES HEALTHHONORS TO ADVANCE SUSTAINED ENGAGEMENT IN HEALTHY BEHAVIORS

NASHVILLE, Tenn. – October 14, 2009 – Healthways, Inc. (NASDAQ: HWAY) today announced the acquisition of HealthHonors, a market-leading behavioral economics company that specializes in behavior change science and optimized use of incentives, in a cash for stock transaction. Healthways will integrate the HealthHonors science and technology into Embrace™, Healthways' comprehensive information system, to enhance sustained engagement in healthy behaviors.

"Just as Healthways has led the industry in applying behavior change science, now we will lead the market in offering scientifically based incentive programs," said Ben R. Leedle, Jr., Healthways chief executive officer. "Integration of HealthHonors' innovative incentive strategy will boost our overall engagement and adherence to clinical and behavioral regimens."

The purchase price includes an upfront cash payment of $14.7 million and a multi-year earn-out arrangement. Although the financial impact of the acquisition is expected to be a net cost of $0.02 per diluted share in Healthways' fourth quarter of 2009, the Company's previously provided full-year earnings guidance remains unchanged.

One key differentiator offered by HealthHonors is their Dynamic Intermittent Reinforcement™ proprietary software that determines the lowest economic reinforcement necessary for an individual, based on behavioral patterns, to maintain his or her healthy behavior. HealthHonors has been able to show, in trial and commercial environments, a range of 33 to 56 percent increase in sustained adherence to targeted behaviors, while decreasing incentive budgets.

"HealthHonors' technology was developed by physician-scientists to help people achieve their best health," said John Sheehan, president and chief executive officer of HealthHonors. "By integrating our strong science, knowledge and technology infrastructure with Healthways' solutions, we will be able to scale to millions of people." HealthHonors will continue to sell, service and expand their business with pharmaceutical manufacturers and others to improve medication adherence and compliance.

Safe Harbor Provisions
This press release contains forward-looking statements, including our guidance and financial expectations for future periods, which are based upon current expectations and involve a number of risks and uncertainties. Those forward-looking statements include all statements that

- MORE -

developed Dynamic Intermittent Reinforcement™ software, which would be integrated into the Embrace platform and determine the lowest economic reinforcement necessary to persuade an individual to maintain healthy behavior. At the time of the acquisition, HealthHonors had published outcomes that showed a 33 to 56 percent increase in adherence to desired health behaviors while decreasing incentive budgets.[8] "Before the

Healthways acquired HealthHonors in 2009, a company that specialized in behavior change science through the use of incentives.

Contact:
Melissa Wyllie
(615) 614-4486
melissa.wyllie@healthways.com

Christina Klaubert (for MedNetworks)
(781) 791-4561
mednetworks@inkhouse.net

EXCLUSIVE PARTNERSHIP BETWEEN HEALTHWAYS, MEDNETWORKS UTILIZES POWER OF SOCIAL NETWORKS TO IMPROVE HEALTH, WELL-BEING

Relationship to Connect Work of MedNetworks Co-Founder and Harvard Scientist Nicholas Christakis to Healthways Well-Being Improvement Solutions

NASHVILLE, Tenn., and NEWTON, Mass. – Aug. 25, 2010 – Healthways, Inc. (NASDAQ: HWAY), today announced an exclusive, strategic partnership with MedNetworks, Inc., a company commercializing social network mapping analytics and technology developed by physician, social scientist and Harvard professor Nicholas Christakis, M.D., Ph.D. MedNetworks has an exclusive license from Harvard University to use the Christakis technology in the healthcare sector.

Healthways and MedNetworks will apply the science of social network mapping to population health management. The understanding of social network structures and dynamics will inform the design of Healthways intervention strategies to improve well-being by showing the relationships and degrees of influence between individuals, providers and organizations, such as employers within a given community.

MedNetworks offers a first-of-its-kind method for analyzing real-life social networks to identify patterns of influence. Using sophisticated analytics, MedNetworks maps social networks, evaluates strength and dynamic development of connections of members of these networks, ranks individual influence, and performs predictive modeling. Research has revealed that influencing an individual's behavior can be enhanced by changing the behavior of someone else in his or her network of relationships. Healthways will utilize the partnership to bring this science of social networks to its market-leading behavior change and engagement models to increase the rate and sustainability of behavior change and to do so with increased efficiency.

"At Healthways, we've known instinctively the power that social networks have on health and well-being. We've seen those networks enable thousands of people to quit smoking through Healthways QuitNet virtual community, and we know that members of Healthways SilverSneakers Fitness Program experience improvement not only to their physical health, but also their social and emotional health through the relationships formed with other program participants," said Ben R. Leedle, Jr., Healthways CEO. "We look forward to this partnership and working together to purposefully create new ways of improving well-being, lowering costs, and increasing work-force performance."

- MORE -

Specializing in the commercialization of social network mapping analytics and technology, MedNetworks agreed to engage in an exclusive relationship with Healthways in 2010.

HealthHonors software was developed, companies would conduct incentive programs without any knowledge of what incentives people would respond to or how large or small they needed to be in order to be effective," Janet Calhoun noted.

Healthways gained additional capability strength in mid-2010 with the successful negotiation of an exclusive relationship with MedNetworks, a company commercializing social network mapping analytics and technology developed by physician, social scientist, and Harvard professor Nicholas Christakis, MD, PhD. MedNetworks has an exclusive license from Harvard University to use the Christakis technology in the health care sector.

The successful negotiation with MedNetworks was driven by the company's increasing understanding of the contributors to well-being that were revealed by the cumulative data from the Gallup-Healthways Well-Being Index®. In a press release announcing the partnership, Leedle said: "We've known instinctively the power that social networks have on health and well-being. We've seen these networks enable thousands to quit smoking through Healthways' QuitNet virtual community, and we know that members of Healthways SilverSneakers® Fitness Program experience improvement not only [in] their physical health but also their social and emotional health through the relationships formed with other program participants."

Christakis agreed, noting "the likelihood of health risks like obesity and smoking is affected by your social network and in turn affects the health of those around you. You are influenced not just by your friends but by your friends' friends and their friends, whom you may not even know."

In a related move, Healthways capitalized a new subsidiary—MeYou Health—with the scientists and programmers who had created the company's industry-leading and award-winning QuitNet smoking cessation program. "We are convinced that it's critical for us to know not only who is in a network and how influence in that network flows, but also how best to help create and sustain virtual networks for an increasingly 'connected' society," Leedle noted. He added:

MeYou Health was created and is dedicated to helping people pursue, achieve, and maintain a healthy lifestyle by helping them engage their social networks for support and introducing them to small actions they can accomplish every day through fun interactive web and mobile applications.

We needed rapid cycle development of social media tools that we could use to increase the longitudinal engagement of people using our solution to make their participation fun and worthwhile. We believe that the best way to achieve that development is to give the developers as much freedom from the parent bureaucracy as possible.

The approach worked well. MeYou Health's Community Clash™ online card game was one of the select few projects showcased at the June 2010 Community Health Data Forum sponsored by the National Academy of Science's Institute of Medicine and the US Department of Health and Human Services.

A fourth major initiative, undertaken by Healthways in early 2010, was also aimed at capturing the power of community in helping people achieve and maintain the healthy lifestyles and behaviors that the Gallup-Healthways Well-Being Index® increasingly revealed were key components of overall well-being. The conclusion wasn't surprising. People spend about half of their waking hours on the job and about 80 percent of their time within a 30-mile radius of their home. While the company had proven approaches for individuals and employers, improving well-being at a community level was uncharted territory.

But not for *National Geographic* researcher and author Dan Buettner, best known for his research into variables common to communities around the globe where an unusually large percentage of the population live to be 100 or older. Buettner published his findings in the best-selling book *The Blue Zones* and went on to lead a team that would pilot instilling those factors and behaviors in a community change project in Albert Lea, Minnesota. The results were excellent, but Buettner did not have the resources to scale up the effort for testing in other communities. Healthways did.

The Internet-based QuitNet quickly became the most successful smoking cessation program in the nation, with over 300,000 users.

I N 2010, HEALTHWAYS TEAMED WITH AUTHOR AND LONGEVITY EXPERT DAN BUETTNER TO create Blue Zones Communities—comprehensive, geography-based wellness areas. Buettner wrote the book *The Blue Zones*, which explored areas around the world in which the population lived longer than average and the keys to their success. That, combined with Healthways' experience in creating the structure around wellness and lifestyle changes, provided a powerful combination.

The Healthways–Blue Zone Vitality Quest℠ was based on a pilot that Buettner undertook in 2009. Using Buettner's theories, the city of Albert Lea, Minnesota, made changes in its environmental policy. Restaurant menus were revised, community gardens were added, and walking clubs were created.

In all, 60 percent of its restaurants, half of its employers, all of its schools, and 27 percent of its citizens participated. These changes helped the population drop an average of two pounds per resident, and brought a 20-percent reduction in absenteeism among key employers. They also raised life expectancy 3.1 years.

Media attention on Buettner's pilot program led

Dan Buettner, author of *The Blue Zones*, discussed his findings at the 2010 Healthways Well-Being Summit. Buettner teamed with Healthways to create the Blue Zones Communities project.

numerous other cities to inquire about bringing something similar to their communities. Buettner turned to Healthways, which had years of proven results in improving lifestyle, health, and wellness.

"Through this partnership, we will be helping communities improve their health and well-being by putting the neighborhood concept back into health," Buettner said in a statement at the time. "We know from deep science that when communities embrace certain principles and implement sustainable policy and environmental changes, it makes it easier for individuals, businesses, and government entities within those communities to support one another, driving real, long-term, meaningful

Together, Buettner and Healthways formed a new entity—the Healthways–Blue Zones Vitality Quest℠ and its Blue Zones Communities project—to partner with

communities whose business and elected leaders were prepared to actively support an effort to improve well-being for the entire community. The program calls on

improvement. Healthways has the tools, capabilities, mission, and experience to scale Vitality Quest^{SM} to more and larger communities than Blue Zones has yet engaged."[1]

Cities selected to be a "Blue Zones Community" would benefit from the combined capabilities of a Blue Zone—with its expertise in longevity—and Healthways' proven solutions for improving well-being. The Gallup-Healthways Well-Being Index® would be used to establish a baseline and measure progress.

Employers would be assisted in creating healthier workplaces. Schools would be taught to provide nutritional meals and engage the community. Restaurants would be helped to transform menus with healthier options. Governmental policies and infrastructure would be assessed. Community groups would be encouraged. And special events and speakers would attempt to engage the entire population.

"Healthways has already achieved a tremendous amount of success bringing behavioral economic and clinical science to

real world applications, helping individuals better manage their health and well-being," said Ben Leedle. "We know that well-being is composed of social, emotional, and physical health, and this partnership affords us an opportunity to develop a wider set of community interventions and access to an impressive range of experts and proven techniques. The combination of our collective abilities as companies to engage whole environments will accelerate the achievement of improved well-being for entire communities."[2]

Numerous cities applied to be named the lead Blue Zones Community, and three finalists were selected: Asheville, North Carolina, and its surrounding area; a section of Central Florida; and the Beach Cities of Southern California. By late 2010, the Beach Cities had emerged as the lead pilot area, and programs were under way. The first task was assessing the current state of well-being in the communities, which provided the blueprint for the personal, business, and infrastructure change processes that began early in 2011.

Healthways CEO Ben Leedle discusses longevity and wellness at the 2010 Healthways Well-Being Summit.

community leaders from government, business, academia, nonprofit organizations, and locally influential groups to take small steps to create a community in

which inhabitants are healthier, have lower health care needs and costs, and live longer. The benefits for the community include a competitive advantage in economic

Left and center: As part of Healthways' commitment to fitness, colleagues around the country often participate in local marathons. Nashville colleagues (left) participated in the Country Music Marathon, while those in the Phoenix business office (center) ran in the Rock 'n' Roll Marathon.

Right: The lawn outside company headquarters is used for kickball games at lunchtime.

development, greater productivity and business results for employers, and a better quality of life for all its residents.

Despite the continuing recession, the project received applications from more than 55 cities that wanted to be selected as the first Blue Zones Community and were willing to make a multimillion dollar commitment to support that effort. The selected city would receive the attention and expertise of Buettner and Healthways plus access to the Gallup-Healthways Well-Being Index®. It would also receive what one magazine called "an 'A Team' of public health policy experts,"[9] including a specialist on walk-ability and bike-ability, another skilled at changing environments and menus in food facilities ranging from restaurants to school cafeterias to kitchen pantries in the home, and an expert on social networks in the real world.

From the more than 55 communities that applied to be named the lead Blue Zones Community, three finalists were selected: Asheville, North Carolina, and its surrounding area; a section of central Florida; and the Beach Communities of Southern California. By late 2010, Southern California's Beach Communities were chosen as the winner, and program work

was soon under way. The first step was to evaluate the current state of well-being in the communities, which supplied the blueprint for the community change processes that would soon be initiated.

Eating What It Cooks

When Healthways made the transition from hospital-based diabetes centers of excellence to diabetes disease management, Bristol-Myers Squibb provided the living laboratory in which the new solution could be tested, modified, and validated. It was a critical step in the creation of the disease management market and one that Healthways couldn't undertake itself due to its relatively small number of colleagues.

With its ensuing growth, however, size wasn't an issue for the company in testing the elements of the emerging Well-Being Improvement Solution. With the acquisition of Health IQ Diagnostics, Healthways began making its programs available to its colleagues, evaluating what did and didn't work. Originally using the Health IQ survey to determine which colleagues might have future health problems—based on various quantifiable measures such as body mass index (BMI), cholesterol levels, and tobacco use—the company switched to the WBA as soon as it had been developed and validated. Started as a voluntary program, the improvement in colleague health was so striking that the company soon made participation in the annual assessment process a condition for receiving health benefits.

Recognizing that nutrition and exercise were also critical to overall well-being, the company tried to provide a supportive environment by offering healthy choices in the cafeteria and banning fried foods from the menu. Healthways colleagues were encouraged to take exercise breaks during the day and pursue any number of company-supported fitness activities. At the headquarters in Franklin, Tennessee, a well-organized kickball league plays on the lawn in front of the office, and the driveway leading to the loading zone has been marked off for basketball. In addition, the main parking structure includes an area where colleagues play cricket, and a significant number of colleagues regularly walk or run together. This focus on well-being isn't limited to the headquarters

group. At the request of Healthways colleagues in Phoenix, the design of the new facility that opened in 2009 included bike racks and showers so that colleagues could ride their bikes to work.[10]

Leedle, who began his career as an exercise specialist, often felt that he had come full circle:

The country and the world are spending a whole lot of money on people who have already developed conditions and disease. Some of that is genetic, and some people get dealt a bad set of cards. But the majority is manufactured as a result of really bad lifestyle choices. You know, what do you and I eat every day? How well do we make our choices of food that we eat? How do we handle stress and cope with it? How strong is our social support system? How do we choose to interact with it? How active are we? Those are fundamental elements of health, and their relationship to well-being is just incredible. The challenge we face is in designing and delivering a solution that will help people deal effectively with these issues and any combination of them. We have to find better ways to consistently help people to do better across the board in all of those areas.[11]

Renewed Government Activity

At the beginning of 2010, Healthways was still in negotiations with various federal agencies and departments with respect to an appropriate settlement of fee claims arising from its participation in the

Company events took on a wellness tone during the opening of the Center for Health Action in San Antonio, Texas, which kept the menu healthy. This Care Enhancement Center stands out due to the presence and involvement of Medco pharmacists as part of Healthways strategic channel partnership with the company.

Medicare Health Support (MHS) program. Although there was mounting evidence that the company had, in fact, achieved all of the performance targets set out for that program, management elected not to disclose those findings while the settlement discussions were still under way.

Elsewhere in the capitol, however, other agencies were seeking solutions to the same sorts of issues related to health care and cost that were plaguing employers in the private sector, and the company was successful in landing two landmark contracts to provide services for federal government employees, both military and civilian.

The first of these contracts was with Defense Department contractor International SOS. Awarded with the specific approval of the Pentagon, this contract would bring Healthways' disease management capabilities to the department's overseas TRICARE Prime Remote beneficiaries. The second agreement, won through an intensely competitive RFP process, was with the US Office of Personnel Management, the agency responsible for administering health benefits for all federal employees.

Finally, in September 2010, Healthways could begin the process of writing a successful finis to its Medicare Health Support efforts. At a DC meeting of the Center for Health Transformation (CHT), the company announced the CMS' independent contractors' findings on performance, which concluded, as Leedle had predicted 33 months earlier, that

Healthways had met all of the performance targets with respect to clinical improvement; beneficiary and provider satisfaction with the program; and most importantly, savings. In releasing the findings, Leedle noted:

The current and rapidly increasing cost of health care has been identified as the principal cause of the nation's deficit, a significant threat to our economy, and a real barrier to our competitiveness in a global market. While there are real savings that can be achieved through improvements to process and quality in the delivery system, this research demonstrates that solutions designed to improve well-being, and thereby reduce the demand for services, are effective; can be provided at scale; and can be easily delivered, both domestically and internationally.[12]

At the CHT meeting, the findings with respect to Healthways' performance in the MHS program, along with the results of other studies of both domestic and international disease management and wellness programs for seniors, were discussed by a panel that included former House Speaker Newt Gingrich, former Senate Majority Leader Tom Daschle, and former Deputy Assistant Secretary of HHS Dr. Ken Thorpe.

All three panelists underscored the importance of the findings. "We've got to seize the moment. If we have a best practice, it is utterly immoral to wait to start it until age 65," Gingrich said. "Shouldn't we adopt best practices from conception on? And shouldn't we try to encourage

positive behaviors so that whatever stage you are [at], you're optimizing your health and minimizing sickness?"

Daschle concurred: "These studies offer a sweeping illustration of what can be done to affect cost and quality. We need to create greater pressure, greater momentum to move in this direction more quickly. Let's make this the national model it deserves to be."[13]

Thorpe also suggested that the findings should be implemented nationally—and rapidly. "The findings add to the increasing weight of evidence that we don't have to wait another five to 10 years to do more pilots. We have a body of research out there on what's going on in the commercial market and what's going on in the Medicare market—approaches that over the next two to four years we can scale up and replicate in the Medicare program nationally."[14]

Finally, at the end of 2010, the company announced it had reached a settlement with CMS with respect to its MHS pilot performance. The settlement resulted in the company booking $22.3 million in additional revenue, which translated to a 38 cent increase in earnings per share.

Setting the Stage for Growth

To prepare the company for a return to growth in 2011 and beyond, Leedle made important changes in the management team during 2010. Chris Cigarran, longtime leader of the company's Human Resources group, took on the role as head of the direct-to-employer business. Clay Richards, formerly in-house general counsel, assumed responsibility for the company's health plan business, and, in anticipation of Stefen Brueckner's planned retirement, Tom Cox was promoted to the

Solutions Liaison Gerrye Stegall has been with Healthways since 2001.

position of chief operating officer. Planned retirement also saw the departure of long-term chief financial officer Mary Chaput, whose position was filled by former chief accounting officer Alfred Lumsdaine.

While many organizations dealing with the types of challenges faced by Healthways during the events of 2008—which were compounded by the subsequent economic crisis and recession—would have hunkered down, waited for the storm to pass, and hoped things would get better, that is not the Healthways way. Instead, the company's leadership drove forward with the plans for the Well-Being Improvement Solution, making significant investments to prepare the market for the new offering and to assure that the critical components would be in place and tested when the market came to recognize that the Well-Being Improvement Solution was exactly what it was looking for.

"As a company, we are not averse to putting our money where our mouth is and making things better, and we don't necessarily live by the maxim 'if it ain't broke, don't fix it,'" said Gerrye Stegall. "We favor the 'forever improving' approach because that's really what the market expects—that you're staying ahead of the game."[15]

"Hope is not a strategy for achieving great things," Tom Cigarran noted. "It is in times of great challenge that the true character of organizations and individuals is revealed, and the board and I could not be prouder of the way the colleagues of this company stayed true to our purpose during these very difficult three years."

While not yet out of the woods, staying true to its purpose appears to have once again been the right choice. During the 2010 year-end company conference call, Leedle told analysts that evidence of the company's success in creating its third new market would be found in announcements of "transformational agreements with health plans, employers, and governments, both domestically and internationally, and as a result of health reform in the United States—even provider organizations."

He predicted these announcements would reflect one or more of five emerging market trends:

1) Health plan preparation for the implementation of state insurance exchanges, which is expected to cause significant disruption of their individual and small group fully insured business;

2) Change from a volume-based to a performance-based payment system, and the associated shift of financial risk and responsibility for cost and quality from health plans to providers;

3) Increasing payer requests for a comprehensive, integrated solution that addresses longitudinal health risk and care needs for total populations;

4) Global adoption of population health management by both foreign government and foreign private sector health organizations; and

5) Large employers' recognition of the expanded value of improved well-being in reducing medical cost and improving individual and company productivity and performance.

In the last days of 2010 and the first four months of 2011, the company was able to make four such announcements about four of these types of agreements. The first was a new 10-year agreement with long-term customer Hawaii Medical Service Association (HMSA), under which the health plan would transfer its health management functions and other health and wellness programs to Healthways. Healthways also assumed responsibility for HMSA's health research functions, pharmacy benefit management, disease management, and care management.

"HMSA and Healthways have a long history of jointly developed and implemented innovations designed to improve the health and well-being of our members while reducing the cost of care," said Michael A. Gold, HMSA executive vice president and chief operating officer. "Our new arrangement will enable us to put more focus on supporting the patient-physician relationship and is a major step forward in pursuit of our goal to have the healthiest members in the nation by

providing them with the country's most affordable, highest quality health care and best customer experience."[16]

The second transformational agreement Healthways announced was its selection by the Government of New South Wales, Australia, to provide telephonic interventions to approximately 43,000 individuals with chronic and complex care needs.[17] In announcing this agreement, Leedle pointed out three elements that made this agreement significant for the company:

- *As a direct contract with a government entity, this [contract] builds on the international success we have had in partnership with the private-side agents of health care in a number of countries.*
- *This contract continues to validate the growth pattern we expect in our international business.*

At an event in Hawaii in 2011, Healthways and longtime customer Hawaii Medical Service Association (HMSA) announced a 10-year agreement that would transfer HMSA's health management functions and other programs to Healthways. Shown here are Healthways Corporate Medical Director Dr. Rich Lachiver (left) and HMSA Executive Vice President and Chief Financial Officer Steve Van Ribbink (right).

• *The service model represented by this contract requires deep integration with hospitals, physicians, and other providers, and, as such, can serve as an emerging model to be leveraged in the United States as health plans, hospitals, and physician groups seek to provide highly integrated, value-based solutions.*

The third transformational contract also came from the international division, which announced the company's selection by the French national health insurer, Caisse Nationale d'Assurance Maladie des Travailleurs Salariés (CNAMTS), to significantly expand France's diabetes management program to include an estimated 1.9 million citizens in France and its overseas territories. In addition, the contract called for the addition of programs for two more chronic diseases during its term.

Commenting on the company's selection by CNAMTS after an exhaustive and highly competitive, seven-month RFP process, Healthways International President Matt Kelliher observed, "The decision by CNAMTS to award this contract to Healthways is a highly meaningful validation of the depth and breadth of both our comprehensive well-being solution and of our Embrace platform. Clearly, our solutions are the world-class benchmark, capable of meeting the needs of millions of individuals threatened by the challenge of living with a long-term condition."[18]

The fourth transformational agreement announced by Healthways was with long-term customer CareFirst to partner with the health plan in delivering its network-wide Primary Care Medical Home (PCMH) model.[19] In announcing the new contract, Leedle said, "We will work with CareFirst's entire book of business as its care coordination arm, integrating deeply with the primary care providers who are participating in the CareFirst PCMH model. This contract is an example of the positive implication of emerging trends, with health plans reshaping their service offerings as the implementation of health care reform moves forward."[20]

Two other key events in early 2011 also signaled the market's new focus on Healthways and well-being. The first was the publication of a special edition of *Population Health Management* containing six peer-reviewed articles

documenting the findings with respect to MHS and its other seniors programs that the company had released the previous September. In a companion editorial column, journal editor David Nash, MD, wrote, "The takeaway message is clear. The country's vision should be toward optimizing each citizen's health over a lifetime rather than starting at age 65. This supplement is one indication that we have identified best practices, developed and tested models, and built an evidence base. Now is the time to fund prevention through the public health trust fund and other avenues made available through health care reform. Good policy over the coming decade will facilitate—and perhaps accelerate—this process."

The other event of note was the international expansion of the Gallup-Healthways Well-Being Index®. Launched in the United Kingdom in January, the partnership was invited to a special meeting of the Royal Society for the Encouragement of Arts, Manufactures and Commerce (RSA) to present the results from the first quarter of polling. The presentation, titled "New Metrics for a New Era," was moderated by Matthew Taylor, chief executive of RSA, and included commentary by Dr. David Halpern, director of the Cabinet Office Behavioural Insight Team, and Paul Allin, director of the National Well-Being Project at the Office for National Statistics.

Within 100 days of Leedle's guiding analysis to five emerging market trends, Healthways made six major announcements with respect to new agreements and activities reflecting four of them. In the company's 2011 first quarter call, Leedle told analysts that the company expected "to sign additional contracts within this framework during 2011."

Leedle's prediction was accurate. Just three weeks shy of its 30th anniversary,

The first quarter results of the Gallup-Healthways Well-Being Index® UK were announced at the Royal Society for the Encouragement of Arts, Manufactures and Commerce session in 2011. Left to right: Dr. David Halpern, director, Cabinet Office Behavioural Insight Team; Paul Allin, director, National Well-Being Project, Office for National Statistics; RSA Chair Matthew Taylor; Jim Clifton, CEO, Gallup; Ben Leedle, CEO, Healthways; and Jim Harter, PhD, Gallup chief scientist.

Creating a healthier world,
one person at a time

HEALTHWAYS

Healthways announced a major expansion and extension of its agreement with Wellmark (Blue Cross and Blue Shield of Iowa) in support of the Healthiest State Initiative announced by Iowa Governor Terry Branstad. This initiative is the nation's first statewide comprehensive well-being improvement program and is designed to help Iowa become the number 1-ranked state for well-being as measured by the Gallup-Healthways Well-Being Index® within five years.

The centerpiece of this business-led, government-endorsed effort is a 10-community Blue Zones Project, which represents the largest comprehensive well-being improvement initiative ever launched. The Iowa Healthiest State Initiative is expected to help Iowans live longer, healthier, and more productive lives while also enabling the state to redirect billions of dollars currently spent on health care to efforts that will further grow the state's economy.

In the final transaction of its 30th year, Healthways announced the acquisition of Navvis, one of the nation's leading and most respected consulting firms to hospital and physician organizations, including six of the top ten health care systems in the country.

Commenting on the acquisition, Leedle noted:

As we predicted late last year, health care systems and insurers are recognizing the need for significant transformation in the structure and operation of the delivery system in response to the increased financial risk and future relevance associated with the impending shift from a volume-based to a value-based payment system. In response, health care systems and health plans are seeking total population health solutions that will improve quality, reduce cost, and spread the financial risk over the entire population in their market, not just areas among those who are ill. Visioning, designing, implementing, and supporting the operation of these new models require a significant degree of expert support. With our acquisition of Navvis, Healthways will substantially enhance its capability to provide that support seamlessly to health care systems, many of which are actively seeking our assistance.

Opposite: With its evolution from hospital management to disease management, to well-being improvement, Healthways ultimately found its place as a company that focuses on the individual, regardless of his or her health status; a belief reflected in its purpose: to be universally recognized for creating a healthier world, one person at a time.

A Final Word

Purpose makes decisions simpler—not easier—to make, to scale, and to execute.

—Roy Spence

Looking Back

The story of Healthways first 30 years began with purpose. Our Purpose is the definitive statement of the difference we are trying to make in the world. It is the touchstone that enables our customers to know, without any doubt, that our intent is honorable. Purpose is our anchor in tough times—and the wind in our sails when times are good.

Each step in Healthways' journey from a hospital ownership and management company to the well-being improvement company we have become today, has been a step in pursuit of our Purpose. Each step, whether taken to add new capabilities, to create new markets, or to expand our value proposition, has enabled us to make a difference for more and more people.

But Purpose is only the beginning of our story. The values which we have adopted to guide how we interact with each other and with our customers are the foundation for our chosen culture—a culture specifically designed to ensure that Healthways creates and maintains an environment in which each colleague can do his or her best work. Our Purpose, and the well-being of the millions of individuals our customers entrust to us, demands no less.

Healthways' Purpose, Values, and Culture have unfailingly attracted colleagues who are second to none in their capabilities, commitment, skills, and passion. It is our colleagues who give our Purpose life and who, in turn, are enriched in knowing that their every action serves to make someone else's life better. Roy Spence once told our colleagues, "You don't know how special you really are." That may be true, but each and every individual whose well-being they help to improve certainly does.

While the road we have travelled over the past 30 years has not always been smooth or the decisions always been simple, our collective alignment in pursuit of our Purpose has permitted us to positively impact the lives of literally millions of people, both domestically and overseas. That is a great gift and a great accomplishment, but it is not enough. There is more—much more—to do. And we will.

Looking Forward

Just as the story of Healthways' first 30 years begins with Purpose, so does the story of our future. The good news is that our Purpose doesn't change. The bad news is that the social, economic, health, and environmental stresses being felt around the globe make it even more important that we are successful. The best news is that Healthways is prepared for the challenge.

At the beginning of 2011, Healthways identified five market changers:

- Preparation for Health Insurance Exchanges
- Transition to a Value-Based Payment System
- Demand for Data, Analysis, Service, and Value Integration
- International Adoption of Population Health
- Demand for Expanded Value (Cost and Performance)

The company predicted that the need of those at risk for health care and/or organizational outcomes to rapidly address these factors would drive demand for proven population health management solutions and increase adoption of its Well-Being Improvement Solution. During the course of 2011, the company entered into seven agreements that were the direct result of organizations recognizing the need to quickly and effectively respond to one or more of those trends. That demand continues to increase.

There can be no question that these emerging market factors are driving significant realignment in the health care industry. In the past year, we have witnessed the re-emergence of integrated health systems and physician organizations as major future players in the delivery of population health services. We have also seen significant changes in the competitive landscape as companies large and small seek to expand their capabilities to provide the "general contractor" services that will be required for successful integration of services and capabilities necessary to deliver a population health solution.

Healthways' investments over the past decade have positioned us uniquely to respond to these new market demands. The capabilities, experience, science, and strategic partnerships that have been brought to bear in the design of our Well-Being Improvement Solution have brought us to exactly the right place at exactly the right time. Not only are we uniquely capable of providing the general contractor services, but also, in the right circumstances with the right customers, we can extend our involvement to be their ongoing co-architect, integrated service provider, and risk partner, setting the stage for the collaborative innovation that will be required to make population health increasingly more effective and efficient.

Ten years ago, on the occasion of Healthways' 20th anniversary, Tom Cigarran expressed his conviction that Healthways would become a great American company. Over the past decade we have taken major steps in that direction and also encountered some challenges that have slowed our progress. Today, we are poised, as never before, to take the next step in making Tom's prediction come true. Focused by our Purpose, supported by our Values and Culture, executed by our exceptional, aligned, and passionate colleagues, our path forward is clear.

So, stay tuned … and be well.

Ben

Ben
September 1, 2011
Franklin, Tennessee

Healthways Colleagues

If I were running a company today, I would have one priority above all others: to acquire as many of the best people as I could.

—Jim Collins, *Good to Great*

OVER THE PAST 30 YEARS, 13,329 INDIVIDUALS HAVE SHARED THE title Healthways Colleague. Energized by purpose, united by a chosen culture, and guided by shared values, each of these colleagues has made a unique contribution to the company's growth and success. The Healthways story—yesterday, today, and tomorrow—is their story. We hope we've told it well.

A

Aaron, Katie
Abadie, Ben R.
Abadie, Patricia
Abarientos, Esther
Abarquez, Pacita S.
Abas, Veryle Z.
Abbley, Enora S.
Abbott, Denise
Abbott, James A.
Abbott, Rachel Kirsten
Abbruzzese, Karen
Abdur-Rahman, Lendo
Abe, Janice
Abel, Ashley A.
Abel, Janelle
Abell, Sheri A.
Abelove, William A.
Abels, Melissa M.
Abernathy, Verlivia
Able, Norma P.
Ables, Robert L.
Ablorh, Deborah Darkua
Abner, Melissa
Abrahall, Judi-Lynn B.
Abraham, Deborah
Abrams, Vickie Lee
Abramson, Joni
Aburaad, Marijana Popadic
Achterman, Kathryn D.
Acker, Michael L.
Ackerman, Jill M.
Ackles, Bonnie J.
Acred, Erica B.
Adair, Michael A.
Adam, Gail Lynn
Adamczyk, Alicia
Adams, Benjamin E.
Adams, Beth A.
Adams, Candis M.
Adams, Charlotte
Adams, Colleen
Adams, Deanna Sue

Adams, Elizabeth A.
Adams, Erika
Adams, Joann R.
Adams, Kristin
Adams, Kristina
Adams, Linda R.
Adams, Lorraine A.
Adams, Mary A.
Adams, Phillip T.
Adams, Sandra J.
Adams, Sherrie
Adams, Sherry
Adams, Stephanie A.
Adams, Tonya M.
Adams, Tracy L.
Adams, Virginia Jan
Adamson, Kevin M.
Adamson, Linda
Adamus, Deborah L.
Adan, Marilou
Adcock, Brenda
Adcock, Elizabeth A.
Adcox, Vickie Rhena
Addis, Karen K.
Addison, Dianna L.
Addison, Jason L.
Addy, Katrice M.
Aderogba, Samuel A.
Adey, JoAnne
Adhimoolam, Abirami
Adkins, Alisa K.
Adkins, Christie
Adkins, Lorna N.
Adkisson, Sharis
Adriaansz, Robert
Affield, Tracy L.
Agans, Melissa S.
Agard, Chereese L.
Agee, Brian D.
Agnew, Crystal Isabella-Grace
Agruso, Donna J.
Aguada, Philip Lawrence
Aguiar, Roxana G.
Aguila, Vivian
Agus, Cristina L.

Ahana, Naomi K.
Ahern, Michael J.
Ahern, Sharon M.
Ahlborg, Robert
Ahlgren, Vickie Weiman
Ahmad, Maria Antonina Lindsey
Ahmadi, Shiva B.
Aiello, Amy M.
Aiello, John J.
Aiken, Julie A.
Ainscough, Rosanne G.
Aitken, Nancy L.
Ajayi, Mona L.
Ajayi, Victoria O.
Ajemian, Jan
Akana, Victoria
Akerejah, Toyin I.
Akers, Christian H.
Akers, Darci D.
Akers-Smith, Lisa Marie
Akiens, Linda M.
Akindana, Adeola O.
Akins, Maria
Akiyama, Katherine H.
Akrobettoe, Naki C.
Alaba, Victoria T.
Aladeselu, Olubunmi O.
Alafa, Sylvia
Alam, Towhid U.
Albawwab, Mohammad A.
Albert, Cynthia A.
Albert, Lynn
Alberts, Mindy
Albertson, Annette L.
Albiston, Wyatt D.
Albitz, Beth Ann
Albright, Jaclyn
Albright, Nancy M.
Alcorn, Linda D.
Alcorn, Pamela G.
Alcorn, Teresa E.
Alday-Plaza, Gloria
Alden, Kenneth
Alden, Lisa A.
Aleman, Monica

Alexander, Dale
Alexander, Jennifer C.
Alexander, Kathy L.
Alexander, Maureen
Alexander, Shirley Dean
Alexander, Susan
Alexandroni, Theresa N.
Alfano, Genie
Alford, Alethia D.
Alford, Patricia
Algozzini, Sue
Al-Hasib, Hamid
Alicar, Madeleine V.
Aljets, Samantha L.
Allbee, Kelly A.
Allen, Alicia A.
Allen, Barbara B.
Allen, Bill
Allen, Brenda J.
Allen, Carolyn Yvonne
Allen, Cynthia A.
Allen, Dana E.
Allen, Darlene E.
Allen, Elizabeth A.
Allen, Kathryn
Allen, Leanetta
Allen, Lillian M.
Allen, Linda
Allen, Margot C.
Allen, Maureen
Allen, Megan A.
Allen, Patricia
Allen, Ronald
Allen, Shirley
Allen-Schmidt, Janelle M.
Allen-Wright, Imelda
Allerdice, Trisha Lee
Alleyne, Cecile Jacqueline
Allgeyer, Patricia K.
Allgood, James C.
Alling, Tristan J.
Allison, Diane
Allison, Katherine J.
Allison, Lori J.
Allison, Marilyn G.

Allman, Carol M.
Allred, Andrea
Almanza, Silvia I.
Almerini, Elizabeth A.
Almond, Julie
Alonsagay, Arline B.
Alonte, Rosie D.
Alousyes, Sheeba
Alsalami, Waleed S.
Alsmeyer, Robert W.
Alspach, Letitia M.
Alston, Glory M.
Alt, Mary
Altman, Ilene
Alton, Bianca R.
Alvarez, Adrian J.
Alvarez, Aurora M.
Alvarez, Jorge A.
Alvarez, Otilia B.
Alvarez, Rosanna
Alvord, Donna Lynn
Ambayec, Senen
Amberson, Margret K.
Ambord, Jeff
Ambrose, Barbara
Ambrose, Elizabeth
Ambur, Nancy
America, Linda M.
Amico, Richard
Amirault, Jaime
Ammon, James W.
Ammons, Kay
Amos, Elaine
Amos, Martha
Amos, Merry
Ampulski, Marjorie R.
Amrhein, David B.
Amsinger, Kara C.
Amstutz, Holly R.
Anastasio, Patricia
Ancira, Grace B.
Anda, Kim
Anderasen, Doug
Anders, Willie
Andersen, Constance A.

Andersen, James P.
Andersen, Steven
Anderson Guice, Philip
Anderson, Adam
Anderson, Amy K.
Anderson, Andrea I.
Anderson, Apphia
Anderson, Barbara L.
Anderson, Bret R.
Anderson, Coralynn
Anderson, Cynthia
Anderson, Debbie
Anderson, Douglas
Anderson, Eric M.
Anderson, Eva L.
Anderson, Gaye A.
Anderson, Heather
Anderson, Janet S.
Anderson, John
Anderson, Julie
Anderson, Karen
Anderson, Katherine
Anderson, Kathleen
Anderson, Kathryn A.
Anderson, Kimberly
Anderson, Linda
Anderson, Lois D.
Anderson, Lydia L.
Anderson, Marissa A.
Anderson, Paulette D.
Anderson, Phyllis
Anderson, Randy S.
Anderson, Sharon J.
Anderson, Sheila
Anderson, Susan M.
Anderson, Terrence L.
Anderson, Tiffany P.
Anderssen, Linda G.
Andrade, Cathryn D.
Andrade, Mary M.
Andrae, Richard M.
Andreasen, Doug
Andrews, David M.
Andrews, Jackie
Andrews, Lisa
Andrews, Nelson C.
Andrews, Patricia M.
Andrews, Rachel Leah
Andrews, Teresa A.
Andrews, Veva
Andrews, Wilma C.
Andrisani, Donna
Andsel, Michael
Ang, Desiree G.
Angel, R. Neal
Angelo, Deborah R.
Angelo, Patricia E.
Angelucci, Pauline M.
Angle, Linda C.
Anglin, Rebecca
Anglo, Susanne
Angus, Daphne R.
Aniska, Cheryl A.
Ansara, Lynne M.
Ansel, Michael L.
Ansorge, Charmaine A.
Anssel, Michael
Anthony, Jo Ann
Anthony, Kara L.
Anthony, Lynn Ann
Anthony, Norma I.
Antista, Della
Antoine, Loretta I.
Anton, Polly C.
Antonazzo, Mary J.
Antone, Kasey
Antoni, Denise A.
Antonini, Marilyn
Antoniuc, Karen
Antony, Mary
Antwi, Alfred
Anvik, Katherine M.
Aparajithan, Srivathsan
Apolinario, Milagros M.
Aponte, Juan C.
Aponte, Julie M.

Appel, Adriana
Appell, Stacey K.
Apple, Tara
Aproberts, Kathleen P.
Aragon, Donna G.
Arakaki, Ami
Arakaki, Leeann M.
Arakelian, Mary
Arbeiter, Mary Frances
Arceci, Jean M.
Archer, Cynthia N.
Archer, Sharvaughn L.
Archibald, Wesley J.
Archila, Carlos M.
Arellano, Leonida
Argo, Cynthia
Argudo, Rhianna M.
Argue, Virginia M.
Arias, Thelma F.
Ark, Kimberly D.
Armantrout, Gail R.
Armendariz, Annette
Armendariz, Stephanie D.
Armistead, Anita L.
Armistead, Stacey M.
Armstrong, Ann
Armstrong, Eva Patricia
Armstrong, Jaime L.
Armstrong, Jerry L.
Armstrong, Lois J.
Armstrong, Lorraine J.
Armstrong, Rebecca M.
Arnal, Jessica R.
Arndt, Martha Lewis Childs
Arner, Melissa
Arnett, Erin L.
Arnett, James A.
Arnett, Jennifer Lynn
Arnholt, Linda D.
Arnold, Angela G.
Arnold, Carole R.
Arnold, Charles
Arnold, Deana M.
Arnold, Edgar B.
Arnold, Elizabeth Yvonne
Arnold, Kai M.
Arnold, Mary Ellen
Arora, Sumeet S.
Arori, Christopher N.
Arrington, Darrow D.
Arrowsmith, Katherine K.
Artates, Antonio
Arteaga, Jessica Robyn Pena
Artibee, Kay Jackson
Artison, Arletta P.
Artz, Timothy E.
Arvinger, Ce'Aira
Arzenti, Lori
Asah, Patricia Esi
Ash, Cathy J.
Ashbaugh, Bridget
Ashford, Mary L.
Ashley, Ann B.
Ashley, Quincy J.
Ashley, Sandra Kay
Ashley, Shivonne
Ashmore, Jeffrey L.
Ashworth, Diane
Asis, Joshelynn D.
Asker, Cathleen
Askey, James H.
Aslam, Mohammad
Aspholm, Cheryl A.
Assink, Michael Lee
Astrike, Debra
Atai, Gay S.
Atchison, Monica
Atherton, Bradley
Atkerson, Gary W.
Atkins, Linda
Atkinson, Penny J.
Aubert, Karen
Aubert-Butterfield, Sylvia M.
Aubrey, Stephanie
Aubut, Patricia
Auciello, Eric D.

Audley, Deborah Sauls
Auer, John E.
Auer, Kelly L.
Auer, Michael D.
August, Garry L.
Augustin, Adjanie C.
Augustyniak, Jodi Lyn
Ault, Susan M.
Austen, Lisa M.
Austin, Cheryl A.
Austin, Donna L.
Austin, Shirley T.
Austin-Zawacki, Judie L.
Auten, Kimberly
Autrieth, Audrey I.
Avadhuta, Niranjan R.
Avant, Kerry B.
Avent, Nancy Marlene
Averitt, Laura Ann
Avery, Sandra S.
Avinger, Robert L.
Awaal-Hartman, Hanan H.
Axelson, Michele L.
Axford, Judith M.
Axtell, Nancy D.
Ayala, Rosemary
Ayers, Charles A.
Ayers, Nancy E.
Ayers, Olivia J.
Aylor, Candace A.
Aylward, Patricia A.
Aysien, Sharon A.

B

Babai-Siahdohoni, Nader
Babbrah, Pooja K.
Babbs, Laura Ann
Babcock, Amber L.
Babcock, Sandra
Baber, Suzanne B.
Baca, Cynthia A.
Baccash, Mona M.
Bach, Laurie
Bach, Othello
Bachman, Sheryl
Back-Brehm, Laura A.
Backer, Gary
Bacon Martinez, Roberta
Bacon, Antonia M.
Bacon, Elbert
Bacon, Keisha S.
Bactista, Sheryl L.
Bader Sapp, Krista
Badertscher, Tammy J.
Badia, Matilde L.
Baer, Barbara F.
Baer, Edwadine J.
Baertschi, Rebecca L.
Baeza, Irma
Baggett, Diana G.
Baggott, Alcy
Bagley, James T.
Bagnulo, Carol-Ann
Bahou, Melinda M.
Bailer, Rita R.
Bailes, Aaron G.
Bailey, Anne E.
Bailey, Craig
Bailey, Cynthia L.
Bailey, Erin L.
Bailey, Glenda M.
Bailey, Jennifer Lynn
Bailey, Melody
Bailey, Melva B.
Bailey, Michael R.
Bailey, Richard
Bailey, Sheree L.
Baille, Lisa
Bain, Petulia R.
Bair, Vivian V.
Baity, Cara L.
Baji, Mayuresh
Baker, Amanda E.
Baker, Deborah J.
Baker, Elizabeth

Baker, Jennifer J.
Baker, John R.
Baker, Julie A.
Baker, Kara
Baker, Kellie M.
Baker, Michael
Baker, Nancy A.
Baker, Nicole
Baker, Patricia B.
Baker, Patrick A.
Baker, Richard
Baker, Roberta S.
Baker, Sherry R.
Baker, Stephen P.
Baker, Suzanne R.
Baker, Terri A.
Baker, Valerie
Bakir, Alice M.
Bakkene, Susan L.
Baksh, Randa S.
Balagurchik, Frances L.
Balason, Marlone B.
Balbuena, Irma
Balciunas, Danute Z.
Balderas, Celia J.
Balderrama, Kelly N.
Baldinger, Kathleen A.
Baldree, Elizabeth K.
Baldridge, Roland Keith
Baldwin, Bethora L.
Baldwin, Deborah A.
Baldwin, Emily Suzanne
Baldwin, Holly
Baldwin, Kathleen M.
Baley, April
Balino, Clarence Q.
Balko, Christina K.
Balkon, Tessa
Ball, Adele
Ball, Heather Putman
Ballard, Bonnie R.
Ballard, Elaine C.
Ballard, Faye
Ballard, Mercy
Ballard, Teresa R.
Ballenger, Craig L.
Ballesteros, Marice W.
Ball-Martin, Donna J.
Ballou, Dana
Balog, Nick
Balser, Sarah
Baltazar, Marilyn Johnson
Baluja, Maria
Ban, Eunice E.
Bancroft, Marsha
Baney, Karen S.
Bang, Kathleen
Bangel, Cynthia
Baniul, Bette
Bankert, Brian J.
Banko, Illona R.
Banks, Emily
Banks, Gwendolyn A.
Banks, Kenneth
Banks, Regina L.
Banks, Sheri R.
Banks-Thornton, Keisha T.
Banlowe, Marilyn P.
Bannan, Olivia M.
Bannard, Linda M.
Bannister, Candida
Bannon, Adrienne B.
Bannon, Marybel
Banotai, Mary J.
Bansal, Bindia
Banuelos, Angelina S.
Banuelos, Diana M.
Banuelos, Susan
Baratta, Anna
Barbarotto, Anita C.
Barbas, Matthew J.
Barbato, Christine G.
Barbato, Rose Ann
Barbee, Sharon Serena
Barber, Amanda M.
Barber, Deborah

Barber, Joey
Barber, Kerri
Barber, Patricia G.
Barber, Stephanie C.
Barbosa, Victoria R.
Barbour, Holly R.
Barcinas, Tanya L.
Barclay, Justin P.
Barcome, Joy L.
Bard, Lynda
Bardley, Sherita M.
Barfield, Nancy
Barger, Nancy H.
Barham, Kristal Renee
Barker, Christopher L.
Barndt, Christine P.
Barker, Guy Patrick H.
Barker, Jason V.
Barker, Jennifer A.
Barker, Michaelene
Barker, Roberta D.
Barkin, Victoria
Barkley, Denzil R.
Barksdale, Sandra
Barnard, Guy Patrick H.
Barndt, Christine P.
Barnes, Brian E.
Barnes, Delois
Barnes, Diane C.
Barnes, Gail F.
Barnes, Karen Y.
Barnes, Tracy Jean
Barnett, Michael J.
Barnett, Paticia
Barnett-Chermak, Diane
Barnette, Deborah
Barnette, Marcia L.
Barney, Jane S.
Barney, Karen
Barnhardt, Jayne R.
Barnhart, Joanne M.
Barnwell, Maria M.
Barnwell, Marilyn M.
Baron, Chmere
Baronas, Amanda R.
Barosh, Janice E.
Barot, Lisa
Barr, Ann McKearin
Barr, Christopher C.
Barr, Marjorie A.
Barr, Valerie Daniels
Barragan, Dolores M.
Barrandey, Fatima
Barraza, Blanca
Barraza-Chavez, Blanka E.
Barrenechea, Chris
Barrenechea, Veronica
Barrera, Angela R.
Barrera, Maria E.
Barrett Deporter, Deborah Mae
Barrett, Barbara
Barrett, Estella Maria
Barrett, Robin S.
Barrett, Ryan
Barrett, Tonya
Barretta, Connie J.
Barretto-Jones, Pamela
Barrientos, Leigh A.
Barros, Marie I.
Barrows, Mary Bridget
Barry, Brittny C.
Barry, Carolyn S.
Barry, Christina M.
Barry, Pamela A.
Barry, Robin
Bartanen, Wendy Sue
Bartels, Barbara Jean
Barthel, Theresa L.
Bartholomew, Sallie P.
Bartholomew, Sandra
Bartholomew, Wanda F.
Bartlett, Emily S.
Bartlett, Linda
Barton, Amy L.
Barton, Neal J.
Barton, Sharon
Barua, Jayanta L.
Barwig, Jean L.

Basara, Linda A.
Basham, Audrey N.
Basil, June
Baskin, Daniel Benson
Baskin, Kathleen M.
Baskin, Lucretia B.
Baskin, Mark A.
Basnight, Delores A.
Bass, Jennifer
Bassitt, Gary Dean
Bastyr, Peggy A.
Bateman, Stacey
Bates, Cristina Renette
Bates, Heather L.
Bates, Jackie L.
Bates, Joanne
Bates, Julie Piano
Bates, Mary C.
Bates, Terry Lynn
Batra, Reeta
Batsuk, Yevgeniy
Battaglia, Sandra L.
Battenberg, Ruth Ann
Battin, Charles D.
Batts, Cheniu L.
Batumalai, Saroja
Baty, Virginia C.
Baudelaire, Maia
Baudler, Katherine
Bauer, Gail
Bauer, Hana M.
Baulch, Josh R.
Baulder, Katherine
Bauman, Molly A.
Bauman, Susan A.
Baumann, Betty Jane
Baumeister, Jerry J.
Baumer, Elizabeth J.
Baumgartner, Leslie
Baumhooger, Deborah
Baxley, Christopher K.
Baxter, Anna M.
Baxter, Jerid C.
Baxter, Linda L.
Bayang, Debbylynn J.
Bayer, James E.
Bayless, Mark
Bayless, Wendy F.
Bayudan, Kelly Ann S.
Beal, Davena
Beale, Janet
Beall, Melinda
Bealyer, Irmatine S.
Beam, Jan M.
Bean, Chad G.
Bear, Christopher J.
Bearce, Dori A.
Beard, Debra L.
Beard, Mary
Beard, Randall S.
Beard, Sheila J.
Beard, Suzanne M.
Bearden, Kathy
Beardsley, Lynda J.
Bearnson, Robert W.
Beasley, Christine R.
Beatty, Heather
Beatty, Monet M.
Beaty, Helen Cathy
Beaty, Tina
Beaubeaux, Terri L.
Beauchamp, Janice M.
Beaudin, Robin G.
Beaudoin, Greg
Beccaria, Lorna
Bechard, Tatiana
Beck, Brenda M.
Beck, Collin
Beck, Greg
Becker, Caryn Denise
Becker, Christine R.
Becker, Julie A.
Becker, Mary
Becker, Sheryl E.
Becker, Tamara M.
Beckmann, Terri

Beckwith, Christine A.
Becus, Lucie C.
Beddingfield, Milton O.
Bedillion, Laurie D.
Bedingfield, Milton O.
Bedner, Kelly J.
Bedner, Kimberly S.
Bedock, Lorianne
Bedsole, Keri A.
Bedwell, Michele
Beecher, Jacqueline M.
Beeler, Lisa C.
Beene, Erin
Beene, Tracey
Beers, Kristin
Beeson, Elizabeth A.
Beeson, Jessie H.
Beeson, Kim
Begay-Sullivan, Marie
Behar, Teri
Beharry, Adam W.
Behler, Paula J.
Behm, Patricia Ann
Behr, Mary
Behrens, Anastasia L.
Behrens, Brenda A.
Behyan, Sandra Lee
Beidelman, Cynthia L.
Beiler, Jay
Bein, Myrna E.
Beitman, Mary A.
Beladi, Kimberly A.
Belan, Joyce
Belanger, Darlene N.
Belanger, Delores R.
Belanger, Patricia A.
Belanger, Sharree A.
Belcher, Allan Raeanne
Belcher, Steven Lane
Belew, Mitchell L.
Belisle, Susan
Bell, Barbara B.
Bell, Catherine A.
Bell, Denise L.
Bell, Diana P.
Bell, Emma
Bell, Erin M.
Bell, Ferne
Bell, Janis S.
Bell, Melanie C.
Bell, Michael E.
Bell, Ricardo D.
Bell, Ronda
Bell, Sandra
Bell, Sharon K.
Bell, Wanda C.
Bellack, Sherry
Bellais, Alison
Bellamy, Sarah J.
Belland, Christine
Bellard, Diane
Bellard, Tanya L.
Bell-Dzide, Dodzi
Belle, Michelle P.
Bellefeuille, Sheri L.
Belles, Sally
Belli, Shauna M.
Bello, Elizabeth
Bellone, Alumine M.
Belotti, Marian L.
Belton, George R.
Beltran, Angelita
Beltran, Yvonne M.
Benavidez, Catherine
Benavidez, Elizabeth T.
Bender, Donna Odell
Bender, Lori
Bender, Lorraine
Bender, Marilyn A.
Bender, Rebecca S.
Bendict, Mary C.
Bendig, Ann M.
Bene, Christina B.
Benedict, Gary
Benedict, Joanna Kendall
Benedict, Paula

Benes, Amanda E.
Benesh, Susan J.
Benison, Lelia
Benites, Nora L.
Benitez, Diana
Benitez, Gladys
Benjamin, Alicia
Benjamin, Sheryl J.
Benman, Nannette
Bennett, Chandler E.
Bennett, Connie Lee
Bennett, Corinne C.
Bennett, Deborah
Bennett, Diane
Bennett, Elizabeth G. H.
Bennett, Ester M.
Bennett, Jolene M.
Bennett, Michael A.
Bennett, Regina F.
Bennett, Rita L.
Bennett, Sima C.
Bennett, Stephanie
Bennett, Tonia M.
Benneyworth, David L.
Bennion, Daniel H.
Bennion, Reagan Nichole
Benoist, Teresa A.
Benoit, Barbara
Benoit, Joan K.
Benoit, Susan
Bense, Dawn E.
Benske, Melanie Marie
Benson, Bonnie
Benson, Dayle C.
Benson, Susan L.
Benston, Linda Kay
Bentley, Blake S.
Bentley, Justin
Bentley, Karen Lee
Bentley, Nicole K.
Benton, Janice
Bentson, Amy E.
Bentz, Colleen
Berg, Susan M.
Berge, Shannon I.
Berger, Christopher Niles
Berger, Lisa P.
Berger, Stephen F.
Berger, Susan J.
Bergeron, Brian O.
Berggren, Gail Maria
Bergh, Bonnie K.
Bergman, Dawn M.
Bergman, Jennifer
Bergstrom, Marianne L.
Beringer, Beth L.
Berkat, Kimberly S.
Berkebile, Barbara
Berkheimer, Dorothy
Berkheimer, Sharon M.
Berkow, Bethany A.
Berkowitz, Ivonne Marie
Berman, Janet B.
Berman, Shari S.
Berman, Stuart
Bermudez, Denis G.
Bernacki, Felicity B.
Bernard, Jennifer Rene
Bernard, Micahel S.
Bernardino, Jedaliah T.
Berney, Karen L.
Bernick, Joan M.
Bernier, Lori A.
Bernotas, Stacy L.
Berns, Lacey
Berry, Barbara
Berry, Diane K.
Berryhill, Karen J.
Bertino, Selena R.
Bertolasio, Lisa
Bertolina, Amy
Bertram, Bethlyn K.
Bertrand, Sarah E.
Beshears, Edward A.
Bess, Cynthia L.
Bessette, Jeffrey

Best, Ruby D.
Beth, Susan L.
Betkis, Bobette S.
Betz, Janice L.
Betzler, Carol
Beyers, Melissa R.
Beyler, Anita
Bhadury, Mala
Bhamidipati, Shanti
Bialecki, Timothy Alvin
Bias, Stefanie N.
Bibyk, Connie Louise
Bicknell, Jean R.
Bicknell, Summer L.
Biederman, Phyllis W.
Biehler, Madeline A.
Bielefeld, Mary E.
Bielenberg, Susan K.
Bielon, Douglas G.
Bigam, Ann E.
Bigam, Kimberly R.
Bigaouette, Kathryn A.
Bigelow, Marcia
Biggs, Steven L.
Bihum, Charles W.
Bilings, John C.
Billal, Dyan
Billings, Gregory
Billings, John C.
Billingsley, Brian Eugene
Billingsley, Dawn K.
Billups, Danielle S.
Binder, Cathleen A.
Binder, Joan
Binder, Joanne
Binegar, Dani
Binette, Bruce R.
Bingham, Alan W.
Bingham, Jason D.
Bingham, Kay
Bingham, Sherry A.
Binhack, Marylynn
Binkley, Janet C.
Binning, Christal S.
Binnington, Jeannine A.
Binstock, Cathy
Birch, Jennifer C.
Bird, Kathryn
Bird, Keisha
Bird, Stephanie A.
Birk, Amanda M.
Birk, Benjamin A.
Birkelo, Marilyn
Birmingham, Gail C.
Bischoff, Judith M.
Bishop, Coral Z.
Bishop, Donna K.
Bishop, Jacqueline
Bishop, Joyce C.
Bishop, Rita J.
Bissonette, Susan
Bitler, Donald R.
Bitsoie, Jason W.
Bjornson, Carrie J.
Black, April
Black, Carl R.
Black, Diane E.
Black, Erika L.
Black, Linda S.
Black, Mary
Black, Mary E.
Black, Mary M.
Black, Michael V.
Black, Scott J.
Black, Sonja
Blackburn, Paul
Blackburn, Tracy
Blackmore, Christine
Blackstock, Kimberly Dawn
Blackwell, Mary K.
Blackwell, Scott R.
Blackwell, Tierra Nicole
Blackwood, Deri L.
Blaha, Janet M.
Blair, Danny Lee
Blair, Dennis James

Blair, Yun Kim
Blair-Robinson, Alberta L.
Blaisdell, Lynne
Blake, Lisette M.
Blake, Robert E.
Blakely, Richard
Blakemore, Christy L.
Blakemore, Yvette
Blakeney, Jakarta A.
Blalock, Anita C.
Blancas, Nancy S.
Blanchard, Dawn
Blanchette, Crispin S.
Bland, Belinda A.
Bland, Bernadette
Bland, David W.
Bland, Lori
Bland, Robert P.
Blangero, Jason
Blanke, Valerie L.
Blankenfeld, G'nette
Blankenship, Donanne
Blankenship, Sandra J.
Blankman, Greta
Blann, Jane A.
Blansett, Stephanie
Blanton, Margaret Palmer
Blasko, Pamela Ann
Blaszak, Michelle
Blaufuss, William F.
Blaugrund, Kevin D.
Blauth, Patricia Ann
Blaylock, Charlotte S.
Blaylock, Connie E.
Blaylock, Donna
Bleeckert, Susan M.
Blevins, Carrie Anne
Blezek, Kim
Bliffen, James E.
Blinder, Carol
Blinkhorn, Kara M.
Blissett, Christy L.
Blissett, Sasha G.
Blocher, Christopher R.
Block, Patrick A.
Blocker, Adene D.
Blocker, Cindy
Blocker, Shirlene
Blohm, Laura L.
Bloir, Muriel A.
Bloom, Michael
Blue, Sonya D.
Bluementhal, Martin
Blume, Betsy
Blume, Linda Schlamowitz
Blumenthal, Marian
Boarman, Ryan C.
Boase, Janice C.
Boateng, Vida Mae
Bobb, Christine
Bobbitt, Michelle
Bode, Alicia K.
Bodin, Deborah
Bodnar, Judith
Boecker, Dirk
Boehme, Odee Ann
Boersing, Catherine
Boersma, Robert Benjamin
Boes, John S.
Boesen, Lori J.
Boet, John B.
Boettcher, Marcia L.
Boggiano, Charles W.
Bogin, Esther L.
Bognar, Wendi W.
Bogolea, Christie L.
Boham, Kevin Lee
Bohanan, Amanda B.
Bohannon, Michael Kenneth
Bohen, Matthew
Bohman, Terre M.
Bohrman, Sherrie G.
Bojorquez, Dominic P.
Bojorquez, Melissa C.
Bolan, Lynda Hope
Boland, Ciria D.

Bolden, Daphne R.
Bolden, Johnnetta D.
Bolden, Judy W.
Boldrey, Joan M.
Bolds, Jacqueline Coston
Boles, Sonya L.
Boley, Sheree
Bolinger, Fredia
Bolser, Kimberly
Bolton, Carol Marie
Bombace, Theresa A.
Bommarito, Connie J.
Bommarito, James J.
Bond, Anthony
Bondeson, Jennifer A.
Bone, Michael C.
Bone, Robert C.
Boneberg, Cecelia A.
Boney, Krystina
BonGiorni, Joa
Bonilla-Ochoa, Karen I.
Boniog, Rhona C.
Bonner, Debra
Bonnett, Rhonda S.
Bonnett, Tamara L.
Bonney, Joel
Bonoan, Eugenia A.
Booker, Charles W.
Booker, Teresa
Booker, Toni V.
Boone, Kimberly D.
Boonsue, Kelly A.
Boore, Pamela
Booth, Nancy
Booth, Ulla
Borchert, Robert P.
Borden, Linda J.
Borkland, Donna
Bornes, Patricia D.
Bornhoft, Kristi M.
Bornt, Jeremy S.
Borough, Andrea A.
Borrego, Anna L.
Borts, Rebecca Lynne
Borusiewicz, Loraine
Bose, Jeremy C.
Boshoff, Marelise
Bosic, Sharon E.
Bosler, Kimberly
Boss, Audrey B.
Bossert, Marie C.
Boswell, James D.
Boswell, Regina D.
Boteler, Lana M.
Boteler, Tamra
Bott, Bridget M.
Bottoms, R. Calvin
Botz, Karen A.
Boughter, Jacqueline Jean
Boulton, Crystal R.
Boulton, Jennifer E.
Bounds, Eric M.
Bourgeault, Jessica M.
Bourgeois, Ina A.
Bourgeois, Melissa W.
Bourgeois, Tina
Bourne, Lorie Ann
Bova, Michelle
Bowen, Angela E.
Bowen, Brenda J.
Bowen, Patricia H.
Bowens, Sylvia M.
Bowerman, Michelle E. L.
Bowers, Linda L.
Bowers, Sabina Anne
Bowery, Kay
Bowker-Davis, Valerie A.
Bowland, Amy R.
Bowland, Thresa J.
Bowler, Ann E.
Bowler, Carol L.
Bowles, Heather B.
Bowling, Kevin R.
Bowman, Glynel Ann
Bowman, Greg
Bowman, Jan

Bowman, Jennifer D.
Bowman, Joseph H.
Bowman, Shelley E.
Bowser, Amy
Box, Kathleen
Box, Ryan
Boyd, Constance Joanne
Boyd, Cynthia L.
Boyd, Gale L.
Boyd, Leonard Thomas
Boyd, Lisa
Boyd, Mark L.
Boyed, Georgia
Boyer, Jamie L.
Boyer, Regina L.
Boyes, Claudia K.
Boyette, Rupert M.
Boyette, Sherri
Boykin, Jeanna M.
Boylan, Marion
Boyle, Ann
Boyle, Beverly K.
Boyle, Bonnie M.
Boyle, Catherine
Boyle, Deborah R.
Bozarth, Lynzee M.
Bozicevich, Mary K.
Bozik, Laura A.
Brabec, Sally A.
Brabson, Danielle D.
Brace, Brandon
Brack, Jeannette Olsen
Brack, John P.
Brack, Mona S.
Brackney, Dana E.
Bracy, Teresa
Bradbury, Linnea M.
Braddock, Leighton M.
Bradford, Elizabeth L.
Bradford, Fay M.
Bradford, Kimberly T.
Bradford, Lynda B.
Bradford, Peter L.
Bradley, Cassius D.
Bradley, Chastity
Bradley, Delaine C.
Bradley, Kathleen S.
Bradley, Melissa F.
Bradley, Nell Hunt
Bradley, Sharon K.
Bradshaw, Keith A.
Bradshaw, Lonnie
Bradshaw, Martha L.
Bradshaw, William Daniel
Brady, Francis M.
Brady, Freddie
Brady, Jennifer A.
Brady, Shirley A.
Brailey, Bonita
Braley, Dawnella M.
Braley, John F.
Braly, Keith Alan
Bramble, Betty Lee
Brancato, Janet
Branch, Shelly
Brandenburg, Mark Conlin
Branders, Kathryn N.
Brandes, Kathryn N.
Brandjes, Bonnie G.
Brandl, Sandra Rosenberg
Brandon, Carole
Brandt, Aulikki M.
Brandt, Cheryl
Brandt, Deborah L.
Brandt, Freida
Brandt, Kathleen
Brannen, Deborah A.
Brannen, Janine
Brannon, Jerry D.
Bransford, Henry M.
Branski, Sherri H.
Branstad, Susan
Branton, Vicky C.
Brashear, Brian
Brashear, Sarah J.
Brasher, Michael R.

Brassell, Kelly J.
Brasswell, Melissa A.
Brast, Amy
Bratcher, Sharon G.
Brau, Jennifer H.
Braucci, Louis J.
Braxmeyer, Debra
Bray, Patricia Ann
Brazelton, A. Ruth
Breckenridge, Kathryn S.
Breda, Linda
Bredeson, Nicole A.
Breece, Lara L.
Breece, Russell
Breen, Teresa M.
Brehmer, Marcella
Breinig, Diane M.
Breiten, Ella Louise
Brekke, Paula
Bremer, David A.
Brenberger, Mark L.
Brennan, Angela Acquista
Brennan, Brenda
Brennan, Thomas
Brenneman-Bell, Sherri
Brenner, Linda K.
Bressler, Sharlene Lee
Brethauer, Cathleen F.
Brett, Georgeann
Brett, Melinda
Bretz, Jennifer E.
Breunig, Sarah E. F.
Brewer, Julie K.
Brewer, Kimberly Ann
Brewer, Michael M.
Brewer, Regina
Brewitz, Marlo Marie
Brewster, BobbieJo
Brewster, Teresa
Brian, Kathleen
Brick, Malinda S.
Brickl, Craig J.
Bridges, Cynthia V.
Bridges, Krista
Briggs, Angela D.
Briggs, Lee
Briggs, Nancy
Bright, Donna L.
Briley, Idella
Bringley, Patrice R.
Brink, Carol E.
Brink, Judy
Brink, Prentice L.
Brinkman, Erin M.
Brisco, Vanessa
Briscoe, Tita S.
Briscoe, Vanessa Jones
Briseno, Barbara J.
Brissette, Matthew P.
Bristow, James M.
Bristow, Nancy
Brito, Magna
Britt, Carrie Louise
Brittain, Jennifer S.
Brittain, Susanne
Britton, Meredith E.
Brletic, Jeri S.
Broadhurst, Craig M.
Broadus, Eric S.
Brocato, Laurie K.
Broccolino, Donna
Brock, Mayveline S.
Brock, Shana Lynne
Brocklehurst, Laura L.
Brockman, Melanie J.
Brockmann, Michelle T.
Broderick, Adealia
Brodwin, Andrea
Brogley, Jennifer L.
Bronshteyn, Katerina
Bronson, Tina R.
Brooks, Anne
Brooks, Celetta M.
Brooks, Denise C.
Brooks, Donna W.
Brooks, Eleanor Lockwood

Brooks, Jasmine G.
Brooks, Laurence E.
Brooks, Leigh A.
Brooks, Leigh Ann
Brooks, Nicole K.
Brooks, Rehonna E.
Brooks, Sandra L.
Brooks, Stephen
Brooks, Teresa
Brooks, Vanetta J.
Brooks, William
Broom, Carolyn M.
Broome, Richard G.
Brosnahan, Gary W.
Brost, Bonita M.
Brost, Mary
Broster, Sally J.
Brothers, James S.
Brotherton, Joyce R.
Brotherton, Pamela D.
Brotmeyer, Celeste C.
Brougham, Alice
Broughton, Jane
Broughton, Saran S.
Brouillette, Joseph
Broussard, Martha J.
Broussard, Michelle
Broussard, Sandra
Brown, Adam M.
Brown, Amber Rose
Brown, Andrea Yvette
Brown, Anita L.
Brown, Audra L.
Brown, Brenda
Brown, Carolyn A.
Brown, Christopher W.
Brown, Claudia H.
Brown, Deborah M.
Brown, Denise K.
Brown, Diana W.
Brown, Donald B.
Brown, Donna J.
Brown, Elaine
Brown, Elizabeth
Brown, Eufa J.
Brown, Gary L.
Brown, Heavenly
Brown, Helleen D.
Brown, Holly L.
Brown, Jacqueline
Brown, Jane H.
Brown, Joan E.
Brown, Karen
Brown, Katherine G.
Brown, Katina Lorise
Brown, Katrainer L.
Brown, Kelly J.
Brown, Keyonda K.
Brown, Lavell A.
Brown, Lawrence D.
Brown, Linda
Brown, Marla R.
Brown, Michael David
Brown, Michele R.
Brown, Nancy Wingate
Brown, Natalie R.
Brown, Page
Brown, Pamela J.
Brown, Rachel G.
Brown, Richard
Brown, Ronald E.
Brown, Ruma J.
Brown, Ryan P.
Brown, Sabrina
Brown, Sharnell
Brown, Sharon R.
Brown, Shirley A.
Brown, Susanne J.
Brown, Tamara T.
Brown, Tammy H.
Brown, Terri
Brown, Tracy Ellen
Brown, Valerie
Brown, Verbest S.
Brown, William Z.
Browne-Williams, Marilyn E.

Browning, Jan
Browning, Jean
Brownlee, Crystal Elaine
Brownlow, Kimberly M.
Brown-Ratcliff, Kiah M.
Brozek, Sally A.
Brubaker, Stephanie A.
Bruce, Kesa
Bruce, Phyllis
Bruce, William J.
Bruckert, Rebecca S.
Bruder, Mary Ann
Brueckner, Stefen F.
Bruehl, Christine L.
Bruenger, Ellen Sue
Brugman, Peggy Ann
Bruick, Carol A.
Bruick, Susan C.
Brumbach, Edward
Brumit, Tricia D.
Brumm, Jennifer M.
Brune, Lori L.
Bruno, Anthony G.
Bruno, Phyllis A.
Brunotte, Carol A.
Bruns, Brittany
Bruns, Jeanette
Bryan, Bryson T.
Bryan, Carol J.
Bryan, Charles J.
Bryan, Tammy L.
Bryant, Daraunda L.
Bryant, Delphane A.
Bryant, Holly J.
Bryant, Jennifer B.
Bryant, Karen M.
Bryant, Kenneth G.
Bryant, Lucinia K.
Bryant, Martha L.
Bryant, Ronata N.
Bryant, Rosemary
Bryant, Taisha W.
Bryngelson, Mary
Brynildson, Amy D.
Bryson, Katherine S.
Buabeng, Yvonne A.
Bucci, Kathleen M.
Buccilli, Elena Maria
Buchan, Bobbie J.
Buchanan, Angela R.
Buchanan, Brandi E.
Buchanan, Deborah M.
Buchanan, Donna M.
Buchanan, Haylee I.
Buchanan, Jamie M.
Bucher, Jr., Robert L.
Buck, Rebecca R.
Buckingham, Michelle
Buckley, Alicia
Buckley, Sharon
Buckley, Suzanne
Buckner, Kenneth R.
Buckner, Matthew M.
Budd, Susan J.
Budge, Eldon J.
Budgett, Marsha
Budness, Ann Marie
Bueler, Michelle
Bueltel, Blake K.
Bueno, Linda S.
Buffaloe, Chaundra M.
Buffington, Jaclyn A.
Bufford, Crystal J.
Bukhin, Mike
Bukva, Emir
Bull, Deborah D.
Bulot, Carolyn D.
Bunch, Kim Kuziola
Bundren, Bernice M.
Bunkers-Lawson, Theresa
Buno, Loreto
Buntin, E. Frazer
Bunting, Chandra N.
Bunting, Chanel D.
Bunty, Kathy
Bunty, Ryan M.

Buntyn, Miriam C.
Buonincontro, Angela R.
Burch, Carol C.
Burch, Mary Ann
Burch, Melvin W.
Burch, Michael N.
Burch, Terri
Burden, Lezlie W.
Burden, Lisa Marie
Burdette, Brett R.
Burdine, Wilma D.
Bureau, Pamela M.
Buren, Elizabeth A.
Burfeind, Philip A.
Burgan, Michelle J.
Burgan, Scott W.
Burger, Alice May S.
Burgeson, Pamela
Burgeson, Robin E.
Burgess, Annetta S.
Burgess, Debra J.
Burgess, Erna C.
Burgess, R. Jerry
Burgess, Timothy W.
Burgesson, Pamela
Burghduff, Tammi J.
Burgher, Beverly
Burgler, Traci M.
Burgos, Lori A.
Burgoyne, Susan
Burhans, Patricia J.
Buritsch, Kathleen L.
Burk, Alice R.
Burkard, Christina M.
Burke, Michele M.
Burke, Victoria A.
Burkemper, Robin M.
Burkey, James C.
Burkhart, John W.
Burkhead, Leslie
Burkhouse, Michael D.
Burks, James K.
Burks, William E.
Burlakoff, Terry
Burlette, Cynthia S.
Burley, B. Diane
Burley, Donna
Burlingham, Mary Lou
Burlison, Lori
Burmeister, Robert J.
Burn, Cora
Burn, Patton B.
Burner, David Nelson
Burnett, Sharon
Burnette, Andrea M.
Burnette, Heidi L.
Burney, Angela M.
Burnham, Amy R.
Burnham, Christine E.
Burno, Tonnitra R.
Burns, Eric J.
Burns, Ginny
Burns, Jeanne A.
Burns, Joanne
Burns, Jonathan A.
Burns, Sandy
Burreau, Pamela M.
Burrell, Shana
Burrell, Thomas S.
Burroughs, Jill
Burrous, Jennifer N.
Burrus, Cynthia G.
Burson, Ernest N.
Burson, Linda W.
Burton, Angela
Burton, Annette
Burton, Barbara A.
Burton, Corey D.
Burton, Deborah J.
Burton, Karen J.
Burton, Kiela
Burwell Phillips, Chowan
Busby, Leanne
Busch, Sarah
Busche, Jr., Arthur F.
Buscher, Robert

Bush, Carri
Bush, Donna Kay
Bush, James
Bush, Janet A.
Bush, Jason P.
Bush-Foster, Sydney H.
Bushman, Lori
Bushno, Delores J.
Buskohl, Debra A.
Buss, Megan K.
Bussard, Lisa J.
Busser, Karen
Bustria, Trini
Butcher, Laura L.
Buterbaugh, Yvonne
Butkovich, Judith A.
Butler, Denise E.
Butler, Jacob
Butler, Jean L.
Butler, John
Butler, Joy
Butler, Karen Olson
Butler, Lyndsey N.
Butler, Michelle
Butler, Nancy L.
Butler, Susan L.
Butler, Teresa L.
Butterfield, Alleene L.
Butterworth, Carolyn A.
Button, Elaine
Buttry, Kyle M.
Butts, Kristi R.
Butts, Ronald E.
Butturini, Russell N.
Butym, Diane M.
Butzow, Robert E.
Buyze, Michael T.
Byas, Kimberly R.
Byerly, Michele
Byers, Susan C.
Bynum, Matthew D.
Byrd, Douglas D.
Byrd, Lori H.
Byrd, Patrick D.
Byrne, Patricia Ann
Byrnes, Elena K.
Byrnes, Kelly

C

Cabacungan, Lou
Cable, James S.
Cable, Jerri
Cabradilla, Madeline G.
Cabreros, Anita S.
Caccavaro, John
Caddell, Stephanie Jones
Cadelina, Rosita
Cadman, Elaine E.
Cadorette, Lynne J.
Cadwell, John W.
Caffey, Susan A.
Cagan, Andrew
Cagle, Jessica E.
Cahalin, Britney
Chacon, Martha L.
Cahill, Kirsten L.
Chambers, Sandy
Caiafa, Kelli L.
Cain, Candace S.
Cain, Cynthia J.
Cain, Kimberly
Cain, Marjorie B.
Cain, Martha
Cain, William R.
Cairns, Jeffrey A.
Cairns, Susan E.
Calabrese, Thomas
Calanchi, Silvia
Calcaterra, Andrea E.
Calcaterra, Ellen M.
Caldwell, Heather L.
Caldwell, La Sondra Roshay
Caldwell, Rebecca M.
Caldwell, Robert
Caldwell-McEwen, Cristan M.

Calefate, Elizabeth M.
Caless, Patricia K.
Calhoun, Janet
Calhoun, Janet S.
Calhoun, Krisann
Calise, Diane
Calivo, Leilani Ann C.
Calkins, Lauren M.
Callahan, Janice
Callahan, Judith Ann
Callaway, Everett R.
Callea, Nancy L.
Callerstrom, Mary A.
Calliste, Sandra C.
Callowborgeson, Carl H.
Calton, Amy K.
Calvert, Denise Ann
Calvert, Kristen N.
Calvert, Roger W.
Calvert, Tamara J.
Calvin, Cindy
Calvin, Janie
Calvo, Alicia
Camacho, Anna M.
Camacho, Maria Cristina
Cambridge, Carole
Cambronero, Jovi O.
Cameron, Kimberly C.
Camesi, Karen J.
Campanella, Patricia Ann
Campbell, Alan B.
Campbell, Amy L.
Campbell, Bernadette A.
Campbell, Carolyn S.
Campbell, Catherine J.
Campbell, Craig R.
Campbell, Emily E.
Campbell, George
Campbell, Hilary Beth
Campbell, Julia
Campbell, Kelly A.
Campbell, Marie H.
Campbell, Mary Ellen K.
Campbell, Mozelle M.
Campbell, Nina L.
Campbell, Patti Elaine
Campbell, Rita M.
Campbell, Stacey R.
Campbell, Stephen P.
Campbell, Susan A.
Campbell, Tonia D.
Campbell, Tracey M.
Camper, Samuel L.
Campos, Cheryl L.
Campos, Lani
Campos, Mary L.
Canaan, Joyce A.
Canclini, Kathleen M.
Candini, Susan R.
Cannavo, Valerie J.
Cannefax, Donna Sue
Cannella, Jerome Jay
Cannella, Melaca M.
Cannella, Rita
Cannizzo, Colleen A.
Cannon, Heidi L.
Cannon, Jennifer L.
Cannon, Kerri K.
Cannon, Sean J.
Cannon, Tonya Juel
Canova, Debra L.
Cantrell, Carrie B.
Cantrell, Ronald K.
Cantwell, Brook A.
Canty, Thelma
Canyette, Cory N.
Cape, Jeremy
Cape, Scarlett S.
Capella, Sandra
Capelle, Angela R.
Capezzuto, Elaine S.
Capili, Cynthia O.
Caplan, Laurel G.
Capley, Carlon D.
Carbone, Mary K.
Carbone, Susan J.

Carden, Barbara H.
Carden, Judith Ann
Carden, Mallory Lynn
Carder, Ann Marie
Cardinal, Dorcas A.
Cardinale, Mary M.
Cardoze, Victoria N.
Carey, Bernellyn M.
Carey, Georgia S.
Carey, LeAnna J.
Carey, Margaret
Carey, Roger J.
Carey, Susan E.
Carl, Kathleen
Carl, Martha
Carl, Rebecca L.
Carleton, Stephanie
Carlis, Cherry
Carlisle Whitney, Virginia A.
Carlisle, Christie
Carlisle, Michelle M.
Carlos, Geraldine G.
Carlotto, Rita R.
Carlson, Allison
Carlson, Eric L.
Carlson, Gary C.
Carlson, Kathy
Carlson, Lois
Carlson, Lorrie R.
Carlson, Madonna M.
Carlson, Mary C.
Carlson, Rachael M.
Carlson, William Y.
Carlsson, Mary A.
Carlton, John Patrick
Carlton, Tracey L.
Carlton, Trisha Deverne
Carlz, Susan E.
Carmack, David L.
Carman, Teresa A.
Carmichael, Lori J.
Carmicle, Marcus
Carmody, Susan
Carmona, Marco A.
Carney, Bettie G.
Carney, Dayna F.
Carney, Jane M.
Caron, Noelle S.
Carosso, Nancy A.
Carpenter, Angie M.
Carpenter, Carol A.
Carpenter, Cheryl
Carpenter, Christy
Carpenter, Edna M.
Carpenter, Elizabeth J.
Carpenter, Lee Charles
Carpenter, Lori D.
Carpenter, N.
Carpenter, Patricia Lynn
Carpenter, Sandra
Carper, Norma E.
Carr, Amy
Carr, Carol J.
Carr, Christopher M.
Carr, David W.
Carr, Debra L.
Carr, Holly
Carr, James M.
Carr, Julie K.
Carr, Lori Q.
Carr, Mindy
Carr, Susan P.
Carragher, Jennifer A.
Carrasco, Donald G.
Carreira, Virginia
Carreon, Hector M.
Carrick, Terence Noel
Carrier, Brenda J.
Carrillo, Daniela N.
Carrington, Joan M.
Carrizal, Maria D.
Carroll, Donna C.
Carroll, Frances P.
Carroll, Lyndsay E.
Carroll, Nancy E.
Carroll, Rick

Carroll, Walter James
Carroll-Grant, Patricia
Carruth, Tyler R.
Carruthers, Donna J.
Carsky-Schroeder, Cecelia
Carson, Gail
Carson, Matthew G.
Carson, Stephanye A.
Carstarphen, William M.
Carter, Andrew W.
Carter, Annetta S.
Carter, Arlene K.
Carter, Barbara Jean
Carter, Carol V.
Carter, Daniel
Carter, Deborah L.
Carter, Frank F.
Carter, Gloria J.
Carter, Karen L.
Carter, Loletta D.
Carter, Mary P.
Carter, Michelle Pateece
Carter, Paul Derrick
Carter, Wetona
Carter-Coleman, Debra J.
Cartter, Christian T.
Cartwright, Ann Moore
Cartwright, Catherine
Carver, Thomas G.
Carville, Karen G.
Cary, Tiara T.
Carzoli-Gupta, Sonia
Casalone, Donna G.
Casanova, Kristin
Casazza, Regina D.
Casbarar, Patricia
Case, Ann
Case, Mary Lou
Case, Paula J.
Case, Theresa D.
Casey, Cheryl Russell
Casey, Kathleen
Cash-Finamore, Carlotta
Cashion, Rebecca
Cashiotta-Munn, Monica
Casper, Tricia A.
Cassada, Jerri R.
Cassada, William E.
Cassavant, Thomas John
Casse, Virginia H.
Cassel, Jennifer L.
Cassel, Kathryn L.
Cassiday, Brian S.
Cassoday, Peggy L.
Nunez, Orestes E.
Castaneda, Melissa
Casteneda, Sylvia
Castle, Trinity A.
Castner, Nancy
Castracane, Josephine M.
Castro, Joy
Castro, Marilou S.
Castrow, Henry C.
Cataldi, Dana M.
Catchings, Monica
Cates, Deanna L.
Cates, Tina L.
Cathcart, Cheryle
Catherman, Kelly L.
Cathey, Kathleen F.
Catlett, Linda
Catliff, Stacie
Cato, Sheila
Catrow, Henry C.
Catton, Elizabeth A.
Caudill, Janet
Caudill, Melissa G.
Cavaliere, Cynthia A.
Cavanaugh, Susan D.
Cavender, Keith A.
Caver-Werts, Bathrenia Arllentia
Cawthon, Catherine
Cazares, Sarah E.
Cearfoss, Victoria L.
Cedeno, Sonia M.
Cela, Thelma

Celania, Lee Ann
Celis, Josephine
Celko, Virginia
Cellers, Deborah O.
Cephus, Alexandria R.
Cerbo, H. Grace I.
Cereno, Glenn L.
Ceresini, Rita
Cerrillo, Gilbert C.
Cervola, Paul J.
Chabot, Andre
Chacon, Martha L.
Chadwell, Lesley L.
Chadwick, Sarah Ruth
Chafatelli, Joseph A.
Chaffin, James E.
Chaffin, Robert J.
Chahal, Jasvir K.
Chahanovich, Ellen P.
Chahanovich, Kelly C.
Chaisitiphol, Emily L.
Chalupa, Patricia A.
Chambers, James Chance
Chambers, Sandy
Chan, Allison E.
Chan, Henry H.
Chanandin, Aasif M.
Chandler, Andrea K.
Chandler, Grace L.
Chandler, Jordan
Chandler, Mary Jo
Chandler, Nancy
Chandler, Nicola V.
Chandler, Ogie
Chandler, Philip L.
Chandler, Sarah M.
Chandra, Madhuri Lata
Chandrakumar, Nirusha
Chaney, Jennifer G.
Channabasappa, Monica
Channabasappa, Sneha
Channell, Kathi G.
Channer, Maryflor C.
Chaparro, Jessica
Chapin Patch, Emilie A.
Chapin, Gail
Chapman, Ileana
Chapman, Jane A.
Chapman, Lara
Chapman, Sheila
Chapman, Yvonne A.
Chaput, Catherine A.
Chaput, Mary
Chaput, Robert L.
Charchenko, Bradley J.
Chardon, Ana M.
Charles, Clarisia K.
Charles, Marylyn E.
Charles, Rosemary
Charlesworth, Deborah
Charlinski, Pauline M.
Charmok, Monica A.
Charmoli, Michael J.
Charnell, Kathleen A.
Chase, Melanie L.
Chasse, Virginia H.
Chastain, Lorraine
Chatterjee, Ripple A.
Chattopadhyay, Pranjali
Chau, Pauline
Chavez, Julia A.
Chavez, Leonor
Chavez, Valerie
Chavez, Vikki
Cheek, Cheryl
Cheek, Elizabeth A.
Cheeseman, Janice
Cheeves, Deborah H.
Cheney, Jean
Cheney, Jessica L.
Chenoweth, Jane H.
Cherette-Accilien, Mirielle
Chermak, Kim M.
Cherry, Tonita J.
Chesnut, John G.
Chester, Mike

Chester, Regina Gail
Chester, Tina Marie
Cheuvront, Michelle
Chevalier, Louise G.
Chiavetta, Eileen P.
Chiesa-Gaul, Maureen
Chiguluri, Srinivas
Chilcoat, Anita B.
Chilcote, Lisa
Childers, Dona
Childress, Leslie T.
Childress, Lillian Sue
Childs, Belinda L.
Childs, Cheryl A.
Childs, James N.
Chippendale, Renee L.
Chirrey, Carolyn
Chischillie, Rose A.
Chitwood, Martha M.
Chivalette, Frank
Choate, Jeanette M.
Choi, Seunghee
Choice, Chinyere A.
Choueiri, Peter
Chow, Teenie
Christensen, Camille
Christensen, Cole M.
Christensen, Janie
Christensen, Joanne L.
Christensen, Lora L.
Christenson, Grant A.
Christian, Cherrel A.
Christian, Deborah
Christiansen, Kenner Roy
Christianson, Alan L.
Christodoulou, Kathleen
Christol, Jeremy B.
Christopher, Corliss A.
Christy, Anne
Chu, Linda T.
Chun, Davelynn C. N.
Chung, Richard S.
Chunnu, Pauline
Church, Martha Jo
Church, Melissa L.
Church, Paula A.
Churchward, Estela A.
Chute, Kimberley I.
Chyan, Chieh-Chieh
Chylack, Kristina
Chyung, Jay H.
Ciallella, Lisa
Cianchini, Margarita
Cianfrone, Carolyn
Cichocki, Brenda M.
Ciciora, Cindy
Cielieska, Mary
Ciestelka, Robert
Cigarran, Christopher
Cigarran, Thomas G.
Cimonetti, Marilyn S.
Cinlar, Teresa Maria
Cintron de Alvarez, Iris N.
Ciranowicz, Marlene M.
Cisneros, Raziel
Claiborne, Linda Debra
Clair, Rosemarie R.
Clamp, Sherri L.
Clancy, Crystal C.
Clancy, Joan M.
Clancy, Stephen B.
Clapp, Deborah A.
Clapper, Mary
Clare, Eileen J.
Clarin, Lynn
Clark, Alicia L.
Clark, Ann S.
Clark, Bobby L.
Clark, Christopher L.
Clark, Cynthia S.
Clark, Dana K.
Clark, Dana M.
Clark, Deanna
Clark, Delores
Clark, Derick L.
Clark, Grant A.

Clark, Karen L.
Clark, Karon L.
Clark, Katharine
Clark, Kathryn L.
Clark, Kimberly D.
Clark, Lindsay E.
Clark, Lisa P.
Clark, Michelle Diane
Clark, Patricia
Clark, Pindi P.
Clark, Sandra J.
Clark, Stacey J.
Clark, Susan
Clark, Talitha D.
Clark, William
Clarke, Charla M.
Clarke, Dana H.
Clarke, Marsha L.
Clarke, Ronald D.
Clarke, Sue Ellin G.
Clatfelter, Evan L.
Claudio, Virginia
Claudon, Barbara Ann
Clauser, Elizabeth A.
Clawson, April J.
Claxton, Violet E.
Claypool, Sally L.
Clayton, Karlin G.
Clayton, Melissa Anne
Clayton, Rebecca
Clayton, Rosalie M.
Clayton, Wanda S.
Clear, Timothy
Cleary, Dian
Cleary, Timothy P.
Clegg, Robert L.
Cleland, Linda J.
Clemens, Brenda Kay
Clemenshaw, Jennifer Ann
Clement, Idie E.
Clements, Cherilyn M.
Clements, Darla J.
Clements, Idie E.
Clements, Kathryn E.
Clements, Michelle J.
Clements, Nancy A.
Clemons, Amber B.
Clemons, Gregory R.
Clemons, Lizbeth L.
Cleveland, Denise M.
Clevenger, Patricia D.
Clevenger, Sandra
Clever, Mary
Clever, Teresa F.
Clines, Peter A.
Clinton, Rita F.
Cloutier, Kristy
Coach, Antonia R.
Coate, Joy
Cobb, Janice D.
Cobb, Mary Ellen
Cobb, Nathan
Cobbett, Jane
Coberley, Carter Ray
Coberley, Sadie S.
Cobian, Janelle
Coburn, Chanese L.
Coburn, Dolly S.
Cochran, Amy T.
Cochran, Donna L.
Cochran, Jacqueline L.
Cochran, Jeffrey T.
Cochran, Mark A.
Cochran, Mary Elizabeth
Cochran, Tara
Coco, Kathy Ann
Codalata, John
Codd, Maryann
Codney, Catherine A.
Cody, Barbara A.
Cody, Sarah A.
Cody-Hunnefeld, Sarah
Coe, Emily S.
Coerver, Robert
Coetzer, Henriette E.
Coffey, William S.
Coffman Humphreys, Carol

Coffman, Madonna A.
Cogar, Karon L.
Cogdell, Susan W.
Cohen, Barry M.
Cohen, Dianne W.
Cohen, Erica L.
Cohen, Jaimie L.
Cohen, Leonard M.
Cohen, Robert A.
Cohen, Sandra H.
Coker, Jill A.
Colagiovanni, Tara D.
Colberg, Sheri
Colbert, Ana Ming
Colbert, Chimere R.
Colbert, Cindy K.
Colby, Jennifer Downs
Coldiron, Laura L.
Cole, Bryan R.
Cole, Danielle H.
Cole, Donna Lee
Cole, Elizabeth H.
Cole, Judy C.
Cole, Kathryn
Cole, Lorraine
Cole, Ronnie D.
Cole, Teresa M.
Cole-Jackson, Celestine W.
Coleman, Alean W.
Coleman, Cheryll Lynne
Coleman, Kevin R.
Coleman, Lillie
Coleman, Melanee J.
Coleman, Melissa L.
Coleman, Robin
Coles, Sheila
Coley, Latonia M.
Colgan, Kelli C.
Colin, Michele
Collar, Keith T.
Collier, Peggy A.
Collier, Tamera L.
Collier, Theresa A.
Collier, Tijuana N.
Collings, Zarita A.
Collins, Anjanette
Collins, Arlethea
Collins, Bernadette K.
Collins, Brenda L.
Collins, Candice M.
Collins, Catherine A.
Collins, Cecilia A.
Collins, Cheryl Gilchrist
Collins, Christian E.
Collins, Christy S.
Collins, Dee-Anne A.
Collins, Dia S.
Collins, Gene
Collins, Heather D.
Collins, Jessica Danielle
Collins, Kim
Collins, Kristi J.
Collins, Melanie H.
Collins, Ruth L.
Collins, Sandra K.
Collins, Shane
Collins, Vincen
Collom, Marri P.
Colon, Jose
Colon, Norma
Colquitt, Kendra K.
Colston, Barbara C.
Colton, Karen L.
Coltoon, Barbara J.
Comas, Marie H.
Combass, Elizabeth F.
Combs, Camille P.
Comer, Connie
Comer, David D.
Comiskey, Laura Burrow
Commito, Michael A.
Compau, Thomas P.
Compiseno, Elizabeth A.
Compton, Timothy
Comstock, Deborah
Concepcion Acevedo, Wanda Ivette

Concepcion, Elisa A.
Conco, Diana
Conde, Veronica A.
Cone, Robert M.
Conell, Jill R.
Coneys, Charlene M.
Confalone, Kenneth
Confer, Eva M.
Conger, Leslie A.
Conklin, Amanda M.
Conklin, Christina
Conley, Carla L.
Conley, Cherie
Conley, Jennifer S.
Conley, Jonathan
Conley, Kirby
Conley, Nadine S.
Conley, Nicole C.
Conley, Shelly
Conlin, Tammy C.
Conly, Elizabeth M.
Connally, Gena Hunt
Connelly, Patti W.
Connelly, Shirley V.
Connelly, Suni M.
Connelly, William P.
Conner, Kelly R.
Conner, Kenneth R.
Conner, Margaret D.
Connor, Anne M.
Connor, Brownie A.
Connor, Georgette E.
Conrad, Eliza Eve
Conrad, Michael
Conroy, Patricia M.
Constantine, Judith M.
Constantino, Janet R.
Conti, Lisa A.
Contreras, Gaudiosa S.
Controy, Jason P.
Conway, Casey Nicole
Conyer-McNaught, Julie G.
Cook, Andrew P.
Cook, Barbara A.
Cook, Danielle A.
Cook, Darlene Elizabeth
Cook, Doris A.
Cook, Elizabeth
Cook, Emily N.
Cook, Gail P.
Cook, John Charles
Cook, Karen
Cook, Kathleen L.
Cook, Kay Carlette
Cook, Lindsay B.
Cook, Lynn
Cook, Maureen
Cook, Nancy
Cook, Paula D.
Cook, Rebecca V.
Cook, Rutha J.
Cook, Sarah Joy
Cool, Amanda M.
Cooley, Susan M.
Coomber, Josephine L.
Coombs, Debbie L.
Coombs, Diana J.
Cooper, Celeste A.
Cooper, Cynthia L.
Cooper, D'Lee B. M.
Cooper, Dawn
Cooper, Deborah Kay
Cooper, Donna J.
Cooper, Linda A.
Cooper, Russ
Cooper, Steven M.
Cooper, Theresa Annette
Coopersmith, Jeral
Copeland, Bert O.
Copeland, Janet J.
Copenbarger, Ginger
Coppedge, Debra A.
Coppess, Douglas
Corbett, Victor
Corbin, Heather B.
Corcoran, Eileen Marie

Corcoran, MaryJo
Cordell, Garrett
Cordell, Janet L.
Cordero, Edwina B.
Cordova, Ronnie Daniel
Core, Jennifer Chelsea
Core, Teresa King
Corea, Michael
Corison, Deborah
Corlett, Doris D.
Corley, Diane M.
Corley, Teresa A.
Corliss, Carrie J.
Cornejo, Karrie
Cornelison, Marie W.
Cornelius, Mark
Cornell, Jill Renae
Cornett, Victor
Cornwell, Bridget L.
Corpuz, Eugenio
Corral, Marthaelena
Correll, Julie E.
Corso, Melanie
Cortes, Daisy V.
Cortes, Regina A.
Cortese, Gail M.
Cortese, Janero
Cortese, Maureen
Corwin, Susan
Corya, Steven G.
Cosby, Peggy L.
Cosgriff, Joni
Cosgrove, Christopher
Cossia, Kimberly R.
Cossman, Wendy S.
Costa, Darlene R.
Costa, Donald E.
Costa, Nancy K.
Coste, Elizabeth D.
Costello, Brooke A.
Costello, Donna L.
Coster, Patricia
Cothrine, Burnett
Cottle, Jasmin L.
Cottrell, Regina G.
Couchman, Kathleen
Coughlin, John
Coughlin, Linda L.
Countess, Rebecca R.
Couper, Beth
Courington, Shelley
Coursey, Melissa
Coval, Lisa D.
Covarrubias, Jacqueline C.
Covey, Judy E.
Cowan, Aaron
Cowan, Catherine Anne
Cowan, Christopher D.
Cowan, Debra B.
Cowan, Heather L.
Cowan, Linda A.
Cowan, Norbert
Cowan, Robert R.
Cowan, Theresa
Cowart, Melinda B.
Cowell, Kimberly
Cowhig, Cheryl
Cox, Barbara L.
Cox, Brenda
Cox, Dawn C.
Cox, Dolores A.
Cox, Jacquelin L.
Cox, James C.
Cox, Kathryn D.
Cox, Laurie L.
Cox, Layne N.
Cox, Lisa J.
Cox, Michelle L.
Cox, Paul
Cox, Rebecca L.
Cox, Shirley M.
Cox, Thomas F.
Cox, Toni H.
Cox, Wendy K.
Cozart Royster, Stariline Gaye
Crabb, Shannon

Crabtree, Dawn H.
Crabtree, Patricia H.
Crader, Amanda L.
Crafton, Charles R.
Craig, Cody J.
Craig, Eileen E.
Craig, Joanne M.
Cramer, Donald
Cramer, Kathryn I.
Cramer, Steven
Crandell, Deborah K.
Crane, Dana Charlene
Crane, Teri M.
Crank-Datka, Michelle L.
Craven, Kimberly A.
Craven, Marlene
Cravens, Cynthia K.
Crawford, Aleah M.
Crawford, Ann L.
Crawford, Brian
Crawford, Gwendolyn L.
Crawford, Karra E.
Crawford, Nicole G.
Creech, Ann M.
Creegan, Mary Ann
Creekbaum II, George E.
Creighton, Judy A.
Crenshaw, Holly Rachel
Crenshaw, Latanjia L.
Cress, Sally A.
Crews, Christopher A.
Crews, Penny N.
Crews, Shirley Mae Green
Critchley, Donnie
Crittenden, Pamela J.
Critz, Kimberly L.
Croarkin, Kathleen O.
Crocetta, Karen
Crocker, Claudia Jean
Crocker, Kyle
Croft, Patti L.
Croley, Deborah J.
Cromley, Helen E.
Cromley, Peggy L.
Cromley, Thomas L.
Cronin, Jessica J.
Cronin, Pamela E.
Cronkite, Susan L.
Cronomtz, Mary K.
Cropp, David
Crosby, Bruce C.
Crosby, Kathryn G.
Crosby, Latoya Y.
Crosby, Mary Kate
Cross, Anita B.
Cross, Barbara D.
Cross, Deborah S.
Cross, Katherine E.
Cross, Tammy
Cross, Terri L.
Crossland-Coon, Freida G.
Crossman, Ashley F.
Crosthwait, Margaret
Crouch, Vickie
Crowe, Nicole M.
Crowell, Connie
Crowley, Linda
Crume, Joanne L.
Crumley, Juaneese
Crupi, Jessica A.
Cruse, Tracy Ann
Cruz, Berenice Rivera
Cruz, Christine
Cruz, Evangeline O.
Cruz, Lydia C.
Cruz, Remedios D.
Cryer, Linda
Cuba, Lori J.
Cude, Lori E.
Cudney, Alan E.
Cuello, Lisa A.
Cuervo, Dolores
Cuizon, Jamie J.
Culbertson, Anita C.
Culbertson, Cathi R.
Cullcy, Thomas

Culligan, Christine E.
Cullinan, Nancy
Culpepper, Deborah L.
Cummings, Davida E.
Cummings, Edward J.
Cummings, Iris
Cummings, Judith P.
Cummings, Judy M.
Cummings, Julie G.
Cummings, Linda R.
Cummings, Paul G.
Cummings, Paula J.
Cummins, Carol M.
Cummins, Sandra J.
Cundiff, Heatherann
Cunningham, Eleanor E.
Cunningham, Hollie M.
Cunningham, Janice S.
Cunningham, Kathryn R.
Cunningham, Ladonna L.
Cunningham, Renee C.
Cunningham, Sharon B.
Cunto, Silvia Lou
Cupelli, Richard
Cupp, Penny C.
Curcuro, Pamela
Curevich, Obera
Curley, Robert
Currey, Kenneth D.
Currie, Janice F.
Currie, Mark R.
Currin, Cheryl S.
Curry, Kathleen L.
Curtin, Cynthia J.
Curtis, Cheryl
Curtis, Eleonora
Curtis, Sandra
Curtiss, Janeen R.
Cushing, Norma
Cusker, Teresa
Cutler, Sharon F.
Cutrell, Dee
Cutshaw, Amy Jo
Cyphers, Allison A.
Cyphers, Ellen R.
Cyr, Aenam
Cyronek, Danita A.
Czajka, Karen
Czapansky, Christina

D

D'Alessandro, Paul L.
D'Amato, Sheila F.
D'Ambrosio, Catherine M.
D'Ambrosio, Gregory A.
D'Amico, Kathleen
d'antona, Nicholas E.
D'Assalenaux, Debra L.
D'Elia, Deborah C.
Dacanay, Charlayne M.
Dacosta, Janet M.
Dade, Rebecca Elaine
Dadson, Norma E.
Dagley, Janet
Dagley, Lauren E.
Dagostino, Beth A.
Dahl, Denise C.
Dahl, Sandra
Dahlberg, Kathleen S.
Dahlberg, Sondra
Dahlen, Susan E.
Dahlman, Roger A.
Dahrens, Jill
Dailey III, George
Dailey, Kimberly J.
Daily, Leslie A.
Dale, Kathy G.
Dale, Rodney
Dales, Maria T.
Daley, Marilyn
Dalien-Meister, Rachel
Dalinis, Frieda M.
Dalton, Melissa S.
Dalton, Sheryl L.
Dalton, Subrenia T.

Daly, Sherry L.
Dambaugh, Jennie
Damery, Natalie J.
Damiani, Judith C.
Dammu, Johnson
Damron, Mark S.
Danahy, Jeanne M.
Dandan, Ghassan
Danels, Jacob W.
Danet, Linda
Danford, Amanda B.
Daniel, Dorothy I.
Daniel, Marita A.
Daniel, Robin R.
Danielewicz, Regina K.
Daniels, Claudia M.
Daniels, Denise R.
Daniels, Lauren M.
Daniels, Stacy L.
Daniels-Cobb, Danita E.
Danielson, Barbara M.
Danner, Karen A.
Danowski, Marilyn F.
Dansie, Chris
Dansie, Gary L.
Dansie, Mason
Dansie, Tucker T.
Dansro, Denise
Danzig, Debbie
Darahpour, Cynthia
Darby, Chenel A.
Darby, Deborah
Darby, Lateshia S.
Darby, Tranice M.
Dardeau, Yvonne
Darden, Robin
Dario, Bethany A.
Darmour, Dawn
Darnell-Thomas, Stephanie
Darrah, Margaret J.
Darrow, Geralyn Marie
Dase, Marjory K.
DaSilva, Heather
Dather, Rhonda L.
Daughdrill, Kelli D.
Daugherty, Carol
Daugherty, Deborah M.
Daugherty, Diane L.
Daugherty, Shannon R.
Daugherty, Tracy M.
Daughtrey, Linda A.
Davenport, Ashley N.
Davenport, Hannah J.
Davenport, Krystee Tanelle
Davenport, Linda
Davenport, Robin V.
Davidson, Angela
Davidson, Anne-Marie
Davidson, Eric P.
Davidson, Maria A.
Davidson, Nina M.
Davidson, Paul
Davidson, Paula
Davidson, Steven M.
Davidson, Thomas
Davie, Cynthia
Davignon, Margaret
Davin, Roger E.
Davis, Akebia
Davis, Andre R.
Davis, Bette Lou
Davis, Brenda
Davis, Brian J.
Davis, Cara M.
Davis, Celia A.
Davis, Constance Carver
Davis, D'Arcy J.
Davis, Diana
Davis, Gina Cobb
Davis, Harry S.
Davis, Helen M.
Davis, James
Davis, Jana
Davis, Jean
Davis, Jeffery C.
Davis, Jessica

Davis, Karen Denise
Davis, Kathie
Davis, Kenneth Paul
Davis, Kimberley L.
Davis, Leslie C.
Davis, Lisa C.
Davis, Lois J.
Davis, Loralie
Davis, Lori
Davis, Lynda K.
Davis, Melissa L.
Davis, Michael W.
Davis, Mischel L.
Davis, Ramona J.
Davis, Rebecca
Davis, Rhonda
Davis, Robin S.
Davis, Sherry L.
Davis, Shirley
Davis, Steven C.
Davis, Tiffany
Davis, Zipporah L.
Davis-Lawson, Victoria K.
Davy-McClure, Kim M.
Dawe, Andrew
Dawes, Connie J.
Dawes, Connie M.
Dawkins, Jenifer E. Reeve
Dawn, Karen R.
Dawolo, Esther Nyamah
Dawson, Darius
Dawson, Margaret
Dawson, Michelle K.
Dawson-Butcher, Lisa J.
Day, Melissa D.
Day, Sheryl S.
Dayvault, Joyce
De Castro, Nina C.
De Guia, Esther D.
De Haven, Matthew R.
de Los Santos, Patricia E.
De Moss, Alisha Lewis
De Vaughn, Sharon
de Vera, Marilou A.
De Yong, Teresa M.
Deal, James A.
Dean, Benjamin L.
Dean, Dana C.
Dean, James R.
Dean, Janis E.
Dean, Joel K.
Dean, Megan L.
Dean, Vanessa
Deangelis, Tara S.
Deans, Judy Bright
Deans, Kay
Deatherage, Sharon
Debaufre, Charity Blevins
Debe, Heather J.
DeBenedict, Angela
DeBranski, Catherine C.
Debro, Tanya M.
Decarlo, Chantal M.
Decker, Andrea E.
Decker, Elaine
DeCounter, Catharine L.
deDeugd, Vicki W.
Deere, David G.
Dees, Nichole R.
Deffinbaugh, Linda H.
Defrancesco, Ruth Ann
Degelsmith, Steven P.
Degnan, Connie
Deguia, Esther D.
Dehart, Melanie M.
DeHaven, Scott D.
Dehyan, Sandra Spears
Deirmendjian, Aram
Deitering, Holly J.
Dejaegher, Joseph
Dejong, Janice
DeKornfeld, Nathan D.
Del Aguila Nino, Grisel A.
Del Aguila, Arturo N.
Del Corro, Deborah T.
Del Mundo, Faye M.

Del Vallejo, Maria
Dela Cruz, Jonathan T.
Delac, Susan D.
Delaney, Jeanee M.
Delans, Mary A.
Delarosa, Alecia M.
Delaune, Patricia S.
Deleon, Joanna L.
Deleonibus, Michele A.
Delester, Jason
Delgado, Claudia L.
Dellinger, Debra F.
Dellinger-Hunn, Wendy E.
DeLoach, David S.
DeLong, Donna V.
Delorenzo, David
Delouis, Cynthia
Demarco, Colleen
Demarco, Teresa E.
Dematt, Kathryn A.
Demling, Diane H.
DeMont, Mary A.
Demorvelle, James
Dempsey, Dorothy J.
Dempsey, Shana Lynne
Demski, Joyce P.
Denardi, Lisa M.
Denney, Tracy
Denninger, Laurel
Dennis, Jacquelynn
Dennis, Kandi Lyn
Dennis, Sharon A.
Dennis, Tanya M.
Dennis, Walter Matthew
Denniston, Colleen Ann
Denny, Benjamin W.
Denny, Ella M.
Denowski, Joel R.
Deogade, Chaitanya B.
Depalma, Wanda
Departie, Deborah
Depriest, Janet E.
Derbidge, Christopher Dale
Derickson, Rhonda
Derow, Janet M.
Derr, Edith B.
Derrick, Clarissa
DeSavatore III, William J.
DeShazo, Barry M.
DeShazor, Stephanie L.
DeShong, Kari A.
Deshpande, Anuradha K.
Deshpande, Shailendra P.
Desico, Lisa M.
Desimon, Lisa A.
Dessau, Melinda L.
DeStefano, Elinor K.
Determan, Steven J.
Dethloff, Steven B.
Detig, Rebecca E.
Dettenmayer, Sandra
Detting, Cindy
Dettlebach, Shirley K.
Dettman, Judy
Deutschman, Susan
Devane, Jane
DeVasher, Sandra Michelle
Devenyi, Mari T.
Devereux, Susan M.
Devers, Eda L.
Devin, Ellen
Devin, Julie A.
Devine, Patricia A.
Devore, Dana
Devriend, Julie C.
Dew, Kari Sue
Dew, Kathryn
Dew, Larry G.
DeWeese, Pamela J.
Dewitt, Laura
Dexter, Diane S.
Dexter, Rebecca L.
DeYonker, Clare A.
Deyoung, Joanne J.
Di Cristofaro, Katherine J.
Di Meo, Daniel P.

Di Peppe, Marsha
Dial, Janika M.
Diamond, Kelly L.
Diane, Theresa
Dias, Mara K.
Diatz, Heather C.
Diaz, Rebecca
Dibble, Denise
Dice, Mary R.
Dickerson, Bradley C.
Dickhens, Patricia A.
Dickinson, Dave
Dickinson, Loraine S.
Dickinson, Melinda
Dickinson, Miles S.
Dickman, Sarah E.
Dickson, Paula
Dicorte, Mary J.
Dicus, Jane
Dicus, JoAnn
Dicus, Sallie A.
Dieckmann, Kay L.
Diehl, Shelly
Dienes, Robert C.
Dierking, Linda K.
Dieter, Jennifer L.
Dietrich, Donna
Dietrich, Vicki L.
Dietz, Jane A.
Digby, Benjamin M.
Dilamarter, Cynthia A.
Dillahunty, Mary Lou
Dillard, Connie F.
Dillard, Katy
Dillard, Mark
Dillman, Andrea L.
Dillon, Alicia R.
Dillon, Cari L.
Dillon, Kristal K.
Dillon, Melissa W.
DiLonardo, Janet M.
DiMaria, Tyla
Dimengo, Josephine
Dinkins, Margo K.
Dinkins, Shannon E.
Dion, Brian L.
Dion, Claudia
Dioquino, Elvin G.
Diorio, Joan E.
Dioso, Lilibeth
Dipasquale, Carmen M.
Dipietro, Patricia E.
Dippy, Joanna
Dirden, Kimberly C.
Dirks, Corbin W.
Dirrim, Lorraine A.
Dise, Amber
Ditzler, Ann M.
Divincenzo, Linda J.
Dixon, Dena M.
Dixon, John David
Dixon, Latrina T.
Dixon, Layne Halstead
Dixon, Linda
Dixon, Lisa R.
Dixon, Margaret
Dixon, Marilyn R.
Dixon, Melanie
Dixon, Nicole A.
Dixon, Rebecca D.
Dixon, Sandra K.
Dixson, Drew L.
Djabbarah, Paula J.
Djordjevic, Milan
Do, Christine
Dobbins, Carol B.
Dobbs, Angela C.
Dobbs, Michael T.
Dobbs, Nancy J.
Dobersen, Deborah T.
Dobransky, Julie
Dobratz, Donald
Dobrowolski, Paula M.
Dobson, Karen
Docks, Sherrie Lynn
Dodd, Elizabeth A.

Dodds, Elaine M.
Dodds, Michele
Dodge, Colleen F.
Dodson, Crystal Heath
Dodson, Karen L.
Dodson, Kirk J.
Dodson, Sharon R.
Doelger, Lisa A.
Dohanyos, Barbara A.
Dohanyos, Joseph P.
Doheny, Mary T.
Doherty, Margaret M.
Doherty, Mary E.
Dohler, Ann E.
Doi, Phillip A.
Doimeadios, Esther
Dokken, Christen Rae
Dolan, Brenda K.
Dolechek, Tina R.
Dolinger, Angela S.
Doliveira, Ann M.
Doll, Susan M.
Dombrowski, Linda
Dominguez, Alcira E.
Dominguez, Derek A.
Dommer, Brenda R.
Donahoo, Carolyn S.
Donahower, Nicole Rae
Donahue, Robert G.
Donaldson, Lisa E.
Donatelli, Barbara
Donatelli, Jeane W.
Donatelli, Kathryn A.
Donato, Dauna R.
Donchatz, Constance R.
Doney, Sherry Ann
Donham, Shae
Donham, Sherrie L.
Donica, Barbara L.
Donohoe, Linda Simmons
Donohue, Barbara L.
Donohue, Lenore C.
Donohue, Mary J.
Donovan, Cynthia
Donovan, Fran
Donovan, Kevin D.
Doolittle, Christopher S.
Doolittle, Jaclyn M.
Doormann, Gayle
Dore, Maureen P.
Dorgan, Mary Kay
Dorgan, Sara Elizabeth
Doriath, Linda Genevieve
Dorn, Chad A.
Dornenburg, Barbara A.
Dorner, Gail
Dorney, William P.
Dornhecker, Lynn
Dorr, Kim D.
Dorris, Sarah E.
Dorsett, Norma
Dorsey, Dwayne A.
Dortch, Jennifer Lee
Dortch, Michael B.
Doss, Jessica R.
Dotson, Deborah J.
Dottore, Carla N.
Doucet, Karla
Doucet, Sara
Dougherty, Alicia
Dougherty, Janis Marie
Douglas, Joanne
Douglas, Joshua D.
Doutre, Joshua P.
Doval, Jacqueline A.
Dove, Lillian O.
Dovenbarger, Joel A.
Dover, Cheryl
Dowdell, Donna
Dowell, Daryle R.
Dowell, Jacobia C.
Dowell, Janice
Dower, Maura T.
Dowl, Barbara
Dowlen, Kayron Y.
Dowling, Glenna

Dowling, Mark
Downard, Lynn L.
Downey, Melinda
Downie, Kenneth J.
Downing, Patricia A.
Downs, Eleanor L.
Dowridge, Dawn A.
Doxon, Kayla J.
Doyle, Cathy S.
Doyle, David P.
Doyle, Michael S.
Doyle, Nadine
Dozier, Alice
Dozier, Dona P.
Dozier, Rebekah
Dragon, Terry L.
Dragovich, Nancianne
Drake, Clarice
Drake, Cynthia
Drake, Debra Jean
Drake, Kim
Drane, Jennifer R.
Draper, Kristi L.
Dreiling, Russell L.
Dress, Lorraine P.
Dressler, Chadwick M.
Drew, Debra L.
Drick, Deanna M.
Drick, Kathy L.
Driscoll, Barara A.
Driscoll, Linda B.
Driscoll, Michael P.
Driver, Carla A.
Driver, Carol J.
Driver, Jason B.
Driver, Mary D.
Driver, Michelle W.
Drowne, Laura
Druash-Gladys, Mauri L.
Drum, Karen A.
Drummond, Laurie
Dubcak, Jerri P.
Dubin, Eileen S.
Dubin, Samantha Nicole
Dubner, Anne L.
Dubois, Wanda
Ducharme, Jessica M.
Duchesne, Edna
Duckworth, Tramond L.
Duda, Carol Robert
Duda, Suzanne C.
Duddukuri, Venkataswara R.
Dudgeon, Jennifer
Dudik, Rollie M.
Dudley, Melissa E.
Dudoit, Carmen L.
Duerksen, Debra A.
Duermeyer, Carol Ruth
Duerson, Leslie R.
Dues, Kimberly M.
Dufault, Joan
Duff, Tonya Renee
Duffy, Cynthia L.
Duffy, Debra
Duffy, James Patrick
Duggan, Andrea Nicole
Duggin, Pamela J.
Duhn, Betsy J.
Duing, Missy A.
Duke, Janice
Duke, Sarah L.
Duker, Paulina N.
Dull, Diana C.
Dullin, Linda L.
Dulsky, Helen
Dumas, Marguerite E.
Dumas, Peggy
Dunaway, Laura S.
Duncan, Alexandria R.
Duncan, Carol O.
Duncan, Lee Ann
Duncan, Marilyn C.
Duncan, Maureen A.
Duncan, Sherry G.
Duncan, Timothy R.
Duncan, William

Dungan, Mark S.
Dungins, Shevon
Dunham, Bonnie L.
Dunlap, Dawn A.
Dunmire, Vanessa Lee
Dunn, Andrea E.
Dunn, Carla L.
Dunn, David A.
Dunn, Kelly Marie
Dunn, Linda
Dunn, Patti K.
Dunn, Stephanie Anne
Duong, Trulphuong T.
Dupay, Mark D.
Dupont, Ana U.
Dupree, Audrey M.
DuPriest, Jennifer L.
Duquette, Anne-Marie
Duran, James Andrew
Durbin, Bonnie
Durbin, Joann W.
Durco, Anna R.
Durham, Lorraine C.
Durkan, Maureen J.
Duron, Vivian
Durst, Joseph R.
Durussel, Leesa
Dusek, Sheryl J.
Dusevic, Judith D.
Duss, Nancy R.
Dusterhoff, Susan
Dutcher, Patricia K.
Dutton, Joshua M.
Dutton, Nancy J.
Duvall, Deanne
Dwyer, Keri A.
Dwyer, Michael
Dyament, Esther E.
Dyche, Emily Lee
Dye, Catherine A.
Dye, Victoria
Dyer, Deborah
Dyer, Susan H.
Dykstra, Jana L.
Dyrhaug, Sandra L.
Dziubinski, Marybeth
Dzuranin, Jody Gahman

E

Eads, Janet W.
Eads, Jesse F.
Eagan, Aaron
Eagan, Michael Kevin
Earl, Rebecca
Earley, Tania S.
Farnest, Stephanie
Earwood, Avery A.
Earwood, Gretchen M.
Easky, Karen A.
Eason, Nancy H.
Eason, Paula M.
Eastep, Jill
Eastman, Donia D.
Easton, Lillian M.
Easton, Sandra L.
Eastridge, Kevin D.
Eaton, Andrea L.
Eaton, Kelly Jane
Eaves, Tracey
Eavey, Marylynn
Ebanks, Deborah L.
Ebaugh, Helen J.
Ebbert, Kathy S.
Ebel, Cathy
Ebeling, Dee A.
Eberenz, Patricia
Eberlin, Ryan P.
Ebey, Karen R.
Eccher, David
Echevarria, Nancy
Echols, Robert
Echols, Vickie
Eckers, Phyllis
Eckert, Beth
Eckert, Michele A.

Eckler, Margaret
Eddleman, Donald W.
Eddy, Dawn Ella
Edelbrock, Randi Dawn
Edelson, Gary
Eden, Kathleen M.
Eden, Kimberly M.
Edens, Jacquelyn
Edge, Erin P.
Edgerson, Patricia M.
Edgett-Underwood, Ronna
Edison, Jemina R.
Edison, Joanne P.
Edmondson, Debra R.
Edner, Elisabeth
Ednie, Angela Rose
Ednie, James R.
Edson, Donna S.
Edwards, A. Karen
Edwards, Alecia J.
Edwards, Ambrosia
Edwards, Carolyn
Edwards, Charlotte
Edwards, Daryl
Edwards, E. R.
Edwards, Gloria P.
Edwards, Karen A.
Edwards, Kathryn
Edwards, Lawrence A.
Edwards, Linda
Edwards, Lynette K.
Edwards, Marsha M.
Edwards, Mary
Edwards, Neal
Edwards, Robert E.
Edwards, Robin F.
Edwards, Rose Yvonne
Edwards, Wendy
Effa, Christiana A.
Egan, Susan
Egan, Timothy P.
Egeto, Linda Marie
Eggleston, Stacey C.
Ehle, Corinne V.
Ehlen, K. James
Ehlert, Catherine M.
Ehm, Carolyn
Ehrenberger, Arlene C.
Eich, Marynda N.
Eichelberger, Jaclyn M.
Eickenberg, Brett A.
Eike, Susan A.
Eikren, Lori J.
Eiland, Shantilly M.
Eilering Symsack, Bonnie J.
Eisbrenner, Jane B.
Eisel, Lisa M.
Eisenbeck, Kyla
Eisenberg, Barbara
Eisenhuth, Lisa W.
Eiswirth, Louise P.
Eitze, Karen G.
Ekborg Hagmeier, Dolores Magdalena
Ekdahl-Lopez, Janet E.
Elam IV, Roy O.
Elbert, Margo A.
Eldeeb, Kathleen R.
Elder, Amy M.
Elder, Lizbeth Kay
Elder, Stanley W.
Eldred, Deborah
Eldredge, Brice C.
Eldridge-Bell, Phyllis
Eleff, Jeanette L.
Eleuterio, Erin L.
Eley, Tonya P.
Elgin, Wendy
Elia, Kori K. H.
Elkin, Mathew R.
Elkin, Nancy K.
Elkins, Eric
Elkins, Jeffrey
Elkins, Linda
Ellefsen, Eric
Ellifson, Barbara D.
Ellington Guido, Rene

Elliott, Craig R.
Elliott, Louise A.
Ellis, Amanda R.
Ellis, Amy Lynn
Ellis, De'jon A.
Ellis, Elizabeth A.
Ellis, Helen H.
Ellis, James C.
Ellis, Joel M.
Ellis, Judith A.
Ellis, Kea A.
Ellis, Laveeda L.
Ellis, Melody W.
Ellis, Patricia R.
Ellis, Paula
Ellis, Shannon N.
Ellis, Stephen J.
Ellis, Susan E.
Ellis, Valerie
Ellison, Joetta Jean
Ellison, Rebekah
Ellison, Rodney C.
Elliston, Ellen J.
Ello, Eileen M.
Ellsweig, Polly W.
Ellsworth, Deborah Darlene
Elmerick, Bonnie B.
Elmore, Andrea J.
Elmore, Chris
Elmore, Paul
Elofson, Robin B.
Elovitz, Charlene F.
El-Platt, Deborah D.
Elrod, James W.
Elsaesser, Kathryn N.
Elsarelli, Dena R.
Elson, Evelyn
Ely, John P.
Elyea, Mark L.
Elyea, Mary Kathleen
Embrey, Christine
Emerson, Janet
Emerson, Peter G.
Emery, Frederick C.
Emery, Heather Marie
Emery, Marilyn
Emmeneggcr, Amy
Emmer, Royce
Emmert, Millicent
Emory, Marcie L.
Emreschak, Patricia A.
Emry, David
Endermuhle, Kelly S.
Engberg, Erik
Engebretson, Kathy
Engel, Jennifer N.
Engelhart, Cornelia A.
England, Ronnie Dale
England, Wendy D.
Engle, Edna M.
Engle, Karen E.
English, Norah C.
English, Roger
Engram, Stacey L.
Enns, Pamela Y.
Enright, Gloria J.
Enright, Joshua
Enriguez, Ines E.
Ensmenger, Patricia E.
Epker, Melissa A.
Erath, Leigh K.
Erb, Audrey A.
Erb, Jessica Tovrog
Erdman, Kristine Anna
Erfle, Katherine B.
Erger, Bob
Erickson, Barbara L.
Erickson, James P.
Erickson, Judith I.
Erickson, Melody S.
Erickson, Susan M.
Ericson, Rebecca I.
Eriksen, Austen C.
Erkes, Leslie E.
Erla, Julie A.
Ernst, Manuela K.

Eross, Linda
Erramuzpe, Kelly
Ervin, Theresa
Erwin, Janette G.
Erwin, Joan E.
Erwin, Nancy H.
Esbri, Marta M.
Escalera, Tamu
Escalona, Mary Ruth G.
Escamilla, Gayle W.
Escamilla, Jacqueline
Escobar Rodriguez, Elizabeth
Escobar, Jessica I.
Escriva, Moma M.
Escue, Sherlyn
Esetes, Gay S.
Espensen, Maureen
Espey, Pam
Espinal, August G.
Esposito, Diane
Esposito, Dustin A.
Esquivel, Isaac M.
Essa, Wadade
Essavi, Caroline E.
Estacio, Roseanna
Esters, Nettie G.
Estes, Eva S.
Estes, Gay S.
Estes, Justin Michael
Estes, Katrena D.
Estill, Jacqueline C.
Estrada, Elsa P.
Ethan, Juan
Etheridge, Rosalind
Etheridge, Yvette W.
Ethridge, Nancy C.
Eubanks, Carol A.
Evangelista, Angelo O.
Evans, Barbara J.
Evans, Benjamin
Evans, Charlotte Elaine
Evans, Cheryl L.
Evans, Darlene M.
Evans, Debra D.
Evans, Delores L.
Evans, Donna L.
Evans, Janet L.
Evans, Linda S.
Evans, Matthew
Evans, Maureen
Evans, Nachelle C.
Evans, Paul A.
Evans, Sara A.
Evans, Tonya Wong
Evans, William S.
Eveland, Joanne L.
Evensen, Stacy K.
Everett, Synovia S.
Everist, Mary Alice
Ewig, Joan A.
Ewig, Joanna A.
Ewing, Anita G.
Ewing, Jacqueline
Ewing, Sheleta S.
Ewings, Anita G.
Ezell, Kristin F.

F

Faber, Marna
Faber, Nancy
Fabina, Judith L.
Fabish, Leslie A.
Fabiszewski, Robert
Fadden, Catherine
Fadik, Mark Paul
Fagan, Brooks
Fagg, Mesha
Fain, Julie A.
Fair, Cindy
Fair, Deborah Kay
Fair, Rebecca
Faison, Joan
Faison, LaTonya N.
Faith, Gary
Fajardo, Ariana A.

Fajardo, Rolina
Fakult, Ryan F.
Falbo, Michele L.
Falcon, Joanne M.
Falconi, Yamina
Falde, Tara D.
Falk, Robyn H.
Fallon, Stephanie
Falls, Cassandra D.
Fallstead, Lori
Farb, Harriet A.
Farber, Kathleen M.
Farber, Susan
Farder, Susan
Farenbach, Linda
Farias, Nancy K.
Farin, Leslie
Farkas, Shirley
Farkash, Glen
Farley, Elizabeth P.
Farley, Karen Louise
Farley, Sheila M.
Farlow, Melanie L.
Farmer, Deanna D.
Farmer, Elaine Prewitt
Faro, Stephen
Farquhar, Jody A.
Farrell, Angela D.
Farrell, Eileen F.
Farrell, Mary P.
Farrell, Richard
Farrell, Therese
Farrell, Thomas M.
Farrell, Tracy
Farrer, Susan Jane
Farrior, Lisa M.
Farris, Melanie
Fasano, Sandra K.
Fate, Keri Renee
Fatigate, Ilonka S.
Fauber, Nelson
Faught, Melanie W.
Fauntz, Deborah
Faust, Charlotte B.
Faust, Elizabeth Jeanette
Faust, Wendy
Favor, Kristi R.
Fay, Catherine
Fayer, Lois
Fayling, Hazel
Fazio, Terri M.
Fearrington, Wanda Clark
Federoff, Frederick
Fedrick, Kimberly Ann
Feehan, Jessica
Fehlenberg, Judith McGhee
Fehler, Helen M.
Fehling, Joanne
Fein, Joyce
Feingold, Jif
Feintein, Marla
Feist, Mary P.
Feka, Annette
Feka, Anthony M.
Felder, Eileen
Feldhake, Sandra D.
Felipe, Regina
Feliz, Karina Y.
Feller, Dana M.
Fellner, Kenneth
Felt, Susan C.
Feltan, Joan
Feltman, Amber L.
Felton, Lorraine Anita
Felton, Tamicka Renee
Feltovich, Mary A.
Felts, Donald
Felts, Vickie Cowell
Fendall, Donna Rose
Fenley, Arleen
Fensteracher, Susan
Fenzlaff, Audry E.
Ference, Laura L.
Fergason, Carol
Ferguson, Carrin M.

Ferguson, Daniel E.
Ferguson, Diana M.
Ferguson, Ellena L.
Ferguson, Linda Sue
Ferguson, Scott
Ferguson, Stephen
Ferianc, Cheryl L.
Fernald, Gerri Lynn
Fernandes, Ana Maria
Fernandez, Carolyn L.
Fernandez, Daryle J.
Fernandez, Lourdes
Fernandez, Presenia
Fernandez, Vivian T.
Ferranti, Deborah J.
Ferrara, Donna C.
Ferrari, Dawn E.
Ferrari, Denise M.
Ferrari, Edward M.
Ferrell, Cynthia
Ferrer, Lois A.
Ferrer, Patrick E.
Ferro, John J.
Ferron, Mary J.
Fessler, Janet
Fetters, Connie L.
Feucht, Donna
Fiedman, Joanne F.
Fieg, Karen L.
Fiegen, Kathleen N.
Fields, Calandra
Fields, Cynthia Ann
Fields, David C.
Fields, Diane E.
Fields, Doris B.
Fields, Eldon
Fields, Elizabeth A.
Fields, Patricia S.
Fields, Patrick A.
Fields, Preston Bell
Fields, Raynell N.
Fields, Robert M.
Fieldson, Mark
Fifer, Elizabeth
Figueroa, Cristy D.
Figueroa, Joaquin R.
Fimple, Lillian G.
Finch, Ann M.
Finch, Rebecca A.
Fincher, Brenda K.
Finder, Helen C.
Findley, Donna J.
Fine-Schmidt, Jennifer A.
Finley, Anecia N.
Finley, Bettye L.
Finley, Mary Y.
Finn, Kathleen P.
Finner, Valla F.
Finney, Theresa
Fiore, Caroline M.
Fiorini, Sharon L.
Firely, David M.
Firth, Sharon M.
Fischer, Connie L.
Fischer, Deborah
Fischer, Jill L.
Fischer, Karl G.
Fischer, Linda S.
Fischer, Penelope L.
Fischer, Scott E.
Fischer, Sue A.
Fischer, William R.
Fish, Bonnie
Fish, Susan K.
Fisher, Barbara
Fisher, Carol Jo
Fisher, Cheri L.
Fisher, Daniel J.
Fisher, Deborah
Fisher, Jennifer L.
Fisher, Jonathan R.
Fisher, Kimberly L.
Fisher, Linda D.
Fisher, Mark Edward
Fisher, Robin A.
Fisher, Teresa A.

Fisher, Trudy A.
Fisk, April
Fisk, Maria
Fiske, Christine
Fitch, DaRhonda L.
Fite, Lydia D.
Fitton, Travis J.
Fitzgerald, Edward A.
Fitzgerald, Jennifer M.
Fitzgerald, Joseph
Fitzgerald, Richard
Fitzgerald, Sandra J.
Fitzgibbons, Michael R.
Fitzpatrick, Beatrice
Flaherty, Judith A.
Flaherty, Lisa Michelle
Flanagan, Betty
Flanagan, Chris
Flanagan, Terrence M.
Flannelly-Waits, Michelle A.
Flannery, Kathy
Flatt, John P.
Fleek, Michael E.
Fleenor, Nancy K.
Fleeton, Cicely N.
Fleming, Charles S.
Fleming, Deborah Gwen
Fleming, Jeri
Fleming, Liselotte
Fleming, Michelle R.
Flener, Charlotte R.
Fletcher, Brenda
Fletcher, Carolyn
Fletcher, Cynthia
Fletcher, David A.
Fletcher, DeAnna Christine
Fletcher, Jay L.
Fletcher, Karen L.
Fletcher, Kristi
Fleury-Milfort, Evelyne
Flinn, Diana
Flint, Cheryl A.
Flipse, Mary
Flock, Lois J.
Floornoy, Linda L.
Flora, Derrick Brandon
Flora, Elizabeth K.
Flora, Laurie A.
Flores, Annette L.
Flores, Arlene G.
Flores, Clarissa
Flores, Cynthia A.
Flores, Delia
Flores, Tresa L.
Flores, Valerie Denise
Flores, Veronica M.
Flowers, Ella M.
Floyd, Laverne W.
Floyd, Mary K.
Floyd, Michael A.
Floyd, Pearl L.
Floyd, Stella L.
Fluet, Charlene
Fly, Elizabeth B.
Flynn, Diana L.
Flynn, Kathleen N.
Flynn, Kelly M.
Flynn, Kimberly A.
Focer, Marilyn
Focks, Terry A.
Fogle, Angela Y.
Foley, Jean
Foley, Kathleen E.
Folgner, Claus-Peter
Folk, Summer D.
Folkmire, Mary P.
Folley, Edna
Follman, Debra P.
Folta, Tammy L.
Foltz, Karl D.
Fondern, Raenicha
Fones, Anne-Taylor Smith
Fones, Christina Lee
Fontana, Sara Guidroz
Fontanelli, Nancy
Fontenot, Nicole E.

Footh, John H.
Forbes, Elizabeth M.
Forbes, Kathy L.
Forbes, Kevin M.
Forbes, Rebecca A.
Ford, Amber
Ford, Christine B.
Ford, Denise
Ford, Lisa Elaine
Ford, Melissa Yvonne
Ford, Rick
Ford, Sheila
Ford, Suzanne P.
Ford, Willie M.
Fore, Brooke
Fore, Dorian B.
Foresman, Julie
Forgay, Johnny
Forkrud, Janice K.
Forman, Cheryl R.
Forman, Melanie
Forman, Samuel
Forney III, Roy Charles
Forrest, Cordell
Forrest, Donna S.
Forrest, Kristin
Forrester, Betty
Forrester, Kathy H.
Forrester, Lynn Marie
Forsberg, Suzanne
Forti, Jean
Fortin, Linda M.
Fortner, Jennifer Leigh
Fosaaen, Christine R.
Foss-Harris, Jan M.
Foster, Deborah A.
Foster, Diana Kay
Foster, Jeanette
Foster, Jessie L.
Foster, Kathryn G.
Foster, Kimberly A.
Foster, Margaret J.
Foster, Mercedes
Foster, Ralph C.
Foster, Vivienne A.
Foster, Vonnetta N.
Foucher, Sharon
Fouhy, Robert C.
Foulke, Ed
Foulkrod, William
Fountain, Nichol J.
Fountain-Beilfuss, Laurel A.
Fowler, Amy E.
Fowler, Beth T.
Fowler, Brian D.
Fowler, Lisa A.
Fowler, Mary
Fowler, Pamela P.
Fowler, Patricia
Fox, Barbara Jean
Fox, Donna C.
Fox, Eileen M.
Fox, Elvia
Fox, Gregory C.
Fox, Jennifer
Fox, Rachel
Fox, Randall D.
Foxhoven, Karen
Fragelli, Mariana
Frahm, Dena
Fraim, Teresa
Fraley, Gabrielle M.
Francisco, Lenore Prince
Franco, Mary M.
Francois-Smith, Cheryl
Frank, Gail C.
Frank, Kendall
Frank, Stephan P.
Franke, Antionette
Franklin, Caroline M.
Franklin, Catherine
Franklin, James
Franklin, Jazmyn A.
Franklin, Kathleen H.
Franklin, Laura L.
Franklin, Mechelle T.

Franklin, Priscilla
Franklin, Tammy L.
Franz, Cheryl M.
Franz, Debra
Franzen, David D.
Frasca, Lori Anne
Fraser, Dan
Fraysier, Donna C.
Frazee, Tim
Frazer, Nancy
Frazier Roney, Linda
Frazier, Altone L.
Frazier, Angela B.
Frazier, Christine A.
Frazier, Christy N.
Frazier, Darlene M.
Frazier, Pamela J.
Frazier, Patricia
Freckman, Jack
Frederick, Kate C.
Frederick, Mary
Fredrickson, Gary R.
Free, Alaine M.
Free, Carla C.
Freeborn, Carol
Freed, Derek W.
Freed, Sara A.
Freed, Stacey J.
Freed-Knisley, Ruth K.
Freedman, Terralyn Lee
Freeland, Cherie A.
Freeland, Jenifer R.
Freels, Miake Jo Anne
Freeman, Angela
Freeman, Angie M.
Freeman, Anna
Freeman, Frank M.
Freeman, Helen Cole
Freeman, Judy K.
Freeman, Laura A.
Freeman, Susan
Freeman, Susanne
Freeman, Vicki L.
Freetly, Julie J.
Freitag, Leslie A.
French, Cynthia E.
French, Jane
French, Jennifer Teresa
French, Julie K.
French, Katherine L.
French, Kathi P.
French, Kenneth M.
French, Lisa L.
French, Mary G.
French, Michele R.
French, Nitzia T.
French, Tina
Frenzel, Sheila K.
Frerking, Don N.
Fretter, Paula Denine-Graham
Freund, Linda D.
Freund, Susan Diane
Fricano, Alaine
Fridley, Tammy L.
Friedersoorf, Karen
Friedman, Barbara
Friedman, Christine M.
Friedman, Cynthia A.
Friedman, Diane
Friedman, Joanne F.
Friedrich, Dorothy
Friend, Cindy
Friend, Cynthia
Friesen, Judy A.
Friesz, Mary C.
Fritsch, Dawn M.
Fritz, Barbara J.
Frizzelle, Pamela S.
Frodl, Dee Ann
Froehlich, John
Froman, Deborah M.
Frontera, Michelle
Frontiero, Leigh C.
Frosen, Mary D.
Frost, Cheryl R.
Frost, Cindy J.

Frost, Margaret J.
Fry, Amy E.
Fry, Christine M.
Frye, Steven T.
Fuchs, Jayne M.
Fuchs, Madeline I.
Fuentes, Barbara
Fuentes, Lilia A.
Fugate, Judy Marie
Fugh, Karen
Fuhrmeister, Erin L.
Fujita, Tracy K.
Fukuda, Patrice
Fuller, Barbara J.
Fuller, Mary W.
Fuller, Sally J.
Fuller, Stephen S.
Fuller, Tammy R.
Fulmore, Philline L.
Fultcher, Charretta S.
Fulton, Amy E.
Fulton, Julie C.
Fultz, Robin S.
Fulwider, Robyn S.
Fulwider, Stephanie D.
Funk, Kristine L.
Funk, Ruby D.
Fuqua, Dustin J.
Fuqua, Laurel
Furlong, Erin M.
Furry, Elizabeth A.
Futterer, Danne F.
Fyffe, Janet

G

Gabriel, Deborah A.
Gadd, Claire T.
Gade, Mary Susheela R.
Gadoua, Leo
Gaffney, Crystal Lee
Gaffney, Jean
Gaffney, Lisa E.
Gafford, Pamela S.
Gage, Maria C.
Gager, Sherrie L.
Gager, Tonya
Gahimer, Karen A.
Gaines, David B.
Gaines, Mary E.
Gaines, Stephanie L.
Gaither, Joseph S.
Galamay, Sharolyn D.
Galante, Mary Anne
Galarneau, Jill
Galase, Deliah
Galdun, Michael J.
Gallagher, Dawn
Gallagher, Elizabeth
Gallagher, Glenna B.
Gallagher, Thomas
Gallagher, Valerie A.
Gallardo, Christine
Gallardo, Jose
Gallegos, Andrea M.
Gallegos, Raymond W.
Gallegos, Teresa L.
Gallo, Mary E.
Galloway, Gwen
Gallupe, Barbara D.
Gambino, Michael
Gambosi, Joanne R.
Gambrel, Steven A.
Gamiao, Lawrence M.
Gandaio, Claudio B.
Gandy, Albert P.
Gandy, Susan
Gandy, William
Ganey, Judith S.
Ganger, Christopher J.
Gangestad, Melanie A.
Gangi, Rita S.
Ganley, Noreen M.
Gann, Christopher Lee
Gann, Robert D.
Gann, Tara E.

Gannon, Chantelle N.
Gannon, Nora I.
Gannon, Tom
Gantala, Matthew L.
Gantt, Rebecca L.
Garbarino, Joseph A.
Garber, Phillip A.
Garcia, Adriana
Garcia, Angel M.
Garcia, Juan P.
Garcia, Juliana
Garcia, Kaleo S. T.
Garcia, Margaret C.
Garcia, Marion
Garcia, Mary Ellen
Garcia, Mary Kara C.
Garcia, Patricia Reider
Garcia, Peggy
Garcia, Rosa O.
Garcia, Theresa M.
Garda, Jane Bell
Garda, Janet B.
Gardine, Michael
Gardiola, Christian N.
Gardner, Cristin L.
Gardner, Deborah L.
Gardner, Karen
Gardner, Kim Y.
Gardner, Lee
Gardner, Lisa
Gardner, Roger
Gardner, Shirley A.
Gardner, Terrence L.
Gargione, Laurie J.
Gariepy, Debra J.
Garison, Mary D. C.
Garman, Victoria S.
Garnder, Kim Y.
Garner, Beth C.
Garner, Caleb A.
Garner, David R.
Garner, Donna I.
Garner, Greg
Garner, James
Garner, Linda M.
Garner, Mary K.
Garner, Michael C.
Garner, Stacey Joyce
Garnett, Judalon
Garnic, Susan A.
Garnon, Colette
Garrett, Barbara
Garrett, Gregory A.
Garrett, Jewel Dean
Garrett, Kimberly A.
Garrett, Linda Loanne
Garrett, Nita R.
Garrison, Eva
Garrison, Kylana N.
Garsha, Matthew S.
Garstang, Patricia Angelica
Garver, Julie N.
Garver, Justine Marie
Garvey, James
Garvey, Maria D.
Garvin, William C.
Gary, William H.
Garza, Antonina M.
Garza, Evangelina
Garza, Jennifer
Garza, Karen
Garza, Maria T.
Garza-Perez, Isabella
Gass, Julia L.
Gast, Linda
Gatchell, Julie
Gates, Nancy S.
Gatlin, Michelle R.
Gatter-Judy, Susan C.
Gatto, Audrey J.
Gaudet, Roger
Gaudia, Vanja V.
Gaudio, Christine M.
Gaunder, Leora B.
Gausz, Regina
Gauthier-Mann, Julie

Gautier, Sheila
Gaver, Susan
Gavigan, Robert T.
Gavigan, William M.
Gavin, Jesse C.
Gavin, Shirley Marie
Gavino, Rosa
Gay, David R.
Gay, Marcia A.
Gay, Marlene S.
Gay, Melodie
Gay, Shari L.
Gaydos, Carolyn
Gayle, Jacqueline Evadne
Gayle, Phillip A.
Gaytan, Lorena C.
Gazey, Priscilla J.
Gburski, Heidi A.
Geadelmann, Eric A.
Geasy, Dennis
Gedaly, Rochelle
Gehlhaar, Tiffany D.
Geller, Lee Andrew
Gellerstedt, Erik L.
Gellin, Sharon G.
Gemperle, Louann
Genet, Amanda L.
Gennert, Tiiu E.
Gennuso, Eric J.
Gent, Felicia R.
Gentili, Mary W.
Gentle, Christine M.
Gentry, Bethany K.
Gentry, Paula
Gentry, Tammany J.
Geobel, Pamela V.
George, Charles Matthew
George, Florine
George, Karen A.
George, Kellie Kay
George, Mary
George, Phyllistine
George, Raymond
George, Susan
George-Max, Sheila P.
Gepford, Alma
Gepford, Charles
Gerardi, Janet
Geraty, Patrick
Gerber, Leslie
Gerbrands, Wendy M.
Geringer, Julia A.
Gerken, Alice M.
Gerlach, Jason
Germain, Jamie P.
Germer, Cheryl J.
Germinario, Annette G.
Germony, Laradean Joyce
Gernatt, Sandra
Gerney, Jill M.
Gershen, Ellie
Gershunova, Anna
Gertz, Brian N.
Gertzman, Jerilyn D.
Gervais, Mary Rose
Geter, Tonya J.
Gett, Curwin Marie
Getz, Susan L.
Gharacholou, Marjan M.
Gharse, Anita
Giacomino, Judith D.
Giambalvo, Jeanette
Gianetto, Evelyn A.
Giannetto, Bryan C.
Gibb, Olivia
Gibberman, Jamie
Gibbons, Ann
Gibbons, Annetta M.
Gibbons, Guy H.
Gibbons, Valorie R.
Gibbs, Diana L.
Gibbs, Janet
Gibbs, Janis M.
Gibbs, Marsia Vaune
Gibbs, Terrie E.
Gibbs, Valerie

Gibo, Kalauahi H.
Gibson, Ellen
Gibson, Ethlyn M.
Gibson, Jolynn M.
Gibson, Karen S.
Gibson, Kimberly
Gibson, Laura
Gibson, Marcella
Gibson, Nancy
Gibson, Patricia K.
Gibson, Susan G.
Gibson, Walter
Gibson-Fagg, Nancy
Giddings, Susan
Gider, Sinan
Giglio, Brenda
Giglio, Rogelia K.
Gil, Iris
Gil, Margarita M.
Gil, Rossina
Gilbert, Charles
Gilbert, John J.
Gilbert, Jonathan N.
Gilbert, Julie C.
Gilbert, Lynda
Gilbert, Pamela
Gilbert, Sonia R.
Gilbert, Virginia L.
Gilbody, Catherine J.
Gilbody, Steve
Gilburn, Patricia
Gilda, Janet L.
Gile-Daniels, Susan
Giles, Karen I.
Giles, Patrick O.
Gilfillian-Bennett, Vickie S.
Gill, Daniel S.
Gill, Julie A.
Gill, Kathryn
Gill, Martha M.
Gill, Sandra S.
Gillen, Karen
Gillen, Susan
Gillespie, Debbie
Gillespie, Debra L.
Gillespie, Ronald K.
Gillespie, Sandra J.
Gilley, Julie Anne
Gilley, Terrie Lynn
Gilliam, Debra S.
Gilliam, Mary
Gillick, Glenda
Gilligan, Cheryl
Gillihan, Janice Della
Gilliland, Katherine J.
Gilliland, Natalie Denise
Gilling, Danette Melanie
Gillotti, Debbie L.
Gilman, Bonnie L.
Gilman, Cathi
Gilmartin, Cari
Gilmer, Tonia S.
Gilmore, Cheryl A.
Gilmore, Cynthia B.
Gilmore, Kristen Nicole
Gilmore, Patricia Ann
Gilmore, Sharon K.
Gilreath, Lisa S.
Gilsrud, Jana K.
Ginsberg, Marilyn R.
Ginsburg, Carol
Giordano, Barbara L.
Giordano, Susan
Gipe, Douglas F.
Gipson, Alonzo L.
Gipson, Hilary J.
Giraldez, Brenda
Girard, Patricia A.
Gird, Karen B.
Girsch, Betty Hall
Giuliani, Cynthia M.
Givens, Daniel
Givens, Laura D.
Givens, Matthew R.
Gladney, Tammy A.
Glanders, Jerri D.

Glaser, Tina
Glasgow, Andrea D.
Glass, Ann P.
Glass, Cheryl
Glass, Naomi R.
Glass, Patti G.
Glasscock, Michael E.
Glasser, Carole C.
Glasser, Robin K.
Glatt, Angela R.
Glatter, Susan
Glatter-Judy, Susan C.
Glavan, Rosemary
Glaze, Delmonica
Glazer, Bonnie L.
Gleason, James M.
Gleason, Kathy L.
Gleason-Edwartowski, Barbara
Gleaves, Barbara E.
Gleeson III, William
Gleeson, Susan M.
Gleich, Sheryl
Glendenning, Connie
Glenn, Cristin K.
Glenn, Theresa L.
Glenn, William
Glennon, Michael L.
Glennon, Susan J.
Glidewell, John
Gliori, Christy Sudberry
Glock, Sharon P.
Glore, Elizabeth J.
Glover, Eunice M.
Glover, Sylvia Maxine
Glover-Adegbaye, Beverly A.
Glovsky, Lisa K.
Glowacki, Cindy
Glowacki, Mary
Glubka, Benjamin J.
Glueck, Rebecca Joy
Glynn, Kevin
Gnewikow, Debra A.
Gnuse, Jacquelyn A.
Goad, Kathy J.
Goad, Kriste
Goad, Michelle C.
Gobble, Cathy S.
Goble, Donald H.
Godby, Loraine A.
Godfrey-Olson, Jill
Godfrey-Roberts, Maria T.
Godley, Mary K.
Goebel, Pamela
Goeders, Patty A.
Goessele, Kimberly D.
Goff, Beverly
Goffo, Bonnie J.
Goggins, Joan E.
Goggins, Morris
Gohlke, Robert B.
Goidel, Rita
Goin, Gary L.
Goins, Lora L.
Goins, Stephen
Goins, Verdean L.
Golaszewski, Lori A.
Gold, Lauren H.
Gold, William R.
Goldade, Sandra S.
Golden, Karen L.
Golden, Mark
Golder, Jonina G.
Goldey, Karen
Goldman, Marjorie Ellen
Goldsmith, Jennifer A.
Goldsmith, Ruthanne
Goldstein, Freda
Goldstein, Jason
Goldstein, Joyce E.
Goldstein, Marcie I.
Goldstein, Miriam E.
Gomes, Pearl
Gomez, Maria
Gonder, Claire E.
Goniea, Ashley N.
Gonzales, Brooke

Gonzales, Criselda
Gonzales, Ernestine G.
Gonzales, Eva H.
Gonzales, Jerry P.
Gonzales, Martha A.
Gonzales, Michael M.
Gonzales, Monica
Gonzales, Nic
Gonzalez, Christina L.
Gonzalez, Cynthia F.
Gonzalez, Ivan A.
Gonzalez, Lilian
Gonzalez, Martha A.
Gonzalez, Norma L.
Gonzalez, Orlando
Gonzalez, Susan M.
Gonzalez, Valeri Tate
Gooch, Karen T.
Good, Robert W.
Goodale, Nanci Rae
Goode, Denise L.
Goode, Jonathan G.
Goode, Kimberly A.
Gooding, Doreen
Goodlow, Carol D.
Goodman, Anne
Goodman, Dolores P.
Goodman, Kelly
Goodman, Vicki L.
Goodman, Victoria W.
Goodner, Mary F.
Goodnight, Vicki D.
Goodrich, Margaret C.
Goodrich, Susan
Goodrum, Julia
Goodspeed, David M.
Goodwin, Karen
Goon, Crystal S.
Gopin, Maria Natal
Goralewicz, Elana L.
Gorberg, Abbe R.
Gordish, Amanda S.
Gordon, Charmaine E.
Gordon, Melba
Gore, Judy W.
Gore, Karen L.
Gore, Sarojini
Gorell, Angela R.
Gorgos, Diana M.
Gorham, Patricia
Gorlewski, Arlene D.
Gorman, Joanna
Gorsline, Patricia A.
Gorzovalitis, Marilyn
Goshert, Jan
Goslowsky, Anna M.
Gosney, Erin
Gospodarski, Sheree R.
Gossage, Wendy M.
Gottlieb, Donna L.
Gottschalk, Robert
Gottschall, Debra A.
Gotwald, Susie H.
Gould, Kathryn C.
Gourash, Christopher J.
Gouveia, Julie M.
Govea, Rafael M.
Gower, Jr., Carey
Gower, Thomas M.
Goyette-Cook, Cynthia L.
Gozzard, Mary
Grabel, Sharon Nancy
Graber, Bridget H.
Grabski, Sandra L.
Grace, Loretta M.
Grace, Patricia A.
Grady, Alison
Grady, David P.
Grady, Eileen
Grady, Sandra F.
Grady, Virginia Kathleen
Graefe, Beth J.
Graefe, Debora
Graf, Mary K.
Graf, Michael S.
Graffis, Jordan D.

Graham, Annette T.
Graham, Carla
Graham, Carolyn J.
Graham, Claudia
Graham, Elizabeth A.
Graham, Janice E.
Graham, Kathy J.
Graham, Nicholas
Graham, Tom E.
Graham-Williams, Cheryl A.
Gralinski, Nancy
Grames, Donald E.
Grammer, Allison L.
Grana, Kerry
Granderson, Kenneth A.
Grandon, Glenda D.
Granger, Diane
Granieri, Elena M.
Grant, Beth
Grant, Caroline Baugh
Grant, Horace W.
Grant, Jason F.
Grant, Rebecca
Grant, Stephen C.
Grassman, Jayne M.
Graverson, Glenna Bell
Graves, Daniel L.
Graves, Gay
Gray, Anna N.
Gray, Barbara B.
Gray, Deborah
Gray, Dina J.
Gray, Jillian M.
Gray, Jo Lynn
Gray, Judith M.
Gray, Sharon
Gray, Teresa D.
Grayson, Tricia W.
Greco, Linda Y.
Greco, Margaret
Greek, Janessa A.
Green Turner, Tacanesha Caprece
Green, Adrienne R.
Green, Allison D.
Green, Ashley C.
Green, Carol A.
Green, Daphne K.
Green, Donna
Green, Eric L.
Green, Holly
Green, Janet Marie
Green, Jennifer
Green, John Hays
Green, Joy M.
Green, Kim
Green, Patricia
Green, Ronald W.
Green, Rosemarie
Green, Samantha E.
Greenblatt, Lynda
Green-Blicher, Emily
Green-Blicher, Ronald W.
Greene, Joan
Greene, Margaret B.
Greene, Rose K.
Greenfeder, Barbara
Green-Hadden, Joy M.
Greenham, Marjorie A.
Greenhow, Debora A.
Greenlee, Lorraine
Greenlee, Troy
Greenler, Lorriane
Greenwalt, William C.
Greenway, Carrie
Greenway, Janet
Greenwood, Dona C.
Greenwood, Louise
Greenwood, Maude E.
Greer, Elizabeth J.
Greer, Lynn Webster
Greer, Mary Ellen
Greer, Nancy M.
Greer, Thomas M.
Greer, Wendy S.
Greger, Jr., Franky
Gregg, Denise E.

Gregg, Edward
Gregg, Jon P.
Gregory, Cassandra
Gregory, Colleen L.
Gregory, Michele A.
Gregory, Rosa M.
Gregory, Susan
Greider, Valerie
Greiner, Barbara J.
Grenne, Joan
Grenne, Margaret B.
Gresh, Mark N.
Greulich, Larissa A.
Greve, Kimberly B.
Grewing-Ambrose, Laurie L.
Gridley, Ray T.
Griedersdorf, Karen
Griego, Janet
Grier, Lorraine
Griffin, Angela L.
Griffin, Barbara A.
Griffin, Carolyn A.
Griffin, Daniel K.
Griffin, David
Griffin, Delores S.
Griffin, Demetria M.
Griffin, Donna
Griffin, Jeffrey W.
Griffin, Karen D.
Griffin, Linda P.
Griffin, Lise J.
Griffin, Maryann
Griffin, Michelle L.
Griffin, Paula Jane
Griffin, Ruth
Griffith, Denise Dahn
Griggs, Debra R.
Griggs, Karen F.
Grijalva, Zoila A.
Grillot, Terrie
Grim, Winnie G.
Grimes, Amity H.
Grimes, Elizabeth
Grimes, Stephanie L.
Grimes, Tracey A.
Grimm, Shauna S.
Grimm, Shelley L.
Grimm, Shelley Lynn
Griser, Regina E.
Grisham, Corinne O.
Griskenas, Rasyte T.
Griswold, Gwen
Gritz, Dawn M.
Grobe, Heide
Groce, Marsha A.
Grocki, Verna
Grodecki, Barbara
Groff, Sherrie
Groff, Tammy L.
Grogan, Sue E.
Groninger, Emily M.
Gronostajski, Susanne B.
Groom, Randall L.
Grooms, Eileen A.
Grooters, Deon N.
Groover, Terri L.
Gross, Jackie J.
Gross, Jessica
Gross, Lisa D.
Gross, Patricia
Gross, Sandra
Gross, Susanne P.
Grossman, Patricia M.
Grote, Jennifer R.
Grove, Cathy
Groves, Amanda Michelle
Grubb, Deborah
Gruber, Carol L.
Gruendler, Brenda
Gruss, Rosemary
Gruszczynski, Ellen H.
Guardiani, Jennifer A.
Guarriello, Andrea J.
Guberman, Dana
Gueldner, Kelly Osten
Guenther, Julie A.

Guerra, Jan C.
Guerra, Petra
Guerrero, Claudia Lorena
Guerrero, Joan
Guerrero, Mary C.
Guerrero-Trinidad, Jennifer
Guest, Sarah Jan
Guettler, Terese
Guevara, Sonia
Guiang, Kathleen C.
Guicheteau, Maureen
Guidice, Isabel
Guido, Patricia E.
Guilfoil, Eileen
Guilmette, Jennifer L.
Guindon, Thomas L.
Guinter, Sandra
Guinther, L. Penny
Guitierrez, Ana
Gulla, Lindsay N.
Gullett, Cody R.
Gulley, Chassity M.
Gulmi, Claire M.
Gunder, Kristin
Gunderman, Annette K.
Gunderson, Heidi
Gunkle, Charlotte L.
Gunnarson, Patricia L.
Gupton, Adrien
Gurgiolo, Patricia A.
Gurley, Virginia F.
Gurney, Ellen D.
Gust, Angela I.
Gustafson, Pamela D.
Gustin, Laura Ann
Gustoff, Mark E.
Guthrie, Cathleen B.
Guthrie, Diana W.
Guthrie, Joyce M.
Guthrie, Justine
Guthrie, Richard H.
Gutierrez, Ernest J.
Gutierrez, Michele E.
Gutstadt, Barbara J.
Guy, Deborah D.
Guy, Linda R.
Guyader, Sharon E.
Guyan, Janan
Guzman, April
Guzman, Carla R.
Guzman, Crystal L.
Guzman, Cynthia
Gwyn, Sherry Deloris

H

Haaf, Andreas
Haag, Mary Ann
Haak, Tina M.
Haake, Mary Frances
Haas, Carolyn
Haas, Joseph A.
Haas, Mary S.
Haas, Wanda
Habing, Larissa A.
Hable, Sharon K.
Hackbarth, Jandy
Hacker, Cathy
Hacker, Jo Ann
Hacker, Judith A.
Hackman, Mark
Hackney, Kimberly E.
Haddad, Fouad Georges
Haddad, Janice
Haddad, Stephen
Haddaway, Sheryl Ann
Hadden, Dawn M.
Haddix, Shannon C.
Haddock, Barbara Anne
Haden, Mark
Hadley, Jennifer Lynn
Haenftling, Deborah
Haes, Melisa Lynn
Hafezi, Darling H.
Hafner, Judy D.
Hafner, Sandra L.

Haft, Deborah
Hagan, Jamey D.
Hagan, Lisa
Hagan, Stephen W.
Hagan, Thomas
Hagansick, Margaret
Hagedorn, Patrick K.
Hagemann, Debra M.
Hagemann, Dennis C.
Hagemann, Eileen A.
Hagemann, Eric N.
Hagemann, Kevin T.
Hagensick, Margaret
Hager, Marcia L.
Hagerich, Barbara
Hagewood, Lori Lea
Hagley, Marcia
Hague, Sarah Elizabeth
Hahlen, Melissa L.
Hahn, Cynthia S.
Hahn, Heather
Hahn, Kathy
Hahn, Kristina
Hainer, John
Haines, Susan
Haines, William R.
Hakanen, Anisa
Haken, Jan
Halcomb, Rhonda
Hale, Christi
Hale, Ellen L.
Hale, Kendra D.
Hale, Lauren A.
Hale, Patrick
Hale, William E.
Hales, Susan
Haley, Cheryl M.
Halgren, Laurie
Hall, Barbara
Hall, Barbara A.
Hall, Barbara J.
Hall, Beth A.
Hall, Beverly D.
Hall, Byron D.
Hall, Cara
Hall, Carole
Hall, Christine
Hall, Dorothy R.
Hall, Frankie J.
Hall, Gina Pomeroy
Hall, Janet
Hall, Jennifer Lynne
Hall, Joan K.
Hall, Jonathan
Hall, Kenya M.
Hall, Kimberly S.
Hall, Laura
Hall, Leslie Brook
Hall, Loralie
Hall, Mark
Hall, Michelle R.
Hall, Phyllis Patricia
Hall, Sandra M.
Hall, Stanley J.
Hall, Susan M.
Hallberg, Joan L.
Haller, Lynn M.
Halley, Lois M.
Halliday, Jeni Ellis
Halloway, Reggie Carol
Halprin, Jonathan B.
Halsey, Vaughn A.
Halstead, Josephine M.
Haluzan, Susan
Halvorson, Sandra K.
Ham, Emily W.
Hamana, Nancy
Hamann, Cynthia J.
Hamann, Kristina M.
Hamann, Robin Y.
Hamar, Guy B.
Hamati, Kristien D.
Hamber, Joyce M.
Hamblen, Diana L.
Hamer, Angella
Hamer, June

Hamilton, Brenda W.
Hamilton, Cheryle A.
Hamilton, Cynthia A.
Hamilton, Deborah J.
Hamilton, Donald R.
Hamilton, Donna K.
Hamilton, Elaine Crosby
Hamilton, Gail Jean
Hamilton, Janice Kay
Hamilton, Kenneth R.
Hamilton, Montane Christopher
Hamilton, Patricia A.
Hamilton, Sandra B.
Hamlet, Karen S.
Hamley, Yolonda F.
Hamlin, Melanie K.
Hamlin, Shari
Hammer, Nancy T.
Hammerschmidt, Tina M.
Hammett, Betty
Hammock, Mark A.
Hammond, Linda A.
Hammond, Rachel
Hammond, William Frederick
Hammons, Barry L.
Hampson, Eileen
Hampson, Janet S.
Hampton, Barbara
Hampton, Joseph
Hampton, Kathryn R.
Hampton, Vanessa
Hampton-Holt, Lucretia
Hamrick, Jacob C.
Hamspon, Eileen
Han, Mingzhu
Hanaoka, Christine N.
Hanashiro, Kingsada
Hanchette, Kimberly C.
Hancock, Billy Ray
Hancock, Marie
Hancock, Ruth H.
Hand, Patricia S.
Hand, Sharon Lee
Handel, Donna
Handel, Linda A.
Handel, Shiela
Handmaker, Christine
Handwork, Patrick
Handyside, Nancy
Hanes, Mary A.
Haney, Christine E.
Hanisch, Robert
Hank, Mary E.
Hankins Irwin, Kimberly Ann
Hankins, Emily F.
Hankins, Nancy
Hankins, Ricky Lee
Hankins, Shelley R.
Hanko, Lori K.
Hanks, Judy E.
Hanks, Mary E.
Hanks, Robert B.
Hanley, Donna
Hanlon, Darlene M.
Hann, Diane L.
Hanna, Debbie R.
Hanna, Katherine J.
Hannah, Dabney Dawn
Hannah, Tamira D.
Hannes, Jodie Ray
Hannington, Lori L.
Hannon, Diane H.
Hanover, Francine M.
Hanrahan, F. Caroline
Hanrahan, Patricia
Hansen, Beverly
Hansen, Brenda
Hansen, Eliza
Hansen, Frances Jean
Hansen, Lisa Ann
Hansen, Patty A.
Hansen, Roberta J.
Hansford, Maite
Hansley, Margaret
Hanson, Christy N.
Hanson, Laurie A.

Hanson, Meredith T.
Hanson, Patricia C.
Hanssen, Heidi
Hantsch, Robert
Hapke, Susan C.
Hara, Harrison A.
Hara, Pam
Harano, Emily Ann
Harbaugh, Diane M.
Harberson, Tish J.
Harbertson, Charee H.
Hardacker, Lisa M.
Hardcopf, Sharlene E.
Harden, Darla G.
Hardieway, Tracey L.
Hardin, Bonnie
Hardin, Erica L.
Hardin, Pamela E.
Hardman, Tammy
Hardrick, Stephanie
Hardy, Carol M.
Hardy, Glenda
Hardy, Janet
Hardy, Joanne M.
Hardy, Valerie T.
Hare, Allison Scott
Hare, Charles C.
Harenski, Karen
Hargens, Stephen J.
Hargis, Joy
Hargreaves, Glenn A.
Hargrove, Sandra
Harkabus, Kimberly W.
Harker, Sandra
Harkins, Sandra J.
Harkness, Michael B.
Harlan, Debra L.
Harman, Diane
Harmon, Jenica R.
Harmon, Justin W.
Harmon, Kathy A.
Harmon, Pamela A.
Harmon, Susan
Harnack, Dawn S.
Harner, Doris E.
Harp, Shelby A.
Harper, Mary T.
Harper, Sunny
Harrel, Shaye E.
Harrell, Chad
Harrell, Jane S.
Harrell, Jill
Harrell, Pamela
Harrell, Royce D.
Harrell, William
Harriel, Theresa
Harrington, Kathryn L.
Harrington, Rebecca L.
Harris, Alisa
Harris, Barbara E.
Harris, Carolyn L.
Harris, Daphne C.
Harris, Dave
Harris, David Lee
Harris, Derric C.
Harris, Diann S.
Harris, Donnie
Harris, Ebony S.
Harris, Eddy R.
Harris, Glenda L.
Harris, Ina
Harris, Jennifer L.
Harris, Jo Ann
Harris, John
Harris, Karen Ransom
Harris, Kathy K.
Harris, Kevin
Harris, Latoya R.
Harris, Laura A.
Harris, Louann
Harris, Luke Anthony
Harris, Malik V.
Harris, Margaret T.
Harris, Maurice
Harris, Melissa N.
Harris, Neal C.

Harris, Pamela Y.
Harris, Phyllis L.
Harris, Regina S.
Harris, Ronal M.
Harris, Sharon K.
Harris, Shena S.
Harris, Sue Jane
Harris, Susan L.
Harris, Tina
Harrison, Barbara
Harrison, Betty Sue
Harrison, Donna M.
Harrison, Jane
Harrison, Jeffrey O.
Harrison, Jessica E.
Harrison, Karen A.
Harrison, Larisa
Harrison, Patrice A.
Harrison, Patricia L.
Harrison, Sallie Louise
Harrison, Stacie Nicole
Harrold, Holly Ann
Harrold, Kimberly
Harrold, Molly A.
Harrow, Cynthia J.
Harrower, Pete M.
Harry, Teresa
Harry, Ursula D.
Hart, Lee A.
Hart, Patricia
Hart, Roger B.
Hart, Sharolyn Irene
Harter, Barbara Ruth
Hartley, Amber M.
Hartman, Amy F.
Hartman, James Thomas
Hartman, Leslie J.
Hartman, Terri
Hartstein, Barbara K.
Hartwell, Joanne B.
Harvery, Linda
Harvey, Ann E.
Harvey, Chad M.
Harvey, Dawn
Harvey, Linda
Harvey, Richard J.
Harvey, Stephanie M.
Harvey, William J.
Harvey, Winston P.
Harville, Maria D.
Harwell, Charlotte A.
Harwell, Paula M.
Harwood, Gretchen M.
Hasenwinkel, Joel A.
Hashi, Gail Y.
Haskins, Michael L.
Hassler, Shirley C.
Hast, Cheryl
Hastert, Molly A.
Hasting, William D.
Hastings, John Todd
Hasty, Holly Elizabeth
Hatam, Mary P.
Hatch, Gwendolyn
Hatch, Jody D.
Hatch, Sandra H.
Hatcher, Debra N.
Hatcher, Lisa G.
Hatcher, Matthew A.
Hatchett, Amanda L.
Hatchett, Kwawieta
Hates, Sheila Downs
Hatfield, Carrie F.
Hatfield, Danielle
Hathaway, Cynthia A.
Hathcock, Jennifer L.
Hatley, Tiffany C.
Hattman, Charles
Hatton, Cara R.
Hatton, Carol A.
Hatton, Jennifer
Hauge, Stephanie A.
Hauschel, Richard
Hauser, Linda E.
Hausmann, Karri L.
Havelock, Rhonda J.

Havens, Dorothy
Haverty, Marleen
Hawk, Amalia
Hawk, Patricia Ann
Hawkins, Candace D.
Hawkins, Deborah
Hawkins, Denise M.
Hawkins, Kelley L.
Hawkins, Lauren E.
Hawkins, Marcia Y.
Hawley, Signe E.
Haws, Brian
Hayashi, Ann M.
Hayat, Gurpreet Z.
Haycock, Margaret
Hayden, James
Hayek, Rosa M.
Hayer, Kamal K.
Hayes, Ashley L.
Hayes, Charlotte Ann
Hayes, Cynthia O.
Hayes, Daniel Wilson
Hayes, Keeley D.
Hayes, Marcia
Hayes, Sheila D.
Hayes, Stephen M.
Hayes-Ortiz, Laura S.
Haynes, Carolyn Marie
Haynes, Charlotte Ann
Haynes, Crista
Haynes, Sandra Diane
Haynes, Stanley F.
Haynie, Amy P.
Haynie, Esther R.
Hays, Jean T.
Hays, Kelly A.
Hayward, Kelly J.
Hayward, Lauren M.
Hazelwood, Lisa
Hazerjian, Aram M.
Hazzard, Carolyn C.
Hazzard, Sheri
Head, Ann M.
Head, Ashley B.
Head, Dorothy J.
Headman, Sidney
Healy, Barbara F.
Healy, Cynthia A.
Healy, Katherine L.
Heap, Amie
Hearne, Heather M.
Hearnsberger, Marilyn E.
Heartfield, Valencia
Heastings, Tammy L.
Heath, David W.
Heaton, Carolyn C.
Hebb, Joshua D.
Hebda, Danette D.
Hebden, Lael
Heber, Melisa J.
Hebert, Diane
Hebert, Elizabeth J.
Heckart, Sallie Lou
Heckart, Teresa L.
Heckel, Patricia A.
Hedberg, Katherine
Hedelius, Richard Leroy
Hedgepeth, Shira C.
Hedges-Hurst, Angela Kristine
Hedrington, Le'Velle T.
Hee, Jerolyn C.
Heebner, David
Heeren, Jennifer
Heffernan, Michele E. J.
Heffner-Henkel, Patricia A.
Heflin, Emily W.
Heft, Sherry S.
Heh, Tair Ping
Hehn, Barbara A.
Heilskov, Barbara A.
Heim, Terese M.
Heimerl, Phyllis
Hein, Blance
Hein, Terese M.
Heinrich, Francene
Heinrich, Katherine K.

Heinrichs, Marilyn R.
Heins, Janet N.
Heinzel, Elisa A.
Heinzerling, Carol E.
Heiple, Monica G.
Heiple, Sheila
Heise, Paula D.
Heithold, Kelly Rae
Hejduk, Angela Louise
Heldt, Susanne C.
Helen, Sumner
Helfrich, Tiffany L.
Helgerson, Kathryn
Helkowski, Sue
Hellenbrand, Diane A.
Heller, Gail
Heller, Rosanne
Helling, Andy L.
Hellman, Cynthia M.
Helm, Mary Beth
Helms, Cynthia Mae
Helms, Russell A.
Helvey, Sulficia R.
Helwig, Stanley J.
Helzlsouer, Cynthia J.
Helzlsouer, John P.
Hemming, Katherine
Hemsley, Amy S.
Henault, Tracey A.
Hendershot, Karen S.
Henderson, Carolyn
Henderson, Eveline R.
Henderson, Janice
Henderson, Kelly M.
Henderson, Linda J.
Henderson, Steven J.
Henderson, Wendy
Hendricks, Emily C.
Hendricks, Gina R.
Hendricks, Jean N.
Hendricks, Lindsy R.
Hendricks, Miriam
Hendricks, Rochelle
Hendrickson, Janis L.
Hendrickson, Sara
Hendrix, Chad
Hendrix, Dawn M.
Hendrix, Lori A.
Hendry, Christopher J.
Henegar, Laureen
Henkhaus, Beverly Jean
Henley, Cathy
Henley, Lynda D.
Henley, Mitzi D.
Henne, Kathy E.
Hennessey, Martha
Hennessy, Amanda J.
Hennessy, Manfred
Henning, Linda K.
Henricksen, Nancy L.
Henrie, Stacy N.
Henry, Agnes K.
Henry, Danny M.
Henry, Heather M.
Henry, James
Henry, Jessica
Henry, Karen J.
Henry, Lisa S.
Henry, Mary Ann
Henry, Michelle R.
Henry, Nita
Henry, Richard
Henry, Teresa K.
Hensley, Jill
Hensley, Julia A.
Hensley, Nancy B.
Hentsch, David
Hentscher, Julia K.
Heon, Edward C.
Heppner, Anne C.
Heppner, Barbara
Herber, Tina
Herbert, Stephanie N.
Herbert, Travis Kriz
Herbold, Mary Lynn
Herchenroeder, Jennifer A.

Herder, Cheryll L.
Herdt, Christine
Hergenhan, Amy L.
Hering, Russell W.
Herlyn, Heather J.
Hermann, Cindy R.
Herman-Rivera, Beverly A.
Hernandez, Belina
Hernandez, David E.
Hernandez, Matthew P.
Hernandez, Robert W.
Hernandez, Sandra M.
Herold, Jodi
Herr, Henry D.
Herr, Jason T.
Herr, Scott W.
Herren, Jennifer
Herrera, Whitney S.
Herrfeldt, Margaret E.
Herrin, David R.
Herron, Annette
Herron, Duane L.
Herron, Margaret
Herron, Sandra S.
Hersch, Debra J.
Hersh, Patricia A.
Hershberger, Peter
Hershey, Cynthia A.
Hertel, Robin
Herzer, Wanda
Hess, Heather F.
Hess, Linda
Hess, Mark R.
Hesson, Melanie A.
Hester, Anne E.
Hester, Pamela I.
Hethcox, Chad E.
Hetrick, Margaret J.
Hetzel, Mary
Hewes, Florence A.
Hewitson, Donna
Hewitt, Margaret A.
Heymann, Catherine
Heysing, Tamara
Heywood, Richard S.
Hibbert, Al
Hibbett, Cheryl
Hickel, Jane L.
Hickenboth, Linda
Hickcy, Gwendolyn W.
Hickey, Julianne
Hickey, Patricia
Hickman, Mary Allison
Hickok, Cynthia M.
Hicks, Betty J.
Hicks, Diana K.
Hicks, Karen D.
Hicks, Linda B.
Hicks, Lizabeth Ann
Hicks, Marcia J.
Hicks, Nancy
Hieke, Meisha Marie
Hietala, Elizabeth A.
Higginbotham, Jack D.
Higginbotham, Kathryn N.
Higginbotham, Kim L.
Higgins, Kimberly
Higgins, Maria C.
Higgins, Mary K.
Higgins, Patricia
High, Ava
High, Fred J.
Highland, Trisha Lee
Hilaire, Gerard
Hiland, Mary Ellen
Hilbun, Julie
Hilgendorf, Kathleen E.
Hiliard, Belinda B.
Hill, Amy S.
Hill, Barbara
Hill, Charles F.
Hill, Eileen
Hill, Georgette A.
Hill, Geraldine H.
Hill, Josette M.
Hill, Ladonna L.

Hill, Melanie R.
Hill, Richard S.
Hill, Ronald Lee
Hill, Sandra N.
Hill, Sharon
Hill, Stefanie M.
Hill, Subrina
Hill, Susan F.
Hill, Vanessa E.
Hilliard, Laura
Hilliard, Shelia A.
Hills, Alexander C.
Hills, Judith L.
Hillyer, Christopher J.
Hilton, Jane E.
Hilton, Julia A.
Hilton, Robert C.
Himes, Alvenia M.
Himes, Leona
Himes, Robert Lynne
Himmerlreich, Beverly
Hinchcliffe, Gloria L.
Hindmon, Lois E.
Hinds, Hillary J.
Hines, Deborah
Hines, Hilda
Hines, Kirsten L.
Hines, Leeanne Marie
Hines, Robin G.
Hines, Sharon
Hinkis, Jennifer
Hinkle, Sara H.
Hinnen, Deborah A.
Hinojosa, Theresa
Hinton, Dawn W.
Hinton, Joyce M.
Hinton, Nancy
Hinton, Sebrena L.
Hinton, Sharika N.
Hintz, Heather C.
Hintzen, Gina M.
Hinz, Ellen R.
Hipp, Sheila M.
Hirokane, Laurel Lynn
Hirsch, Linda A.
Hirsch, Sue Hamilton
Hirschauer, Kathy
Hisscock, Thomas G.
Hitchcock, Beth
Hitchcock, Lauren A.
Hitchcox, Shirley A.
Hite, Johnny M.
Hite, Victoria J.
Hitzke, Diane Goff
Hixon, David
Hixon, LuAnn
Hixson, Shirley
Hiza, Judith M.
Hjelmgren, Therese A.
Ho, Elvera P.
Ho, Melisa M.
Hoadley, Kathleen A.
Hoang, Michael
Hobbs, Anita Marie
Hobbs, Judeth
Hobbs, Leslie A.
Hobbs, Mary K.
Hobbs, Rebecca L.
Hobgood, Adam Neil
Hoch, Mary M.
Hochstadt, Robin R.
Hockensmith, Terri L.
Hockensmith, Tracy L.
Hockett, Teresa Lynn
Hocking, Mary Kay
Hodgdon, Darren W.
Hodge, Austin
Hodge, Charlotte L.
Hodge, Cline F.
Hodge, Donna K.
Hodge, Janet S.
Hodge, L. Charlotte
Hodges, Krista A.
Hodges, Nathan J.
Hodges, Rena G.
Hodges, William J.

Hodgkin, Harriet P.
Hoefling, Michael R.
Hoehn, Candy K.
Hoelscher, David A.
Hoermann, Jennifer M.
Hoerner, Edward
Hoertkorn, Nicolaus R.
Hoey, Don
Hoffman, Angela S.
Hoffman, Ann C.
Hoffman, Diane M.
Hoffman, Jana G.
Hoffman, Joanna R.
Hoffman, John E.
Hoffman, Mary
Hoffman, Michael
Hoffman, Nita R.
Hoffman, Patricia
Hoffman, Robert W.
Hoffmann, Janice C.
Hofmann, Susan M.
Hofmeister, Matthew W.
Hogan, Ann M.
Hogan, Antonia M.
Hogan, Cary G.
Hogan, Jan
Hogan, Marjorie M.
Hogan, Teresa D.
Hogans, Tina
Hogenmiller, Peg
Hoglund, Ryan F.
Hohertz, Caren L.
Hohm, Janet
Holbrook, Chandra Elizabeth
Holbrook, Mary L.
Holcomb, Sheila G.
Holcombe, Ronda
Holden, Gregory D.
Holden, Scott D.
Holden-Corr, Ursula M.
Holder, Kim L.
Holder, Sandra
Holder, Sheri L.
Holdwick, Giovanna Joann M.
Holifield, Trudee
Holko, Katherine P.
Holko, Susan May
Holland, Cynthia A.
Holland, Faith L.
Holland, Karen T.
Holland, Kathleen P.
Holland, Kimberly Jean
Holland, Lynne A.
Holland, Maria A.
Holland, Ramona Dawn
Holle, Jessica I..
Holler, Cynthia M.
Hollett, Debra A.
Holley, Anita
Hollinrake, Jean Marie
Hollis, Jeannette
Hollis, Mary F.
Hollis, Suzanne
Hollow, Barbara Anne
Holloway, Janine
Holloway, Tracey
Holloway, Vanessa
Hollrah, Teresa Irene
Holmberg, Rachel Louise
Holmen, Kimberly L.
Holmes, Crystal M.
Holmes, Faith Lee
Holmes, Rashee N.
Holmes, Renita K.
Holmes, Vickie L.
Holmes, Volante L.
Holmlund, Julia R.
Holohan, Candice N.
Holoway, Tracey L.
Holroyd, Ronald B.
Holt, Grete C.
Holtkamp, Denise K.
Holtsclaw, Elinor C.
Holtz, Tricia J.
Holtzman, Beverly J.
Hom, Mol

Homa, Valerie M.
Homer, Sammy R.
Homra, Leslie A.
Hone, Francis J.
Honeywell, Lorraine
Honkanen, Christy
Hood, Dina J.
Hood, Judy M.
Hood, Robert Daniel
Hooks, Peggy L.
Hooper, Micshanna C.
Hoover, Allyson
Hoover, Donna M.
Hoover, Gayle I.
Hoover, Jan
Hoover, Mary E.
Hoovler, Marcia J.
Hopkins, David A.
Hopkins, Grettel
Hopkins, John J.
Hopkins, Lois
Hopkins, Rebecca S.
Hopper, Lisa Leigh
Horn, Susan J.
Horne, Alison M.
Horner, Ferne M.
Horner, Holly J.
Horner, Jacob J.
Hornick, Brendan D.
Hornsby, Gay
Hornung, Phyllis T.
Horodeck, Marelle
Horstman, Lindy R.
Horter, Sarah N.
Horton, Leigh-Ann
Horton, Linda R.
Horton, Michael E.
Horton, Millicent R.
Horton, Tabitha Michelle
Horton, Tylena K.
Horvath, Rita C.
Horwat, Catherine
Hoskins, Wende D.
Hostetler, Pamela M.
Hostettler, Jaime L.
Hotchkin, Terry E.
Houck, Patricia M.
Houde, Anita Jean
Houedou, Marie A.
Hough, Holly J.
Hough, Judith L.
Hough, Lori
Hough, Sandra
Houghtling, Virginia M.
Houk, Lara C.
Houk, Nancy J.
House, Angela D.
House, Lou Anna
House, Michael Seraphin
Householder, Charles
Houser, Dan
Houser, Jeanette M.
Houser, Wendy A.
Housteau, Hilda
Howard, Angela Y.
Howard, Avis I.
Howard, Elizabeth
Howard, Genetta A.
Howard, James C.
Howard, Jill M.
Howard, Kristine M.
Howard, LaTonya C.
Howard, Rita K.
Howard, Simone Late
Howard, Tricia Ann
Howard, Trudy
Howe, Rufus
Howell, Angela M.
Howell, James M.
Howell, Luisa B.
Howell, Nathan Tod
Hoxsey, Caitlin M.
Hoyle, Daniel S.
Hoyt, Jeanette White
Hrbek, Robinetta M.
Hrutkay, Kimberly J.

Hryadil, Jacqueline E.
Huang, Kewen
Hubbard, Ada L.
Hubbard, Cheryl L.
Hubbard, Dorinda A.
Hubbard, Pearl A.
Hubbs, Brandon
Hubert, Jody Marie
Huda, Akm N.
Huddleston-Sanders, Carlene Sue
Hudek, Beth A.
Hudson, Helen
Hudson, Joan M.
Hudson, Kristi
Hudson, Laurel R.
Hudson, Robert
Hudson, Sandra J.
Hudson, Zerita H.
Huegerich, Erin L.
Huegle, Daniel S.
Huelsing, Christine M.
Huey, Elizabeth D.
Huey, Kevyn D.
Huff, Ashley
Huff, Carol G.
Huggar, Dianne M.
Huggins, Elizabeth C.
Hughes, Betty
Hughes, Carla
Hughes, Charmelle Y.
Hughes, Dannis J.
Hughes, De Anna R.
Hughes, Dorothy E.
Hughes, Jayne M.
Hughes, Jo P.
Hughes, Joe
Hughes, Karen
Hughes, Linda A.
Hughes, Melinda
Hughes, Myrtle Constantia
Hughley, Anthony
Huie, Rita I.
Huleatt, Tom
Huleisy, Alicia Ahlam
Hulett, John P.
Hulin, Carol U.
Hull, Erin L.
Hull, Glenda
Hultgren, Dorothea A.
Humber, Heidi
Humble, Christina L.
Humiston, Carol J.
Humphrey, Bonnie J.
Humphrey, David A.
Humphrey, Kathleen M.
Humphrey, Kelly E.
Humphrey, Ronnie J.
Humphreys, Eva
Humphries, Elizabeth A.
Humphries, Maria T.
Hunger, Beverly D.
Hunnicutt, Joanne
Hunsucker, Patti
Hunt, Carlos D.
Hunt, Cheryl Christine
Hunt, Debbie
Hunt, Holly Elizabeth
Hunt, Jane A.
Hunt, Jessica
Hunt, Julie
Hunt, Marian L.
Hunt, Maureen B.
Hunt, Molly E.
Hunt, Timothy A.
Hunt, Tonia Y.
Hunteman, Gloria K.
Hunter, Beverly D.
Hunter, Beverly J.
Hunter, Delecia Denee
Hunter, Donna
Hunter, Harry
Hunter, Leonard
Hunter, Margaret
Hunter, Mary
Hunter, Maureen B.
Hunter, Pamela

Hunter-Boerner, Helen
Huntman, Gloria K.
Huq, Carolyn A.
Hurley, Dyanna
Hurney, Jessica J.
Huron, Roy
Hurst, Violette J.
Hurster, Sandra
Hurt, Christina
Hurt, Emma J.
Hurt, Mary Rebecca
Hurteau, Melissa C.
Husband, Karen
Husband-Antis, Kimberly M.
Huskey, Kathy L.
Huskey, Mary K.
Hussaini, Diane Coppedge
Hussein, Linda C.
Hussey, Barbara C.
Husted, Leslie I.
Huston, Edwin Clayton
Huston, Penny L.
Huston, Robert
Husu, Karen
Hutchings, Pamela Jo
Hutchins, Laura K.
Hutchison, Brian
Hutchison, Edward J.
Hutchison, Phyliss
Hutchisson, Celestia J.
Hutfless, Amy K.
Hutkins, Laura
Hutsell, Emily M.
Hutson, Jeanne M.
Hutson, Kenna S.
Hutt, Cheryl K.
Hutt, Nancy Wassom
Huttner, Walter
Hutton, Kathleen Louise
Hvezda, Maria L.
Hwang, Jane Y.
Hwu, Susan
Hyatt, Beverly
Hyde, Francesca G.
Hyland, Rosalea
Hyland, Sarah
Hyman, Lisa
Hymers, Jacqueline J.
Hymes, Kathryn Ann
Hynes, Elizabeth
Hynes, Mary J.

I

Iacovacci, Christine A.
Iampieri, Susanne R.
Iarussi-Donnelly, Mary Jo
Ibanez, Karina
Ibara, Louella U.
Ibarra, Jason J.
Ilo, Chibuzo N.
Iluebbey, Gwendolyn
Im, Hyun C.
Imel, Jed B.
Imlej, Annbeth
Imler, Angela L.
Imler, Janet L.
Immordino, Sabatino
Imperial, Lorna Q.
Ines, Hilda
Infante, Erlinda R.
Ingalls, Suzanne E.
Ingals, Margaret
Ingelson, Kathleen
Ingle, Carolyn
Ingle, Joanne M.
Ingleson, Kathleen
Inglis, Pamela A.
Ingold, Andrea
Ingram, Kala
Ingram, Pamela O.
Ingram, Sonya J.
Ingram-Jones, Cherie
Inniss, Roemayne
Innocentini, John
Inouye, Larry T.

Inyang, Irene A.
Inyang, Rosalind D.
Inyard, Stephanie Y.
Ioannitis, Vasilios-Bill
Ipsa, Lainie
Ireton, Elizabeth
Irie, Sheryl S.
Irlbeck, Catherine
Irons, Mildred A.
Irvin, Lindsay T.
Irvin, Michelle
Irvine, Dora J.
Irvine, Ericka Drake
Irvine, Susan H.
Irving, Melissa D.
Irwin, Barbara
Irwin, Jean P.
Irwin, Nancy H.
Irwin, Tatia
Isaacs, Ann K.
Isaacson, Haylee
Isaacson, Valerie
Isaak-Shapiro, Deborah
Isbell, Lisa M.
Isbell, Shawna Leigh
Isbey, Caroline
Isenhart, Rachel
Isenhower, Janet E.
Ishman, Kennethia R.
Ising, Mary M.
Isom, Jolene M.
Ison, Jordan Dennis
Issa, Martha C.
Istre, Catherine Anne
Ivanic, Dustin B.
Iwamura, Diane
Iyoha, Esohe T.
Izutsu, Marci A.
Izzo, Cecilia S.

J

Jablonski, Joline Ann
Jablonski, Virginia A.
Jackels, Lois Thomas
Jackels, Terry
Jackman, Jahmai
Jackson, Andre
Jackson, Andrew M.
Jackson, April S.
Jackson, Barbara L.
Jackson, Beverly Jane
Jackson, Brenda C.
Jackson, Craig
Jackson, Dennis A.
Jackson, Eulalia D.
Jackson, J. Cole
Jackson, Jacquelyn
Jackson, Jessica Marie
Jackson, Joan J.
Jackson, Jonathan T.
Jackson, Marc A.
Jackson, Mark A.
Jackson, Miriam M.
Jackson, Nancy L.
Jackson, Patricia J.
Jackson, Sally A.
Jackson, Scott
Jackson, Stephanie Renee
Jackson, Tamatha
Jackson, Tobias M.
Jackson, Tracey K.
Jackson, Travis H.
Jacob, Francine
Jacob, Mary Francis
Jacobs, Amy M.
Jacobs, Carla J.
Jacobs, Elizabeth J.
Jacobs, Jill M.
Jacobs, Joan G.
Jacobs, Julie
Jacobs, Monica S.
Jacobs, Phyllis C.
Jacobsen, Kelley J.
Jacobsma, Shelley A.
Jacobson, Ardis K.

Jacobson, Brandy A.
Jacobson, Julia Ann
Jaconetta, Laura M.
Jacques, Richard K.
Jacques, Robert J.
Jacques, Sandra Kay
Jaeger, Mary
Jaekel, Geraldine
Jaggers, Raymonda
Jagiello, William Martin
Jah, Phyllistine
Jain, Amit
Jain, Rinki
Jakowich, Teresa M.
James, Bobbi L.
James, Catherine S.
James, Debra K.
James, Kimberly A.
James, Margaret
James, Pamela Jean
James, Tracy Elizabeth
Jameson, Lisa A.
Jameson, Nancy
Jameson, Nicole E.
Jamieson-Montijo, Patricia
Jamison, Julie A.
Janca, Susanne K.
Jandt, Barbara
Janish, Dianne H.
Jank, Jennifer Kay
Janoske, Amy M.
Jansak, Elaine
Janssen, Elsie
Janusz, Maria J.
Jaramillo, Robin L.
Jarmoluk, David
Jarosz, Kathy
Jarrell, Perry
Jarrett, Barbara L.
Jarvis, Nancy M.
Jarzombek, Nelly S.
Jasinski, Janice M.
Jaskiewicz, Julia A.
Jasper, Shelly S.
Javar, Sandra
Jay, Nancy
Jaynes, Catherine Weatherly
Jean-Latiolais, Joyce
Jeannette, Edward T.
Jedlicka, Virginia L.
Jefferds, Sarah L.
Jefferson, Cicely C.
Jefferson, Jacqueline R.
Jeffery, Jennifer Lynn
Jeffery, Linda
Jeffery, Reanna E.
Jeffrey, Janet L.
Jeffries, Nancy
Jeffs, Kevin
Jenkins, Carolyn
Jenkins, Dana S.
Jenkins, Joyce A.
Jenkins, Kathryn L.
Jenkins, Kerri L.
Jenkins, Kevin W.
Jenkins, Mia L.
Jenkins, Nancy Morgan
Jenkins, Patsy J.
Jenkins, Rebecca W.
Jenkins, Tammy
Jenkins, Tonya Z.
Jenkinson, Desiree M.
Jennings, Debra
Jennings, Jason
Jennings, Nancy C.
Jennings, Shelia
Jennings, Susan R.
Jens, Amy J.
Jensen, Aaron R.
Jensen, Lisa Diane
Jensen, Stacey
Jensen, Tawnie E.
Jenson, Stacey J.
Jeon, Claudia Misun
Jerde, Bruce J.
Jerdee, Vicky H.

Jericho, Kristy
Jerman, Saundra
Jernigan, Jetta Lynn
Jerrell, Vickie L.
Jesionowski, Gloria
Jesse-Petersen, Sue K.
Jeter, Cynthia
Jeter, Mary M.
Jett, Karen R.
Jewell, Anita L.
Jewell, Linda J.
Jewett, Marcia
Jhjelmgren, Tehrese A.
Jimenez, Sandra S.
Jimenez, Teresa L.
Jin, Xin
Jinon, Jay F.
Jirak, Hannah R.
Jirau, Cassaundra H.
Jirik, Treena M.
Jirkovec, Johanna
Jochim, Vivian L.
Johansson, Julie M.
John, Helen
John, Jennifer L.
John, Jenny
Johnbrier, Christine
Johncola, Nancy
Johns, Eleanor Lockwood
Johns, Kenneth C.
Johns, Maryann H.
Johnson Kendall, Annette M.
Johnson, Aida G.
Johnson, Amanda
Johnson, Anne
Johnson, April
Johnson, Beth A.
Johnson, Blair A.
Johnson, Cameron M.
Johnson, Candice A.
Johnson, Carol
Johnson, Cassaundra C.
Johnson, Christine
Johnson, Cindy L.
Johnson, Claressa D.
Johnson, Cynthia Yvonne
Johnson, Damaris L.
Johnson, Dazella
Johnson, Deborah R.
Johnson, Debra C.
Johnson, Dee A.
Johnson, Deirdre L.
Johnson, Dionne
Johnson, Dolores L.
Johnson, Donna
Johnson, Eric David
Johnson, Georganne
Johnson, Geraldine F.
Johnson, Helen M.
Johnson, Irene Y. L.
Johnson, James
Johnson, Janet K.
Johnson, Janine Leigh
Johnson, Jeffrey
Johnson, Jeffrey H.
Johnson, Joel C.
Johnson, Joseph
Johnson, Judith
Johnson, Judy B.
Johnson, Julie Ann
Johnson, Karla J.
Johnson, Karyn L.
Johnson, Katherine E.
Johnson, Keith R.
Johnson, Kelly
Johnson, Kenneth J.
Johnson, Kim M.
Johnson, Koren D.
Johnson, Kristin L.
Johnson, Kristy M.
Johnson, Larry M.
Johnson, Lauren McMurtry
Johnson, Linda
Johnson, Lois Turner
Johnson, Luann M.
Johnson, Margie

Johnson, Marianne Elizabeth
Johnson, Marlys A.
Johnson, Mary M.
Johnson, Mary Mims
Johnson, Megan L. S.
Johnson, Myra S.
Johnson, Nicole Y.
Johnson, Oretha D.
Johnson, Patricia L.
Johnson, Patricia M.
Johnson, Rebecca A.
Johnson, Richard E.
Johnson, Robert A.
Johnson, Robin Lee
Johnson, Sally W.
Johnson, Sharon
Johnson, Susan
Johnson, Tamala Renee
Johnson, Theresa
Johnson, Timothy H.
Johnson, Vickie D.
Johnson-Larosa, Sandra A.
Johnson-Plato, Patricia A.
Johnston, Carolynn
Johnston, Gregory S.
Johnston, Jeannine A.
Johnston, Jennifer G.
Johnston, Judith
Johnston, Katherine
Johnston, Kenton J.
Johnston, Margaret L.
Johnston, Marilyn G.
Johnston, Phillippa L.
Johnston, Sean K.
Johnston, Shelly R.
Johnston, Tanya K.
Joiner, Barbara
Jolley, Jennie L.
Jones Holley, Melissa C.
Jones, Amy
Jones, Anita M.
Jones, Anyah
Jones, Arthur
Jones, Bonnie L.
Jones, Carla M.
Jones, Carole A.
Jones, Catherine R.
Jones, Christine M.
Jones, Danisha R.
Jones, Darren R.
Jones, DeVora L.
Jones, Dianne E.
Jones, Edna L.
Jones, Erica M.
Jones, Evonne G.
Jones, Fawn J.
Jones, Frances L.
Jones, Franklin E.
Jones, Frederick G.
Jones, Gail D.
Jones, Gwenevere C.
Jones, Jacquelyn Y.
Jones, Janet S.
Jones, Janna L.
Jones, Joan
Jones, Joan M.
Jones, JoAnn G.
Jones, Joy E.
Jones, Joyce
Jones, Judy L.
Jones, Justina
Jones, Karen
Jones, Kathleen Marie
Jones, Kathryn R.
Jones, Keith D.
Jones, Kelly
Jones, Kenya C.
Jones, Kimberly S.
Jones, Lois M.
Jones, Lori U.
Jones, Lucas
Jones, Lucas C.
Jones, Mark L.
Jones, Melissa L.
Jones, Melody K.
Jones, Michael L.

Jones, Miranda L.
Jones, Nancy W.
Jones, Norman
Jones, Pamela J.
Jones, Patricia
Jones, Paula
Jones, Ruth
Jones, Sandra
Jones, Shanell R.
Jones, Sharion M.
Jones, Shelia R.
Jones, Tami B.
Jones, Terrie Z.
Jones, Thomas
Jones, Timika S.
Jones, To Lysa Marshea
Jones, Valerie
Jones-Ingram, Cherie
Jones-Romo, Mechelle A.
Jonynas, Titas R.
Jordan, Amy Beth
Jordan, Charles W.
Jordan, Corrine
Jordan, Elizabeth A.
Jordan, Erin E.
Jordan, Kathy L.
Jordan, Phyllis E.
Jordan, Shakundala M.
Jorge, Carmen L.
Jorgensen, Janelle
Jorgensen, Maxine
Jose, Aimee S.
Jose, Linda
Joseph, Antoinette M.
Joseph, Delores
Joseph, Elizabeth A.
Joseph, Laura K.
Joseph, Rolande
Josephs, Cynthia M.
Joshi, Hitanshu H.
Joshi, Richa R.
Jost, Julie Ann
Joyce, Jr., James J.
Joyce, Margaret
Joyce, Patricia
Joyner, Karen K.
Juanengo, Nenette B.
Juarez, Deborah Taira
Jubb-Bichy, Grace M.
Judd, Vanessa A.
Juderjahn, Renae D.
Judge, Karen H.
Julson, Deborah J.
July, Maris
June, Candi Kay
June, Kathryn Ann J.
Jungbauer, Robert
Jungbauer, Robin R.
Jungers, Carol A.
Junkman, Patricia E.
Junor, Josephine
Jurich, John E.
Jurnich, Linda Ann
Jursik, Peter A.
Jussila, Pamela S.
Just, Shari L.
Justen, Leslye
Justice, Phyllus J.
Justus, Lexy

K

Kaarto, Joanne F.
Kabat, Michael
Kabel, Joya
Kacir, Sandra J.
Kadera, Virginia M.
Kahn, Celeste L.
Kahn, Shahla
Kaiman, Marianne
Kaiser, Margaret
Kaiser, Miriam D.
Kalayoglu, Murat
Kalwa, Stephen M.
Kamara, Helen H.
Kaminski, Erin N.

Kampine, Bill
Kampiyil, Dayamole G.
Kampiyil, Jerry T.
Kanapala, Sukeshini
Kane, Jerry A.
Kane, Joan C.
Kane, Toni
Kantanie, Stanley J.
Kanter, Anne Harriet
Kaplan, Debra Nadine
Kaplan, Milca A.
Kaplan, Nancy
Kaplan, Terry
Kapolas, Peter
Kappel, Dolores A.
Karch, Jennifer A.
Karesh, Kimberly O.
Karl, Diane
Karl, Melanie K.
Karlicek, Cynthia
Karman, Angela M.
Karn, Karen L.
Karpenko, Ali E.
Karr, Luana
Karras, Karla
Karrick-Harner, Susan L.
Kasakevics, Shannon M.
Kaschyk, Rosemary
Kasnetz, Karen A.
Kassa, Kelly C.
Kassly, Florence Angela
Kassly, Judith E.
Kassner, Meagen M.
Kastenschmidt, Kimberly A.
Kasun, Jr., Victor N.
Kaszuba, Jacquelynn
Katrdzhyan, Sara
Katz, Fred
Katz, Timothy R.
Kauahi, Barbara D.
Kaufman, Kenneth R.
Kaufman, Stephanie
Kaufmann, Janice E.
Kaur, Jasjeet
Kavanaugh, Megan E.
Kawakami, Valerie
Kawano, Kie O.
Kayarkar, Madhura
Kaylid, Julie D.
Kayser, Margaret A.
Kazmierski-Smith, Amy
Keagy, Diane E.
Keamo, Charlene L.
Kearns, Carol
Kearns, Stephanie
Keast, Greg D.
Keating, Florence
Keck, Susan G.
Keck, Todd W.
Keddie, Susan
Keebler, Leslie
Keech, Cynthia A.
Keegan, Kelly T.
Keel, James W.
Keele, Stephenia
Keeley, Nancy
Keeling, Nicole M.
Keen, April Kay
Keen, Linda A.
Keenan, Christopher J.
Keener, Courtney A.
Keener, Eric W.
Keener, Paula D.
Kegel, John P.
Kegley, Beverly J.
Kehe, Whitney C.
Keil, Patricia
Keita, Cheryl W.
Keith, Nancy M.
Keith, Victoria C.
Keith-Enriquez, Jayleen J.
Keith-Leach, Patricia
Keivens, Karen
Kellams, Pamela J.
Kellar, John
Kelleher, Tom

Keller, Abbie L.
Keller, Barbara
Keller, Barbara J.
Keller, Deborah
Keller, Michelle L.
Keller, Patricia M.
Kelley, Barbara C.
Kelley, Christine
Kelley, Gregory
Kelley, Kimberly A.
Kelley, Martha
Kelley, Martha E.
Kelliher, Matthew
Kelliher, Patrice
Kelling, Paula R.
Kellison, Candice L.
Kellogg, Lisa
Kellum, Bob G.
Kelly, Christine R.
Kelly, Cynthia
Kelly, Debbie I.
Kelly, Deborah
Kelly, Gayle E.
Kelly, Helen V.
Kelly, Juanita J.
Kelly, Karla K.
Kelly, Linda
Kelly, Margo Honen
Kelly, Mary
Kelly, Michelle
Kelly, Mildred Kathleen
Kelly, Patrick S.
Kelly, Robin
Kelly, Sharon M.
Kelly-Jones, Karen
Kelner, Lesley G.
Kelsey, Sylvia A.
Kemper, Jane E.
Kemper, Pamela S.
Kempkes, Sheryl
Kendall, Constance L.
Kendall, Teresa A.
Kendell, Zina
Kendrick, Mary N.
Kenfield, Michael R.
Kennedy, Amanda B.
Kennedy, Debra J.
Kennedy, Donna
Kennedy, Jack
Kennedy, Jeffrey
Kennedy, JoLee D.
Kennedy, Karen Lynn
Kennedy, Mary K.
Kennedy, Michael
Kennedy, Paul
Kennedy, Pauline
Kennedy, Tamara T.
Kennedy, Troy O.
Kenney, Deborah L.
Kenney, Marsha E.
Kenney, Tyrone
Kenny, Christine S.
Kenny, Dawn G.
Kent, Ann E.
Keohokapu, Laraline L.
Kepler, Angela
Kepler, Nancy Jane
Kerbo, Susan Williams
Kern, Juanita Sue
Kernen, Linda
Kerns, Kalvin K.
Kerr, Leo J.
Kerr, Lillian F.
Kerr, Nicole L.
Kerr, Shiela
Kerrigan, Karen F.
Kerstein, Howard J.
Kerwin, Suzanne L.
Kessinger, Leonard
Kessler, Ellen M.
Kessler, Lori
Kessler-Axelrod, Hermine
Ketchens, Erika J.
Ketner, Lisa W.
Keyes, Jennifer R.
Keyser, Beth E.

Keyser, Vivian M.
Kgasi, Linda
Khalaf, Ahmed A.
Khalil, Caroline F.
Khalsa, Idolinda
Khan, Margaret E.
Khan, Ramin
Khan, Shahla
Khanna, Suzanne C.
Khechen, Khaled A.
Khosroshahi, Mitra S.
Kiambao, Jody A.
Kibler, Benjamin
Kibler, Charla Marie
Kidd, Delores
Kidd, Patricia
Kidd, Richard A.
Kieboom-Lopez, Joline
Kiel, Carol
Kiemel, Heidi L.
Kienemann, Karen K.
Kienle, Karen A.
Kiesau, Katie A.
Kiesling, Mary Kay
Kifer, Nancy
Kihu, Emmah
Kiker, Kimberly D.
Kilgo, Robert
Killam, Patricia E.
Killean, David R.
Killingsworth, Dillon T.
Killpack, Becky
Kilma, Jemina R.
Kilpatrick, Renee L.
Kim, Irene Insook
Kim, Jung O.
Kim, Meeye H.
Kim, Talhae
Kimball, Barbara N.
Kimball, Nancy S.
Kimber, Lois A.
Kimble, Deborah L.
Kimble, Kim M.
Kimble, Sharon E.
Kimbler, Joanna N.
Kimm, Joan E.
Kimmel, Mary K.
Kimmel, Susan
Kimmo, Niki Nadine
Kinder, Amanda
Kiner, Stewart M.
King, Ashley B.
King, Betty J.
King, Brandon R.
King, Chantaya M.
King, Cherie
King, David J.
King, Donna M.
King, Dorene A.
King, Gregory O.
King, Jennifer
King, Jerry W.
King, Jesse S.
King, JoAnne M.
King, Jolie
King, Jon P.
King, Jr., Jerry W.
King, Julie Renee
King, Laura E.
King, Linda L.
King, Marilyn
King, Marsha
King, Maryellen
King, Michael H.
King, Nancy M.
King, Nathan D.
King, Shannon Ashley
King, Sherita J.
King, Stephen J.
King, Thomas C.
King, Veronica K.
King, Victor B.
Kingsbury, Shawne R.
Kingsbury, Tammy
Kingston, Kristy
Kingston, Wendy L.

Kinkin, Mary Lou
Kinnaman, Annette C.
Kinnard, David O.
Kinney, Alicia L.
Kinney, Julie
Kinney, Kathy
Kinsella, Bernadette M.
Kinsey, Mary E.
Kiplinger, Gerald D.
Kipp, Dorcas
Kirby, Edith L.
Kirby, Jennifer D.
Kirby, Judy
Kirby, Katie M.
Kirby, Patricia A.
Kirby, William G.
Kirby, Wyn A.
Kirchner, Carol
Kirincich, Kimberly
Kirisits, Beth A.
Kirk, Jamie
Kirk, John
Kirk, Judy A.
Kirk, Kathryn
Kirkland, Robert Alex
Kirkman, Celia
Kirkman, Kristin R.
Kirkpatrick, Brad
Kirkpatrick, David W.
Kirkpatrick, Judith A.
Kirkpatrick, Kevin L.
Kirkpatrick, Linda C.
Kirtland, Karyn J.
Kiser, Donna J.
Kishaba-Leaman, Sheri K.
Kishi, Lloyd T.
Kissling, Kevin M.
Kissner, Michael G.
Kistler, Danielle M.
Kistner, Adrienne P.
Kitamura, Natalie S.
Kittle, Patricia Karen
Kivlin, Merre E.
Kizer, Brandon D.
Kjell, Susan E.
Klain, Nancy K.
Kleffner, Jaime M.
Kleimann, Maria M.
Klein, Deborah P.
Klein, Lois Bede
Klein, Margaret Laura
Klein, Michael
Kleinbeck, Connie
Kleine, Sandy K.
Kleinheksel, Nancy
Kleinrichert, Kelli
Kleinschnitz, Lydia
Klem, Jeff A.
Kleman, Marlene G.
Klemm, Megan Ann
Klemperer, Susan E.
Klenk, Kevin A.
Klepper, Cecelia J.
Kleppick, Mary Ellen
Kliebenstein, Lorraine K.
Klima, Kelly
Klimek, Frank P.
Klimek, Mary A.
Kline, Sabra L.
Klinger, Eric L.
Klingman, Linda
Klink, Diann
Klinkhammer, Erna
Klish, Wendy
Klockow, Colleen A.
Kloehn, Julie
Kloos, Deborah
Klosiewski, Mark C.
Klote, Jeffrey G.
Klotwog, Joyce
Kloven, Cheryl L.
Kluemper, Molly D.
Kmetz, Marla C.
Knapp, Pamela
Knapton, Jason A.
Knapton, Karen F.

Knauer, William J.
Knechtel, Rose J.
Kneipp, Kirsten L.
Knight, Bryana S.
Knight, Cynthia A.
Knight, Freeda M.
Knight, Harriett D.
Knight, Kimberly
Knight, Lisa D.
Knight, Pauline
Knight, Rachel Ann
Knighton, Sharon K.
Knott, Keya
Knotts, Rhonda C.
Knowles, Deborah A.
Knowles, Judy C.
Knowles, Patrick M.
Knudson, Sheila Louise
Knull, Briana K.
Knutson, Eric N.
Knutson, Kristina M.
Kobashigawa, Kelli K.
Kobayashi, Erika A.
Kochanoff, Anita T.
Kochman, Barbara J.
Koehne, Renee Z.
Koeplin, Gerrie L.
Koepp, Deborah Y.
Koeppen, Shirley J.
Koepplinger, Debra K.
Koernke, John S.
Kohen, Kathryn
Kohler, Renee
Kohnen, Betty C.
Kohrman, Gina L.
Koike, Cary K.
Koinis, Jenny N.
Kokal, Erika M.
Kokosza, Kathryn M.
Kokowski, Palma A.
Kolenc, Margaret Jude
Kolida, Sylvia A.
Kolock, Robert A.
Kolodziej, Connie
Koly, Lucian S.
Kolzow, Wendy W.
Kombe, Eninka M.
Komomua, Mary K.
Konakis, Pamela J.
Koncheck, Beverly
Kondo Chun, Joni L.
Kong, Blia
Konig, Janet W.
Konigsberg, Joanne E.
Kono, Joan D.
Konyha, Kathleen
Kopel, Hera D.
Koppe, Martha E.
Koppelman, Theresa
Kordesh, Suzanne
Koren, Kathryn
Kormanik, Erin Marie
Kortemeyer, Jay
Korzec, Lorrie V.
Koska, Rosemarie
Kosmicki, Brandy
Koss, Lisa E.
Kossover, Melvyn F.
Kost, Christine
Kostella, Carol Ann
Kostial, James E.
Kothari, Siddhesh K.
Kovac, Yolanda J.
Koval, Linda B.
Kovaleski, Jean
Kowalski, Patricia A.
Kowalski, Thomas F.
Kozacek, Cynthia E.
Kozak, Kathryn A.
Kozak, Stephen I.
Kozicki, Scott
Kozikoski, Anita L.
Kozlowski, Becki
Kozlowski, Thomas
Krahn, Karol M.
Kramer, Billie

Kramer, Christine A.
Kramme, Karen Alice
Kranenburg, Marion
Krantz, Linda
Krapek, Kimberley J.
Kratoska, Kristyn Marie
Kratter, Eileen G.
Kraus, Eleanor R.
Kraus, Nancy
Krause, Jacqueline Anne
Kreader, John
Krebs, Jeffrey T.
Krebs, Linda E.
Kreiling, Deanna
Krentz, Patricia G.
Kresak, Karen
Kreszenzia, Marykay G.
Kretzer, Terry A.
Krieger, Erin G.
Krieger, Joy Barr
Krikorian, Susan L.
Krishnan, Sindhu
Krispinsky, Sharon L.
Kriss, Kristie L.
Kroeger, Lee A.
Krohn, Bruce W.
Krolick, Karen M.
Kroner, Mary Anne
Kropp, Sarah D.
Kross, Daryl Ann
Kruchinski, Jennifer A.
Krueger, Kathleen M.
Kruger, Kimberly S.
Krulia, Janet M.
Krumholz, Vanessa D.
Krumwiede, Shana Frey
Krusmark, Sandra M.
Krutzner, Carrie A.
Kubas, Karen L.
Kuehler, Gretchen I.
Kuehner, Joseph P.
Kuellenberg, Michael Karl
Kufrin, Susan Irene
Kugel, Barbara A.
Kugler, Anna M.
Kuhar, Diana
Kuhlmann, Becky
Kuhn, Kerry L.
Kuhn, Rosemarie
Kuhn, Sabrina L.
Kuhn, Sarah A.
Kuhn, Tracy Ann
Kulbacki, Debra
Kulchin, Shelley D.
Kulhanek, Daniel J.
Kulkarni, Karmeen
Kulseth, Sherri L.
Kummer, Leslie H.
Kunf, Audra G.
Kunkel, Sherrie
Kunkle, Alexandra C.
Kuno, Joan D.
Kuplic, Kirstin R.
Kuriger, Cynthia L.
Kurtz, Jeanne M.
Kuruvilla, Sarin
Kusluski, Mary Anjanette D.
Kusz, Marilyn
Kuta, Ann Marie
Kutas, Alex
Kutrip, Mary E.
Kutsch, Patricia L.
Kutsko, Catherine M.
Kuwanyaioma, Donna L.
Kuzek, Kelly L.
Kuznetsov, Phillip
Kvasnicka, Ann M.
Kveberg, Constance J.
Kveene, Melissa A.
Kwan, Janessa A.
Kwapien, Adrianna P.
Kwash, Brittany A.
Kwash, Shiree L.
Kyger, Suzanne
Kyle, Suzanne

L

La Master, Walter Cole
Labadie, Eileen
Labani, Robin Lynn
LaBarre, Raymond J.
Labat, Jackie Boucher
Labiner, Ruth
Labishak, Kathleen P.
Labounty, Jeff A.
Labrasca, Donna M.
Labrosse, Martine
Lacatell, Janna L.
Lacava, Wilma
Lacaze, Lynn
Lachiver, Richard M.
Lackey, Kelly
Lackey, Tracy M.
Lacour, Deborah L.
Lacquement, Denise L.
Lacy, Carole
Laffoon, John R.
Laffoon, Melanie D.
LaFleur, Kim L.
LaFrance, Jeanne-Marie
LaFrance, Judith
Lagos, Kathy M.
LaGrone, Cicely N.
Laham, Charles T.
Lahr, Shirley J.
Lai, Pikki
Lain, Teresa
Laine, Rosaire B.
Laird, Mary L.
Lajaune, Kathleen
Lakey, David John
Lakies, Charlotte L.
Lally, Katherine J.
Lam, Lisa
Lamantia, Sylvia Dianne
Lamas-Sheldon, Leida
Lamb, Briana K.
Lamb, June M.
Lamb, Michelle
Lambert, Donna M.
Lambert, Glen A.
Lambert, Mary Jane
Lambert, Valerie A.
Lamberth, Phillip Kevin
Lambeth, Suzanne T.
Lamkin, Sharon R.
Lamm, Tammy B.
Lamma, Lacy L.
Lamont, Carol
Lamontagne, Diana L.
Lampi, Lindsay B.
Lampley, Gerry
Lampley, Wendy G.
Lampman, Marilee L.
Lampo, Susan E.
Lancaster, Kelly P.
Lance, Terry S.
Land, Christina N.
Land, Jared R.
Landavazo, Cynthia G.
Landeen-Carlin, Janet
Lander, Phillip T.
Landin, Rita E.
Landin, Therese A.
Landing, Amy K.
Landini, Susan K.
Landman, Denise M.
Landrum, Julia
Landry, Barbara
Landry, Sean
Landwehr, Edwin Allan
Landy, Beverly
Lane, Arthur
Lane, Catherine H.
Lane, Dixie E.
Lane, Karen
Lane, Pat
Lane, Rosa Bonita
Laney, Vickie L.
Lanfer, Dianna M.

Lang, Adele C.
Lang, Anne L.
Lang, Kathleen
Lange, Barbara Ann
Lange, Carol
Lange, Jennifer L.
Langer, Carolyn Lynn
Langford, Janice S.
Langley, Anita B.
Langner, Helen J.
Lanham, Alexander B.
Lanham, Brian L.
Lanier, Margaret O.
Lanius, Tina M.
Lankford, Davetta
Lanning, Justin W.
Lanning, Linda B.
Lanove, Tammy S.
Lanque, Tammy Sue
Lansdorf, Lawrence L.
Lantz, Lisanne
Lanz, Karla J.
Lanzrath, Robert N.
Lapcevich, Nancy
LaPlant, Lisa M.
Laplante, John
Laposta, Angela M.
Lara, Carmelia D.
Lara, Carmelita A.
Laraway, Karen
Larkin, Angela Maria
Larkin, Katherine Anne
Larkin, Mary
Larochelle, Sandra L.
Larsen, Bette M.
Larsen, Ellen
Larsen, Julie
Larsen, Lynne
Larsen, Mabel M.
Larsen, Sharay
Larsen, Shelly
Larson, Bonnie M.
Larson, Debra L.
Larson, Doris J.
Larson, Julie A.
Larson, Kristin J.
Larson, Susan G.
Larue, Gary
Lasher, Nancy A.
Lashley, Paula D.
Laska, Joan B.
Lasko, Leah
Lassiter, Betty
Lassiter, James
Lassiter, Katherine
Lasure, Eileen J.
Lata, Miranda
Lategano, Cheryl S.
Latham, Linda
Latham, Nancy
Latham-Hosey, Amy M.
Latino, Beth L.
Lau, Grace
Lau, Rose L.
Lau, William C.
Laubenthal, Diana
Lauer, Barbara J.
Lauer, Janet
Lauerman, Carol A.
Laureys, Sandra J.
Laurin, Maryjane
Lauterbach, Jennifer N.
Laux, Karen A.
Lavarias, Rodney P.
Lavender, Ida
Lavender, Iris
Lavender, May
Lavent, Fran
Lavin, Sharon
Lavorico, Donna
Lawhead, J. F.
Lawler, Kevin
Lawler, Linda
Lawler, Nancy
Lawler, William C.
Lawrence, Amy R.

Lawrence, Jason R.
Lawrence, Michelle
Lawrence, Samuel
Lawrence, Ursula
Laws, Nathaniel
Lawson, Amy J.
Lawson, Brian M.
Lawson, Eliza J.
Lawson, Glover E.
Lawson, Grover C.
Lawson, James Eric
Lawson, Janet L.
Lawson, Jenifer A.
Lawson, Nanette C.
Lawson, Nicole A.
Lawton, Seth
Lay, Betty Ann
Lay, Margaret A.
Layne, Christine
Layne, Mary E.
Layton, Kathleen M.
Lazar, Mary
Lazzori, Kathirose
Le Boutillier, Jean-Baptiste
Le, Thuy Tien Pham
Leach, Kate
Leach, Paul Garfield
Leal, Marisol
Leao, Michele H. F.
Learned, Velma J.
Leasure, Carolyn L.
Leavitt, Kathleen
Lebo, Candace L.
Lebo, William Charles
Lebow, Marlene
Lecates, Janice
Lechmanik, Kathryn Mary
Lecomte, Amy E.
Lecuyer, Nancy K.
Ledbetter, Janet E.
Lede, Maria
Lederman, Alex R.
Ledford, Rebecca J.
Ledgerwood, Adrienne Michele
Ledney, Christine M.
Ledsetter, Janet E.
Lee, Allison
Lee, Carolyn M.
Lee, Cynthia S.
Lee, David A.
Lee, Gregory
Lee, Gretchen F.
Lee, Karensa C.
Lee, Kathy T.
Lee, Keisa M.
Lee, Kelly J.
Lee, Kristi R.
Lee, Lai W.
Lee, Laura C.
Lee, Lisa A.
Lee, Mary Jo
Lee, Maureen
Lee, Monica E.
Lee, Sandra S.
Lee, Sheilla K.
Lee, Ting Ting
Lee, Willis R.
Lee, Zyrion R.
Leedle, Ben R.
Leedle, Jordan R.
Leenay, John
Leeson, Shannon S.
Lee-Van Houten, Mary Jo
Leff, Candy K.
Lefors, Deborah D.
Leftenant, Jacqueline
Legenzoski, Raymond J.
Legrand Jameel, Ronda
Lehan, Jane Macy
Lehman, Benjamin
Lehman, Carla
Lehman, L. Diane
Lehman, Lorrie Diane
Lehman, Matthew J.
Lehman, Sharon A.
Leichnauer, Colleen M.

Leichsenring, Mary E.
Leidheisr, Shannon M.
Leinwand, Martin R.
Leiske, Kelly Ann
Leitner, Richard J.
Leitz, Sandra
Leko, Annie E.
Lells, Julie G.
Lemaire, Suzanne
Lemen, John E.
LeMin, Jonathan R.
Lemond, Alva P.
Lemonds, Phoebe J.
Lemons, Sheila R.
Lempka, Sheila M.
Lengemann, Lynn A.
Lengl, Anna
Lenhardt, Kathryn A.
Lenk, Holly M.
Lennick, Amanda B.
Lennon, Timothy
Lennon, Tori S.
Lent, Hazel
Lent, Sherry A.
Lenzen, Sandra
Lenzi, Julie A.
Leon, Nicole A.
Leon, Yesenia T.
Leonard, Dana E.
Leonard, Eva
Leonard, James J.
Leonard, Joan E.
Leonard, Linda F.
Leong, Jon R.
Leon-Gonzalez, Carlos N.
Leonhard, Karen
Lepore, Marlyn
Leshley, Kimberly Beth
Lesko, Judith
Leslie, Jeanne M.
Leslie, Sonya E.
Lesmes, Gloria M.
Lesnick, Sandra
Lessar, Susan
Lester, Anicia Q.
Lester-Porner, Deborah A.
Lettow, Ryan C.
Leung, Lok M.
Leuthold, Elisabeth Susan
Levario, Baltazar G.
Lever, Julia
Leversee, Matthew D.
Levertov, Leonid
Levesque, Celia M.
Levin, Diane L.
Levin, Joanne V.
Levin, Margot A.
Levin, Rick
Levine, Jody Bell
Levine, Sandra
Levitan, Susan P.
Levy, Rachel C.
Lewallen, Lynne P.
Lewally, Augusta B.
Lewandowski, Brian J.
Lewandowski, Thomas G.
Lewis Huber, Virginia L.
Lewis, Christine
Lewis, Claudia L.
Lewis, Debra Kaplan
Lewis, Dorothy D.
Lewis, Faith
Lewis, Gina
Lewis, Joshua T.
Lewis, Jovan M.
Lewis, Katherine J.
Lewis, Kathleen Lynn
Lewis, Kellie
Lewis, Kristine A.
Lewis, Maria G.
Lewis, Marjorie A.
Lewis, Matilde L.
Lewis, Maureen T.
Lewis, Patricia S.
Lewis, Samiya
Lewis, Samuel

Lewis, Sandra J.
Lewis, Shelley A.
Lewis, Susan M.
Lewis, Suzanne L.
Lewis, Tamara A.
Lewis, Tracey
Lewis, Valerie
Lewis, Victoria
Lewis, Wendy M.
Lezcano, Jayne
Lheureux, Pamela
Li, Yongjian
Liabenow, Tanya Marie
Lias, Grashelle
Libao, Shannon K.
Libster, Elena Simeon
Licata, Carol E.
Liddell, Beulah E.
Liddell, Meta B.
Lieberg, Christian A.
Liebert, Kimberly R.
Lieser-Shepherd, Jane M.
Liford, Diana K.
Lifschitz, Mervyn L.
Liggitt, Ashley N.
Light, Katy B.
Lightfoot, Cynthia Cooper
Lighthall, Jay T.
Liko, Helen A.
Lilly, Teresa M.
Lim, Maria Cordelia L.
Linam, Denise
Lincoln, Gail H.
Lincoln, Laura Rose
Lincoln, Stacy Anne
Lind, Kimberly
Lindberg, Bernadette V.
Lindberg, Lisa
Lindberg, Yvette R.
Lindberry, Lorrie C.
Lindeman, Wayne W.
Lindgren, Barbara A.
Lindsay, Michael
Lindsay, Randall B.
Lindsay, Stacy A.
Lindsay, Sybil
Lindsay-Long, Shelley
Lindsey, Anna M.
Lindsey, Kari L.
Lindsey, Laura
Lindsey, Scott A.
Lindstrom, Glenna K.
Lindstrom, Janice A.
Lindstrom, Stephanie A.
Lindstrom, Stephen A.
Linhome, Sarah
Links, Alissa L.
Linn, Guy
Linonge, Fatmata B.
Linscott, Jana Davis
Lippello, Anita L.
Lipscomb, Angela M.
Lira, Elizabeth
Lira, Ruth A.
Liszak, Kathleen
Liszt, Suzanne D.
Litecky, Robert M.
Litteken, Kate O.
Little, Barbara A.
Little, Dana L.
Little, Joanne S.
Little, Nancy A.
Littlefield, Deborah L.
Littlefield, Jennifer
Littler, Nancy
Littles, Alonda J.
Litton, James F.
Littwin, Timothy B.
Litzenblatt, Ira
Livas, Erik J.
Livingston, Mark D.
Livingston, Rose Marie
Lledford, Rebecca J.
Lloyd, Sonophia
Lloyd, Vanessa M.
Lloyd, Weston

Llwewllyn, Josephine
Loch, Jill M.
Lockamy, Linda J.
Locke, Maria Josefina G.
Locke, Susan M.
Lockett, William E.
Lockhart, Janice G.
Lockhart, Katie S.
Lodholz, Steven G.
Loeb, Lisa
Loehr, Cathy
Loertscher, Lisa
Loewen, Cindy L.
Loftis, Sylvia
Lofton, Kevin B.
Lofton, Sharon
Loftus, Judy L.
Loftus, Michael E.
Loftus, Raymond R.
Logan, Alina
Logan, Deon M.
Logan, Kathy
Logan, Nicole Leigh
Logan, Norman B.
Logan, Teresa A.
Loggins, Sandra
Lohmann, Carla
Lohoff, Nancy
Lois-Decker, Elaine
Lollar, Karen L.
Lonacre, Linda
Londergan Gay, Patricia A.
London Brown, Allison
London, Jessica E.
Long, Barbara
Long, Christie L.
Long, Deanna L.
Long, Deborah A.
Long, Gabrielle
Long, Jeanne T.
Long, Joan R.
Long, Karen
Long, Lisa G.
Long, Nita
Long, Patricia
Long, Sharon S.
Long, Stacy M.
Long, Tracey
Long-Lucero, Laura A.
Longmire, Rose Badgett
Longnecker, Natalie
Longoria, Gabriel R.
Longwith, Virginia
Lonsdale, Karen Lynn
Looney, Jon
Loper, Judy L.
Lopes, Beverly A.
Lopez, Anita J.
Lopez, Celeste L.
Lopez, Elizabeth
Lopez, Joline Kieboom
Lopez, Mark Anthony
Lopez, Mary F.
Lopez, Robert
Lopez, Victoria T.
Lopez, Yvonne M.
Loprete Langlais, Susan
Lord, Elizabeth R.
Loredo, Alma Gloria
Loring, Kelly S.
Lormand, John E.
Lortrakul, Donna Y. M.
Losi, Judith Anne
Losito, Joanne M.
Losowski, Amanda
Lotito, Mary Sue
Lott, Richshell
Loubser, Shannon Marie
Loughner, Deborah A.
Louis-LaPierre, Sonia
Lounsbury, Patricia D.
Love, Albretta L.
Love, Kari L.
Love, Melinda D.
Love, Tonya N.
Loveless, Deborah

Lovett, Cheryl L.
Love-Walker, Tracy
Loving, Andrew M.
Lovvorn, Kim R.
Lowe, Carolyn
Lowenstein, Nicki
Lower, Theresa Ann
Lowery, Juliette M.
Lowery, Martin
Lowery, Patricia
Lowney, Malinda A.
Lowrey, Lisa A.
Lowry, Mary
Lowry, Shelia Y.
Loya, Emily R.
Loyd, Susan M.
Lozano, Virginia
Lubin, William J.
Lubitz, Michael D.
Luby, Monica W.
Lucas, Amber L.
Lucas, Carla
Lucas, Karen Pandullo
Lucas, Lisa A.
Lucas, Monique
Lucas, Tanya Kae
Luciano, Catherine A.
Luck, Shoneen
Ludlam, Paul Michael
Ludwick, Alyson H.
Luebbe, Angela M.
Lueders, Karen R.
Luetkenhaus, Gail Ann
Luge, Lauren L.
Luginski, Mary A.
Lugo, Christina M.
Luibel-Hulen, Anne Marie
Lukemire, Johanne W.
Lumetta, Jennifer E.
Lumsdaine, Alfred
Lumsden, Cheryl A.
Luna, Deborah K.
Luna, Judy
Lunce, Fred
Lund, Marc
Lundak, Mary K.
Lundgren, Esther R.
Lundy, Victor
Lunn, Glorianna
Lunn, Rodney H.
Lupo, Debra A.
Luqua, Laurel Lynn
Lusain, Debra A.
Luster, Susan M.
Lutcher, Christine
Luther, Beverly
Luther, Elaine G.
Luther, Madeline
Luther, Robin Leah
Luther, Robyn J.
Lutz, Lisa M.
Luzius, Nancy E.
Luznar, Catherine
Ly, Sherry Y.
Lyford, Joanne
Lyman, Joan
Lyman, Stacia Marilew
Lynch, Bonnie
Lynch, Jane
Lynch, Joanne M.
Lynch, Laura
Lynch, Maura
Lynch, Patricia M.
Lynch, Sheila L.
Lynch, Susan P.
Lynes, Henry A.
Lynn, Jeffery D.
Lynn, Jordan D.
Lynn, Kimberly R.
Lynn, Mary F.
Lynn, Rodney H.
Lyon, Barbara L.
Lyon, Michelle M.
Lyons, Nichole Y.
Lyons, Schrelle
Lyster, Jennifer J.

Lyston, Sally W.
Lytle, Lisa H.
Lytle, Sherri

M

Mabbitt, Larry A.
Mabry, Mary A.
Mabry, Matthew
Mabry, Teresa
Macali, Jennifer L.
Macaller-Dawson, Tami A.
Macchiaroli, Kristina N.
MacConnell, Teresa
Maccord, Carolyn Marie
MacCrakin, Laura E.
MacDonald, Elaine
MacDonald, Jamie
Macfarlane, Nicole M.
MacGregor, Daryl T.
Mach, Suzanne B.
Machara, Lori J.
Macharsky, Jennifer W.
Mack, Lynne P.
Mack, Michele L.
Mack, Sedric
Macke, Ginger L.
MacKenty, Michael
Mackenzie, Kristin J.
Mackey, Angelica L.
Mackey, Mikaela G.
Mack-Finch, Joyce A.
Mackie, Sheryl A.
Macklin, Corliss Lee
Macleane, Barbara A.
Macmillan, Barbara P.
Macmillan, Kelley R.
Macy, Carol
Macy, Margaret
Madden, Elmira
Madden, Lorrie D.
Madden, Marcia Anne
Maddox, Christopher R.
Maddox, Marylynn
Maddux, Alice
Madenwald, Nettie Darlene
Mader, Judith
Madera, Maria B.
Madewell, Alison N.
Madha, Sarah
Madikoto-Owusu, Marjorie R.
Madison, Teresa G.
Madrid, Yolanda
Madrigal, Patricia
Madsen, Linda B.
Madson, Mardelle
Madux, Alice
Maez, Deon S.
Maffey, Janet C.
Magaha, Marilyn
Magalee, Shamika
Magana, Yanelle
Magaro, Norman P.
Magat, Kristine M.
Magdaro, Colleen M.
Magee, J. Sample
Maggard, Amy Lynn
Magill, Cathleen R.
Maginness, Jamie L.
Magnificent, Lori A.
Magnusen, Ellen G.
Magpuri, Perpetua
Magruder, LaVon J.
Magura-Scarberry, Kathleen W.
Magyar, Jane
Magyar, Susan L.
Mahaffey, Dani R.
Mahaffey, Douglas S.
Mahajan, Rajendra R.
Mahan, Daniel S.
Mahan, Linda
Maheshwari, Sumit
Mahler, Susan M. R.
Mahlmann, Ann Marie
Mahoney, June
Mahoney, Kathleen

Mahoney, Linda S.
Mahutte, Kees
Maier, Jeffrey L.
Mailloux, Jerome A.
Main, Margaret A.
Maines, Gail D.
Maines, Jennifer A.
Majewski, Nichole Renee
Majors, Jammie C.
Majors, Misty D.
Mak, Kevin
Makizuru, Wade Y.
Makos, April Lynn
Makris, Meredyth J.
Makuakane, Faith
Malaikham, Pone
Malamatos, Mary Beth
Malanchuk, Megan C.
Malaney, Diane F.
Malaskovitz, Amanda Joyce
Malaskovitz, Joyce
Malaspino, Linda
Malatest, Patricia
Malbone, Jami
Malcom, Lora L.
Maldonado, Erma
Malhotra, Taniya
Malik, Constance W.
Malik, Monica
Malik, Sandra Elizabeth
Malinoff, Marylee
Malinoff, Rochelle L.
Malinowski, Ann
Malinowski, Kelly
Malkin, Ellery S.
Malkoch, Gracie A.
Mallery, Sarah
Mallinder, Joy
Mallon, Walter K.
Mallory, Yvette C.
Malloy, Diana L.
Malloy, Mike
Maloch, Lori B.
Malone, Della
Malone, Katherine M.
Malone, Krista R.
Malone, Marion C.
Malone, Susan K.
Malone, Therese
Malone, William Charles
Maloney, David J.
Malsy, Amelia
Malugin, Shawn Christopher
Malum, Donna J.
Mammoser, Anita
Mancilla, Esther
Mancina, Joanne
Mandel, Ellen D.
Mandrell, Judy K.
Maneri, Alisa A.
Manges, Jeremy M.
Mangino, Gloria
Mangio, Connie J.
Mangold, Michael J.
Mangold, Nancy B.
Mangold, Nancy D.
Manier, Gwendolyn
Manigault, Carolyn A.
Manion, Mary Jane
Manly, Benjamin P.
Mann, Diane L.
Mann, Julie
Mann, Myrna L.
Mann, Scott R.
Manning, Cassandra H.
Manning, David L.
Manning, Joan
Manning, Robert David
Mans, Jean
Manson, Susan C.
Mansour, Amgad M.
Mantle, Clarissa M.
Mantovani, Sylvia L.
Manuel, Ryan T.
Manus, Mandy
Manusani, Bindu M.

Maple, Morris
Maples, Amanda
Maples, Kevin R.
Maples, Morris
Marbley, Mary
Marbury, Candice M.
Marceau, Angela
Marcella, Marian
Marcelli, Melissa A.
Marchus, Claudia
Marciniak, Brenda A.
Marconi, Toni Ann
Marcu, Gary J.
Marcuccelli, Monica L.
Marcus, Bobby G.
Marcus, Rosalyn P.
Marcyjanik, Frances J.
Mardell, Stephen R.
Marenghi, Amanda J.
Margolis, Steven J.
Mariana, Carol Ann
Mariano, Jomar
Marietta, Amanda Amaya
Marin, Delia
Marino, Christopher J.
Markelz, John
Markendorf, Joyce F.
Markham, Debra
Marklein, James E.
Markotay, Vicki
Markovich, Lehiwa N.
Markowitz, Lynda S.
Markowitz, Susan
Marks, Paula Frances
Marks, Susanne C.
Markus, Kathy Ann
Markuson, Ann E.
Markworth, Bonney
Marlar, Janet
Marlow, David B.
Marlowe, Arleita
Marlowe, Sarah Jayne
Marok, Lindsey M.
Marotta, Michael A.
Marotto, Marybeth
Marple, Claire E.
Marquand, Judith A.
Marquez, Evelyn
Marquez, Laura C.
Marquez, Maureen R.
Marquez, Patricia
Marrero, Virginia
Marsch, Debra S.
Marsh, Amy N.
Marsh, Jeffrey A.
Marsh, Philip J.
Marsh, Shirlie
Marshall, AnneMarie L.
Marshall, Avril C.
Marshall, Cynthia
Marshall, Detra V.
Marshall, Douglas
Marshall, Jessica Quinn
Marshall, Katheryn A.
Marshall, Kathy
Marshall, Kelly
Marshall, Linda
Marshall, Richard W.
Marshall, Sally A.
Marshall, Sharon Ann
Marshel, Florine
Marston, Mary Patricia
Marszal, Dawn Sauter
Marszalek, Phyllis B.
Martchenko, Nelli
Martelli, Maria J.
Marten, Courtney D.
Marth, Kelly S.
Marth, Mel
Martich, Dawn
Martin, Amanda M.
Martin, Ann N.
Martin, Cheryl L.
Martin, Christine
Martin, Colleen K.
Martin, Connie

Martin, Daniel R.
Martin, Dinah
Martin, Emma M.
Martin, Esther
Martin, Faustine
Martin, Glory
Martin, Janice
Martin, Jessica J.
Martin, John
Martin, Joyce A.
Martin, Katherine S.
Martin, Kendra
Martin, Kendra E.
Martin, Leonard V.
Martin, Linda Kay
Martin, Lisa
Martin, Lisanne J.
Martin, Marilyn Kay
Martin, Matthew H.
Martin, Michelle S.
Martin, Nadine Mary
Martin, Nan
Martin, Paul A.
Martin, Paula K.
Martin, Robert L.
Martin, Roberta I.
Martin, Sean C.
Martin, Susan
Martin, Tamara K.
Martin, Tara
Martin, Valorie R.
Martin, Virginia L.
Martineau, Jennifer L.
Martinez, Angelique M.
Martinez, Deo
Martinez, Hector R.
Martinez, Ismael J.
Martinez, Jennifer L.
Martinez, LaVonda D.
Martinez, Ricardo A.
Martino, Laura
Martins, Jeremy N.
Martz, Christy A.
Martz, Michele A.
Marvel, Joann M.
Marvel, Wendy C.
Marvin, Dana
Marvin, Jeffrey
Marvin, Kim
Marye, Roberta I.
Marzicola, Francey K.
Mascaro-Corwin, Mary Beth
Masenri, Lisa
Mashburn, Janice D.
Masih, Sylve S.
Masley, Cindy A.
Masneri, Lisa
Mason, Andrea
Mason, Carl R.
Mason, Christopher M.
Mason, Danielle M.
Mason, Diane
Mason, Dorothy
Mason, Glenda
Mason, Idallas M.
Mason, Jacquelyn M.
Mason, Kayla D.
Mason, Mary A.
Mason, Olive
Mason, Susan A.
Masood, Jennifer A.
Mass, Carolee
Mass, Sandra A.
Massa, Christine
Masset, Grace E.
Massetto, Karen E.
Massey, Cynthia Beth
Massey, Gary Lynn
Massey, Sharon R.
Massey-DeMonbreun, Lori
Massengill, Nina B.
Masters, Emily J.
Masterson, Susan L.
Masterson, Tara A.
Mastraieni, Adrian S.
Masztak, Dean

Matern, Linda B.
Matheson, Della L.
Mathews, Deborah L.
Mathews, Hiram J.
Mathews, Linda H.
Mathews, Patricia
Mathews, Tina F.
Mathis, Georgiana J.
Mathis, Rebecca
Matlock, Cindy O.
Matotek, Michael T.
Mattes, Joan E.
Matthais, Sheilan M.
Matthews, Deborah W.
Matthews, Kimberlee D.
Matthews, Kristen Irene
Matthews, Lori J.
Matthews, Shantel
Matthis, Lisa M.
Mattingly, Victor
Mattison, Sandra S.
Mattox, Terra D.
Matulovich, Kristie L.
Mau, Lisa
Mauldin, Brooke
Mauldin, Carroll
Maunakea, Kimberly K.
Mauser, Nancy E.
Mautz, Melinda
Mawk, Kathleen
Maxey, Alan H.
Maxwell, Evon
Maxwell, Joann C.
Maxwell, Peggy E.
Maxwell, Susan
May, Bradley S.
May, Candi Kay
May, Maris
May, Wayne
Mayberry, Dana E.
Mayberry, Paul D.
Mayer, Ann Goulet
Mayers, Joel E.
Mayes, Courtney N.
Mayes, Peri Anne
Maynard, John D.
Maynard, Sharlln H.
Maynard, Timothy
Mayone, Claire A.
Mayr, Mark A.
Mayton, Jean K.
Mazat, Jeanne R.
Mazur, Carolyn
Mbakwe, Eberechi
McAdams, Jr., Daniel W.
McAdoo, Catrina D.
McAdoo, Kacey Crowley
McAliley, Susan M.
McAllister, Irene
McAllister, Paul D.
McAlpine, Deymeon D.
McArthur, Sandra W.
McAtee, Martha Aileen
McAtee, Verlisa Jean
McAulay, Robin Ann
McAuley, Anne
McBrian, Lisa
McBride, Doreen
McBride, Kevin M.
McBride, Suzanne Marie
McCabe, Marsha G.
McCaffrey, Patricia G.
McCaig, William T.
McCaleb, Angela H.
McCaleb, June M.
McCall, Patsy A.
McCall, Stephen S.
McCallister, Terry L.
McCallum, Patsy Ann
McCallum, Wendy Lynn
McCallus, Cynthia M.
McCammon, Carl
McCammon, Carolyn
McCammon, Jennifer
McCann, Mary Elizabeth
McCann, Peter N.

McCann, Suzen Hutchison
McCarter, Cathy A.
McCarter, Jane
McCarter, Tonya K.
McCarther, Kimberly B.
McCarthy, Chad D.
McCarthy, Kellie J.
McCarthy, Linda J.
McCarthy, Mary
McCarthy, Mary Anne
McCarthy, Parker J.
McCartney, Sarah R.
McCarty, Lucille C.
McCarty, NaShawn A.
McCary, Stephanie N.
McClain, Angela
McClain, Janice
McClain, Jennifer R.
McClain, Kathryn A.
McClain, LaFonda Chicole
McClain, Leslie D.
McClard, Carol J.
McClarey, Bryan
McClarey, Deborah F.
McCleary, Andrea E.
McCleary, Nancy
McClellan, Debra N.
McClellan, Donald L.
McClelland, Warren Spence
McClendon, Cassandra L.
McClendon, Dawn M.
McClendon, Jacquelyn J.
McClenithan, Scott L.
McCloskey, Joyce A.
McCloskey, Sheila
McClosky, Kari
McClure, Twila B.
McCollam, Resa
McCollum, Donna Lynn
McConahy, Breanna L.
McConahy, Lonnie L.
McConnell, C. Don
McConnell, Donna C.
McConnell, James M.
McConnell, Lori Ann
McConville, Susan
McCool, James P.
McCool, Margaret M.
McCorkle, Joyce M.
McCormack, Kristen Marie
McCormick, Erin
McCormick, Joan
McCormick, Judith A.
McCormick, Kim C.
McCorry, Sandra
McCoy, Jeanine F.
McCoy, Kathleen Mary
McCoy, Patricia
McCracken, Michelle L.
McCracken, Ryan A.
McCrary, Adrian N.
McCray, Kimberly R.
McCrea, Celia
McCrea, Deborah
McCrimmon, Catherine E.
McCulloch, Kelly
McCullough, Bobbi A.
McCullough, Jeffrey D.
McCullough, Julie A.
McCullough, Troy B.
McCullough, Tyler B.
McCune, Frank
McCurdy, JoAnn C.
McCurtain-Talbert, Diana
McDade, Anne Marie
McDaniel, Adrienne L.
McDaniel, Beatriz M.
McDaniel, Brenda
McDaniel, Elizabeth A.
McDaniel, Florence A.
McDaniel, Gloria
McDaniel, Martha Jayne
McDaniel, Tina C.
McDaniel, Wendy D.
McDonald, Austine
McDonald, Cheryl A.

McDonald, Edward J.
McDonald, Gaye
McDonald, John
McDonald, Kathleen V.
McDonald, Ken P.
McDonald, Mary B.
McDonald, Milo
McDonald, Patty Ann
McDonald, Peggy A.
McDonald, Rebecca N.
McDonald, Renee
McDonald, Ricka E.
McDonald, Rita A.
McDonald, Peggy
McDonnell, Catherine J.
McDonnell, Cathy
McDonnell, Robert C.
McDonough, Tammy
McDowell, Deborah A.
McDowell, Michael D.
McDowell, Patricia A.
McElewee, Michelle
McElfresh, Darla C.
McElhaney, Sherri
McElheny, Kathleen
McElhone, Susan M.
McElwee, Frances
McEver, David L.
McEwen, Inara
McFadden, Alysa D.
McFall, Shannon
McFarland, Debbie D.
McFarland, Douglas G.
McFarland, Lucinda
McFarland, Margaret S.
McFerrin, Cheryl I.
McFerrin, Suzanne A.
McGarry, Erin M.
McGary, Judith Ann
McGee, Amanda M.
McGee, Jennifer L.
McGee, Kathleen A.
McGee, Lynn B.
McGeever, Patricia A.
McGehee, Lillian Jeanette
McGhee, Shirell
McGill, Jennifer L.
McGill, Nanette Louise
McGill, Richard D.
McGinley, Geraldine
McGinley, Geraldine
McGinnis, Matthew A.
McGinnis, Matthew A.
McGonigle, Rosemary
McGovern, Steven J.
McGowan, Maureen P.
McGrane, Maggie L.
McGrath, Jane
McGrath, Lisa R.
McGrath, Paula M.
McGraw, Patrick
McGraw, Susan
McGregor, Susie
McGregor-Landerkin, Leslie
McGregory, Rhonda K.
McGrone, Contessa N.
McGuigan, Brian
McGuire, Denise
McGuire, Gail L.
McGuire, Judith M.
McGuire, Karen Y.
McHale, Ann E.
McHale, Jean Marie
McHale, Susan R.
McHaney, Racheal N.
McInnes, Elaine M.
McIntosh, Darryl W.
McIntyre, Donna K.
McIntyre, Marilyn R.
McIver, Ruth Johnson
McKain, Donald E.
McKain-Yancey, Denise P.
McKay, Beverly Ann
McKay, Helen J.
McKee, Shirley M.
McKeehan, Martha

McKeller, Malika
McKelley, Andrew R.
McKenna, Ann K.
McKenna, Lindsay A.
McKenna, Marguerite
McKenna, Mary E.
McKennan, Eleanor
McKenney, Lisa M.
McKenzie, Tami Lynn
McKibbin, Carolyn J.
McKim, Robert V.
McKinney, Kenya
McKinnie, Laura J.
McKinnon, Gail H.
McKnelly, Casey Ann
McKnight, Karen
McKoy, Sabrina L.
McLain, Linda
McLamb, Carol L.
McLane, Mary A.
McLaren, Tina M.
McLarty, Katie A.
McLaughlin, Eugene
McLaughlin, Jane
McLaughlin, Lynda B.
McLaughlin, Mary
McLaughlin, Marylynn A.
McLaughlin, Michael
McLay, Wanda P.
McLean, Esther Nyamah
McLenon, Rani L.
McLeod, Martha
McMahon, Jean M.
McMahon, Linda
McMahon, Marie C.
McMahon, Sims
McManaman, Kevin
McManus, Denise
McMeans, Melinda H.
McMenamin, Debra D.
McMillan, Debbie K.
McMillan, Michael L.
McMillan, Rebecca D.
McMillan, Wendy L.
McMorrow, Patricia
McMullen, Debra J.
McMullen, Ruth
McMurray, Elizabeth
McMurray, Latoya T.
McNabb, Jennifer Anne
McNair, Corrina Rebekah
McNally, Kathleen A.
McNally, Mario R.
McNally, Mary E.
McNally, Michelle M.
McNally, Susan
McNally, Tracy Lee
McNamee, Christina M.
McNany, Norman
McNear-Watkins, Deborah D.
McNeely, Amanda H.
McNeely, Carol
McNeil, Claudia J.
McNeil, Mary N.
McNeil, Patricia D.
McNeill, Mary N.
McNelis, Michele M.
McNicholas, Imelda
McNutt, Judith Will
McPeak, Shirley
McPhee, Ersel E.
McPhee, Melanie A.
McPherson, Kimberly S.
McPherson, Trent Michael
McRedmond, Alice Marie
McRedmond, Mary A.
McReynolds, Robert L.
McShane, Bernadine M.
McTaggart, Judy L.
McVay, Laura L.
McVay, Thomas
McVeigh, James T.
McVey, Karla R.
McVicker, Jenae A.
McVicker, Karen J.
McWaters, Michael

McWhorter, Jason W.
McWhorter, Mark H.
Meacham, Kelly J.
Mead, Connie L.
Mead, Janna L.
Mead, Lois
Mead, Mary
Meade, Tanesha R.
Meador, Marybeth S.
Meadows, Barbara
Meadows, Connie L.
Meadows, Jayne Katy
Means, Donna M.
Means, Linda A.
Means, Melissa
Mears, Susan
Mecham, Jennifer J.
Mechnik, Sandra R.
Medanich, Virginia P.
Meddleton, Cheryl
Meder, Gertrude
Medford, Cynthia C.
Medina, Marjorie K.
Medina, Melca A.
Medlen, Joanne E.
Medley, Marie
Medwid, Amber M.
Meehan, Vickie J.
Meehleib, Arlene E.
Meeks, Keifer
Meenach, Jonathan
Megahan, Donald Bruce
Meggs, Barbara J.
Mehan, Natalie
Mehta, Cheryl L.
Mcier, Norma J.
Meiners, Rebecca A.
Meirelles, Janet
Meis, Martha M.
Meisenhelder-Smith, Jodee
Meisner, Gary B.
Meister, Angela K.
Meitz, Deborah Ann
Mejia, Monica N.
Meketa, Antares
Mekush, Amber
Melcher, Brian J.
Melder, Christine
Melegari, Jason D.
Melgaard, Marylen
Mellick, Elizabeth
Mellon, Judith Lorraine
Melnikov, Gretchen
Melson, Daniel L.
Melton, Fredrick
Meltzer, Jeffrey A.
Melville, Mark B.
Melvin, Alaina S.
Melvin, Carol B.
Melvin, Cathy
Melvin, Hugh S.
Membreno, Maria
Menard, Christine M.
Menck, Sheila Boyle
Mendenhall, Heather J.
Mendez, Marco A.
Mendonsa, Betty J.
Mendoza, Kathie A.
Mendoza, Nancy E.
Mercer, Joe T.
Mercer, Judy A.
Mercer, Julie A.
Mercer-LeBlanc, Lauraine E.
Merchant, Jeremy S.
Merchant, Julie
Merchant, Richard Kuziola
Merenich, Micheal J.
Mergaert, Wendy M.
Merges, Diane
Mericle, Katherine B.
Meriwether, Mary Ellen
Meriwether, Roderick D.
Merlau, Kathleen W.
Merlenbach, Tina M.
Mero, Doreen E. L.
Mero, Susan

Meron, Irit
Merrill, Kristine
Merrill, Stacey
Merritt, Catherine C.
Merritt, Erika Robin
Merryman, Catherine J.
Mervosh, Mary Lynn
Merwarth, Catherine A.
Mesch, Susan A.
Meseberg, Margaret
Messer, Susan E.
Messer, Tricia J.
Messick, Alina M.
Messick, M. Gwen
Messier, Donald W.
Messier, Natacha F.
Messinger, Joyanna
Messmer, Mary Beth
Metcalf, Kimberly Grace
Metcalf, Paula
Metter, Patricia P.
Mettler, Lindsay C.
Metts, Peggy J.
Mettukuru, Srikanth
Metzger, Janice L.
Metzig, Debra
Metzler, Cheryl Ann
Meyer, Cheryl
Meyer, Chrystie M.
Meyer, Corinne
Meyer, Crystal M.
Meyer, Hope M.
Meyer, Iris
Meyer, James M.
Meyer, Karen V.
Meyer, Laura
Meyer, Paula June
Meyer, Phillip A.
Meyer, Wallace M.
Meysing, Larry
Meysing, Tamara
Michael, Bonnie
Michael, Susan R.
Michail, Nina
Michal, Ellen
Michela, Matthew A.
Micheletto, Wendi Ellen
Michette, Barbara J.
Mick, Cynthia M.
Mick, Linda
Mickel, Courtney D.
Mickelsen, Aaron D.
Middlebrooks, Bruce M.
Middlesworth, W. M.
Middleton, Patricia A.
Middleton, Stephanie J.
Midgett, Marilynn M.
Midyette, Sandra Kay
Miedema, Joanne
Miesner, Jeffrey B.
Mikaelian, John
Mikits, Karrie A.
Milana, Carol
Milanowski, Barbara
Milashoski, Susan K.
Milatovic, Kylie C.
Milburn, Ryan G.
Miler, Anna V.
Miles, Carlene
Miles, Debra M.
Miles, Julie R.
Miles-Moghadom, Sheila E.
Miley, Kimberly L.
Millage, Diana
Millan, Geri Caryl
Millan, Stephanie
Millanes, Juliet E.
Millard, Nadine K.
Millender-Lassister, Barbara
Miller, Alan
Miller, Amy
Miller, Andrea
Miller, Ann H.
Miller, Anna V.
Miller, Anthony W.
Miller, Ashley

Miller, Bettijean
Miller, Brianna B.
Miller, Carson
Miller, Christine
Miller, Connie M.
Miller, Daniel
Miller, David L.
Miller, Deborah
Miller, Deedra D.
Miller, Eboni
Miller, Elizabeth
Miller, Erik R.
Miller, Garrett V.
Miller, Grace L.
Miller, Ian
Miller, James
Miller, Janet R.
Miller, Jill L.
Miller, Joanne K.
Miller, Julie
Miller, Kathleen E.
Miller, Kirk K.
Miller, Laura J.
Miller, Linda
Miller, Lo-Rita C.
Miller, Margaret
Miller, Mari-Ann
Miller, Mary
Miller, Maxine L.
Miller, Melissa
Miller, Nancy
Miller, Nicholas S.
Miller, Pamela F.
Miller, Paul
Miller, Paula
Miller, Richard L.
Miller, Robert
Miller, Robin G.
Miller, Shannon B.
Miller, Sheryl A.
Miller, Stephen W.
Miller, Steve
Miller, Susan
Miller, Taunja Lea
Miller, Teresa
Miller, Tracy Lynn
Miller, Travis J.
Miller, Wui K.
Millerton, Yvonne M.
Millet, Josie B.
Milligan, Lori M.
Milligan, Wendy L.
Mills, Angela M.
Mills, Beth
Mills, Cherylann M.
Mills, Cortney L.
Mills, Kathleen M.
Mills, Steven R.
Milman, Aleksandr
Milner, Patricia L.
Milone, Carmela
Milroy, Casey R.
Milsap, Michelle C.
Milstone, Craig
Minear, Joan R.
Minear, Justin
Minich, Vickie J.
Minks, Carla
Minnehan, Rosemary E.
Minnella, Patricia A.
Minton, Daniel J.
Minturn, Jocelyn Lee
Minzer, Lisa M.
Mio, Franella M.
Miranda, Mark Anthony
Mirasolo, Josephine
Misity, Marie L.
Miskovsky, Vicki A.
Misleh, Matthew J.
Misso, Francesca A.
Mistrangelo, Mary Ann
Mistry, Pari
Mitcham, Tausha N.
Mitchell, Aaron Reynolds
Mitchell, Amanda G.
Mitchell, Bernadette C.

Mitchell, Bethany Anne
Mitchell, Dinah F.
Mitchell, Doris
Mitchell, Gaynelle Marie
Mitchell, Lucy J.
Mitchell, Lynnette
Mitchell, Marilee A.
Mitchell, Marta
Mitchell, Rebecca
Mitchell, Richard Ronald
Mitchell, Terri H.
Mitchell, Tracy L.
Mitchell, Tyrece L.
Mitch-Lynn, Loretta
Mitchner, Carrie Lee
Mittelstaedt, Vivian
Mixon, Elias R.
Miyashiro, Cindy T.
Mize, Jamayca D.
Mizrahi, Bonnie
Mkandawire, Selina C.
Mlinac, Ashley M.
Mlinac, Gary
Moak, Jennifer
Moats, Andrew D.
Moats, Jerri A.
Mock, Brenda Kay
Mockler, Nicole C.
Mockmore, Raymond Lee
Modean, Valerie A.
Moe, Jeanne E.
Moellenberg, Kathy
Moen, Michael
Moen, Stephanie
Moench, Laura
Moeslein, Timothy
Mofarrahi, Cheryl S.
Moffatt, Lee
Moffitt, Frank O.
Mohl, Daniel J.
Mohr, Heidi J.
Mohr, Linda M.
Mohringer, Johanna
Mohta, Aditya S.
Moilan, Mary E.
Moix, Karen
Moldawski, Mitchell R.
Moldenhauer, Laura
Molfino, Susan M.
Moline, Eneida
Mollenhauer, Patricia A.
Molly, Stephanie
Molyneaux, Donna R.
Momeno, Barbara J.
Monachino, Janice R.
Monagle, Jeannine
Monarch, Amy N.
Monat, Michael K.
Monczewski, Trudy A.
Mondragon, Rosio M.
Monette, Rachelle J.
Moneymaker, Lisa
Monroe, Andrea B.
Monrotus, Aimee M.
Monrotus, Rosemary T.
Monstwil, Stefanie L.
Montalto, Rita Marie
Monteiro, Edith M.
Monteiro, Robert
Montellano, Jesus C.
Montesa-Lujan, Jennifer
Montgomery, Angela
Montgomery, Elizabeth M.
Montgomery, Joel C.
Montgomery, Marjean H.
Montgomery, Patricia L.
Montgomery, Paula
Montgomery-Krechel, Kathleen Ann
Montijo, Michael F.
Montini, Susan M.
Montoya, Gayle P.
Moody, Amy J.
Moody, Jackie L.
Moody, James
Moody, Myra Denise
Moody, Nila L.

Mooers, Gerldine Rang
Moon, Mercedes P.
Mooney, Janice V.
Moor, Terry L.
Moore, Amy
Moore, Andrea L.
Moore, Billye J.
Moore, Cathleen Bell
Moore, Chandrica Newton
Moore, Charles D.
Moore, Cheryl Lynn
Moore, Christopher Douglas
Moore, Darin R.
Moore, Debra
Moore, Debrorah K.
Moore, DeLois T.
Moore, Diana Montoya
Moore, Diana V.
Moore, Diane L.
Moore, Donna J.
Moore, Edith K.
Moore, Ellen G.
Moore, Janis L.
Moore, Jay
Moore, Jeanne
Moore, Jennifer
Moore, John Troy
Moore, Kelley
Moore, Linda
Moore, Lora A.
Moore, Lynda Diane
Moore, Martha
Moore, Mary Ann
Moore, Melanie
Moore, Ornita G.
Moore, Paula
Moore, Rayburn
Moore, Renee C.
Moore, Ruth Ann
Moore, Samuel E.
Moore, Sonya
Moore, Tamera K.
Moore, Teresa M.
Moore, Terrence W.
Moore, Todd D.
Moore, Vicki L.
Moore, Wanda M.
Moore, William
Moore, Yvonne E.
Moorehead, Christine M.
Mooring-Howard, Evelyn Y.
Mor, Joanne M.
Moraca, Debra L.
Moragne El, Janet S.
Morales, Kathleen A.
Morales, Lisa E.
Moran, Rosann M.
Morar, Rekha
Moray, Pamela
Morciglio, Myrta M.
More, Lynda Diane
Moreau, Deborah
Morehart, Lisa E.
Morehouse, Christopher L.
Morel, Sharon V.
Moreshead, Susan B.
Morgan, Angela R.
Morgan, Deborah Gleason
Morgan, Diane
Morgan, Ellen
Morgan, Judy B.
Morgan, Lawrence
Morgan, Patricia M.
Morgan, Steven G.
Morgenroth, Gary
Mori, Janie
Moribe, Andrea
Moring, Marjorie E.
Morkel, Constance J.
Morley, Melinda A.
Morley, Nick F.
Morlock, Desiree Orvette
Moron, Melody
Morphy, Timothy
Morrell, Valerie J.
Morris, Crystal H.

Morris, Edith Ann
Morris, Ellen J.
Morris, Julie
Morris, June A.
Morris, Lesley K.
Morris, Mary
Morris, Michael J.
Morris, Sheila D.
Morrisey, Nancy L.
Morrison, June A.
Morrison, Karen D.
Morrison, Linda J.
Morrison, Mark
Morrison, Mary V.
Morrissey, Jennifer L.
Morrissey, Kathryn M.
Morrissey, Nancy L.
Morrow, Gregory M.
Morrow, Kristi L.
Morrow, Lisa F.
Morrow, Scott D.
Morrow, Sibyl
Morse, Jean L.
Mortensen, Ellen H.
Mortenson, Kathleen G.
Morton, Diane A.
Moser, Brandon D.
Moses, Emily Morgan
Moses, Ryan M.
Moses, Zachary M.
Mosier, Sherri E.
Moskowitz, Leslie A.
Mosley, Michelle L.
Mosley, Paul
Moss, Donna J.
Moss, Kristy
Mossak, Ann M.
Moten, Sharron C.
Motheral, Brenda Renee
Motheramgari, Rajeshwar
Motsinger, Sebyl Colleen
Mottern, Kathleen B.
Motto, George S.
Mount, Donna M.
Mounthongdy, Khampeng
Moushon, Jessica L.
Mowery, Jennifer L.
Moy Joseph, Hestor E.
Moy, Esterlina R.
Moy, Meilie
Moyer, Molly Ann
Moyer, Pamela
Moyo, Bekezela
Mruczek, Wanda A.
Mubiru, Phillip Balimunsi
Muchnick, Sandra R.
Mudgal, Manish
Mudiam, Satya L.
Mueller, C. Robert
Mueller, Holly M.
Mueller, Robert C.
Muenz, Janet
Mugar, Antoinette M.
Mugnier, Marcia Michelle
Mugo, Ann W.
Muhammad, Nicole D.
Muhly, Frederick W.
Mulherin, Katherine L.
Mullen, Kathleen D.
Mulleneaux, Steven T.
Mulligan, Elizabeth A.
Mulligan, Katherine
Mullihan-Post, Chantel
Mullinax, Barbara
Mullings, Yvonne
Mullinix, Morgan E.
Mullins, Chasity
Mullins, Dawn E.
Mullins, Janis G.
Mullooly, Catherine A.
Mumm, Joan L.
Mumphrey, Regina L.
Muncrief, Mary M.
Mundorff, Harry H.
Mundy, Melissa Kathryn
Mundy, Toshiko

Mungin, Al
Mungin, James A.
Munguia, Barbara C.
Muniz, Irma Bell
Munn, Rebecca W.
Munoz, Bryan P.
Munoz, Zulma
Munoz-Ross, Esther
Munroe, Linda L.
Munson, Jennifer L.
Munz, Patricia
Murabito, Pamela Dorothy
Murata, Noreen S.
Murdaugh, Myra
Murdic, Deborah Washington
Murdock, Amy J.
Murdock, Carol A.
Murgi, Lynda M.
Muro, Marisol
Murphy, Dawn M.
Murphy, Donna
Murphy, Eileen C.
Murphy, Janice K.
Murphy, Jennifer M.
Murphy, Kara S.
Murphy, Melinda G.
Murphy, Neil
Murphy, Patricia
Murphy, Sally
Murphy, Semaj A.
Murphy, Shirley
Murphy, Teresa H.
Murphy, Valerie T.
Murphy, Virginia I.
Murray, Brenda W.
Murray, Cheryl J.
Murray, Debra D.
Murray, Hattie M.
Murray, Jaye K.
Murray, Jena G.
Murray, Kristin R.
Murray, Margaret P.
Murray, Raymond
Murray, Robert
Murray, Sandra D.
Murray, Sherry
Murrell, Glenda D.
Murrell, Jacqueline E.
Murrell, Sharon J.
Murtagh, Sister Eilish
Murtaugh, Nancy E.
Murtin, Kathleen M.
Mushinsky, Robert C.
Mushti, Sirisha N.
Musial, Dorothy I.
Mussler, Richard B.
Mutisya, Brenda W.
Muunz, Patricia
Myers, Amy
Myers, Catherine F.
Myers, Cheryl K.
Myers, Elizabeth V.
Myers, Gwendolyn M.
Myers, Jake
Myers, Joyce Ann
Myers, Jr., Robert E.
Myers, Karen B.
Myers, Katie A.
Myers, Lisa S.
Myers, Mary J.
Myers, Rita L.
Myers, Ruth R.
Myers, Yvonne J.
Myles, Marcie L.
Myllymaki, Melanie C.
Mzik, Kellie L.

N

Naegele, Elaine
Nagel, April M.
Nagel, Laurie C.
Nagle, Mark Allen
Nagle-McDonald, Marianne
Nagrant, Nancy J.
Nagurny, Kristina

Naguszewski, Tanya L.
Nagy, Martin J.
Nagy-Scroggins, Jessica L.
Naito, Joanne N.
Najera, Michael A.
Najor, Sheila
Nakamura, Colleen M.
Nakata, Holly J.
Nalesnick, JoAnn
Nalley, Jeannine T.
Nalley, Sharon L.
Nance, David
Nance, Jacqueline
Nansel, Shaylen R.
Nap, Ann
Napier, Janice
Napoliello, Sally Ann
Napovanice, Melanie Kaye
Napovanice, Terra Michelle
Napper-Owen, Gloria E.
Nappi, Lisa S.
Narayanaswamy, Vivek
Narayandas, Harikrishna
Narchet, Marie-Berthe
Narciso, Lerrie Joy M.
Narmore, Lynn
Narr, William
Nash, Doris A.
Nash, Sue P.
Natcher, Charles
Nater, Denise
Nathamuni Balaji, Vignesh
Nathan, Carol L.
Natividad, Leonarda
Naughton, Bonita S.
Nauman, Ann E.
Nauman, Tiffany Marie
Naunheim Hipps, Julia
Navarra, Peter I.
Navarrete, Deyanire
Navarro, Bernadette
Navarro, Diana M.
Navarro, Michelle
Navarro, Tomas J.
Navasu, Vera
Naylor, Joseph C.
Nazemi, Sylvia D.
Neagley, Betsy
Neal, Mary V.
Neal, Matthew J.
Neal, Roy Clayton
Neal, Sally A.
Necciai, David T.
Neckes, Susan
Nee, Paula
Needham, Judy
Needs, Debra Anne
Neel, Yaronda P.
Neely, Andrea M.
Neely, Matthew J.
Neese, Ashley L.
Neese-Harbolt, Theresa
Neftzger, Amy Lynn
Negovan, Shylah
Nehlsen, Darren P.
Neideffer, Donald W.
Neidich, Mary L.
Neifeld, Alma M.
Neifeld, Bella
Neil, Murphy
Neill, Jennifer Elizabeth
Neis, Beatrix H.
Neitzert, Nancy E.
Nekula, Barbara J.
Nekula, Linda S.
Nelligan, Patrick
Nelms, Margaret R.
Nelson, Alicia M.
Nelson, Carol L.
Nelson, Catherine
Nelson, Cheryl K.
Nelson, Debra
Nelson, Donna J.
Nelson, Douglas G.
Nelson, Gail
Nelson, Heather A.

Nelson, Iona V.
Nelson, James A.
Nelson, Jennifer A.
Nelson, Lori A.
Nelson, Marilee
Nelson, Marina C.
Nelson, Mary Jo
Nelson, Michele
Nelson, Nan
Nelson, Nancy R.
Nelson, Rebecca L.
Nelson, Ryan W.
Nelson, Suzanne M.
Nelson, Theresa
Nelson, Zachary C.
Nelson-Cram, Sandra S.
Nemetsky, Cheryl M.
Nensley, Julia Anne
Nepple, Laura C.
Nesbitt, Marilyn
Neslund, Ryan K.
Nesmith, Laurie
Nesselroad, Gail R.
Nessler, Jennifer A.
Nestell, Regina
Nester, Kimberly B.
Nestor, Ella
Netz, Katherine Ellen
Neu, Erika L.
Neufeld, Ronald
Neuharth, Tamara Jolee
Neuschwander, Sally I.
Neusen, Sharon L.
Neusse, Sue C.
New, Rebecca A.
Newberry, Aerste A.
Newborn, Rhonda G.
Newby, Allison P.
Newby, Diane G.
Newcomb, Emily J.
Newell, Alfred
Newell, Katie Marie
Newell, William J.
Newkirk, Benjamin E.
Newman, Laura L.
Newman, Margie M.
Newman, Vanessa A.
Newsom, JoAnn
Newton, Bryan James
Newton, Emily
Nguyen, Ann H.
Nguyen, Quoc M.
Nguyen, Ruth Elizabeth
Nguyen, Tien T.
Niblett, Jeff S.
Nicewarner, Sally A.
Nicholas, Clayton J.
Nicholas, L. Louise
Nichols, Christine
Nichols, Darlene J.
Nichols, Donna
Nichols, Douglas J.
Nichols, Toni K.
Nicholson, Erik B.
Nicholson, Jill E.
Nicholson, Karen L. C.
Nicholson, Lisa
Nicholson, Lisa L.
Nicholson, Rebecca
Nickas, Tina
Nickels, Gaye N.
Nickels, Sherry I.
Nickens, Charlotte A.
Nickerson, Joan
Nickerson, Lorene
Nicklaw, Maureen F.
Nicklin, Barbara Y.
Nicolaus, Margaret M.
Nicoll, Jean
Nicoll, Jeanette
Nicoll, Robyn
Nicoll, Tara R.
Nidetz, Sheldon A.
Niduaza, Nanette T.
Nielsen, April E.
Nielsen, Enid L.

Niemann, Melissa Kaye
Nieweg, Leslee G.
Nightengale, Sharon K.
Nikolou, Jennifer L.
Niland, Mary Ellen
Nimmo, Niki Nadine
Nipp, Linda Gray
Nisbet, Mary A.
Nishimura, Lee Rachel A.
Nissen, Austin M.
Niven, Jason Ryan
Nixon, Brenda F.
Nixon, Virginia L.
Njelmgren, Therese A.
Noah-Wilson, Natalie M.
Noble, Kathy K.
Noble, Kelli
Noble, Tracy A.
Noble, Yvonne M.
Noe, Sarah Jane
Noel, Sandra F.
Noelting, Bernard Wiliam
Noelting, Margo T.
Noftsger, Rodney J.
Nolan, Charity L.
Nolette, Michael J.
Nollenberger, Elise
Nolte, Alison Joy
Nolting, Mark H.
Noonan, Eileen G.
Noonan, Jenna K.
Norberg, Carrie
Norbury, Diana C.
Nord, Bonnie
Nordstrom, Nikki A.
Norgaard, Rosella Rose
Norman, Coley D.
Norman, Darlena
Norman, Jane B.
Norman, Renee S.
Normann, Kimberly L.
Norris, Barbara Porter
Norris, Carolyn Terry
Norris, Leigh
Norris, Terry E.
Norris, Thomas J.
Norris-Porter, Barbara
North, Jettie Moore
Northern, Shonnette P.
Norton, Shirley A.
Norton-Gunther, April C.
Norwood, Matthew A.
Nottoli, Bonnie B.
Nouwen, Henny M.
Novak, Amy G.
Novak, Karen
Nowak, Patricia G.
Nowakowski, Dana
Nowik, Amy L.
Nowik, George
Nubee, Maryam Zainab
Nuckols, Cardwell C.
Nugent, Gregory
Nunez, Karla R.
Nunez, Martha
Nungester, Betty
Nunley, Charles N.
Nwosu, Valentina
Nwosu, Victoria N.
Nybladh, Emily J.
Nyquist, Traci J.

O

O'Brien, Anthea E.
O'Brien, Carolyn S.
O'Brien, Corinna Jo
O'Brien, Cynthia L.
O'Brien, Ilse
O'Brien, Katherine
O'Brien, Kerri
O'Brien, Marureen Beron
O'Brien, Matthew H.
O'Brien, Megan K.
O'Brien, Patricia Margaret
O'Brien, Vincent

O'Bryan, Kathleen Marie
O'Bryan, Sherri Anne
O'Bryant, Darrel S.
O'Connell, Heather Ann
O'Connell, Paulette
O'Connor, Anna J.
O'Connor, Erin
O'Connor, Janet
O'Connor, Kelly
O'Connor, Lawrence N.
O'Connor, Mary M.
O'Connor, Marylen M.
O'Connor, Melissa Kass
O'Connor, Michelle
O'Dell, Velena H.
O'Donnell, John J.
O'Donnell, Meghan
O'Donnell, Richard
O'Donnell, Walter A.
O'Hagan, Judy F.
O'Hara, Joann M.
O'Hara, Rosamond
O'Hare, Sharon D.
O'Hearn, Lillian V.
O'Kane, Kimberly
O'Keefe, Elizabeth R.
O'Keefe, Kathleen A.
O'Keefe, Thomas
O'Malley, Brenda
O'Malley, Brendan
O'Malley, Christine M.
O'Malley, Ellen
O'Malley, Richard P.
O'Neal, Beth Stallings
O'Neal, Cathryn K.
O'Neal, Connie Melissa
O'Neal, Janet S.
O'Neil, Ina M.
O'Neil, Michael
O'Neil, Sara B.
O'Neill, Brian P.
O'Neill, Mary E.
O'Reilly, Carla L.
O'Shaughnessy, Christine
Oakley, Cheryl F.
Oakley, Janet G.
Oakley, Leanne M.
Oakley, Leigh
Obbrovac, Holly L.
Obenauf, Gail
Obenchain, Janet
Oberlin, Amy C.
Oberlin, Mary C.
Obiecunas, Marilyn
Obike, Mercy N.
Obiorah, Nneka O.
Obravac, Holly L.
Obrovac, Holly L.
Och, Erma
Och, Thomas
Ocharo, Eva
Odea, Carol
Odlum, Susan J.
Odom, Walter C.
Odum, Marcie Clayton
Oertel, Pascale
Oetting, Cindy
Ofcarcik, Jill A.
Officer, Lisa M.
Ogbonna, Celia U.
Ogborn, Kevin D.
Ogden, Florence C.
Oglesby, Christopher R.
Ognibene, Brigid
Ohearn, Lillian V.
Ohl, Kelli
Ohloff, Carmella
Ohlsen, Traci S.
Ojeda, Narcissa Yvette
Okafor, Ngozi N.
Okereke, Gloria
Okoli, Ladonna L.
Okon, Uduak D.
Olagoke, Joyce Tojuiyayi
Oldham, Joanne
Olechowicz, Linda L.

Olenick, Leon
Olinger, Amy L.
Oliphant, Charlotte
Olivas, Cynthia L.
Olivas, Lori A.
Oliver, Arica
Oliver, Brandy J.
Oliver, Jane E.
Oliver, Lylwellyn T.
Oliver, Marjorie
Oliver, Stephanie L.
Olivere, Linda
Oliveros, Aurora
Olivo, Alexandria D.
Ollerhead, Nancy T.
Ollis, Joyce
Olmstead, Jeffery B.
Olmstead, Roberta
Olmstead, Suzanne McGhee
Olodort, Keith D.
Olokodana, Victoria O.
Olsen, Donna L.
Olsen, Sylvi
Olshenske, Elizabeth J.
Olson, Beth Ann
Olson, Holly M.
Olson, Jane D.
Olson, Kimberly Lynn
Olson, Lynne
Olson, Mona Mcgee
Olson, Pamela J.
Olson, Richard
Olson, Susan K.
Olszewski, Karen
Olviedo, Olga
Oman, Connie
Oney, NaJla K.
Onfroy, Lorraine
Ong, Evangeline N.
Ongert, Susan A.
Onken, Ruth M.
Onosaki-Yabes, Jana
Opel, Deborah H.
Opett, Jeannine M.
Opon, David J.
Oppus, Jeffrey
Optekar, Denise
Opun, David J.
Orange, Shirley E.
Orange, Tamarh
Oravetz, Judith
Orbiso, Cynthia
Orbovich, Catherine
Ording, Beatrice A.
Orefice, Jr., Joseph F.
Oreiet, Patricia
Orengo, Xavier
Orensteen, Susan
Oriet, Patricia B.
Oriji, Mary Ann
Ormel, Corry A.
Ormont, Joseph A.
Ornelas, Julie W.
Ornelas, Luis A.
Orozco, Dawn A.
Orr, Brenda Lou
Orr, Grethlyn A.
Orr, Patricia Warren
Orr, Patty M.
Ortali, Claudia
Ortelli, Tracy A.
Orth, Alice
Orth-Hutchinson, Michelle
Ortiz, Allicia
Ortiz, Elizabeth O.
Ortiz, Francisca G.
Ortiz, Jorge H.
Ortiz, Judith
Ortiz, Karla Y.
Ortman, Angela D.
Ortmann III, Fred W.
Orvis, Catherine
Osborn, Francine L.
Osborn, Linda C.
Osborne, Annette
Osborne, David E.

Osborne, Diane M.
Osborne, Jerry W.
Osborne, LaKeesha
Osborne, Linda
Osburn, Janet L.
Osgard, Faith U.
Osgood, Duane B.
Osgood, Susan B.
Osiecki, Thomas R.
Osler, Dana D.
Osler, Jenneth L.
Ostlund, Sheryl J.
Ostroski, Josephine
Ostrowski, Annette
Oswald, Johanna
Otero, Leslie V.
Othoudt, Paula
Otis, Carol B.
Ott, Linda Nix
Ott, Mary Creppon
Ott, Susan L.
Ott, Sylvia A.
Ottinger, Nina R.
Ottmann, Sally
Otts, Ana E.
Otway, Jane
Ouellette, Susan M.
Oumaye, Wendell Y.
Overall, Victor R.
Overbey, Lynn O.
Overbey, Mary Jane
Overby, Cody D.
Overby, Katherine D.
Overby, Shannon A.
Overholt, Justin R.
Overrey, Lynn O.
Overstreet, Debra L.
Overstreet, Mary A.
Overthrow, Karen A.
Overturf, Cynthia Marie
Overybey, Lynn O.
Owen, Anna R.
Owen, Malissa B.
Owens, Latoya R.
Owens, Patrina M.
Owens, Susan
Owens, Wendy B.

P

Paccione, Susan Ellen
Pace, Alexias B.
Pace, Heather L.
Pacheco, Diana
Pack, Dana E.
Pack, Karen L.
Pack, Laura E.
Packard, Denise
Packett, Anne A.
Pack-Kifer, Mary L.
Padach, Linda M.
Padberg, Nancy
Paddock, Betty M.
Padilla, Cristina O.
Padilla, James M.
Padilla, Lucia
Padjen, Sandra L.
Paez, Raquel
Pagan, Olga
Page, Arnita C.
Page, Jenny H.
Pagels, Jeffrey M.
Pagersky-Roberts, Carol
Pagoaga, Michelle A.
Pagoga, Mickey L.
Pagurayan, Jacqueline B.
Paige, Mary
Paige, Marylen
Paige, Sallie F.
Paikin, Katherine
Paine, George Carter
Paine, Michele L.
Painter, Hayley R.
Palacios, Grace
Paladino, Cynthia A.
Palavios, Grace

Palgi, Yehoshua
Pallas, William C.
Palmer, Cori
Palmer, Diane E.
Palmer, Elizabeth A.
Palmer, Lauren C.
Palmer, Robert L.
Palmiere, Kathleen
Palmore, Tammy T.
Palumbo, Christine
Palumbo, Shanna
Pampena, Melanie A.
Pan, Joan J.
Panarese, Justin M.
Panish, Joanne
Pantaleo, Theodore
Panter, Joy
Paone-Trimbur, Valerie A.
Papantonio, Kathryn
Papciak, Michael E.
Pape, Jeffrey
Pappo, Miriam
Paradise, Kristen R.
Pardeshi, Anurag R.
Paredes, Gabrielle
Parenteau, Heather N.
Parikh, Gina M.
Paris, Faye
Parish, Sheryl L.
Parisi, Marie J.
Park, Arlene H.
Park, Beverly Ann
Park, Deborah
Park, Polly A.
Parker, Bonnie B.
Parker, Charles E.
Parker, Gertrude B.
Parker, Gloria
Parker, Gracen Harrison
Parker, Jamie M.
Parker, Jessawynne A. L.
Parker, Karen P.
Parker, Kimberly
Parker, Leslie D.
Parker, Lynda C.
Parker, Lynn W.
Parker, Maureen
Parker, Megan J.
Parker, Michael
Parker, Nisheba M.
Parker, Phyllis L.
Parker, Sharon K.
Parker, Theresa A.
Parker-Richardson, Naquita R.
Parkhurst, Flora
Parks, Christopher A.
Parks, Debra
Parks, Joyce
Parks, Pamela
Parks, Stephanie R.
Parks, Suzanne
Parks, Theresa A.
Parks, Wendy M.
Parkway, Laura Lynn
Parlier, Christine R.
Parnala, Edilyn
Parnell, Janice M.
Parodi, Vivien Andrea
Parrer, Sharon R.
Parrett, Anne L.
Parris, Caroline M.
Parrish, Sheila A.
Parrot, Christopher M.
Parsay, Farinaz
Parsells, Stacie Ann
Parsley, Bettie J.
Parsley, Stephanie D.
Parson, Barbara A.
Parsons, Barbara
Parsons, Beneta O.
Parsons, Cecilia D.
Parsons, Diane M.
Parsons, Donna Kay
Parsons, Josie A.
Partamian, Jean
Partin, Edith G.

Parton, Esther M.
Paschal, Rhonda M.
Pashia, Debra S.
Pasieka, Lorraine
Passafiume, Alice J.
Passerin, Faith
Passey, Damon J.
Pastore, Jeanne M.
Pate, David B.
Pate, Jennifer
Patel, Anisha P.
Patel, Bina D.
Patel, Karen
Patel, Kinjal C.
Patil, Venkatesh
Patino, Mary Ann
Patino, Ricardo F.
Pato, Lynn M.
Patopea, Christine E.
Patrick, Julie L.
Patrick, Sheri L.
Patrick, Sherry Jean
Patt, Mary Ava
Patten, Eric F.
Patten, Ruth M.
Patterson, Brenda L.
Patterson, Carron W.
Patterson, Cassandra A.
Patterson, Dan
Patterson, Dana
Patterson, Dianne M.
Patterson, Gregory L.
Patterson, Jessica L.
Patterson, Kimberly
Patterson, Linda G.
Patterson, Mary E.
Patterson, Michael J.
Patterson, Peggy T.
Pattillo, Cynthia A.
Patton, Angela R.
Patton, Melinda J.
Patton, Susan E.
Patuto, Michelle
Pau, Anela U.
Paul, Alice M.
Paul, Carleen
Paul, Cynthia J.
Paul, Doreen Carol
Paul, Felecia R.
Paul, Jeffrey R.
Paul, Karen M.
Paul, Mark E.
Paul, Marsha
Paul-Blanc, Chantal M.
Paulik, Crystal J.
Paulik, Kevin L.
Paulin, Julie L.
Paulino, Ivania
Paulsness, Susan A.
Paulson, Amy C.
Paulson, Bonita T.
Paulson, Rita A.
Pavelik, Michael S.
Pavlak, Diane J.
Pavuk, Corinne M.
Paxton, Margaret A.
Paylor, Vanikki
Payne, Billie A.
Payne, Bonnie J.
Payne, Brandyn L.
Payne, Brenda
Payne, Chanta L.
Payne, Chiquita A.
Payne, Diane Elizabeth
Payne, Mark A.
Payne, Mary K.
Payne, Stephanie M.
Pazin, Carol C.
Peabody, Andrea L.
Peabody, Vicky
Peacher, Carolyn L.
Peacock, Kimberly H.
Peaks, Kasandra Louise Page
Pearce, Cheryl N.
Pearce, Edna Q.
Pearce, Tammy R.

Pearson, Bonna L.
Pearson, Jake I.
Pearson, Kimberley K.
Pearson, Lou E.
Peck, Deborah
Peck, Stephanie Kay
Pecoraro, Charlene J.
Pecoraro, Suzanne
Pecsok, Amy N.
Pecsok, Vicki L.
Peddecord, Particia D.
Pedersen, Annette Lou
Pedersen, Wanda L.
Pederson, Annette L.
Pederson, Diane M.
Pederson, Joseph R.
Pederson, Tina Ranee
Pedigo, James W.
Pedroso, Lourdes A.
Peebles, Kathryn
Peebles, Molly E.
Peebles, Susan D.
Peek, Sherry
Peeler, Darnell
Pefferman, Diane Kay
Pegel, Donna S.
Pegosh, Nadine
Pegosh, Rena
Peicher, Jack
Peirce, Emily K.
Peitz, Judith
Pelham, Leanna M.
Pelino, Carol
Pellicane, Joyce
Pellicci, Deanna
Peloquin, William A.
Pelt, Tiffany T.
Pembridge, Richard L.
Pembridge, Shari L.
Pena, Angela M.
Pena, Rhiannon C.
Pena-Resendez, Ponciana
Pencak, Sandra R.
Pence, Diane Lynn
Pencek, Eileen M.
Pendergast, Sharon R.
Pendergrass, Constance
Pendergrass, Labeth M.
Penland, Holly D.
Penley, Katherine Lindsey Gray
Penn, Alexis K.
Penna, Kevin
Penner, Beverly
Penninger, Linda
Pennington, Elizabeth
Pennington, Janis
Pennington, Joseph L.
Penrod, Genise
Pentony, Deidere A.
Pentz, Sheri L.
Pepper, Donna
Perala, Julia
Peraldo, Betty
Perdue, Janet S.
Pereira, Blancalicia
Pereira, Varinia J.
Perez, Andres
Perez, Antoinette
Perez, Eric A.
Perez, Ernest
Perez, Isabella G.
Perez, Laurie
Perez, Linda M.
Perez, Melissa A.
Perez, Patricia S.
Perez, Peter
Perez, Susan Lynn
Perez-Benitoa, Manruco
Perez-Blizzard, Irene B.
Peri, Kamesh
Perkins, Cydni Y.
Perkins, Erin B.
Perkins, Helen W.
Perkins, James E.
Perkins, Jeanna Ann
Perkins, Lashanda

Perkins, Laura Tarumianz
Perkins, Ronald G.
Perko, Sandra L.
Perley, Michael J.
Perlmutter, Michael D.
Perlow, Joseph
Pernack, Brenda L.
Pernell, Chris
Perrigo, Terry L.
Perrin, Patricia M.
Perrone, Carolyn R.
Perry, Andrea B.
Perry, Dorene
Perry, Jean
Perry, Jimmy T.
Perry, John
Perry, Laura
Perry, Mary Ellen
Perry, Nancy Anne
Perry, Staisha R.
Perry, Tammy A.
Perry, Theodore L.
Perry, Vivian
Perryman, Naketa N.
Persichetti, Barbara J.
Persico, Joseph M.
Persigehl, Matthew David
Person, Edward E.
Persson, Jeffrey
Persson, William J.
Pertino, Rosemary A.
Pertranovich, Tamara J.
Peruski, Heidi L.
Peshel, Dennis A.
Pesyna, Ellen
Pete, Loretta Diann
Peters, Alan S.
Peters, Bryan N.
Peters, Glenn A.
Peters, Kimberly J.
Peters, Margaret S.
Peters, Mary E.
Peters, Philip J.
Petersen, Daniel J.
Peterson, Delores A.
Peterson, Donna L.
Peterson, Eric T.
Peterson, G. Paige
Peterson, Gregg T.
Peterson, Jan M.
Peterson, Jane Marie
Peterson, Joan
Peterson, Leigh A.
Peterson, Lisa A.
Peterson, Paul P.
Peterson, Rachel C.
Peterson, Rachelle A.
Petkervich, Claudia L.
Petno, Diana
Petranovich, Tamara J.
Petree Nye, Kimberly A.
Petree, Paul
Petrich, Robin L.
Petrie, Monika B.
Petrik, Hollie A.
Petrillo, Sloane
Petrini, Andrew
Petrino, Tenly
Petro, Katherine A.
Petrosino, Angela L.
Petrossian, Patricia
Petruzzelli, Michael A.
Petryk, Susan M.
Pettaway, Tammi A.
Pettiford, Linda M.
Pettineo, Elizabeth
Pettit, Thomas C.
Pettus, Debbie
Petty, Craig A.
Petty, Larry
Petty, Laura
Pewitt, Julie K.
Pewitt, Robert Howard
Pfau, Cherry J.
Pfeffer, Mary
Pfeiffer, Kathleen

Pfleegor, Heather J.
Pflum, Sue Ann
Phan, Kelvin Trong
Phelps, Leanne P.
Phillip, Cynthia
Phillips, Amy J.
Phillips, Anne M.
Phillips, Carrie A.
Phillips, Janice M.
Phillips, Joy L.
Phillips, Karen R.
Phillips, Kristi Ann
Phillips, Leann
Phillips, Lynette G.
Phillips, Patricia A.
Phillips, Roger L.
Phillips, Stephen L.
Phillips, Tamara L.
Phillipsen, Edwin
Philson, Carolyn
Phimma, Shoua Elizabeth
Phmajevich, Lisa
Pholar, Margaret
Phommahaxay, Manny
Piaskoski, Diane
Piazza, Karen Lynn
Picha, Christopher P.
Pickell, Melissa B.
Pickelmann, Amie M.
Pickens, Barbara A.
Pickens, Jennifer Lynn
Pickett, Troy A.
Piechowski, Rashel
Piepho, Yvonne
Pierce, Art C.
Pierce, Cynthia M.
Pierce, Emily K.
Pierce, Jean G.
Pierce, Loretta V.
Pierce, Malinda S.
Pierce, Paula G.
Pierce, Sherry D.
Pierre, Vanessa R.
Pierson, Joni
Pierson, Jonie
Pierson, Reba R.
Pietig, Vicki L.
Pietrowsky, Karen S.
Pietrzak, Carole A.
Pietz, Judith
Pigott, Laura B.
Pigott, Sherry B.
Pilapil, Leticia L.
Pilarczyk, Rosemarie
Pilcher, Mary R.
Piliwale, Corallene L.
Pilling, Jennifer L.
Pimentel, Ana M.
Pimentel, Juan Luis
Pineda, Marisol
Pinkall, Jason D.
Pinkerton, Lawanna J.
Pinkham, Stephanie Rae
Pinkston, Beverly L.
Pinnick, Bret
Pino, Ann Young
Pinter, Janet A.
Pinto, Erika S.
Pioth, Angela G. M.
Piotrowski, Sheila T.
Piper, Susie V.
Pirotta, Michael J.
Pirozek, Lisa
Pisko, John
Pita, Julio C.
Pithers, Jane Ann
Pitkow, Barbara F.
Pitner, Vicki
Piton, Carisha Cruz
Pitter-Jones, Michelle K.
Pittman, Diane G.
Pitts, Kimberly
Pitts, Lillie M.
Pixley, Susan
Pizzella, Shelly R.
Plado, Alexander Q.

Plain, Carol Ann
Plansinis, Karen L.
Plasencia, Julie
Platt, Melinda L.
Plaxico, Nancy B.
Pleasant, Sheralyn L.
Plocek, Jodi Marie
Plotzke, Geraldene
Pludeman, Alissa A.
Plumley, Susan
Plummer, Deri L.
Plummer, Dora D.
Plummer, Joyce F.
Plunkett, Brian
Po, Zarleemaine K.
Pochadt, Todd Arthur
Podeszwa, Sharon
Poe, Susan T.
Poellot, Susan S.
Pogue, Albert S.
Pogue, Louie C.
Pogue, Scott A.
Pohmajevich, Lisa
Poirier, Josee
Poisall, Mark E.
Pokorny, Lisa Margretta
Pokorny, Michael S.
Polakiewicz, Pansy B.
Polancich, Margaret S.
Poland, Kathy
Polas, Marcia A.
Polcyn, Sheila M.
Polen, Amber N.
Polen, Rosemary
Polidan, Sheryl L.
Polit, Michelle R.
Polite, Jr., Nelson M.
Polite, Tiffany N.
Polk, Martha A.
Polkinghorne, Barbara
Pollard, Sharon O.
Polley, Fredricka L.
Pollick, Karrie
Pollock, Amity Rachel
Pollock, Heather M.
Pollock, Weston A
Polo, Marilurdes
Polomski, Susan
Poluszek, Tamara A.
Poluszek, Tamara Ann
Pomeroy, Gina L.
Pomrenke, Connie L.
Pond, Robert B.
Pong, Joseph K.
Pontius, Charlotte
Pool, Gentrie L.
Poole, Brodie
Poole, Radeana T.
Poole, Sharon
Pope, Bonnie L.
Pope, James
Pope, Raphaela
Popek, Vickie
Popkin, Pauline
Popp, Tammy M.
Poquette, Linda A.
Poremski, Michalean C.
Pori, Daria T.
Porter, Barbara
Porter, Claudia G.
Porter, Cory N.
Porter, Faye E.
Porter, Joyce A.
Porter, Julie
Porter, Krystal A.
Porter, Robert S.
Porterfield, Jay K.
Porterfield, Tamara J.
Porter-Shaw, Cheryl
Porto, Kristine U.
Poseley, Lori M.
Poseley, Patricia M.
Posey, Dorothy
Posey, Helen T.
Poskevich, Lenore J. M.
Posner, Michelle

Post, Beverly
Post, Janis L.
Posten, Jean E.
Posterick, Kathleen A.
Postlewaite, Janet R.
Poston, Kimberly A.
Poteat, Betsy G.
Poteet, Kathy A.
Potje, Stephen R.
Potter, Sharon E.
Potterton, Sara Whitwell
Potts, Deborah L.
Potts, Tammie A.
Potts, Virginia Lee
Poukhovskaia, Natali Nickolaevna
Powell, Antoinette O.
Powell, Cheryl D.
Powell, Joy S.
Powell, Kimberly P.
Powell, Margaret
Powell, Martha
Powell, Nancy
Powell, Patricia A.
Powell, Shawn M.
Powell, Valorie C.
Powell-Mack, Margaret R.
Powers, Gregory L.
Powers, Jane
Powers, Julia F.
Powers, Mark
Powers, Sarah Jayne
Powers, Stephanie Darlene
Prabha, Aruna
Prado-Domingo, Charla K.
Praino, Sandra J.
Pratt, Jill M.
Preble, Harry E.
Preiss, Carrie A.
Preist, Suzanne L.
Prendergast, Linda
Presseller, Susanna
Presser, Bobbi
Preston, Bryan E.
Preston, Carol P.
Preston, Uvalune Diane
Prewitt, Elaine N.
Prewitt, John Daniel
Prewitt-Farmer, Elaine
Price, Beverly
Price, Cassandra R.
Price, Connie A.
Price, Deborah S.
Price, Diana Mae
Price, Donald A.
Price, Emily
Price, Frances M.
Price, Jacob D.
Price, Jean P.
Price, Lynn W.
Price, Stephanie R.
Price, Todd
Priddy, Jennifer L.
Pride, Jeanne B.
Pridmore, Scott A.
Prier, David L.
Priest, Herb
Priest, Suzanne L.
Primavera, Roya
Primrose, Louise
Prince, William T.
Pritchett, Debbie J.
Pritzel, Wendell L.
Priver, Rita S.
Privott, James D.
Probeck, Sandra K.
Proctor, Christopher R.
Proctor, Jennifer L.
Proctor, Lester Everett
Procupp, Janice L.
Proenza, Lourdes A.
Prokop, Anne M.
Propster, Thomas A.
Prosen, Beverly J.
Provost, Gene L.
Provost, Mary N.
Provost, Sudonna P.

Prucey, Denise L.
Pruett, Amy S.
Pruitt, C. Grayling
Pryor, Jeffrey Porter
Pucci, Nicole
Puchtler, Cynthia
Puckett, Brian
Pudans, Carol L.
Puent, Debbie H.
Puett, James T.
Pugh, Karen
Pulizzi, Jodi L.
Pupel, Bernard C.
Puri, Melissa S.
Puri, Shalini S.
Purkey, Charla F.
Pursley, Amanda L.
Purvis, James C.
Puryear, Deanna P.
Putnam, Gregory M.
Putnam, Tammy
Pyant, Sandra
Pyle, John
Pyles, Debra L.
Pyrdum, Patricia A.
Pyzia, Monica

Q

Quaas, Barbara J.
Qualls, Beverly D.
Qualls, Ellen S.
Qualls, Karla L.
Qualls, Robert
Quandt, Robert L.
Quarles, Susan May
Quattrone, Linda
Quave, David R.
Quebral, Jocelyn
Quemado, Elvie Marie Pascual
Quiamco, Cynthia
Quick, Cynthia P.
Quickel, Bruce L.
Quigley, Gail
Quiles, Luz N.
Quilter, Lyndsay A.
Quinlan, Nicole R.
Quinlan, Steven E.
Quinn, Eileen
Quinn, Erol Spencer
Quinn, James
Quinn, Phoebe
Quinn, Susan C.
Quiñones, Olga
Quintana, Virginia M.
Quirk, Liane M.
Quiroz, Carol S.
Qulini, Claire M.

R

Raabe, Jeannie Christine
Rabara, Kathleen Marie
Rabe, Margo E.
Rabune, Catherine G.
Raby, Claudia G.
Radcliffe, Patricia L.
Rader, Amy L.
Radford, Diana M.
Radford, Laurie A.
Radick, Todd M.
Radoff, Steven
Radowick, Brandy Jo
Rafalik, Theresa A.
Raftery, Jennifer R.
Ragan, Helen
Raggs, Vernetta M.
Raghavan, Veena
Ragle, Sarah
Ragnetti, Kenneth P.
Ragnetti, Theresa
Ragsdale, Diana Michelle
Raich, Amanda D.
Raiford, Elizabeth
Rajaratnam, Augustine S.
Rakowski, Richard

Ram, Nina
Raman, Pamela A.
Ramelb, Jovites A.
Ramenofsky Stewart, Jane B.
Ramer, Barbara B.
Ramey, Brenda A.
Ramey, Katelyn Renee
Ramey-Smith, Annie M.
Ramirez, Anna M.
Ramirez, Christopher S.
Ramirez, Gabriel
Ramirez, Hilda M.
Ramirez, Juan
Ramirez, Lisa J.
Ramirez, Marsha M.
Ramirez, Regina L.
Ramos, Alicia
Ramos, Henry
Ramos, Jose G.
Ramos, Marilyn P.
Ramos, Rosana Ouibido
Ramos, Sandra E.
Ramos, Tara E.
Ramos, Tomas
Rampacek, Chris
Ramsay, Mary K.
Ramsbey, Heath E.
Ramsdell, Mary F.
Ramsey, Carolyn M.
Ramsey, Daphne L.
Ramsey, James D.
Ramsey, John M.
Ramsey, Reginald N.
Ramsey, Timothy P.
Ramthun, Sarah Jean
Randall, James B.
Randall, Jennifer K.
Randgaard, Sherri A.
Randolph, Carol
Randolph, Leslie A.
Rang, Geraldine L.
Rangarajan, Mitra J.
Rangel, Michael
Raniero, Kathy Lois
Rank, Mary Beth
Rankin, April L.
Ransom, Kamber A.
Rapp, Carla
Rapp, Jacquelyn
Rapp, Marlene
Rasberry, Jamie E.
Rash, Courtney E.
Raskopf, Vaune
Rasmussen, Jean
Rasmussen, Reva R.
Rasnetz, Karen
Rastelli, Raymond H.
RataJeski, Grace
Ratcliff, Lillian D.
Ratcliff, Sharon K.
Rath, Diane D.
Rath, William R.
Rathburn, Patricia A.
Ratliff, Dawn L.
Rattay, Carla
Raulerson, April Lee
Rawaan, Spenta Roshan
Rawlings, Carol Kenahan
Rawlins, Jason
Ray, Deborah L.
Ray, Gerald
Ray, Holly G.
Ray, James Donald
Ray, Rob
Ray, Tomeka L.
Ray, Valinda
Rayburn, Andrew J.
Rayburn, Joseph H.
Rayes, Shannon M.
Rayford, Kelli Edwards
Raymond, Kent Alexander
Raymond, Melinda Lowry
Razuri, Maria D.
Rea, Mary Ann
Rea, Pamela A.
Read, Jean

Read, Linda
Read, Megan T.
Readen, Alyson Jones
Reagan, Elizabeth
Reagen, Mark
Realph, Christine A.
Reames, Jennifer M.
Reaney, Patricia A.
Reano, Terri L.
Reardon, Laurie J.
Reaser, Mary E.
Reath, Phyllis J.
Reau, Jennifer A.
Reavell, Judith A.
Reaves, Letitia O.
Rebham, Margaret A.
Recor, Jane M.
Redar, Sue
Reddan, L. Paige
Redder, Deborah
Redding, Kimberly T.
Redfern, Lee Ann
Redman, Theresia R.
Redmiles, Jacqueline N.
Redmond, Mildred Conrad
Redoble, Jane N.
Redwine, Rachel
Reeck, Donna Marie
Reed, Denise A.
Reed, Eleanor Ann
Reed, Elizabeth L.
Reed, Francis J.
Reed, Janelle S.
Reed, John C.
Reed, Kelly
Reed, Kimberly L.
Reed, Lisa R.
Reed, Mary A.
Reed, Rene E.
Reed, Rosalyn D.
Reed, Sonja L.
Reed, Verbena E.
Reed-Tomlin, Kimberely
Reefer, Carol R.
Reese, Annette M.
Reese, Beverly
Reese, Karen W.
Reese, Michael F.
Reese, Patricia A.
Reeves, David S.
Reeves, Natalie I.
Regan, Christine
Regan, John
Regensburger, Travis H.
Reginald, Gaye W.
Rehagen, Harold W.
Rehnert, Candace
Reich, Karol S.
Reich, Marya A.
Reichhardtt, Laura
Reicks, Jennifer M.
Reid, Angela M.
Reid, Beverly
Reid, Deborah
Reid, Edward L.
Reid, Glenn C.
Reid, Kristen Noelle
Reid, Tonja
Reid, Zelinda E.
Reid-Young, Keir D.
Reiken, Michelle F.
Reilly, Helen A.
Reilly, Karen
Reimers, Tyler J.
Reinard, Jane Marie
Reiner, Karen H.
Reinheimer, Kathy
Reise, Denice
Reiser, Charlene
Reisinger, Gentry L.
Reisinger, Terry L.
Reiss, Rebecca A.
Reissmueller, Shelley A.
Reiter, Patricia A.
Relihan, Joanne M.
Reliman, Joanne M.

Rembisz, Kathleen S.
Remick, Maria
Remmers, Joan A.
Rencher, Sherelynn L.
Rene, Patricia
Renken, Lizabeth
Renna, Mark W.
Rennert, Jennifer N.
Renquist, Martha T.
Renshaw, Doreen F.
Renth, Naomi Katherine
Rentmeester, Anna M.
Renwick, Anne C.
Renzaglia, Jennifer R.
Repasky, Larry J.
Rerstein, Howard J.
Resendez, Ponciana
Resnick, Trina S.
Rethman, Vaughna L.
Rethwisch, Kay
Reuter, Joan A.
Reuther, Carol Anne
Revilla, Elaine U.
Rewkowski, Jennifer L.
Reyes, Julissa I.
Reyes, Luis A.
Reyes, Samantha M.
Reyla-Lau, Raenell K.
Reyna, Patricia
Reynolds, Barbara
Reynolds, Brenda L.
Reynolds, Dianne
Reynolds, Elaine B.
Reynolds, Felice
Reynolds, Linda L.
Reynolds, Marie C.
Reynolds, Sandra L.
Reynolds, Sherry Booker
Reynolds, Stuart R.
Reynolds, William Scott
Rezende, Valeria G.
Reznichenko, Vitaliy A.
Reznick, Barrett M.
Reznikova, Gail
Rhein, Brenda J.
Rhew, Sharon D.
Rhinehart, Margaret
Rhinehart, Richard A.
Rhoades, Jonathon M.
Rhodes, Elizabeth
Rhodes, Judith S.
Rhodes, Melissa L.
Rice, Angela Farr
Rice, Deborah L.
Rice, Elaine D.
Rice, Erica C.
Rice, Jamie E.
Rice, Jeffrey J.
Rice, Roy F.
Rice, Tami
Rich, Ann G.
Rich, Karen L.
Rich, Lisa Kaydell
Rich, Rosemary A.
Rich, Sandra R.
Richard, Darren
Richard, Diane M.
Richard, Gregory M.
Richard, Mary D.
Richards, Janetter F.
Richards, LaurieAnn B.
Richards, Rhonda C.
Richards, Ronald C.
Richardson, Carolyn
Richardson, Debra Y.
Richardson, Donna L.
Richardson, Dulcie Renee
Richardson, Elisa Marie
Richardson, Evelyn
Richardson, Gwendolyn
Richardson, Kayla
Richardson, Luann
Richardson, Marsha
Richardson, Marsia V.
Richardson, Mary L.
Richardson, Matt H.

Richardson, Michelle
Richardson, Nancee L.
Richardson, Patricia L.
Richardson, Shaun J.
Richart, Jacquelyn E.
Richburg, Kelly A.
Richer, Jane E.
Richey, Jeremy L.
Richey, Kim
Richmond, John B.
Rickard, Timothy J.
Rickenbacker, Salley
Ricketts, Bryan
Ricketts, Janine L.
Ricks, Chiffon Y.
Riddle, Carol N.
Rideau, Paula M.
Ridgway, Andrea
Ridinger, Mark H. T.
Riedl, Maragret A.
Riedl-Galli, Margaret
Riegel, Ashley N.
Rieger, Catherine A.
Rieger, Laura K.
Riekhof, Karen
Rieman, Yvonne G.
Riesner, Pam L.
Rieth, Regina T.
Rieves, Cheryl
Riggle, Laurie
Riggs, Shari
Riggsbee, Wendy L.
Rigonan, Teresita
Rigor, Elinor N.
Riley, Devin E.
Riley, Donna
Riley, Karen J.
Riley, Khory
Riley, Leah
Riley, Lindsey E.
Riley, Lisa Michelle
Riley, Miranda L.
Riley, Patricia Ann
Rinaldi, Dominic J.
Rinaldi, Dona M.
Rinaldo, Linda J.
Rineer, Paula W.
Rinehart, Jennifer A.
Ringeisen, Lynzee Marie
Ringer, Pamela
Ringley, Melissa J.
Riojas, Marylou
Riordan, Dale Ann
Rios, Nadia P.
Ripan, Monica
Ripley, Aimee LaFreniere
Ripple, John Lawrence
Risher, Melissa D.
Risler, Iris M.
Risley, Mary E.
Risola, Brea A.
Ritter, Amanda
Ritter, David M.
Ritter, Margaret
Riva, Audray
Rivard, Corinne
Rivenbark, Pete G.
Rivera, Noel
Rivera, Ricardo
Rivers, Whitni M.
Rives, Sarah
Rivinius, Lynette
Rix, Lynda
Rizk, Olga Danielle
Rizo, Kellie C.
Rizvi, Jerry M.
Rizzo, Daniel C.
Rizzolo, Ruth Ann
Roach, David
Roach, Deborah C.
Roark, Delaine E.
Roark, Patty Joy
Robbins, Larry B.
Robbins, Loretta S.
Robbins, Pamela
Roberson, Sara T.

Roberson, William M.
Roberto, Linda M.
Roberts, Barry R.
Roberts, Donna Lorene
Roberts, Elizabeth S.
Roberts, Frederick Joseph
Roberts, Jason
Roberts, Karen S.
Roberts, Kathleen R.
Roberts, Leslie J.
Roberts, Lynnae C.
Roberts, Mary L.
Roberts, Patricia
Roberts, Phyllis
Roberts, Sherman D.
Roberts, Tamara L.
Roberts, Thomas G.
Roberts, Victoria L.
Roberts, William S.
Robertson, Elissa R.
Robertson, Jerry B.
Robertson, Judith A.
Robertson, Keith Alan
Robertson, Marcina
Robertson, Mark S.
Robideaux, Rochelle V.
Robine, Frances A.
Robinette, Pamela
Robins, Frances A.
Robinson, Alicia Spezia
Robinson, Andrea S.
Robinson, Chelsea C.
Robinson, Crystal Phylathia
Robinson, Cynthia
Robinson, Donna
Robinson, Dorothy H.
Robinson, Georgette P.
Robinson, Isabel E.
Robinson, Janis M.
Robinson, Jeffery C.
Robinson, Kesha R.
Robinson, Kim Bunch
Robinson, Linda
Robinson, Lorna
Robinson, Maria E.
Robinson, Michael G.
Robinson, Mildred Elaine
Robinson, Nicola J.
Robinson, Pamela L.
Robinson, Patricia A.
Robinson-Antoine, Sabrina
Robison, Marc G.
Robison, Regina E.
Roblejo, Lydia
Robles, Irene T.
Rocamontes, Marilyn D.
Rocha, Deborah
Rocha, Rachel
Roche, Patricia
Rock, Jennifer L.
Rockwell, Jill M.
Roco, Maria Cecilia
Rodefer, William O.
Rodela, Joe A.
Roden, Shirley Ann
Rodgers, Carol B.
Rodgers, Deborah A.
Rodgers, Kathryn J.
Rodgers, Lyndsey K.
Rodgers, Mary Elizabeth
Rodgers, Rosalyn
Rodman, Lois J.
Rodney, Julia
Rodriguez, Amanda K.
Rodriguez, Frances
Rodriguez, Guadalupe
Rodriguez, Marion L.
Rodriguez, Mary Ellen
Rodriguez, Maurilia
Rodriguez, Monica J.
Rodriguez, Nathan A.
Rodriguez, Omelio J.
Rodriguez, Shelby A.
Rodriguez, Veronica R.
Roe, Michelle K.
Roebuck, Antoinette B.

Roeder, Rebecca A.
Roemer, John D.
Roesch, Barbara J.
Roese, Steven Mitchell
Roeser, Marylee E.
Roesler, Robin
Roesler, Tricia
Rogan, Debra H.
Rogan, Kelly A.
Rogers, Ana E.
Rogers, Brandy
Rogers, Charnae D.
Rogers, Doris
Rogers, Ellen
Rogers, Gregory Wyatt
Rogers, Joyce K.
Rogers, Lisa B.
Rogers, Lynell
Rogers, Matt S.
Rogers, Michelle
Rogers, Nita Jo
Rogers, Odessa Broadie
Rogers, Shane A.
Rogers, Sharon A.
Rogers, Sheila K.
Rogers, Susan
Rogers, Thuli M.
Rogers, Vicki R.
Rogers-McMillan, Carolyn J.
Roggiero, Sue
Rohn, Susan G.
Rohrbough, George
Rohrer, Deacon W.
Rohricht, Mark T.
Roht, Robin
Rojas, Chad P.
Rojo, Rosa
Roland, Bradley C.
Roldan, Marcie
Rolen, Brent
Rolla, Evelyn
Rolle, Jr., Othel A.
Roller, Ann A.
Roller, Kathryn
Roller, Kim S.
Rolph, June E.
Roman, Kimberly
Romanek, Lillian
Romano, Jeanne
Romanowski, Desiree D.
Romero, Darlene
Romero, Jacquelyn A.
Romero, Kelly J.
Romero, Renee
Romero, Rosalinda
Romero-Alas, Mercedes
Romine, Megan
Ronald, Karen E.
Ronan, Amanda C.
Rondano, Denise
Rondon, Jessica A.
Ronyha, Kathleen
Rood, Robert Porter
Rooks, Susie P.
Roomets, Michele L.
Rooney, Julia
Rooney, Timothy P.
Roosevelt, Theodore S.
Roosevelt, Todd S.
Rosa, Edith
Rosado, Martha M.
Rosales, Marisella C.
Rosales, Raquel
Roscigno, Karen L.
Rose, Cheri S.
Rose, Christina M.
Rose, Jean
Rose, Joyce A.
Rose, Margaret A.
Rose, Thomas
Rose, Tina R.
Roseen, Lynne D.
Rosen, Charlotte
Rosen, Jacqueline C.
Rosen, Jodi R.
Rosen, Sandra Stalbird

Rosenberg, Sarah A.
Rosenberg, Stacey L.
Rosener, Sarah M.
Rosenfeld, Alan S.
Ross, Bryan
Ross, Elizabeth N.
Ross, Evelyn E.
Ross, Gail L.
Ross, Hilary
Ross, Jason W.
Ross, Susan
Ross, Wytina Carrington
Roston, Elaine S.
Roswall, Jill L.
Roszczyk, Susan
Roten, Geoffrey P.
Roth, Glynn E.
Rothfield, Linda C.
Rothwell, Deanna L.
Rotter, Henry A.
Rottman, Kristin M.
Rotz, Deborah L.
Roudebush, Brittany L.
Rountree-Elliott, Krystal M.
Rouse, Catherine Ann
Rouse, Elsa B.
Rouse, Elsworth Tyrone
Rouse, Kim M.
Roush, Gene D.
Roush, Joyce A.
Roushdi, Anthony
Rousseau, Stephen R.
Rousselot, Gshzelle D.
Routh, Michael
Routh, Patti
Roux, Ann Elizabeth
Roux, Denise
Rovenko, Kathleen E.
Rowan, Anita M.
Rowe, Brandi L.
Rowe, Harvey E.
Rowell, Heather D.
Rowland, Patricia
Roy, William J.
Royal, Kimberly D.
Royal, Lauren S.
Royal, Patricia
Royster, Nancy F.
Royster-Bennett, Tracey A.
Rozar, Inez
Rozema, Susan B.
Ruawhare, Elizabeth J.
Rubadeau, Nancy H.
Rubell, Eric
Rubin, Steve
Rubino, William R.
Rubinstein, Barbra I.
Rubinstein, Sidney Mark
Rubio, Aurora Delgado
Rubio, Lizandra
Ruby, Jacqueline M.
Rucker, Leah J.
Rucker, Vernetta J.
Ruckman, Kathryn A.
Rude, Martha
Rudisill, Elizabeth
Rudman, Mary Rose
Rudo, Dayrn
Rudolph, Joyce
Rudzinski, Roger R.
Rueda Negron, Javier O.
Ruemping, Stacy M.
Ruesskamp, Elizabeth
Rueuther, Carol A.
Rufer, Clyde A.
Ruffato, Robyn L.
Ruggles, Leigh Ann
Ruhl, Carol Dene
Ruhl, Fred R.
Ruiz, Luz R.
Ruiz, Sheryl A.
Ruiz-Flores, Maria C.
Rula, Elizabeth Y.
Rundus, Norma J.
Ruocco, Emilio D.
Rupp, Ann E.

Rusche, Joanne
Rush, Stephen G.
Rush, William E.
Rushe, Regina
Rushing, Lori Lynn
Russ, Lisa E.
Russell, Ashley
Russell, Colleen H.
Russell, Elisabeth J.
Russell, Jeff N.
Russell, Joanne
Russell, Justin M.
Russell, Krista J.
Russell, Leroy
Russell, Mary
Russell, Nancy
Russell, Viola E.
Russo, Lynn
Russo, Michael J.
Rust, Abbey
Rutledge, Gayle E.
Rutledge, Leigh A.
Rutsky, Megan
Ruybalid, Jerald K.
Ruzicka, Karen H.
Ryan, Alison
Ryan, Angela
Ryan, Carol A.
Ryan, Jackie L.
Ryan, Jane E.
Ryan, Julia Frances
Ryan, Leslie
Ryan, Mary Jane
Ryan, Natasha R.
Ryan, Sheila
Ryan, Suzanne M.
Ryan-Turek, Terri
Ryder, Donna K.
Ryder, Sherry A.
Rydholm, Marie L.
Ryland, Kristen L.
Rylander, Barbara
Rymell, Lois
Rynearson, Monique
Ryssel, Mary A.

S

Saab, Christina J.
Sabajkar, Abhishek
Saberton, Ronald L.
Sabin, Stephen
Sable, Merrily S.
Sabram, William
Sacadat, Scott A.
Sachs, Cynthia A.
Sachtleben, Steve
Sacks, Russell L.
Saclolo, Alice
Sadawi, Sonja Gwendolyn
Sadeghi, Janet B.
Sadler, Joni L.
Sadowski, Beth A.
Sadowski, Rita Q.
Saeedpour, Reza
Saegesser, Douglas S.
Saehler, Timothy E.
Sage, Marlene
Sagisi, Alfredo G.
Sai, Stephanie T.
Saiki, Paula K.
Sailer, Rita R.
Saip, Elena A.
Saita, Judith A.
Sakata, Luisa G.
Sakauye, Rachel T.
Salalac, Angela
Salas, Iris
Salas, Monica C.
Salazar, Ana R.
Salazar, Donna Marie
Salberg, Jack R.
Saldivas, Ruby F.
Sale, Paulette L.
Saleeb, Eva
Sales, Erlinda B.

Salgado, Vanessa A.
Salgian, Matthew
Salinas, Juan H.
Saling, Jenny
Salk, Carla
Sallas, Anita M.
Sallings, Beth
Sallow, Lisa A.
Salmons, Laurie A.
Salton, Tracey
Salucci, Patricia A.
Saludo, Kristine W.
Saludo, Rex A.
Salvador, Precy Campos
Salziger, Pamela M.
Samaniego, Jill W.
Samanta, Chinmaya K.
Sambrook, Jillian Marie
Samec, Lawrence
Sami, Seppideth
Samion, Gina
Sammet, Richard
Samples, Stephen G.
Samples, Zackary O.
Sampson, Brenda D.
Sampson, Deborah R.
Sams, Carla
Sams, Elizabeth R.
Samson, David W.
Samson, Kathryn C.
Samuel, Matthew
San Mateo, Angie Bright
Sanchez, Robert J.
Sand, Susan M.
Sandella, Sheela R.
Sander, Brett O.
Sanders, Gabriel J.
Sanders, Gwendolynn A.
Sanders, Heidi
Sanders, John M.
Sanders, Judy
Sanders, Lisa
Sanders, Maria I.
Sanders, Marian I.
Sanders, Michael E.
Sanders, Phillip G.
Sanders, Shakinna
Sanderson, Jerry Tyler
Sanderson, Ruth R.
Sanderson, Sandra
Sandhaus, Sonia
Sandidge, Martha
Sandler, Jeffrey A.
Sandman, Kara A.
Sandoval, Blanca
Sandoval, Carla Rose
Sandoval, Christie C.
Sands, Elaine P.
Sands, Susan L.
Sandwick, Louise N.
Sandwith, Michael T.
Saner, Steven M.
Sanford, April Yvonne
Sanford, Debora
Sanneman, Nancy A.
Santamaria, Carol J.
Santana, Susan
Santandrea, Margaret
Santarcangelo, Melinda
Santiago, Hortense
Santiago, Linda
Santic, Velibor
Santoleri, Joanne E.
Santoro, Tracey M.
Santos, Jessica D.
Santos, Olivia R.
Santos-Lopez, Michelle M.
Santovito, Mary
Sanudo, Brenda E.
Saper Bloom, Lisa
Saphire, Debra
Saputo, Norma J.
Sarchet, Cathy
Sardinha, Carol A.
Sargeant, Linda P.
Sargent, George A.

Sargent, Tracy
Sarno, Lorraine M.
Sarpy, Karen
Sartin, Shirley J.
Sartoris, Denise
Sarver, Julia R.
Sass, Deloris M.
Sasser, Michele
Sassi, Lisa A.
Saterbak, Marie
Sattler, Joan
Saucedo, Sophia R.
Sauer, Marie Deette
Sauerland, Kathleen M.
Sauers, Kay F.
Saulsbury, Lee Ann
Saulsbury, Roy R.
Saunders, Angela M.
Saunders, Ashley
Saunders, Duane M.
Saunders, Gail
Saunders, JoAnn C.
Saunders, Karen L.
Sauro-And, Edith
Sautner, Darlene
Savage, Cheryl A.
Savage, John A.
Savage, Maryann
Savage, Samantha
Savage, Sheila C.
Savoie, Elliot F.
Sawinski, Jennifer A.
Sawyer, Cynthia P.
Sawyer, Hannelore
Sawyer, Robert
Saxon, Peggy
Sayasan, Patty P.
Sayers, Kathy P.
Saylor, Regina
Scaife, Jacqueline R.
Scalercio, Margaret
Scallorn, Wendy L.
Scally, Gretchen R.
Scally, Julie M.
Scalzo, Marcello M.
Scanlan, Elise A.
Scarberry, Barbara
Scarborough, Rosalie
Schaag, Sherre L.
Schab, Julianna A.
Schaberg, Amanda L.
Schablitsky, Carmen
Schacher, Andrea K.
Schachtschneider, Hans L.
Schaefer, Brenda L.
Schaefer, Donna C.
Schaefer, Lisa
Schaefer, Todd D.
Schafer, Sydney
Schaffer, Charlotte
Schaffer, Michelle K.
Schaffner, Nelly
Schall, Rita J.
Schaller, Judy L.
Schamel, Dennis John
Schanen, Andrew Dumas
Schank, Patricia A.
Schardt, David L.
Scharf, Deanna M.
Schatzman, Beth E.
Schauer, Denise Geri
Schaumburg, Dylan W.
Schechter, Bonnie
Scheffner, Jennifer
Scheitlin, Gerard
Schellhorn, Sandra J.
Schempp, Sharon
Schenck, Jennifer
Schenck, Rand
Schenke, Linda
Schensted, Yvonne
Schenzinger, Virginia
Schertl, Therese V.
Scheuren, Lea Anne
Schick, Maria Sue
Schieler, Chris

Schiering, Madelyn
Schild, David
Schiller, Deborah L.
Schilling, Linda
Schine, Amy
Schlakman, Patricia
Schlatter, Stephanie Carol
Schlecht, Steven J.
Schlicht, Sheryl
Schlick, Lynnette
Schlote, Yvonne M.
Schmauder, Beverly W.
Schmidt, Amber B.
Schmidt, Angie M.
Schmidt, Cory E.
Schmidt, Deborah
Schmidt, Dieter
Schmidt, Lindsay T.
Schmidt, Roberta A.
Schmidt, Sue J.
Schmidt, Susan D.
Schmitt, Patricia
Schmitz, Deborah
Schmook, Denise
Schmucker, Enita J.
Schnaak, Jean C.
Schnabel, Susan J.
Schnathorst, April D.
Schneider, Julie L.
Schneider, Lisa M.
Schneider, Marlene S.
Schneider, Nicolie Davis
Schneider, Rachel E.
Schneider, Raymond
Schneider, Wendy R.
Schneiderhan, Jon-Erik
Schneiderman, Michael S.
Schnell, Patrice M.
Schnizer, Diane Kay
Schnmidt, Dieter
Schockey, Jennifer J.
Schoeck, Kathleen M.
Schoen, Mary
Schoepflin, Tami S.
Schofield, Donna M.
Scholar, Bryan
Schols, Vickie
Schoof Knauer, Patricia J.
Schorn, Joan A.
Schorn, Shirley A.
Schrack, Sheila Louise
Schrader, Barbara
Schrader, Carin
Schrader, Karen
Schrader, Leslie
Schrader, Susan K.
Schram, Jennean
Schrankel, Dawn
Schreckengost, Connie A.
Schreier, Ann R.
Schreiner, Elizabeth L.
Schreiner, Jeffrey K.
Schrenker, Brandy P.
Schreter, Anne
Schroeder, Carrie A.
Schroeder, Heather Marie
Schroeder, Jennifer E.
Schroeder, Sarah
Schrumpf, Eric A.
Schuler, Raymond
Schulte, Kelly P.
Schultz, Cassidy J.
Schultz, Deborah
Schultz, Joan
Schultz, Judith M.
Schultz, Kathleen R.
Schultz, Mary E.
Schultz, Nancy A.
Schultz, Patricia A.
Schultz, Peggy
Schultz, Regina M.
Schulz, Jerilynn
Schulz, Lynda G.
Schulze, Beth H.
Schumacher, Christine J.
Schuman, Barbara N.

Schumann, Mary Beth
Schumpert, Bonni
Schuneman, Kristin A.
Schurman, Karen L.
Schusterman, Kurt M.
Schutt, Michelle Ryan
Schutz, Peter F.
Schwaegerl, Jane
Schwanz, Shirley
Schwartz, Kathleen A.
Schwartz, Mindy
Schwarz, Lisa Terry
Schwarz, Sharon
Schwarze, Nora Ann
Schweikert, Mary P.
Schweitzer, Linda
Schwerin, Stacy V.
Schwieters, Mary Ann
Sciacca, Margaret
Sciascia, Elaine M.
Scioscia, Stephen M.
Scobie, Doris
Scocimara, Susan M.
Scoggins, Maren Winters
Scotland, Barbara Tallman
Scott, Allison K.
Scott, Arlene M.
Scott, Benjamin Ross
Scott, Diane
Scott, Donna
Scott, Janice
Scott, Jasmin E.
Scott, Joyce
Scott, Katherine
Scott, Kyla D.
Scott, Lorraine A.
Scott, Melinda G.
Scott, Monica L.
Scott, Phyllis C.
Scott, Rosalind R.
Scott, Ruby H.
Scott, Sherrie L.
Scott, Sheryl M.
Scott, Thomas W.
Scott-McClain, Doris R.
Scotto, Tina
Scovil, Mildred G.
Scowden, Frances P.
Scruggs, Raymond
Scruggs, Rita
Scrutchen, Norma J.
Scudder, Margaret S.
Seaborne, David A.
Seabrooks, Marvin B.
Sealey, Billy J.
Sealey, Veda I.
Seals IV, Issac
Seaman, Diane C.
Seaquist, Lea A.
Searle, Ann Marie
Searls, Christopher R.
Sears, Dawn E.
Sears, Lindsay E.
Sease, Becky A.
Seaver, Margaret E.
Seawright, Anthony
Seay, Jill M.
Seay, Michelle E.
Sebille, Judy A.
Seckinger, Jeremy
Secor, Marcy
Secules, Amy E.
Secules, Jr., Robert
Seftner, Karen A.
Sefton, Grace Y.
Segal-Owens, Arlynn
Seger, Erin K.
Seggerman, Kathleen A.
Segroves, Jon G.
Segura, Michael H.
Seider, Regina M.
Seigel, Amy Fredricka
Seiling, Barbara A.
Sekelik, Grace
Selby, Laura M.
Selby, Rhonda

Selden, Lynn
Self, Karon J.
Self, Lelain Wayne
Selisker, Sally
Sellars, Janice L.
Sellers, Carren H.
Sellers, Dianne
Sellier, Kirsten
Semanko, Helen
Semler, Mary
Semple, Nanci L.
Semrick, Mary
Sena, Elizabeth Marlene
Sendelbach, Debbie
Sengvongxay, Molly
Sensing, Hal D.
Sepada, Genevieve T. S. M.
Sepulveda, Norma
Serafin, Dana
Sergon, Catherine C.
Sergon, Linda
Serquina, Amraphel T.
Serra, Doris M.
Serrano, Neil S.
Servais, Elaine J.
Servarlic, Brandy
Seserman, Sue B.
Sessoms, Wendy P.
Sesson, Judith P.
Sestiaga, Theresa M.
Sethi, Kiran
Setliff, Karen G.
Sevaaetasi, Kristie G.
Severance, Robin B.
Severino, Angela
Severt, Victoria L.
Severtson, Lys E.
Sexton, Patricia A.
Sexton, Sharon A.
Seymour, Nancy R.
Shabi, Richard
Shackleford, Heath
Shade, Elmo
Shadel, Linda J.
Shafer, Laura
Shafer, Nancy
Shafer, Rochelle
Shaffer, Lisa L.
Shah, Bhavinkumar B.
Shah, Viral V.
Shahade, Maryann
Shaheen, Shadiyah C.
Shaik, Sharif
Shake, Rita
Shakes, Uva M.
Shanahan, Lynette M.
Shanbhag, Rukshana
Shankel, Cynthia K.
Shanks, Sarah
Shannon, Everett R.
Shannon, Richard L.
Shapera, Merle
Shapiro, Flora L.
Shapiro, Rhona E.
Shapiro, Susan L.
Share, Brian P.
Sharek, Heather M.
Sharenow, Linda
Shariff, Amal Aamir
Sharma, Chanderkant
Sharma, Sanjay
Sharon, Alberta D.
Sharp, Marilyn
Sharpe, Katherine H.
Sharpe, Vanissa
Sharpless, Lashun R.
Shartel, Joann M.
Shatzer, Bonnie D.
Shaw, Eileen Browdy
Shaw, Francis
Shaw, Kelly P.
Shaw, Rebecca
Shaw, Sheila M.
Shaw, Susan
Shea, Christopher
Shea, Jeffrey M.

Shea, Leah A.
Shea, Sherryl
Shea, Susan Marie
Shearer, Jinny
Shearer, Judy K.
Sheariss, Carrie Ann
Sheasley, Jill
Sheasley, Tammy D.
Sheehan, Carol J.
Sheehan, Deborah Anne
Sheehan, John P.
Sheehan, Richard
Sheffer, Vicki J.
Shelborne, Kathy
Sheldon, Jr., William
Sheldrake, Melanie D.
Shell, Dawn E.
Shell, Gloria J.
Shelley, Theresa G.
Shellhart, Amy Lynn
Shelton, Alicia N.
Shelton, Ann M.
Shelton, Donna J.
Shelton, Jackie
Shelton, Sara
Shemon, Kathleen A.
Shemonia, Joseph
Shenker, Joanne L.
Shepard, Astrida T.
Shepard, Christopher V.
Shepard, Sheila
Shepard, Vicki L.
Shepherd, Carolyn J.
Shepherd, Cynthia C.
Shepherd, Lisa
Sheppard, Frances Y.
Shcrbondy, Julie M.
Sheridan, Michael P.
Sherlock, Sally
Sherlog, Lawrence A.
Sherman, Larry
Sherman, Lola M.
Sherman, Maureen B.
Sherman, Sandra C.
Sherman-Appel, Lori R.
Shern, Robin
Sherouse, Betty
Sherrill, Jeanne C.
Sherrod, Carrie Callis
Sherrod, Kimberly
Sherron, Laura R.
Sherry, Sally
Shevlin, Sheila K.
Shi, Yuyan
Shick, Cheryl
Shields Morton, Taketia L.
Shields, Joe B.
Shields, Tammeron T.
Shields, Tiffany
Shiferaw, Sihin
Shifflett, Tammy M.
Shilow, Dana
Shilts, Mary J.
Shimamoto, Sarah G.
Shimata, Lori S.
Shinagawa, Jodie Y.
Shindel, Sarah A.
Shindnes, Margarita
Shinn, Scott F.
Shinoda, Lei A.
Shipley, Carol
Shipley, Stephanie L.
Shipman, Alane
Shipman, Susanna M.
Shipman-Cortes, Enid
Shippee, Charlotte J.
Shippey, Patricia M.
Shippy, Joyce A.
Shirai, Jared A.
Shirley, Gregory A.
Shirley, Janie P.
Shirley, Sharon E.
Shiroma, Florence
Shiroma, Mary-Jean E.
Shive, Joan E.
Shive, Lori A.

Shivnan, Lucy Anne
Shockey, Jennifer
Shockley, Shelley Racquel
Shoemaker, Elizabeth R.
Shoffner, Deirdre A.
Shoop, Natalie N.
Shope, Bradley N.
Shore, Joseph H.
Shore, Julia Oreto
Shore-Lewinsohn, Jan
Short, Benita
Short, Jason
Short, Louise J.
Short, Sharon
Shorthill, Rita
Shortridge, Kym
Shoup, Penny Jo
Shouse, Janie A.
Shout, Teresa
Showalter, Donna
Showell, Carolyn M.
Showfety, Catherine P.
Shrauger, Erick G.
Shrine, Gardenia
Shrout, Carrie
Shubin, Maria L.
Shultz, Judith M.
Shuman, G. Gayle
Shumway, Glenda Lee
Shuppert, Nathaniel A.
Shurney, Dexter W.
Shuster, Peggy
Sibley, Jo Ann
Sick, Jennifer R.
Sickels, Berry
Sickels, Betty M.
Sickles, Jean Elizabeth
Sidlowe, David A.
Sidney, Betty
Sidney, James A.
Sidney, Martha
Sidwell, Meredith
Siebert, Jodie S.
Siedlinski, Melanie K.
Siefken, Julie
Siegel, Susan
Siegenthaler, Benjamin D.
Siegrist, Frances F.
Siehert, Lisa Ann
Siekanowicz, Sally
Sierk, Angela Faye
Sierra, Austin J.
Siesener, Diane M.
Sigal, Abigail C.
Sigmon, Evaron R.
Silas, Sheila M.
Silberman, Kathryn M.
Silkwood, Christine
Siltanen, Kathy Elizabeth
Silva, Cynthia R.
Silva, Marilyn F.
Silva, Mildred
Silva, Patricia A.
Silver, Audrey
Silver, Constance M.
Silver, Joy
Silver, Regina M.
Silver, Robert D.
Silverman, John L.
Sime, Donice L.
Simerson, Barbara J.
Simisky, Edward M.
Simmons, Deborah J.
Simmons, Emily S. N.
Simmons, Gary
Simmons, Mary E.
Simmons, Michelle D.
Simmons, Rosezetta D.
Simmons, Shannon H.
Simmons, Shawna L.
Simms, TeQuita Brianne
Simon, Christian May T.
Simon, Cindy L.
Simon, Olga M.
Simonovitch, Lawrence W.
Simons, Susan T.

Simpson, Angel M.
Simpson, Jennifer P.
Simpson, Lonie D.
Simpson, Pamela J.
Simpson, Rashida N.
Simpson, Sandra L.
Simpson, Tammy A.
Simpson, Tracy
Simpson, Zana
Sims, Heather W.
Sims, Sarah C.
Sims, Theodora R.
Sin, Mei Ling
Sinclair, John D.
Sinclair, Kim
Sinclair, Kimberly
Sindo, Micki R.
Sinecki, Gina M.
Siner, Christopher M.
Singer, Dorothy P.
Singh, Charanjit
Singh, Diana
Singleton, Carol Ann
Singleton, Cynthia L.
Singleton, Robert C.
Singley, Judith
Sinkeus, Linda D.
Sinnema, Janet
Sinyard, Alyssa F.
Sipher, Mary W.
Sipple, Andrew G.
Sirigos, John J.
Sirk, Jeanine
Sisk, Diane Marie
Sisser, Laurie A.
Siudzinski, Patricia M.
Sivier, Julie
Sivik, Scott J.
Sjogren, Sandra L.
Sjoholm, Gretchen
Skaggs, Tricia A.
Skalitzky, Glenda R.
Skelding, Shirley
Skelly, Cheryl A.
Skelton, Jamie
Skinner, Jason T.
Skinner, Lisa M.
Skogman, Christie
Skomedal, Sarah L.
Slade, Cody B.
Slade, Cynthia H.
Slater, Terese
Slaughter, Darlene Kay
Slaven, Thomas
Sleiman, R. Robert
Sleiman, Robert R.
Slentz, John
Slepinski, Nancy
Slike, Shanley Ann
Slingwine, Patricia
Slinkard, Joe S.
Sloan, Elizabeth M.
Sloan, Ellen J.
Sloan, Judy McPeak
Sloan, Thomas M.
Slone, Jane E.
Slottje, Maureen
Small, Craig L.
Small, Mary P.
Smalls, Herbert
Smallwood, Marie
Smartt, David W.
Smelser, Lorraine M.
Smirl, Laraine V.
Smitchens, Beverly
Smith Wright, Relista
Smith, Aigner R.
Smith, Allen R.
Smith, Andrea G.
Smith, Ann M.
Smith, Barbara A.
Smith, Candice L.
Smith, Carett S.
Smith, Carolyn Sue
Smith, Catherine
Smith, Cecilia M.

Smith, Charlene E.
Smith, Charlotte B.
Smith, Christina L.
Smith, Cindy Amy
Smith, Claudia
Smith, Constance
Smith, Dale T.
Smith, Deborah G.
Smith, Diane B.
Smith, Dianne Lynn
Smith, Donna
Smith, Edward
Smith, Eugene J.
Smith, Evelyn N.
Smith, Frederick D.
Smith, Gary L.
Smith, Geneva
Smith, Harold T.
Smith, Heidi L.
Smith, Holly
Smith, Howard
Smith, James G.
Smith, Jane M.
Smith, Janell
Smith, Janis L.
Smith, Jean
Smith, Jennifer J.
Smith, Joan D.
Smith, Joanne L.
Smith, Jody A.
Smith, Joel T.
Smith, John
Smith, Judith
Smith, Judy A.
Smith, Julie R.
Smith, Justin J.
Smith, Kari A.
Smith, Kathleen L.
Smith, Kimberly A.
Smith, Laura
Smith, Linda
Smith, Lisa L.
Smith, Lorri G.
Smith, Lynn J.
Smith, Maria M.
Smith, Maripaz C.
Smith, Marlene
Smith, Martha J.
Smith, Mary
Smith, Melody
Smith, Michele W.
Smith, Michelle
Smith, Monica
Smith, Mozelle
Smith, Nicole Elizabeth
Smith, Pamela J.
Smith, Patricia
Smith, Perry
Smith, Rachel S.
Smith, Ralph C.
Smith, Rebecca
Smith, Roberta L.
Smith, Ronald R.
Smith, Roseann
Smith, Ryan G.
Smith, Shastah M.
Smith, Sheree J.
Smith, Shirley M.
Smith, Sonia
Smith, Stephanie R.
Smith, Stephen
Smith, Susan A.
Smith, Susannah S.
Smith, Tanikia M.
Smith, Tanya Starkovich
Smith, Tena
Smith, Thomas
Smith, Tonya M.
Smith, Valencia
Smith, Valerie
Smith, Virginia
Smith, Wiliam A.
Smith, Yvette J.
Smith-Condon, Cherry G.
Smithey, David K.
Smith-Mui, Andrew

Smith-Silvera, Kiarnold L.
Smith-Snyder, Cecelia M.
Smith-Snyder, Tonya M.
Smithson, Inge L.
Smithwick, John G.
Smock, Teresa
Smolecki, Agatha B.
Smolen, Isabel A.
Smoot, Trista L.
Smykiel, Grace
Snare, Tracy R.
Snead, Jeanne A.
Sneed, Nita M.
Sneid, David S.
Snell, Gloria Lou
Snell, Molly J.
Sniegowski, Petra K.
Sniff, Stephanie L.
Snively, Barbara A.
Snow, Bryan
Snow, Joanne H.
Snow, Richard A.
Snowfety, Catherine P.
Snyder, Catherine A.
Snyder, Christopher M.
Snyder, Ellen
Snyder, Janet S.
Snyder, Jenny L.
Snyder, Judy
Snyder, Linda
Snyder, Matthew
Snyder, Sharon G.
Snyder, Shirley A.
Soanes, Amanda R.
Sobolewski, Barbara
Sodergren, Rose M.
Sokolik, Ruth I.
Sokolowski, Stacey A.
Solano, Maritza
Soles, Wilbur R.
Soliman, Aidalyn
Solis, Peggy A.
Solis, Sara
Solomin, Deborah A.
Solomon, Hyacinth
Solomon, John P.
Solomon, Linda
Solomon, Marla
Somera, Bernagene R. L.
Somers, Elizabeth Jane
Songer, Sally H.
Songne, Elizabeth A.
Sonnenberg, Rhoda L.
Sonomura, Sherrie S.
Sonsteby, Paula G.
Sopp, Stephen
Sorensen, Bob
Sorensen, Toni
Sorensen, Wendy Michelle
Sorenson, Sherry
Sorg, Kathleen M.
Soriano, Sheryl B.
Sorin, Linda R.
Sorneson, Bob
Sorrentino, Robin Stafford
Soruco, Fernando L.
Sosa, Abdiel
Sosa, John D.
Sotiriadis, Pamela E.
Soto Arras, Joel A.
Soto, Darren P.
Soto, Lourdy M.
Sours, Lisa J.
Southerland, Adrienne E.
Southward, Kathleen
Southwell, Susan W.
Sowerbutts, David J.
Spade, Mary H.
Spaeth, Maria
Spagna, Karen
Spahn, Phyllis
Spain Bey, Yasmin P.
Spak, Myron J.
Spang, James D.
Spann, Carol
Spann, Mary P.

Spann, Micheal A.
Spann, Nancy Britt
Spann, Phyllis
Sparacia, Cathy Mary
Sparacino, Frances B.
Sparby, Anne M.
Sparer, Laura K.
Spargo, Barbara
Sparhawk, Bart M.
Sparhawk, Steven B.
Sparks, Kathy R.
Sparks, Robin E.
Sparrow-Bodenmiller, Janet
Spath, Frances L.
Spearman, Delphine
Spears, Sheila
Speck, Anita L.
Spector, Jason A.
Speed, Felice J.
Speelman, Diana
Speight, Jennifer V.
Speirs, Catherine
Spelle, Lane
Spellman, Carolyn
Spence, Carol
Spence, Erica
Spence, Joann L.
Spence, Shannon M.
Spencer, Judith
Spencer, Laurie
Spencer, Melice E.
Spencer, Ragina F.
Spera, Christopher
Speros, Sarita O.
Sperrazza, Barbara J.
Spetz, Kelly Marie
Spicer, Betty
Spicer, Elisabeth
Spicer, Terri
Spieler, Carol A.
Spillers, Cindy P.
Spindler, Cynthia A.
Spinelli, Cara E.
Spinelli, Maria L.
Spinks, Lorna
Spires, Teresa Y.
Spoonheim, Joel B.
Sporn, Mindy
Spradlin, Cynthia M.
Spragg, Anne Marie
Spragg, Ardi J.
Spray, Elliott J.
Spring, Karen J.
Springer, Donna L.
Springer, Gwen H.
Springs, Judy A.
Sproul, Lucy Jane
Sprowls, Helen S.
Spuhler, Charles F.
Spurgeon, Darrin S.
Spurr, Laura E.
Squiers, Shelley R.
Srinivasan, Peter G.
St. Charles, Ginger
St. Clair, Arilma M.
St. Clair, Fern L.
St. Cyr, Aenam
St. Ours, Joan M.
Stabelfeldt, Martha R.
Stacho, Dave
Stack, Mary Clare
Stack, Sarah S.
Stackhouse, Trelisa D.
Stacy, Raymond C.
Stadler, Sharon A.
Staff, Todd
Stafford, Andrea H.
Stafford, Daniel L.
Stafford, Gayla L.
Stafford, Kristin
Staggs, Greta G.
Stahly, Jeffry D.
Stalder, Sharon A.
Staley, Tara L.
Stallings, Beth
Stam, Nancy

Standiford, Mary K.
Stanek, Susan Lynn
Stanelis, Nicholas Micheal
Stanfill, Donna
Stanford, Janice A.
Stankovic, Deana L.
Stanley, Karen
Stanley, Kirk M.
Stanley, Mary A.
Stanley, Stephanie Lee
Stanley, Swick
Stansfield, Kathleen M.
Stanton, Kathy A.
Stanton, Kim
Stanton, Teresa A.
Stapel, Diane L.
Staples, James G.
Stapleton, Roxanne H.
Starcevich, Cari R.
Starck, Donna J.
Starck, Shannon M.
Stark, Michael K.
Starks, Christina N.
Starnes, Gary S.
Starzetski, Kimberly
Stauder, Martha A.
Stauder, Michael
Stauffer, Margaret C.
Staugaitis, Jane O.
Stead, Megan M.
Stebbins, Valerie
Steckler, Kristan M.
Steed, Carolyn
Steed, Leigh Jean
Steed, Robert D.
Steele, Katherine F.
Steele, Romona D.
Steele, Teresa J.
Steele, Timothy Paul
Steen, Joy E.
Steeves, Thomas H.
Steffen, Jessica L.
Steffen, Teresa B.
Steffes, Carol
Stegall, Gerrye C.
Stegall, Sharon H.
Stegmeir, Diane K.
Steigleman, Amy
Stein, Charlene M.
Steiner, Cortney Lynn
Steiner, Daniel L.
Steiner, Megin M.
Steinhouse, Nancy I.
Steinman, Joanna
Steinman, Linnet
Steinmeyer, Julie Ann
Stekloff, Debbie S.
Stelter, Tawyna L.
Stender, Robin L.
Stennett Brantley, Tiffany
Stenson, Susan A.
Stephens, Christina M.
Stephens, Elisa
Stephens, Georgina Y.
Stephens, Jeffery H.
Stephens, Jennie
Stephens, Roberta Kathleen
Stephens, Rosemary A.
Stephens, Rosie
Stephens, Shanna L.
Stephens, Stephanie A.
Stephens, Tammy
Stephenson, Carol A.
Stepp, Michael D.
Sterling, Chanda J.
Stern, Leslie M.
Stetter, Heather M.
Stevens, Carole Diane
Stevens, Jacquelyn
Stevens, Katie L.
Stevens, Marilyn M.
Stevens, Terra L.
Stevens, Terri C.
Stevenson, Brandi
Stevinson, Edward P.
Steward, Geralyn D.

Steward, Michael
Stewart, Anne M.
Stewart, Caitlin R.
Stewart, Candace A.
Stewart, Dawn
Stewart, Dianne K.
Stewart, Emy A.
Stewart, Esther M.
Stewart, Geralyn D.
Stewart, Herman Alvin
Stewart, Jacquelyn M.
Stewart, Julianne
Stewart, Kathleen
Stewart, Kathryn C.
Stewart, Laura
Stewart, Leah K.
Stewart, Lehiwa N.
Stewart, Linda D.
Stewart, Pieper R.
Stewart, Sharon
Stewart, Susan B.
Stewart, Teresa Madison
Stielstra, Gregory E.
Stifler, Rita
Stika, Matthew E.
Stinger, Kristy A.
Stinson, Debra L.
Stinson, Jamie D.
Stinson, Jan A.
Stinson, Marta
Stintzi, Dawna J.
Stiteler, Linda K.
Stitt, Karleen M.
Stjernberg, Shelley R.
Stockdale, Leah P.
Stockhausen, Janet C.
Stockholm, Terry L.
Stoddard, Melony M.
Stoelzel, Judith F.
Stofel, Diana R.
Stoker, James J.
Stokes, Amanda M.
Stokes, Andrea
Stokes, Bridget B.
Stokes, Carolyn
Stolar, John C.
Stolar, Sue C.
Stoll, Denise Rita
Stoll, Eileen H.
Stoll, Katherine
Stoll-Mooyoung, Trisha M.
Stolzenbach, Carol S.
Stomer, Jeanetta Renee
Stone, Carolyn
Stone, Earl A.
Stone, Jacquelyn
Stone, Jane G.
Stone, Jeremy
Stone, Jonathan
Stone, Krisandra M.
Stone, Robert E.
Stonebraker, Cheryll Lynne
Stooksbury, Krista L.
Stooksbury, LeeAnn L.
Stores, Seth M.
Storhaug, Colleen J.
Storms, Kathleen A.
Storrie, Ashley N.
Storvik, Philip
Story, Janis
Story, Robyn K.
Stouffer, Kristin A.
Stough, Barbara J.
Stout, Joyce W.
Stovall, Burton E.
Stover, Desiree E.
Stowe, Lisa
Stoyer, Leslie A.
Strachan, Lora A.
Strader, Wilbur
Strader, William J.
Strahm, Jedediah Michael
Strait, Jennifer
Stranaghan, Laurel C. B.
Strang, Stephanie
Straub, Teresa R.

Straus, Frances C.
Straus, Pamela
Straus, Teresa R.
Strauser, Patricia Lee
Strawbridge, Tisha M.
Streater, Gayle
Streater, Kim Shows
Streater, Laura G.
Streber, Barbara K.
Strecker, Linda E.
Street, Brenda H.
Street, Marian Rene
Street, Polly A.
Streeter, Carolynn P.
Streeter, Felice Olivette
Strickland, Aubrey A.
Strickland, Joanne Irene
Strickland, Theresa M.
Strickling-Hart, Susan E.
Stritehoff, Charlotte Elizabeth
Stritzel, Julie Ann
Strobl, Robert
Stroble, Jeffrey C.
Stroker, Starlit
Strom, Amy B.
Strong, Anthony P.
Strong, Kathleen M.
Stroud, Alice Fredricka
Strowman, Hanna P.
Strub, Elizabeth Bell
Struck, Lauren J.
Stuard, Lisa Renee S.
Stuart, Jordan
Stuart, Lois C.
Stuart, Philip R.
Stubbs, Sara A.
Stubbs, Tamsin R.
Stuckey, Pamela L.
Stude, Mary Ann
Stueckel, Cheryl L.
Stuepfert, Kathleen M.
Stull, Brittany L.
Stull, Daryl S.
Sturm, Brian E.
Suarez, Marayxa
Suart, Philip R.
Sucher, Robert L.
Sudermann, Michael E.
Suedekum, Jeri
Suellentrop, Linda R.
Suffian, Lauren
Suffridge, Jeanne M.
Suits, Barbara C.
Sukel, Claudia Ann
Sukram, Bibi Z.
Sullivan, Angela
Sullivan, Bobbie Lynn
Sullivan, Bridget W.
Sullivan, Cecilia
Sullivan, James A.
Sullivan, Janet M.
Sullivan, Jill M.
Sullivan, Melissa J.
Sullivan, Nancy P.
Sullivan, Patricia
Sullivan, Rebekah D.
Sullivan, Sally J.
Sullivan, Tonya
Sum, Becky L.
Sumida, Flower
Sumida, Michael S.
Summerford, Quo-Vades
Summers, Wallis Kay
Summerville, Glenda
Sumpter, Rebecca S.
Sunday, Bonnie K.
Sundt, Kati K.
Sunko-Imhof, Patricia A.
Suren, Louise S.
Surgeon, Ramona P.
Suria, Angela R.
Suriani, Nancy L.
Surman, Denise
Sushil, Mary
Susman, Paul E.
Suter, Pamela J.

Sutherland, Jason M.
Sutphin, Stacey
Sutton, Gary
Sutton, Gerald W.
Sutton, Margaret J.
Sutton, Martha
Sutton, Susan K.
Sutyak, Wendy
Sutz, Raeanne
Suzuki, Lola L. B.
Swader, Patricia A.
Swails, Etta L.
Swan, David W.
Swan, Valerie J.
Swanson, Gregory R.
Swanson, Rebecca
Swanson, Surgena C.
Swarmer, Sherry
Sweeney, Howard E.
Sweeney, Linda
Sweeny, Catherine A.
Sweet, Sara Elizabeth
Sweet, Wanda
Swendiman, Shawna L.
Swenson, Catherine A.
Swiecinski, Johanne Hey
Swiercinsky, Stacey J.
Swietlicki, Nannette I.
Swift, Terry
Swift, William J.
Swint, Denise N.
Swisher, Lou Ann
Swope, James D.
Syamsundar, Aruna
Sydnor, Rhonda M.
Sykes, Janet
Sylvia, Cyndi L.
Syracuse, Donna C.
Szabo, Elroy
Szatkowski, Jacqueline S.
Szenderski, Matt
Szente, John
Szewczyk, Margaret E.
Szramowski, Marilyn L.
Szymanski, Joanne

T

Taamu, Malia Romania
Taber, Vivian L.
Tabron, Deborah L.
Tabur, Christina B.
Tacelli, Catherine M.
Tackmann, Katie T.
Tadesse, Abel
Taffenhart, Rita M.
Tah, Teebeh
Takata, Cheryl Y.
Takata, Kimberly
Talamantes, Mary Ellen
Talano, Catherine N.
Talio, Nancy
Tallada, Jennifer L.
Tamalunas, Jacquelyn J.
Tamargo, Patricia A.
Tamir, Sara L. F.
Tamprateep, Lisa Z.
Tamprateep, Marala
Tamprateep, Shaun
Tandon, Kokil
Tanenberg, Robert
Tanghal, Evelyn A.
Tanguay, Laura
Taniguchi, Myles J.
Tanikawa, Lisa K.
Tanner, Vicky L.
Tanquilut, Elizabeth F.
Tansey, Marian Rita
Tao, Tammy
Tappen, Peter A.
Tappen, Sara F.
Tarasovich, Shirlee A.
Tarasula, Eugene
Targgart, Anita M.
Tart, Teresa H.
Tashiro, Toni M.

Tassin, Rhonda D.
Tataryn, Vicky A.
Tate, Chrisundra
Tate, Doloris Ann
Tate, Jennie R. K.
Tate, Jon Marcus
Tate, Laurel E.
Tate, Phullis F.
Tate, Shandalay L.
Tatpati, Olga A.
Tatsuno, Maya H.
Tauheed, Rajia
Taumua, Tusitala S.
Tautuaa, Sitataila
Taxis, Jean Carole
Taylor Lyphout, Tricia L.
Taylor, Abby
Taylor, Amy
Taylor, Anna M.
Taylor, Arlene
Taylor, Becky Kay
Taylor, Catherine L.
Taylor, Charles
Taylor, Constance G.
Taylor, Deborah M.
Taylor, Debra J.
Taylor, Donald B.
Taylor, Elaine
Taylor, Elizabeth
Taylor, H. David
Taylor, Ila B.
Taylor, Jan S.
Taylor, Jay C.
Taylor, Johnita J.
Taylor, Kathleen J.
Taylor, Keena L.
Taylor, Kelly
Taylor, Leslie Faye
Taylor, Liddie Michelle
Taylor, Lisa L.
Taylor, Mark A.
Taylor, Matthew
Taylor, Megan D.
Taylor, Melanie
Taylor, Michael
Taylor, Michele
Taylor, Mildred
Taylor, Natalie
Taylor, Rosemarie T.
Taylor, Susanna M.
Taylor, Tanya Lee
Taylor, Verna P.
Taylor, William M.
Taylor, Yvonne C.
Taylor-Douglas, Wanda K.
Tays, Mary L.
Te, Sochenda M.
Teague, John L.
Teare, Sean D.
Teaster, Dennis L.
Teats, Angela J.
Teel, Crystal P.
Teel, Glen A.
Tegtmeyer, Amanda Lynn
Teichrow, April J.
Teissen, Lori L.
Teixeira, Jennifer M.
Tekoppel-Jordan, Kathisu
Telford, Peggy A.
Telleria, Susan A.
Templar Bail, Rachel L.
Templar, Cheryl L.
Temple, Mary L.
Temple, Robin Chandler
Tendall, Cynthia
Tengan, Sherrilyn
Tennant, Elizabeth A.
Teply, Cynthia
Teppe, Heather L.
Terranella, Patricia A.
Terranova, Annmignon
Terranova, Nancy
Terrazas, Virginia A.
Terrell, Akeya Y.
Terrell, Crystal Monique
Teslik, Diane C.

Tesone, Jean L.
Tessmann, Ellen H.
Tester, Dennis L.
Teuton, Cher R.
Thaler, Tara K.
Thayer, Susan R.
Thein, Ko Ko
Theis, Michele N. A.
Theisen-Chenchar, Debra S.
Theiss, Anita
Theodoras, Suzanna
Theodotou, Andrew V.
Theriot, Ramona M.
Therrien, Annette E.
Thibault, Tracie R.
Thiel, Kenneth E.
Thielen, Kimberly S.
Thigpen, Kara M.
Thigpen, Sumari F.
Thilenius, Sherry
Thiry, Barbara A.
Thobe, J. Wayne
Thoele, Susan L.
Thoele, Susanna
Thoene, Phyllis
Thogainathan, Anuradha
Thomas Fowler, Kimberly
Thomas, Ashley Nicole
Thomas, Beverly J.
Thomas, Carann L.
Thomas, Carla M.
Thomas, Elizabeth A.
Thomas, Forrest D.
Thomas, Helena Y.
Thomas, Irene
Thomas, Jacob T.
Thomas, Jacqueline E.
Thomas, Jamie W.
Thomas, Janie
Thomas, Jeffrey
Thomas, Jennifer A.
Thomas, Jodie R.
Thomas, John H.
Thomas, Julia Anne
Thomas, Kathryn J.
Thomas, Laura A.
Thomas, Linda
Thomas, Liza J.
Thomas, Lorna
Thomas, Maryann
Thomas, Michelle M.
Thomas, Nancy A.
Thomas, Nancy S.
Thomas, Olivia A.
Thomas, Pamela
Thomas, Patrick A.
Thomas, Propster A.
Thomas, Reginald P.
Thomas, Robert
Thomas, Scott
Thomas, Shirley Hopkins
Thomas, Shron C.
Thomas, Vonda K.
Thomas, William
Thomason, Laura Danielle
Thomas-Ross, Amber S.
Thome, Merilee
Thompkins, Barbara Helen
Thompson, Azilee
Thompson, Barbara K.
Thompson, Courtney E.
Thompson, Dennis A.
Thompson, Diane M.
Thompson, Harold J.
Thompson, Holly C.
Thompson, Jennifer
Thompson, John T.
Thompson, Kimberly S.
Thompson, Linda
Thompson, Lisa J.
Thompson, Marjorie
Thompson, Mark A.
Thompson, Mary B.
Thompson, Marybeth E.
Thompson, Michael L.
Thompson, Nancy L.

Thompson, Rayette L.
Thompson, Rebecca S.
Thompson, Richard L.
Thompson, Rita
Thompson, Russell A.
Thompson, Sandra R.
Thompson, Venus Eve
Thoms, Greg A.
Thomson, Cara Lea
Thomson, Jeri Lynn
Thomson, Latecia
Thomson, Susan
Thornton, Portia I.
Thornton, Robert D.
Thorpe, Ashlye
Threlfall, Jane
Threlkeld, Sheree
Throckmorton, Carol M.
Thrower, James A.
Thuele, Susan L.
Thumbert, Carol Anne
Thurman, Tammy W.
Thursby, Jennifer Longard
Thurston, Blake L.
Thwaits, Vivian
Thyagarajan, Singaram
Thyer, Susanna K.
Tiani, Angela M.
Tibbetts, Catherine J.
Tibbetts, Cathy
Tibbetts, Wendy
Tiblier, Bruce V.
Tiblier, Sherry Lynn
Tibretts, Catherine J.
Tiburcio, Marylinda P.
Tice, Hollie N.
Tickle, Jeanne
Tidd, Simon T.
Tidemann, Karma G.
Tidroski, Sherry
Tidwell, Blake M.
Tidwell, Catheia S.
Tidwell, Jan
Tidwell, Jane
Tidwell, Jean K.
Tiegen, Vivian E.
Tien, Christine P.
Tierney, Mary Beth
Tiessen, Lori L.
Tifre, Jeanette
Tighr, Susan A.
Tigner, Suzi
Tijernia, Noelia
Tikunoff, Nancy L.
Tilak, Elizabeth F.
Tillar, Veronica A.
Tillery, Kristi
Tillery, Martha G.
Tillman, Diana J.
Tillman, Shawn T.
Timbo, Stacey R.
Timmerman, Gloria J.
Timmerman, Jess W.
Tin, Jonathan T.
Tindal, Candace
Tingwald, James O.
Tinsmith, Laurel
Tippett, Amy R.
Tippitt, April Maria
Tipton, Gloria
Tipton, Joshua Dean
Tipton, Kim
Tisdale, Jacqueline
Tish, Donna
Tisher, Jim
Tison, Dan V.
Titus, Debra A.
Tluczek, Lakisha L.
Tobe, Christopher Joseph
Tobey, Richard Downs
Tobias, Richelle D.
Tobin, Ann
Todd, Margaret J.
Todd, Mikel Kent
Todlan, Christian R.
Toennis, Galen Lynn

Togafau, Doris
Togashi, Rose M.
Tokh, Homira
Tokonitz, Christine K.
Tokumoto, Keith K.
Tolbert, Edith S.
Tolbert, Jana
Tolbert, Lisa C.
Toler, Melissa
Toler, Rachel L.
Tolley, Debra Jean
Tolliver, Mara D.
Tom, Christopher P.
Tom, Ellen C. L.
Tomasa, Tod T.
Tomasella, Stephen J.
Tomecek, Lisa A.
Tomich, Frances Ann
Tomlin, James A.
Tommy, Vonjo R.
Toms, Loretta
Tomsett, Giles R.
Ton, Gwaine W.
Tooke, Susan L.
Toothman, Patricia A.
Tootle, Joseph M.
Topp, Katherine
Torgerson, Brianna R.
Torke, Lynn D.
Toronto, Marilyn C.
Torrelli, Donna
Torrente, Barry
Torres, Ana C.
Torres, Annabelle
Torres, David C.
Torres, Jamin C.
Torres, Jesse A.
Torres, Joanna S.
Torres, Lyla
Torres, Maria E.
Torres, Sonia
Torres, Victor Joseph
Tortorello, Victoria A.
Toth, Nicolas
Totin, Bonnie L.
Totten, Margaret L.
Toub, Gail M.
Toungett, Rhonda
Toungette, Brian
Toups, Dorothy
Tovrog, Jessica
Towers, Kevin
Towle, Bradley
Townes, Barry
Townes, Janet
Townley, Glenn David
Townsend, Catherine J.
Toy, Sylvia S.
Tozer, Jorja A.
Trace, Elizabeth
Trace, Marjorie Anne
Tracy, Carol A.
Tracy, Mary F.
Tramble, Shaun
Trammell, Anita
Tramontana, Joan M.
Tran, Leann L.
Tran, Phu Hoang
Tran, Tuan T.
Traugh, Annette
Traunero Gall, Angela Marie
Traupmann, Georgia
Travalini, Jane
Travers, Kimberly Ruth
Traversino, Anthony R.
Traxler, Emilee
Trcka, Leigh B.
Treadway, Keri
Trees, Marie T.
Treese, Laura G.
Tremoulet, Brenda
Trenary, Renee
Trenney, Lynn
Trentmann, Christine Ann
Trevino, Jorge A.
Tribble, Abigail B.

Tribble, Joanne L.
Tribles, Virginia L.
Trice, Yulandra T.
Triesch, Linda B.
Trinkle, Nicholas P.
Triplet, Michael E.
Triplett, Jennifer
Tripp, Michael L.
Trisler, Kathleen
Trivers, Oscar Brion
Triviski, Rosanne
Trocino, John E.
Trocki, Joni L.
Troiani, Nicole Marie
Tropp, Janis E.
Trosko, William M.
Trost, Cecelia M.
Trost, Kritsy
Troupe, Corinne
Trout, Christina M.
Troutman, Barrie Ann
Trow, Heidi M.
Troxler, Kathryn B.
Troy, Kelly
Troyer, Lisa Jane
Truax, Jesse D.
Truax, June
Truax, Loretta
Truex, Dan R.
Truitt, Karen M.
Trujillo, Brenda
Trujillo, Gloria M.
Trumble, Roy Robert
Trunnel, Sherry L.
Truscott, Tara Lynn
Trussell, Jamie Lynn
Tsang, Julia Wai-Chi
Tscherne, David J.
Tschirpke, Barbara
Tseng, Lien-Chou
Tsoutis, Jill Williams
Tubbs, Dana Thomas
Tubbs, Jo L.
Tucker, Carole
Tucker, Gary
Tucker, Ginger K
Tucker, Lara L.
Tucker, Melanie W.
Tucker, Melissa M.
Tucker, Patricia
Tucker, Toni L.
Tucker, Travis
Tudeen, Alan
Tudeen, Marcella
Tudeen, Michael
Tueffel, Nora A.
Tugend, Juliann
Tull, Jeremy
Tullock, Robert Prewitt
Tulodzieski, Barbara A.
Tumbarello, Jean M.
Tumminello, Kevin J.
Tunney, Mary E.
Turek, Adele
Turk, Brian J.
Turkich, Natasha
Turley, Margaret
Turlik, Cheryl A.
Turnbeaugh, Sandra E.
Turner, Alice Kay
Turner, Anna C.
Turner, Carolyn K.
Turner, Charles E.
Turner, Connie R.
Turner, Deborah A.
Turner, Diana
Turner, Georgeanna
Turner, John Eric
Turner, John Michael
Turner, Katie M.
Turner, Lisa
Turner, Marissa L.
Turner, Marsha A.
Turner, Mary E.
Turner, Misah R.
Turner, Nicole J.

Turner, Pamela E.
Turner, Parcilla A.
Turner, Robert
Turock, Steven M.
Turpin, Karen L.
Turton, Maria T.
Tustison, Winston
Tutor, Billy A.
Tutt, Diane W.
Tuzzolo, Sandra J.
Twist, Carrie S.
Twomey, Catherine M.
Tydingco, Carrie R.
Tyler, Jeanne M.
Tyler, Johanna K.
Tyler, Timothy F.
Tyson, Barbara Powell

U

Uddin, Zakia S.
Ugwuadu, Francisca Nkiru
Uhiren, Tori K.
Uhlmansiek, Amanda K.
Uhrine, Jill D.
Uliana, Stephanie
Ullery, Janice
Ullrich, Susan
Ulrich, Carol
Ulrich, Susan
Underwood, Carla J.
Unger, Kara M.
Unger, Theresa
Unglaub, Margaret
Ungs, Janet L.
Unrath, Steven T.
Unruh, Renae Lynn
Upchurch, Sandra
Upham, Marjorie A.
Upjohn, Charles E.
Urbaniak, Victoria R.
Urben, Lauren F.
Uribe, Ana C.
Uriegas, Yvonne R.
Urteaga, Paula E.
Urteaga, Rene
Uson, Rayna A.
Uster, Mary Lee
Utley, Christopher
Uyan, Remedids M.
Uyenishi, Diane

V

Vaccaro-Kish, Joanne
Vachon, Ann-Marie F.
Vadlamani, Lalita D.
Vagnier, Michael L.
Vago, Jill L.
Valdengo, Peggy B.
Valdes, Anthony J.
Valdez, Lisa A.
Valenti, Ida
Valentine, Dandrea
Valentine, Tamara L.
Valenzuela, Dianna L.
Valenzuela, Laura A.
Valfre, Benjamin
Valicoff, Rebecca Mary
Valitzski, Patricia
Valjean, Jacque
Vallejo, Peggy D.
Valulick, Judith
Van Aartsen, Lisa
Van Allen, Kathryn
Van de Water, Barbara
Van Der Merwe, Isabella M.
Van Der Merwe, John H.
Van Every, Cathy C.
Van Fossen-Miller, Mary
Van Gemmert, Colleen L.
Van Haasteren, Gloria
Van Hamme, John L.
Van Horn, Kelly
Van Horn, Kristin
Van Ness, Emily

Van Note, Dorothy
Van Osten, Leticia
Van Schaik-Louis, Barbara
Van Scoik, Andrea Lynn
Van Wyckhouse, Laurie
Van Zuidan, Stacie M.
Vanavery, Janet R.
Vanbrandt Muzquiz, Grace
Vandehey, Kristin R.
VanderMeulen, David L.
VanDusen, Terra A.
Vangrevenhof, Jani A.
Vanhoozer, Joseph
Vanhoozer, Katie J.
Vanlangendon, Lana R.
Vanmatre, Julie
Vanosodol, Janice V.
Vanzante, Gloria
Vanzin, Kira
Varallo, Veronica
Vardaman, Didi M.
Varden, Beverly F.
Vargas, Angela N.
Vargas, Jennifer Marie
Vargas, Sylvia
Vargas, Wendy
Vargo, Keith A.
Varnado, Myra
Varnell, Brandi Lyn
Varvarovsky, Linda L.
Vasbinder, Kent S.
Vasenin, Yuriy
Vasey, Sherry
Vasper, Michael
Vasquez, Maria A.
Vassar, Linda M.
Vaughan, Amy C.
Vaughan, Rhonda A.
Vaughan, Rhonda Adams
Vaughan, Susan L.
Vaughn, Deborah J.
Vaughn, Faith C.
Vaughn, Joseph
Vaughn, Kimberly H.
Vaughn, Marquita Rosalee
Vaughn, Paul
Vavrock, Debra
Vazquez, Adam
Vazquez, Sydney Schwartz
Veach, Anthony R.
Vecchio, Joalice I.
Vecchio, Joshua J.
Vecchry, Carole
Veenstra, Lianne
Vehige, Deborah A.
Veilleux, Ann J.
Veith, Victoria M.
Velazquez III, Carlos
Velez, Erwin A.
Velez, Lillian V.
Velgich, Jennifer L.
Veloso, Glenn S.
Venable, Donna
Vendetta, Kathleen
Venegoni, Judy E.
Venegoni, Vickey L.
Veneman, Amanda L.
Venkannagari, Anitha
Venson, Trina
Venzant, Earvin E.
Vera, Maria T.
Verbeten, Cynthia M.
Verderber, Amy C.
Verdi, Nicholas J.
Verdin, Erica Lorraine
Vernich, Carolyn A.
Vernier, Kimberly
Vernon, Elizabeth M.
Verplank, Diane
Vertison, Dorothy
Via, Barbara Lee
Via, Patricia S.
Vice, Ann G.
Vicenzi, Geraldine N.
Vichaikul, Robin
Vick, Roberta L.

Vickers, Cathy
Vickrey, Ellen K.
Victor, Robin
Vidal, Richard A.
Vidal, Rita G.
Viehoever, Sterling R.
Vieira, Catherine T.
Vifansi, Evelyn
Vigersky, Robert
Viggiano, Bonnie
Vigil, Patricia T.
Vilakazi, Patricia
Vilaverde, Erlina S.
Villacorte, Rosalyn R.
Villagomez, Evangelina
Villagomez, Keren A.
Villamero, Kimberly M.
Villani, Kimberly M.
Villanueva, Diane M.
Villarreal, Monica M.
Villas, Von D.
Villaverde, Linda M.
Villella, Nancy J.
Vilt, Betty
Vincent, Annette Michelle
Vincent, Donna M.
Vincent, Robert W.
Vincent, Sandra Melissa
Vincent, Susan M.
Vincler, Mark S.
Vindedzis, Dana L.
Vinson, Randolph S.
Vinson, Sally
Vinzant, Kelly Kaye
Viola, Kristina K.
Virtudes, Kelly Ann
Viscusi, Susan E.
Viscuso, Maurice J.
Vita, Tina
Vitchitpundhu, Chowtip
Vitez, Cathy L.
Vivant, Amanda Anne
Voci-Reed, Jackson
Voelkel, Baillie Lynn
Voelkle, Sharon
Vogel, Carol L.
Vogel, Karen I.
Vogel, Madonna Marie
Vogel, Norine K.
Vogler, Crista Lynn
Vogler, Diane J.
Vogt, Larry
Voigt, Laura L.
Volckmann, Sarah J.
Volgi, Josephine R.
Volk, Ellen L.
Voloudakis, Michael L.
Von Stroud, Alice F.
Vonklemen, Deborah A.
Vorthman, Mary T.
Vosbein, Beth Spraggins
Voss, Jeffrey M.
Vulli, Pradeep
Vulpis, Patricia M.
Vunk, Sherry
Vye, Nancy
Vyzas, Ben

W

Wachtler, Joseph W.
Waddey, Paula Ellis
Wade, Brett J.
Wade, David J.
Wade, Deborah D.
Wade, Laura
Wade, Revia M.
Wade, Tracy A.
Wadley, Brian James
Waeckerle, Kathleen A.
Wage, Paulette E. T.
Waggoner, Pamela C.
Wagner, Ann C.
Wagner, Christina
Wagner, Darla J.
Wagner, Erin K.

Wagner, Jonathan
Wagner, Lana
Wagner, Leah E.
Wagner, Linda R.
Wagner, Meaghan
Wagner, Mildred L.
Wagner, Patricia A.
Wagner, Vicki
Wagoner, Craig
Wahl, Lawrence H.
Waibel, Kenneth
Waid, Collin
Wainner, Wendel M.
Wainwright, Michael A.
Waite, Barbara A.
Waits, Karen E.
Wakaumi, Merilyn C.
Wakefield, Gail
Wakeley, Rita D.
Wakeman, Teresa M.
Walbert, Nathan
Walburn, Allen Earl
Walburn, Bobbi Marie
Wald, Alice M.
Waldek, Carmen Maria
Waldor, Mario J.
Waldrep, Stephanie
Waldriff, Mary Carolyn
Waldron, Kristie L.
Waldron, Rosemary
Waldrop, Jessica Deann
Walker, Alison Bell
Walker, Betty A.
Walker, Carl D.
Walker, Cathy L.
Walker, Francine Vivian
Walker, Gale M.
Walker, Janet E.
Walker, Jennifer L.
Walker, Johnnie C.
Walker, Kara M.
Walker, Leola P.
Walker, Michelle C.
Walker, Natalie A.
Walker, Rose
Walker, Sandra D.
Walker, Sara
Walker, Shannon M.
Walker, Stewart G.
Walker, Timothy
Walker, William Tracy
Walkston, Cherri L.
Walkuski, Maria
Wall, Cynthia
Wall, James R.
Wall, Janet Oaks
Wall, Melanie
Wall, Paula Timothy
Wall, Tammy J.
Wall, Wendy C.
Wallace, Ann D.
Wallace, Carol A.
Wallace, Deborah M.
Wallace, Don S.
Wallace, Jeffrey R.
Wallace, Joseph F.
Wallace, LaVerne
Wallace, Paul
Wallace, Racheal L.
Wallace, Rebecca Ann
Wallace, Saundra
Wallace, Tiffany A.
Wallbaum, Cynthia L.
Waller, Peggie C.
Walley, Kimberly E.
Walling, Amanda D.
Walling, Barbara
Wallsch-Drury, Sandra M.
Walsh, Christina
Walsh, Colleen M.
Walsh, Ellen D.
Walsh, Kathleen
Walsh, Mark O.
Walston, Cherri L.
Walt, Marie
Walter, Loretta M.

Walter, Trulener
Waltermeyer, April S.
Walters, Courtney F.
Walters, Elaine A.
Walters, John E.
Walters, Kathleen S.
Walters, Marion M.
Walters, Michael
Walters, Rita
Walters, Sharon L.
Walters, Teresa A.
Walther, Julie
Walther, Michael
Walther, Sara
Walthour, Barbara
Walton, Patricia M.
Walton, William F.
Wambach, Nancy
Wambold, Kym S.
Wan, Daisy Y.
Wang, Andrew X.
Wang, QianQian
Wang, Qing
Wannall, Laura
Ward, Anthony A.
Ward, Barry N.
Ward, Elizabeth Y.
Ward, Felicia D.
Ward, John E.
Ward, Joseph F.
Ward, Kathe Y.
Ward, Lorrie
Ward, Margaret L.
Ward, Melanie
Ward, Michelle D.
Ward, Nancy A.
Ward, Sandra A.
Ward, Teresa L.
Ward, Valerie N.
Warden, Christine A.
Wardlaw, Craig
Ware, Katrina Renae
Ware, Rena A.
Warford, Erika N.
Warlick, Justin W.
Warloski, Elizabeth A.
Warman, Deborah W.
Warner, Beverly
Warner, Cherice E.
Warner, Daneen G.
Warner, Linda M.
Warner, Philippa A.
Warner, Susan G.
Warren, Cheryl A.
Warren, Gail
Warren, Grant D.
Warren, Harold E.
Warren, Kenneth S.
Warren, Kristy D.
Warren, Linda A.
Warren, Mary JoAnne
Warren, Sierra D.
Warren, Susan S.
Warren, Timothy R. F.
Warshaw, Hope S.
Warshaw, Rita S.
Wasilowski, Lisa
Wasko, Donna M.
Wassom, Nancy
Waszczenko, Christine
Waters, Autumn
Waters, Jan
Waters, Mary Jane
Waters, Melissa K.
Watkins, Debra Hatcher
Watkins, Jennifer A.
Watkins, Kristine
Watkins, Mary K.
Watkins, Paula
Watkins, Sharla Cherry-Ann
Watkins, Stephen H.
Watkins, Velma E.
Watkins, Victoria A.
Wator, Paula A.
Watson, Audrey D.
Watson, Barbara

Watson, Candace E.
Watson, Crockett
Watson, David K.
Watson, Doris E.
Watson, Kyle N.
Watson, Lavanda
Watson, Mary A.
Watson, Patrick
Watson, Rachel J.
Watson, Sandy
Watson, Sheila
Watson, Shirley Lou
Watson, Sondra
Watson, Stephanie
Watson, Stephen P.
Watson-Bramble, Valencia G.
Watson-Sensky, Pamela G.
Watterson, Annie
Watterson, Nancy M.
Watts, Aaron D.
Watts, Albert R.
Watts, Estrella
Watts, Ruth J.
Waugaman, Nancy A.
Waugh, Elizabeth Ann
Waugh, Tonja
Wavada, Camille M.
Weamer, Meghan C.
Weary, Christina
Weast, Frances K.
Weatherford, Mandie N.
Weatherford, Victoria L.
Weathers, Beth A.
Weaver, Amy P.
Weaver, Angela E.
Weaver, Karen S.
Weaver, Matthew B.
Weaver, Sharon W.
Webb, Allen H.
Webb, Anna
Webb, Beverly J.
Webb, Kimberly W.
Webb, Martha L.
Webb, Misty S.
Webb, Monica O.
Webb-Whitney, Chaliece
Weber, Bridget L.
Weber, Cassandra J.
Weber, Danielle M.
Weber, Mary Kay
Weber, Patricia
Weber, Tina D.
Weber, William
Webster, Janey M.
Webster, Laurel
Webster, Nancy J.
Webster, Stella M.
Webster, Teri D.
Wedderburn, Edwina D.
Weddington, Tisha D.
Wedell, Barbara
Wedgewood, Ann Marie
Weech, Deborah M.
Weeks, Dennis D.
Weeks, Scott
Weeks, Susan E.
Weems, Trevor J.
Weglarz, Walter
Wegscheid, Carol J.
Wehby, Tracy L.
Wehrhagen, Mary K.
Weikel, Sharon S.
Weimer, Nicholas N.
Weinberger, Karen
Weinberger, Ruth L.
Weiner, Robyn
Weinert, Tara P.
Weinland, Donald F.
Weinreb, Lee M.
Weinstein, Sheldon M.
Weintraus, Thea
Weir, Angela
Weir, Brenda Lee
Weir, Gladys
Weis, Ivy M.
Weisensee, Bertha E.

Weiss, Kathleen
Weiszmann, Marcia
Welch, Jamie L.
Welch, Judith Bell
Welch, Kathleen
Welch, Leslie A.
Welk, Nancy J.
Weller, Marc
Wellington, Patricia
Wellman, William
Wells, Aaron R.
Wells, Amy E.
Wells, Ashley A.
Wells, Cynthia
Wells, Diann S.
Wells, Jane
Wells, Jennifer L.
Wells, Judy B.
Wells, Patricia W.
Wells, Sandra Anita
Wells, Wendy
Welsh, Carol G.
Welsh, Debra L.
Welters, Mary D.
Weltzien, Michelle L.
Wenclewicz Henderson, Tiffany M.
Wendel, Jane M.
Wendling, Mark G.
Wendt, Corinna Ann
Wenger, Diana
Wenger, Lucille A.
Wenstrand, Sally S.
Wentink, Judy H.
Wenzel, Rita P.
Werger, Jonathan D.
Werner, Bonnie C.
Werner, Deborah
Werner, Linda M.
Wert, Harry O.
Wertz, Valeria M.
Wesby, Greta
Wesco, Amanda M.
Wesner, Barbara
Wesolek, Emily S.
Wessels, Dorothy
Wessels, Peggy
Wesson, Mathew H.
West, Adele P.
West, Belinda
West, Carlisa Daniella
West, Diana N.
West, Donna J.
West, Eileen
West, Ruth A.
West, Tina Latrice
West, William Keith
Westbrook, Lisa A.
Westenfelder, Bruce
Westerberg, Sally A.
Westerfield, JoAnne
Westergard, Mary
Westfall, Rachel Ann
Westin, Hans Bertil
Weston, C. Sue
Weston, Christine R.
Weston, Lloyd
Wettengel, Wendy L.
Wettergreen, Amy
Wettleson, Joyce
Wetz, Holly A.
Wetzl, Christopher B.
Wetzler, Sheila M.
Wexler, Bruce R.
Whalen, Lorrie P.
Whalen, Rebecca J.
Whaley, James A.
Whayne, Michele L.
Wheeler, Celeste A.
Wheeler, David H.
Wheeler, JoAnn
Wheeler, Kathleen
Wheeler, Staci
Wheeler, Teresa D. McRae
Wheltle, Gail M.
Whetstone, Leigh A.
Whetton, Miriam L.

Whidbee, Angela D.
Whidby, John Bernard
Whisenant, Christine
Whisner, Paula S.
Whitbey, Lorene F.
White, Alesia M.
White, Amber S.
White, Angela M.
White, Barbara S.
White, Carol V.
White, Carolyn
White, Cheri L.
White, Christine
White, Connie J.
White, Cynthia L.
White, David S.
White, Deborah
White, Donna
White, Frank
White, Gloria Falls
White, Indria V.
White, Jeanette L.
White, John C.
White, Katherine Lynn Dineen
White, Kimberly K.
White, Lisa M.
White, Margaret
White, Megan A.
White, Nancy E.
White, Ruth A.
White, Sarah
White, Sharrye
White, Stacy Lindsay
White, Susan M.
White, Tamra L.
White, Thomas Randy
White-Green, Lora E.
Whitehead, Ellen B.
Whitehouse, Rebecca
Whitfield, Alexander R.
Whitfield, Angela L.
Whitfield, Lora
Whitfield, Marilee M.
Whitfield, Willie
Whitley, Dawn
Whitley, Molly
Whitley, Sharon S.
Whitman, Jan Marie
Whitman, Mary T.
Whitman, Michelle C.
Whitmer, William J.
Whitmore, Ana M.
Whitmore, Heather A.
Whitt, Kelly
Whittaker, Cheryl J.
Whittaker, Ramona
Whittier, Alexander
Whitton, Agnes
Wiberg, James J.
Wible, Gary R.
Wible, Gerald
Wiblishauser, Michael Joseph
Wick, Rita B.
Wickes, Amy L.
Wickett, Marsha K.
Wickstrom, Ashley P.
Wickstrom, Kathy J.
Widen, Lynette M.
Widmer, Stephani
Wiechman, Carrie Nicole
Wien, Michelle
Wiener, Jacquelyn
Wienert, Julie
Wienke, Judith Ann
Wier, Amanda K.
Wiersema, Tiffany
Wiese, Craig
Wiese, Sheri A.
Wiesenauer, Jennifer Elizabeth
Wigant, John E.
Wiggan, Sophia L.
Wiggins, Ricky G.
Wiggins, Susan
Wightman, William Robert
Wiisanen, Ada C.
Wilamowski, Linda L.

Wilbanks, Sara
Wilburn, Yvonne D.
Wilcott, Kathleen H.
Wilcox, Jenny C.
Wildberger, Richard
Wilder, Stacey Marie
Wiles, Anna M.
Wiley, Darrell
Wiley, Price H.
Wiley, Vickey L.
Wilhelm, Laura E.
Wilhelm, Stacey M.
Wiliams, Janice L.
Wiliams, Sherri
Wilke, Lisa
Wilkerson, Bettina Delaine
Wilkerson, Denise
Wilkerson, Ernestine
Wilkerson, Ledna R.
Wilkerson, Melissa
Wilkerson, Ploomie
Wilking, Julia G.
Wilkins, Anne
Wilkins, Daniel S.
Wilkins, Jason R.
Wilkins, Julia G.
Wilkins, Lorraine
Wilkins, Margaret D.
Wilkins, Stephen G.
Wilkinson, Karen
Wilkinson, Kassidy R.
Wilkinson, Kathie
Wilkinson, Mary
Wilkison, Sandra
Wilks, Miriam D.
Will, Lark A.
Willardsen, Juliann P.
Wille, Christine L.
Willes, Don G.
Willet, Nancy
Willett, Lisa A.
Willette, Lilah E.
Willey, Beverly
Willey, Carolyn M.
Willey, Christina Joy
Willey, M. Carolyn
William, Dana C.
William, Virginia F.
Williams Piech, Christine
Williams, Amanda B.
Williams, Amy L.
Williams, Angela B.
Williams, Barbara A.
Williams, Bernetta M.
Williams, Candice B.
Williams, Carlos R.
Williams, Carol Y.
Williams, Celesta M.
Williams, Cindy S.
Williams, Clarice
Williams, Clifford J.
Williams, DaKendra Sharron
Williams, Dana C.
Williams, Danita
Williams, David E.
Williams, Delroy L.
Williams, Desiree
Williams, Donald
Williams, Doris M.
Williams, Eleanor R.
Williams, Elizabeth
Williams, Frances
Williams, Greta M.
Williams, Harold E.
Williams, Helen B.
Williams, Jennifer Ann
Williams, Joseph
Williams, Juanica D.
Williams, Judith E.
Williams, Julia K.
Williams, Karen
Williams, Kelly J.
Williams, Kimberly
Williams, Kristi
Williams, Kristina
Williams, La-Gina K.

Williams, Lalita W.
Williams, Linda K.
Williams, Lisa
Williams, Mary Elizabeth
Williams, Maureen
Williams, Melissa M.
Williams, Melonie
Williams, Mineive B.
Williams, Misty
Williams, Myra
Williams, Natasha Rochelle
Williams, Noreen
Williams, Patricia
Williams, Paula J.
Williams, Renee J.
Williams, Rosaline D.
Williams, Russell
Williams, Sharise Lynette
Williams, Shavonne N.
Williams, Shelley
Williams, Sherina M.
Williams, Sherry A.
Williams, Stephanie E.
Williams, Susan
Williams, Teresa M.
Williams, Thomas
Williams, Torie L.
Williams, Tracey L.
Williams, Valerie M.
Williams, Virginia Batson
Williams, Wendy
Williams, Yoncenia
Williams-Briggs, Richard
Williamson, Andrea R.
Williamson, Emily S.
Williamson, Jay
Williamson, Jeanette
Williamson, Laura J.
Williamson, Marcus D.
Williamson, Margaret K.
Williamson, Nancy A.
Williamson, Stephanie
Williamson, Tiana Nichole
Williford, Monica Z.
Willimas, Susan
Willis, Bruce J
Willis, Gerald
Willis, Jessica Dawn
Willis, Karre A.
Willis, Katherine K.
Willis, Kimberly A.
Willis, Mary L.
Willis, Melissa L.
Willis, Rosalind A.
Willison, Kimberly Ann
Willits, Linda
Willley, M. Carolyn
Willmeth, Kimberly J.
Willoughby, Addy
Wills, Marvin B.
Willson, Kelly S.
Wilmot, Norma A.
Wilson Gilbert, Dienese A.
Wilson, Andria J.
Wilson, Anna E.
Wilson, Benvel
Wilson, Bonnie
Wilson, Caroline H.
Wilson, Christy
Wilson, Cindy
Wilson, Cynthia M.
Wilson, Deborah
Wilson, Donna
Wilson, Emily B.
Wilson, Esther M.
Wilson, Ethel A.
Wilson, Floyd
Wilson, Gail C.
Wilson, Greg L.
Wilson, Heide F.
Wilson, Helen
Wilson, Jane M.
Wilson, Janita Gale
Wilson, Joan
Wilson, Joanne
Wilson, Josephine

Wilson, Katherine
Wilson, Kathleen F.
Wilson, Kelly
Wilson, Larney
Wilson, Leticia P.
Wilson, Margaret Avery
Wilson, Marilyn I.
Wilson, Melinda
Wilson, Melissa D.
Wilson, Miriam N.
Wilson, Patricia C.
Wilson, Richard H.
Wilson, Rocky C.
Wilson, Rosalind Cephus
Wilson, Sadie J.
Wilson, Shaidrise M.
Wilson, Sherri S.
Wilson, Susan
Wilson, Teresa
Wilson, Tina R.
Wilson, William G.
Wilson-Henderson, Sherry
Wilson-Johnson, Linda J.
Wilverman, John
Wimber, Marlys J.
Wimer, Margaret M.
Winborg, Brad
Winburn, Amy J.
Winchell, Kami J.
Winchip, Gerelyn
Winderweedle, Patsy Jane
Windham, Charles F.
Windham, Penny
Wineland, Nancy L.
Winfree, Joshua K.
Wingard, Debra
Wingfield, Christine
Wingo, Pamela A.
Winham, Penny W.
Winker, Cynthia A.
Winkler, Annabelle M.
Winningham, Donna
Winstead, Amy McNish
Winstead, Lynette Marie
Winston, Oswanna Lavander
Winter-Bertsch, Renee S.
Winters, John E.
Winters, Leigh Ann
Winters, Linda M.
Winters, Marissa A.
Winters, Paulette
Winters, Ronald Lee
Winters, Walter E.
Winterton, Tami L.
Wintle, Michelle L.
Wirth, Andrea D.
Wise, Carol A.
Wise, Duell O.
Wise, Kathy M.
Wise, Kevin
Wise, Kyle J.
Wiseman, Cynthia M.
Wiseman, Tim S.
Wishner, Kathleen L.
Wishner, William J.
Wisnieski, Barbara L.
Witas, Louise
Witherly, Karen
Witkowski, Kathleen S.
Witt, Brenda
Wittbold, Jill
Witte, Deborah F.
Witte, Faith
Wittgan, Arlette A.
Witting Theiss, Raelynn
Witzer, Sheri L.
Wlson, Melinda
Wochomurka, Charles F.
Woddail, Joseph Downs
Wodele, Andrea Platkin
Woehler, Amy L.
Wohlheiter, Harold W.
Wohlschlegel, Beckie L.
Wohnowski, Rita C.
Wojciechowski, James G.
Wojcik, Elisa

Wojnowski, Rita C.
Woland, John L.
Wolf, Patricia M.
Wolf, Sharon M.
Wolf, Virginia A.
Wolfe, Larry M.
Wolfe, Melissa Renee
Wolff, Anna K.
Wolff, Cindy L.
Wolff, Joan Marie
Wolford, Betsey L.
Wolfsen, Connie
Wolking, Nancy J.
Wollan, Gina M.
Wollenberg, Kathleen J.
Womack, Janice Cowell
Womboldt, Carolyn A.
Wong, Carol A.
Wong, Melisa Mei-Foon
Wong, Stephanie J.
Woo, Alan
Wood, Andrea
Wood, Brandy C.
Wood, Desiree
Wood, Gary
Wood, Geraldine A.
Wood, Judith Joyce
Wood, Kathryn
Wood, Lola L.
Wood, Mary G.
Wood, Nancy C.
Wood, Tressa
Wood, Virginia Margaret
Woodall, Cathey Jo
Woodall, Stephanie S.
Woodard, Brenda O.
Woodard, Donald T.
Woodard, Parker A.
Woodbury, Krista Marie
Woodham, Jill
Woodley, Ferne Bell
Woodrick, Mark A.
Woodroof, Stacey D.
Woods, Daryl R.
Woods, Lisa Denienne
Woods, Mary Kyle
Woods, Robin D.
Woodson-Brown, Rhonda L.
Woods-Ward, Lois
Woodward, Gloria L.
Woodward, Joanne C.
Woodward, Stephen
Woody, Delores
Woody, Valdemira C.
Woolbright, David
Woolridge, Kathleen

Woolsey, Carolyn K.
Wooten, Amber N.
Wooten, Danielle Y.
Worden, Dianna L.
Worden, Sherry Beth
Worek, Aubrey L.
Worf, Ann C.
Work, Judith A.
Workman, Cheryl L.
Workman, Michael L.
Worley, Kali M.
Worlund, Katrina S.
Worrell, Marcella A.
Worster, Nancy J.
Wortham, Rebecca
Wortman, Marla L.
Woyach, Kimberly A.
Wozniak, Rebecca L.
Wray, Jason B.
Wray, Melissa L.
Wray, Suzanne
Wray, Suzanne M.
Wright, Amanda
Wright, Ann Lea
Wright, Christopher O.
Wright, Cinda D.
Wright, David J.
Wright, Elaine
Wright, Gale M.
Wright, John
Wright, Jr., Vincent Milton
Wright, Lana
Wright, Latosha
Wright, Lee
Wright, Linda A.
Wright, Margaret
Wright, Mary Gwendolyn
Wright, Michelle L.
Wright, Pamela
Wright, Pauline C.
Wright, Robin Lynn
Wright, Roger E.
Wright, Tamesia L.
Wright, Wendy W.
Wung, Penny
Wurz, Shay L.
Wyatt, Dixie M.
Wyatt, Janice
Wyatt, Mozelle
Wyatt, Sandra J.
Wyatt, Susan H.
Wygal, Cheryl A.
Wygant, Bonnie M.
Wyley, Andrea H. P.
Wyllie, Melissa S.
Wyman, Jodi T.

Wyman, Kevin J.
Wymer, Jo Ann
Wyndham, Randy D.
Wynne, Michael
Wyszynski, Jane E.

Y

Yacano, Daniel D.
Yadao-lida, Terrilyn M.
Yamada, Tracy E.
Yamamoto, Linda
Yamashita, Paul S.
Yamini, Sedigheh
Yanes, Andres E.
Yanez, Yelina V.
Yang, Jun
Yang, My Saykao
Yaniz, Sylvia M.
Yankura, Patric M.
Yannitelli, Kelly J.
Yardley, Evelin
Yarnell, Carol
Yasin, Najah H.
Yass, Carol
Yates, Cynthia M.
Yates, Judith H.
Yates, Susan
Ybarbo, Mary Jane
Yeadon, Charlotte
Yeager, Stephen L.
Yeager, Terri
Yeager, Yvonne R.
Yee, Cheryl S.
Yellowhair, Angela
Yelverton, Dana E.
Yenser, Lori A.
Yerger, Kathleen G.
Yerramalla, Aruna
Yetsko, Nancy J.
Yevchak, Arthur
Yockey, Jennifer Lynn
Yoder, Jo Marie
Yoder, Nancy A.
Yohn, Belinda A.
Yohn, Donald Dene
Yonek, Linda K.
Yoneshige, Karen Y.
York, Patrick T.
Yost, Amanda J.
Youd-Olson, Jeri
Youel, Janet P.
Young, Bonnie
Young, Carole
Young, Collen T.
Young, Cynthia A.

Young, Deborah Schultz
Young, Ethan K.
Young, Gay S.
Young, Janis B.
Young, Jeri L.
Young, Julie
Young, Melinda A.
Young, Michael R.
Young, Michelle
Young, Robert L.
Young, Rodney K. W.
Young, Sandra
Young, Shana A.
Young, Sherry
Young, Staisy
Young, Susan
Young, Tiffany E.
Young, Yolanda
Youngbar, Sara Jane L.
Youngblood, Caroline J.
Youngman, Karl D.
Younkin, Mary S.
Yount, Patrick
Youssef, Gretchen
Yudiskas, Barbara C.
Yuhaniak, Susan R.
Yuhasz, Karen
Yukes, David A.
Yusko, Christopher J.
Yuson, Caroline
Yutzy, Paula S.
Yzaguirre, Mary Ann

Z

Zaborski, Keith R.
Zacharjasz, Jan
Zagor, Karen Becky
Zahurak, Barbara
Zajdek, Karen H.
Zajfen, Susan
Zakutney, Rachel
Zalewski, Andrea R.
Zalkin, Terri L.
Zamata, Kathlyn Hatcher
Zambrano, Martha M.
Zamora, Sandra Alonzo
Zamudio, Virginia K.
Zancan, Michelle M.
Zane, Barbara J.
Zane, Meribeth
Zanotti, Mary E.
Zapata, Nicole M.
Zarazua, Pedro
Zare, Sete
Zareczny, Karen

Zarley, Kris A.
Zarr, Linda F.
Zaruches, Linda
Zarzeczny, Karen
Zaun, Maryann
Zawacki, Helaine S.
Zawisza, Christopher
Zebell, Lucille
Zehr, Lucille A.
Zeiser, Tammie L.
Zelof, Maher A.
Zeltman, William M.
Zeltwanger, Lisa Kay
Zeng, Huiwen
Zeng, Tom
Zephyr, Vallori N. E.
Zeppieri, Jon
Zerneke, Dawn M.
Zeroth, Kathleen M.
Zewe, Tracey
Zhang, John G.
Zhao, Xing Hua
Zhilyakova, Elena
Ziebol, Mary C.
Ziegelmeyer, Debra C.
Zielinski, Jayson
Zientarski, Karen A.
Zierenberg, Terry
Zighelboim, Jodi
Zillmer, Tommy R.
Zimmerman, Deborah
Zimmerman, Kristin
Zinckgraf, Eric P.
Zinnert, Kathy J.
Zipin, Susan
Ziroli, Mary Lou
Zitelli, Susan F.
Zivkovich, Mary E.
Znavor, Eunice G.
Zobian, Joyce V.
Zoeckler, Denise
Zoet, Lori
Zoller, Judith A.
Zollinger, Gregory Floyd
Zonenberg, Linda S.
Zuazua, Rose M.
Zukowski, Mark A.
Zukowsky, Joan E.
Zumbrun, Linda D.
Zupancic, S. Carol T.
Zuppinger, Astrid H.
Zuro, Carol M.
Zvekan, Irma
Zysk-Mchugh, Kimberly

Notes to Sources

Chapter One

1. Jane Gibbs DuBose, "Health care firm's chairman credits growth to teamwork," *Nashville Banner*, 11 May 1989.
2. Roy Spence, chairman and CEO of GSD&M Idea City, founder of The Purpose Institute.
3. Thomas Cigarran, interview by Jeffrey L. Rodengen, digital recording, 13 May 2008, Write Stuff Enterprises, LLC.
4. Ibid.
5. Jim Buncher, "Message from the President," *Inside HAI*, Hospital Affiliates International, 24 April 1981.
6. Cigarran interview.
7. Henry Herr, agenda, American Healthcorp internal document, 1981.
8. Cigarran interview.
9. Ibid.
10. Albert Cason, "New Hospital Corporation Formed Here," *Tennessean*, 29 September 1981.
11. Ibid.
12. Albert Cason, "New Hospital Firm Receives Credit Lines," *Tennessean*, 24 November 1981.
13. Jane Gibbs DuBose, "Health care firm's chairman credits growth to teamwork," *Nashville Banner*, 11 May 1989.
14. Henry Herr, interview by Jeffrey L. Rodengen, digital recording, 18 May 2009, Write Stuff Enterprises, LLC.
15. Annetta Burgess, "American Healthways 20th Anniversary," 2001, DVD, American Healthways.
16. Thomas W. Mader, Health Services Markets, SRI International, Research Report 647, February 1981.
17. "Malaise Maestro," Investor's Business Daily website, 22 May 2007, http://www.ibdeditorials.com/IBDArticles.aspx?id=264727202278115/.
18. W. Robert Friedman Jr., "Reagan's Impact on the Healthcare Industry," *Surgical Business*, April 1981, page 47.
19. Dana Williams, interview by Jeffrey L. Rodengen, digital recording, 16 September 2008, Write Stuff Enterprises, LLC.
20. American Healthcorp 1981 business plan, page 14.
21. Herr interview.
22. Press release, American Healthcorp, 23 December 1981.
23. Dave Flessner, "Nashville Hospital Group Negotiates To Buy Tepper Hospital and Clinic," *Chattanooga Times*, 14 November 1981.
24. Bob Stone, interview by Jeffrey L. Rodengen, digital recording, 13 May 2008, Write Stuff Enterprises, LLC.
25. John Vass Jr., "American Healthcorp unveils name at former Tepper Hospital," *Chattanooga News-Free Press*, 7 February 1982.
26. "American Healthcorp Reports Acquisition of Medical Center," *Tennessean*, 2 March 1982.
27. Ibid.
28. "Proposed Private Placement of $6 Million Subordinated Notes Due 1994 with Warrants," American Healthcorp, August 1982, page 20.
29. Dana Williams, interview by Jeffrey L. Rodengen, digital recording, 16 September 2008, Write Stuff Enterprises, LLC.
30. Williams interview.
31. "Fourth Firm's Offer is $11.5 Million," *Tullahoma News and Guardian*, 24 March 1982.
32. "3 Firms Now Vying for Hospital," *Tullahoma News and Guardian*, 17 March 1982.
33. Monthly Operating Report, American Healthcorp, Inc., September 1982, page 1.
34. Development Update, American Healthcorp, September 1983, page 8.
35. Ed Gregory, "Hospitals and Health: Hilton Sees Professional Managers as Key Factor," *Tennessean*, 22 January 1984.
36. Minutes of the March 23, 1984 Board Meeting, American Healthcorp, 23 March 1984, page 1.
37. Stone interview.
38. Stone interview.
39. Cigarran interview.
40. Ed Gregory, "Hospitals and Health: Hilton Sees Professional Managers as Key Factor," *Tennessean*, 22 January 1984.
41. National Medical Enterprises Hospital Purchase Agreement, American Healthcorp, page 2.
42. Herr interview.

Chapter One Sidebar: Expanding the Health Care Field

1. "Key Milestones in CMS Programs," Center for Medicare and Medicaid Services website, http://www.cms.hhs.gov/History/Downloads/CMSProgramKeyMilestones.pdf/.
2. Bob Stone, interview by Jeffrey L. Rodengen, digital recording, 13 May 2008, Write Stuff Enterprises, LLC.

3. Henry Herr, interview by Jeffrey L. Rodengen, digital recording, 18 May 2009, Write Stuff Enterprises, LLC.
4. "Nashville Health Care Council Unveils 2008 Family Tree," Nashville Health Care Council press release, 20 October 2008.
5. Ibid.
6. Annual Report 2007–2008, Nashville Health Care Council, page 4.
7. Stone interview.
8. "About Phil," Tennessee state website, http://www.tennesseeanytime.org/governor/About.do/.
9. "About Us," Hope Through Healing Hands website, http://www.hopethroughhealinghands.org/.
10. "Health Care Industry Contributes $30 Billion Annually to Nashville Economy," Nashville Health Care Council press release, 7 July 2010.

Chapter Two

1. Henry Herr, interview by Jeffrey L. Rodengen, digital recording, 18 May 2009, Write Stuff Enterprises, LLC.
2. American Healthcorp business plan, page 7.
3. "Nova January 1983-January 1984" PBS website, http://www.pbs.org/wgbh/nova/listseason/10.html/.
4. "Mrs. Reagan's Crusade," Ronald Reagan Library website, http://www.reaganlibrary.com/reagan/nancy/just_say_no.asp/.
5. American Healthcorp slide presentation, June 1988, page 13.
6. Ibid.
7. Undated American Healthcorp plan, page 9.
8. Ibid, page 1.
9. Ibid, page 18.
10. Thomas Cigarran, interview by Jeffrey L. Rodengen, digital recording, 13 May 2008, Write Stuff Enterprises, LLC.
11. Ed Gregory, "Health Unit Expands Through Purchase," *Tennessean*, 2 February 1984.
12. Ibid.
13. American Healthcorp Strategy Proposal, 19 October 1984, page 2.
14. *Wall Street Transcript* reprint, 13 July 1992.
15. Cathy Schulze, "American Healthcorp sold to execs, Chicago firm," *Nashville Banner*, 26 September 1988.

16. American Healthcorp, Inc., Monthly Operating Report, 31 January 1988, page 2.
17. Cigarran interview.
18. American Healthcorp 1991 Annual Report, page 16.
19. Herr interview.
20. Ibid.

Chapter Three

1. Steve Samples, interview by Jeffrey L. Rodengen, digital recording, 11 February 2009, Write Stuff Enterprises, LLC.
2. Thomas Cigarran, interview by Jeffrey L. Rodengen, digital recording, 13 May 2008, Write Stuff Enterprises, LLC.
3. Ben Leedle, interview by Jeffrey L. Rodengen, digital recording, 13 May 2008, Write Stuff Enterprises, LLC.
4. Proposal submitted to receive bank financing, American Healthcorp, October 1981, page 1.
5. Bob Stone, interview by Jeffrey L. Rodengen, digital recording, 13 May 2008, Write Stuff Enterprises, LLC.
6. Ibid.
7. Henry Herr, interview by Jeffrey L. Rodengen, digital recording, 18 May 2009, Write Stuff Enterprises, LLC.
8. Stone interview.
9. Monthly Operating Report, American Healthcorp, Inc., September 1982, page 3.
10. Stone interview.
11. Ibid.
12. Ibid.
13. Leedle interview.
14. Ibid.
15. Pat Lynch, interview by Jeffrey L. Rodengen, digital recording, 17 September 2008, Write Stuff Enterprises, LLC.
16. Healthways 2006 Annual Report, page 47.
17. American Healthcorp 1991 Annual Report, page 7.
18. Kathy Kirk, interview by Jeffrey L. Rodengen, digital recording, 17 September 2008, Write Stuff Enterprises, LLC.
19. Ibid.
20. Emily Cook, interview by Jeffrey L. Rodengen, digital recording, 16 September 2008, Write Stuff Enterprises, LLC.

21. American Healthcorp 1991 Annual Report, page 1.
22. *Wall Street Transcript* reprint, 13 July 1992.
23. Leedle interview.
24. Ibid.
25. Ibid.
26. Jay S. Skyler, "DCCT: The Study That Forever Changed the Nature of Treatment of Type 1 Diabetes," *British Journal of Diabetes and Vascular Disease*, 23 March 2004.
27. Leedle interview.
28. Hospitals & Health Networks, 20 May 1994, as reported in the American Healthcorp 1994 Annual Report, page 5.
29. American Healthcorp 1994 Annual Report, page 2.
30. Ibid, page 12.
31. Ibid, page 2.
32. Ibid, page 6.
33. Ibid, page 7.
34. Ibid, page 8.
35. Ibid, page 1.
36. Kathy Kirk, interview by Jeffrey L. Rodengen, digital recording, 17 September 2008, Write Stuff Enterprises, LLC.
37. Cook interview.
38. Regina Seider, interview by Jeffrey L. Rodengen, digital recording, 16 September 2008, Write Stuff Enterprises, LLC.

Chapter Three Sidebar: DTCA Foundation Intends to Lead the Way

1. Bob Stone, interview by Jeffrey L. Rodengen, digital recording, 13 May 2008, Write Stuff Enterprises, LLC.
2. Ibid.

Chapter Three Sidebar: Diabetes Increasing Along with Waistlines

1. *Diabetes Trends in the U.S.: 1990-1998*, Centers for Disease Control, September 2000.
2. "Prevalence of Diabetes Rose 5 Percent Annually Since 1990," American Diabetes Association website, http://www.diabetes.org/diabetesnewsarticle.jsp?storyid=15351710&filename=20070623/ADA20070623 1192625856641EDIT.xml/.

3. *Diabetes Trends in the U.S.: 1990–1998,* page 1,280.
4. American Healthcorp 1991 Annual Report, page 2.
5. American Healthcorp 1998 Annual Report, page 1.
6. *Diabetes Trends in the U.S.: 1990–1998,* page 1,281.
7. "Prevelance of Diabetes Rose 5 Percent Annually Since 1990."

Chapter Four

1. *Wall Street Transcript,* reprint, 13 July 1992.
2. American Healthcorp Strategy Proposal, 19 October 1998, page 2.
3. American Healthcorp Strategy Proposal, version 2, page 1.
4. American Healthcorp Strategy Proposal, 19 October 1998, page 1.
5. American Healthcorp Strategy Proposal, version 2, page 2.
6. American Healthcorp Strategy Proposal, 19 October 1998, page 2.
7. American Healthcorp slide presentation, June 1988.
8. Bob Stone, interview by Jeffrey L. Rodengen, digital recording, 13 May 2008, Write Stuff Enterprises, LLC.
9. Ed Gregory, "Diabetes Care Lifts American Healthcorp," *Tennessean,* 7 April 1992, page 1.
10. Thomas Cigarran, interview by Jeffrey L. Rodengen, digital recording, 13 May 2008, Write Stuff Enterprises, LLC.
11. Stone interview.
12. Jane Brody, "Diet That Made Oprah Winfrey Slim Demands Discipline, Specialists Say," *New York Times,* 24 November 1988.
13. Cigarran interview.
14. Penny Ward Moser, "Whole Lotta Shakin' Goin' On," *Sports Illustrated,* 21 October 1991.
15. Cigarran interview
16. Henry Herr, interview by Jeffrey L. Rodengen, digital recording, 18 May 2009, Write Stuff Enterprises, LLC.
17. Tim Tanton, "Healthcorp adds surgery business," *Nashville Banner,* 30 October 1992.
18. American Healthcorp 1995 Annual Report.
19. AmSurg 1997 Annual Report.
20. Ibid
21. UBS Global Research Report, 4 December 1997, page 1.
22. Ibid, page 9.
23. Ibid, page 14.
24. AmSurg 2008 Annual Report.

Chapter Four Sidebar: Changes At The Top

1. Cathy Schultz, "American Healthcorp sold to execs, Chicago firm," *Nashville Banner,* 26 September 1988.
2. Jane Gibbs DuBose, "Fewer firms want public ownership," *Nashville Banner,* 18 November 1987.
3. Thomas Cigarran, interview by Jeffrey L. Rodengen, digital recording, 13 May 2008, Write Stuff Enterprises, LLC.
4. Ibid.
5. Martin J. Koldyke biography, The Frontenac Company website, http://www.frontenac.com/Founders.aspx?id=1&selection=0/.
6. Cigarran interview.
7. "American Healthcorp sold to execs, Chicago firm."
8. Ibid.
9. Tim Tanton, "Stock offering planned," *Nashville Banner,* 23 July 1991.
10. Cigarran interview.
11. "American Healthcorp up on 1st trading day," *Nashville Banner,* 14 August 1991.
12. "Partnership reduces stake in health firm," *Nashville Banner,* 14 January 1993.
13. Cigarran interview.

Chapter Five

1. Janet Calhoun, "The Healthcorp Story," DVD, Healthcorp Inc., 6 February 2008.
2. Ben Leedle, interview by Jeffrey L. Rodengen, digital recording, 13 May 2008, Write Stuff Enterprises, LLC.
3. Oxford University website, http://www.dtu.ox.ac.uk.ukpds_trial/index.php/.
4. Steve Samples, interview by Jeffrey L. Rodengen, digital recording, 11 February 2009, Write Stuff Enterprises, LLC.
5. Janet Calhoun, interview by Jeffrey L. Rodengen, digital recording, 16 September 2008, Write Stuff Enterprises, LLC.
6. Samples interview.
7. Bob Stone, interview by Jeffrey L. Rodengen, digital recording, 13 May 2008, Write Stuff Enterprises, LLC.
8. Thomas Cigarran, interview by Jeffrey L. Rodengen, digital recording, 13 May 2008, Write Stuff Enterprises, LLC.
9. Calhoun interview.
10. Leedle interview.
11. Calhoun interview.
12. American Healthcorp 1995 Annual Report, page 5.
13. Kathy Kirk, interview by Jeffrey L. Rodengen, digital recording, 17 September 2008, Write Stuff Enterprises, LLC.
14. Leedle interview.
15. Ibid.
16. Ibid.
17. Dana Williams, interview by Jeffrey L. Rodengen, digital recording, 16 September 2008, Write Stuff Enterprises, LLC.
18. American Healthcorp 1995 Annual Report, page 5.
19. American Healthcorp 1996 Annual Report, pages 12, 14.
20. Samples interview.
21. Leedle interview.
22. American Healthcorp 1995 Annual Report, page 6.
23. American Healthcorp 1995 Annual Report, page 6.
24. Rick Bailey, interview by Jeffrey L. Rodengen, digital recording, 17 September 2008, Write Stuff Enterprises, LLC.
25. American Healthcorp 1996 Annual Report, page 6.
26. Ibid.
27. Bill Evans, interview by Jeffrey L. Rodengen, digital recording, 17 September 2008, Write Stuff Enterprises, LLC.
28. Bailey interview.
29. Ibid.
30. American Healthcorp 1997 Annual Report, page 6.
31. Evans interview.
32. American Healthcorp 1997 Annual Report, page 5.
33. Ibid, page 9.
34. "A Winning Combination: CIGNA and American Healthways," *Healthcare Business,* sponsored supplement.
35. Ibid.
36. Evans interview.

37. Samples interview.

38. Ibid.

39. Deb Hagemann interview, "Healthways at a Glance," DVD.

40. Robyn Fulwider, interview by Jeffrey L. Rodengen, digital recording, 17 September 2008, Write Stuff Enterprises, LLC.

41. Ibid.

42. American Healthcorp 1998 Annual Report, page 2.

43. Ibid, page 3.

44. Ibid, page 2.

45. Evans interview.

46. American Healthcorp 1998 Annual Report, page 14.

47. Evans interview.

48. "American Healthcorp Study Demonstrates Benefits of Intensive Treatment of Diabetes," American Healthcorp press release, 23 October 1996, page 1.

49. "New Data Show That Investing in Diabetes Care Now Can Save Money and Improve Clinical Outcomes—Fast," American Healthcorp press release, 5 November 1997, page 1.

50. Ibid.

51. Ibid.

52. "American Healthcorp Announces Lewin Study Confirming That Diabetes Treatment Centers of America's Diabetes NetCare™ Program Improves Health Status, Reduces Medical Costs," American Healthcorp press release, 3 August 1998.

53. Kathleen Sullivan, "American Healthcorp Gains on Diabetes Plan," *Bloomberg Forum*, 3 April 1998.

54. American Healthcorp 1998 Annual Report, page 4.

55. Ibid.

56. Ibid.

57. Bailey interview.

58. American Healthcorp 1998 Annual Report, page 3.

59. "American Healthcorp Gains on Diabetes."

60. Ibid.

Chapter Six

1. Thomas Cigarran, "20th Anniversary DVD," American Healthcorp, 2001.

2. Janet Calhoun, interview by Jeffrey L. Rodengen, digital recording, 16 September 2008, Write Stuff Enterprises, LLC.

3. Ben Leedle, interview by Jeffrey L. Rodengen, digital recording, 13 May 2008, Write Stuff Enterprises, LLC.

4. Bob Stone, interview by Jeffrey L. Rodengen, digital recording, 13 May 2008, Write Stuff Enterprises, LLC.

5. Leedle interview.

6. Ibid.

7. "Healthcorp Changing Name to American Healthways To Reflect Expanded Product Line; Nation's Leading Disease Management Company Also Phasing Out Use of the Diabetes Treatment Centers of America Name," American Healthways press release, 13 December 1999.

8. American Healthways 1999 Annual Report, page 13.

9. Leedle interview.

10. Janet Calhoun, interview by Jeffrey L. Rodengen, digital recording, 16 September 2008, Write Stuff Enterprises, LLC.

11. American Healthways 2001 Annual Report, page 13.

12. Lee Holliman, "Call Centers Offer A Healthy Approach to Customer Service," *Call Center* magazine, 5 November 2000.

13. Ibid.

14. Gerrye Stegall, interview by Jeffrey L. Rodengen, digital recording, 12 February 2009, Write Stuff Enterprises, LLC.

15. Ibid.

16. American Healthways 2000 Annual Report, page 12.

17. "American Healthways and Agilent Technologies Announce Agreement for At Home Support for People with Heart Disease," American Healthways press release, 9 May 2000.

18. American Healthways Establishes Advisory Council to Develop Next Generation of Care Management Technologies; Agilent Technologies, Avaya, CareSteps, Compaq, Davox and MCI Worldcom Provide New Integrated Solutions for American Healthways' Care Management Programs," American Healthways press release, 26 July 2000.

19. "American Healthways Signs First Multiple Disease Contract," American Healthways press release, 20 March 2000.

20. American Healthways 2000 Annual Report, page 3.

21. Ibid.

22. Ibid, page 9.

23. Ibid, page 11.

24. Dr. Charles Wilhelm, interview by Jeffrey L. Rodengen, digital recording, 11 May 2009, Write Stuff Enterprises, LLC.

25. "American Healthways Signs First Multiple Disease Contract."

26. Leedle interview.

27. American Healthways 1999 Annual Report, page 4.

28. "CIGNA Healthcare Selects American Healthways to Provide Cardiac Disease Management Services; American Healthways Now Nation's Largest Cardiac Disease Management Provider," American Healthways press release, 20 September 2000.

29. "American Healthways to Provide Diabetes Disease Management Services to Hawaii Medical Service Association," American Healthways press release, 24 May 2000.

30. "New Data Show That Comprehensive Disease Management Programs Can Improve Health Status of Medicare Recipients and Reduce Health Care Costs for the Medicare Program," American Healthways press release, 23 May 2000.

31. Ibid.

32. Leedle interview.

33. American Healthways 2003 Annual Report, page 8.

34. "Healthways, Blue Cross and Blue Shield of Minnesota Win National Partnership Award," American Healthways press release, 27 March 2004.

35. Ibid.

36. American Healthways 2003 Annual Report, page 8.

37. Leedle interview.

38. American Healthways 2003 Annual Report, page 5.

39. Calhoun interview.

40. Natasha Orrick, "Healthways hunting new accounts," *Minneapolis/St. Paul Business Journal*, 16 May 2008.

41. Cigarran interview.

42. Calhoun interview.

43. Leedle interview.

44. Regina Seider, interview by Jeffrey L. Rodengen, digital recording, 16 September 2008, Write Stuff Enterprises, LLC.

45. Molly Cate and Roy Moore, "American Healthways acquires Connecticut research company," *Nashville Business Journal*, 8 June 2001.

46. Ibid.

47. Mary Chaput, interview by Jeffrey L. Rodengen, digital recording, 16 September 2008, Write Stuff Enterprises, LLC.

48. Henry Herr, interview by Jeffrey L. Rodengen, digital recording, 18 May 2009, Write Stuff Enterprises, LLC.

49. Chaput interview.

50. Keith Russell, "Disease Management Strategy Finally Paying Off for American Healthways," *Tennessean*, 22 July 2001.

51. Steve Samples, interview by Jeffrey L. Rodengen, digital recording, 11 February 2009, Write Stuff Enterprises, LLC.

52. "Disease Management Association Honors Industry Leaders At its Recognizing Excellence Awards Ceremony," Disease Management Association of America press release, 16 November 2001.

53. Ibid.

54. Leedle interview.

Chapter Six Sidebar: The Company Embraces a New Look

1. American Healthways 2004 Annual Report, inside front flap.

2. American Healthways 2001 Annual Report, page 2.

3. Ibid, page 1.

Chapter Seven

1. Dr. Charles Wilhelm, interview by Jeffrey L. Rodengen, digital recording, Write Stuff Enterprises, LLC, 11 May 2009.

2. Matt Kelliher, interview by Jeffrey L. Rodengen, digital recording, Write Stuff Enterprises, LLC, 12 February 2009.

3. Kelliher interview.

4. Ibid.

5. Ibid.

6. "Healthways Enters Brazilian Market Through 10-Year Disease Management Service Agreement With Fleury," Healthways press release, 6 March 2008.

7. Ibid.

8. "American Healthways, Regence Group partner to improve health, reduce costs,"

BioTech Week, 31 December 2003, page 35.

9. Healthways 2005 Annual Report, page 16.

10. Chris Rauber, "LifeMaster and Healthways nix $307M merger," *San Francisco Business Journal*, 2 October 2006.

11. Benjamin Nagy, "Contracts may herald 'arrival' of disease management," Managed Healthcare Executive, 1 June 2006.

12. Healthways 2006 Annual Report, page 4.

13. Bob Stone, interview by Jeffrey L. Rodengen, digital recording, 13 May 2008, Write Stuff Enterprises, LLC.

14. Janet Calhoun, interview by Jeffrey L. Rodengen, digital recording, 16 September 2008, Write Stuff Enterprises, LLC.

15. "Healthways announces executive changes to support strategic collaboration with Medco," *Managed Care Weekly Digest*, 16 June 2006.

16. "How it Started," Silver Sneakers website, http://www.silversneakers.com/ Default.aspx?section=About& subsection=HowItStarted/.

17. "Axia Health Management Acquires American WholeHealth Networks Inc.; Acquisition Reinforces Axia's Mission to Become the Premier Direct Prevention Services Company in the U.S.," Axia press release, 21 July 2005.

18. "Axia Health Management Buys Quitnet Inc.," UPI NewsTrack, 20 October 2005.

19. "Harris HealthTrends Inc. Joins Forces with Axia Health Management," Genstar Capital press release, 9 February 2006.

20. "Genstar Capital Portfolio Company, Axia Health Management, Acquires My ePHIT; Acquisition of Internet-Based Health Improvement Company Marks Axia's Fifth Acquisition," Genstar press release, 19 April 2006.

21. "Not retiring type: Lytle leading fast-growing wellness firm," *Indianapolis Business Journal*, 30 January 2006.

22. Ibid.

23. Healthways 2006 Annual Report, page 4.

24. "Healthways to buy Axia Health for $450M," *AFX International Focus*, 11 October 2006.

25. Ibid.

26. Justin Smith, interview by Jeffrey L. Rodengen, digital recording, 11 February 2009, Write Stuff Enterprises, LLC.

27. Alfred Lumsdaine, interview by Jeffrey L. Rodengen, digital recording, 17 September 2008, Write Stuff Enterprises, LLC.

28. Emily Cook, interview by Jeffrey L. Rodengen, digital recording, 16 September 2008, Write Stuff Enterprises, LLC.

29. Rick Bailey, interview by Jeffrey L. Rodengen, digital recording, 17 September 2008, Write Stuff Enterprises, LLC.

30. Cook interview.

31. Mary Hunter, "The Healthways Story," DVD, 6 February 2008.

Chapter Seven Sidebar: Taking Services to Medicare Beneficiaries

1. Marilyn Alva, "Disease Manager Trades Minor Risk for Major (Potential) Reward," *Investor's Business Daily*, 7 July 2005.

2. Ibid.

3. Ibid.

Chapter Seven Sidebar: Strike Up the Band

1. "Healthways' Strat5 Only Local Band Chosen to Compete Saturday in *FORTUNE®*'s Battle of the Corporate Bands," Healthways press release, 13 July 2007.

2. Ibid.

3. Ibid.

Chapter Seven Sidebar: A Building That Matches the Purpose

1. Sue Schmidt, interview by Sandy Smith, digital recording, 29 May 2009, Write Stuff Enterprises, LLC.

2. Ibid.

3. Ibid.

4. Ibid.

5. Ibid.

6. Ibid.

Chapter Eight

1. Emily Cook, "The Healthways Story," DVD, 6 February 2008.

2. Healthways 2007 Annual Report, page 5.

3. Ibid.

4. Ibid, page 2.

5. Ibid, page 1.

6. Healthways 2010 Annual Report, page 10.

7. Matt Kelliher, interview by Jeffrey L. Rodengen, digital recording, 12 February 2009, Write Stuff Enterprises, LLC.

8. Ibid.

9. "Deutsche Angestellten Krankenkasse (DAK) Selects Healthways to Implement Programs for Members with Chronic Diseases," Healthways press release, 30 August 2007.

10. Kelliher interview.

11. Ibid.

12. Healthways 2007 Annual Report, page 1.

13. Kelliher interview.

14. Healthways 2007 Annual Report, page 1.

15. "Healthways SilverSneakers® Fitness Program Proven to Reduce Health Care Costs of Members with Chronic Conditions," Healthways press release, 16 September 2008.

16. Ibid.

17. Ibid.

18. "Curves International and Healthways SilverSneakers® Fitness Program Announce Partnership," Healthways press release, 9 December 2008.

19. Kelliher interview.

20. "New Total Population Agreement with HCF Australia Expands Healthways Global Presence," Healthways press release, 1 December 2008.

21. Kelliher interview.

22. Ben Leedle, interview by Jeffrey L. Rodengen, digital recording, 13 May 2008, Write Stuff Enterprises, LLC.

23. Healthways 2008 Annual Report, page 5.

24. "Gallup, Healthways, Release First-Ever Well Being Results For UK," Healthways press release, 12 April 2011.

25. "A Million People Have Spoken: Gallup, Healthways Unlock The Meaning Of Well-Being," Healthways press release, 10 October 2010.

26. "National Well-Being Measure Finds Majority Struggling," Healthways press release, 29 April 2008.

27. "Healthways 7th Organization Granted Permanent World Health Poll Monitor," Healthways, Healthways press release, 17 September 2008.

28. "Wellmark Blue Cross And Blue Shield First In Nation To Measure Well-Being Of Health Plan Members, Employees," Wellmark press release, 15 October 2008.

29. Ibid.

30. "A Million People Have Spoken: Gallup, Healthways Unlock The Meaning Of Well-Being," Healthways press release, 10 October 2010.

31. Ibid.

Chapter Eight Sidebar: Making Sure the Cultures Fit

1. Mary Chaput, interview by Jeffrey L. Rodengen, digital recording, 16 September 2008, Write Stuff Enterprises, LLC.

2. Chris Cigarran, interview by Jeffrey L. Rodengen, digital recording, 4 June 2009, Write Stuff Enterprises, LLC.

Chapter Nine

1 Ben Leedle, interview by Jeffrey L. Rodengen, digital recording, 13 May 2008, Write Stuff Enterprises, LLC.

2. Healthways 2008 Annual Report, page 5.

3. Ibid.

4. Healthways 2009 Annual Report, page 5.

5. "Healthways Among First in the Nation to Achieve Accreditation for URAC's Comprehensive Wellness Standards and Measures Program," Healthways press release, 19 December 2008.

6. Gallup, Healthways Release First-Ever Well-Being Results For UK," Healthways press release, 12 April 2011.

7. "Healthways Reports Second-Quarter Earnings of $0.26 Per Diluted Share," Healthways press release, 23 July 2009.

8. "Healthways Announces Acquisition of Behavioral Economics Company, HealthHonors," Healthways press release, 14 October 2009.

9. Mark McDermott, "The Vitality Quest," *Beach* magazine, 7 April 2011.

10. Sue Schmidt, interview by Sandy Smith, digital recording, 29 May 2009, Write Stuff Enterprises, LLC.

11. Ben Leedle, interview by Jeffrey L. Rodengen, digital recording, 13 May 2008, Write Stuff Enterprises, LLC.

12. "Well-being improvement initiative reduces costs for seniors domestically and abroad," Healthways press release, 17 February 2011.

13. Ibid.

14. Ibid.

15. Gerrye Stegall, interview by Jeffrey L. Rodengen, digital recording, 12 February 2009, Write Stuff Enterprises, LLC.

16. "HMSA and Healthways announce new 10-year agreement," HMSA press release, 25 January 2011.

17. "Healthways to Provide State Government-Funded Program for Severe Chronic Disease Management in New South Wales, Australia," Healthways press release, 31 January 2011.

18. "Healthways Awarded Contract to Expand National Chronic Disease Management Program in France and France's Overseas Territories," Healthways press release, 7 April 2011.

19. "Healthways Reports First-Quarter Earnings of $0.12 Per Diluted Share and Affirms 2011 Financial Guidance," Healthways press release, 25 April 2011.

20. Ibid.

Chapter Nine Sidebar: Healthways Enters the Blue Zones

1. "Healthways, Blue Zones Enter into Exclusive Agreement to Improve Well-Being of U.S. Communities," Healthways press release, 15 March 2010.

2. Ibid.

Index

Page numbers in italics refer to photographs and illustrations.

Hospital Corporation of America
   (HCA), 14, 16–19, 20, 24, 25
Hospitals & Health Networks
   (magazine), 48
Houston Center for Health
   Promotion, 55, 58–59
HRAs, 144
Humana, 20, 24
Hunter, Mary, xi, 20, 23, *92,*
   107, 121

I

Ingenix (UnitedHealth Group),
   140–141
Iowa Healthiest State Initiative, 159

J

JCAHO (Joint Commission on
   Accreditation of Healthcare
   Organizations), 31, 102
Jefferies & Co., 97
John Deere Health Services, 80
Johns Hopkins University, 31,
   98–99, 101, 130
Johnson & Johnson, 133
Joint Commission on Accreditation
   of Healthcare Organizations
   (JCAHO), 31, 102
Jones, Bonnie, xi
Joslin Diabetes Center, 41
Journal of Clinical
   Endocrinology and
   Metabolism, 66, 82, *83*

K

Kantanie, Stan, xi, *14,* 15, 16, 17, 57
Kelliher, Matthew E. "Matt," xi, 106,
   106, 124–125, 129–130, 156
King, Ashley B., xi

Kirk, Kathy, xi, *43,* 44, 45, 51,
   68, 123
Klein, Michael, xi
Koala Centers, *32, 33,* 33–37, *34,*
   35, 36
Koldyke, Martin J. "Mike," xi, *27, 56,*
   56–57, *82*

L

Lakewood Hospital, 42
Lakey, David, *115*
Lane, Catherine, xi
Lasorda, Tommy, 58
Leedle, Ben, *56, 92, 107, 149,*
   153, 157
   on alliances, 109
   on American Healthcorp, 43
   on behavioral economics,
      134–136
   on behavior modification
      models, 131, 159
   on Bristol-Myers Squibb joint
      development project, 69
   on the DTCA, 40, 63, 67
   on the Embrace technology
      system, 144
   on fitness, 151
   on the future of American
      Healthways, 96
   on the future of Healthways,
      127, 139, 160–161
   on health services delivery
      models, 67
   on Healthways history, 160
   on Healthways market
      reception, 102–103
   on Healthways success, 103,
      139, 142, 154–155
   on his move into
      business development,
      46–47

   on insurer-based disease
      management, 71, 80,
      93–96, 156
   on international business
      growth, 155–156
   on market changing forces,
      154–155, 161
   on the Medicare
      Health Support program,
      110, 111
   on multi-disease management,
      89–90, 93
   on name change, 87
   as president and CEO of
      Healthways, x
   on social networks,
      146, 147
   Roy Spence on, viii
   on success, 47
   on the WBI, 136, 143
   on wellness promotion
      programs, 113, 114–115,
      127–128, 152
Leinwand, Marty,
   114, *115*
Lewin-VHI, Inc. report,
   49, 65, 66, *66, 81,* 82, *83*
Libowitz, Steve, 101
LifeMasters Insurance Services,
   107–108
Lindstrom, Steve, xi
Lowney, Malinda, xi
Lumsdaine, Alfred, xi, 120, 154
Lynch, Patricia "Pat," xi, 43
Lytle, Ben, 116, 117

M

Mangold, Nancy, xi
market creation and development
   process, *28,* 29–31
market-driven solutions, 30–31